Carole Pollard
Ellen Rowley
Natalie de Róiste
Merlo Kelly
Aoife O'Halloran
Shane O'Toole
Aoibheann Ní Mhearáin
Paul Tierney

More than concrete blocks:
Volume 3
1973–99

Dublin city's twentieth-century buildings and their stories

Ellen Rowley and Carole Pollard
(Editors)

Foreword, Michelle Norris		4
Preface: *How to use this book*		6
Acknowledgements		9
About the Editors + Authors		12
About Dublin City Council Heritage Office		17
Series Introduction		18
Overview Essays		
The 1970s by Carole Pollard		22
The 1980s by Ellen Rowley		34
The 1990s by Merlo Kelly		48

Case Studies

1973	Molyneux House (CP)	60
1973	Merrion Hall (CP)	70
1972 + 1975	Bank of Ireland HQ, Baggot Street (CP)	82
1976	Darndale Housing Estate (ER)	94
1971 + 1978	Poolbeg Chimneys (MLK)	106
1978	PMPA (ER)	118
1978	1970s Housing, From Fitzgibbon Court to Ash Grove to City Quay (ER)	128
1978	Church of the Holy Trinity, Donaghmede (ER)	148
1979	Herbert Mews (CP)	162
1979 + 1980	Allied Irish Bank (AIB) Bankcentre (CP)	174
1979	Papal Cross, Phoenix Park (ER)	188
1979	Central Bank (CP)	200
1981	AnCO Training Centre, Finglas (ANíM)	214
1981	Port and Docks HQ (CP)	224
1983	IDA Enterprise Centre, Pearse Street (ANíM)	236
1984	St James's Hospital Energy Centre (CP)	248
1984	Artane Oratory (NdeR)	260
1984 + 1985	Willow Field Housing Scheme (MLK)	274
1978 + 1985	Irish Life Centre (CP)	282
1987	Juvenile Court, Smithfield (MLK)	298
1987	Atrium/Loos Bar, Trinity Dining Hall Restoration, TCD (AoH)	308
1990	Treasury Building (CP)	320
1991	Stanhope Green, Focus Ireland housing (ER)	334
1991 + 1996	Temple Bar Introduction, Framework Plan + Meeting House Square (ER + MLK)	350
1992	Temple Bar, Irish Film Centre/Institute (MLK)	366
1994	Temple Bar, Temple Bar Gallery + Studios (ER)	378
1994	Temple Bar, The Printworks (MLK)	392
1995	British Embassy, Ballsbridge (MLK)	406
1996	Parsons Laboratory, Mechanical Engineering, TCD (MLK)	416
1998	Ranelagh Multi-Denominational School (ANíM)	428
1998	Castle Street Mixed-Use Building (CP)	440

Outline Survey	452
Index	500

Author Legend
CP – Carole Pollard
ER – Ellen Rowley
MLK – Merlo Kelly
ANíM – Aoibheann Ní Mhearáin
NdR – Natalie de Róiste
AoH – Aoife O'Halloran

Foreword

The final instalment in this groundbreaking trilogy on the architectural history of 20th-century Dublin City covers the period from early 1970s until the century's end. This series, edited by Ellen Rowley and commissioned by Dublin City Council, has filled a major gap in scholarship on Irish architectural history, which has hitherto focused largely on the Georgian and Victorian periods. And the publication of this third part of the trilogy enables readers to 'gather on the horizon' and reflect on the architectural development of Dublin over the entire century.

This book examines a particularly volatile period in Dublin and Ireland's economic history, as economic and population growth in the 1960s and early 1970s turned to recession and renewed high emigration in the late 1970s and 1980s before economic and population growth returned in the 1990s. In social and cultural terms, it was a period distinguished by significant conflicts, but also radical change and this book provides fascinating insights into how these developments were reflected in the design of Dublin's residential, commercial, cultural, and religious buildings. For this purpose, the series editor, Rowley has been joined by architect and scholar of the period, Carole Pollard.

The volume illuminates how changes in the confidence of architects and builders and in the capacity of the state, market and non-profit sectors to finance construction were reflected in the buildings constructed over these three decades. The case studies presented in the book illustrate how the period of economic growth in the 1970s inspired tentative confidence expressed in the experiments of architectural modernism commissioned by commercial clients such as Merrion Hall (1972) and Bank of Ireland's new headquarters on Baggot Street (1972–75). This spirit of experimentation was undermined by the 1980s recession but re-emerged as the economy rebounded in the 1990s and the long-term pattern of inner-city depopulation began to finally reverse. The case studies of the regeneration of Temple Bar, the redesign and rebuilding of which was led by the Group 91 consortium of eight architectural practices, suggests that this was the ground-breaking event in this re-emergence, that made room for full-scale reimagining of what contemporary Irish architecture can be and should be.

The design and purpose of key buildings constructed in late-20th century Dublin, as well as the characteristics of those involved in the architectural profession, also holds a mirror to social change during this period. While places of worship (mainly commissioned by the Catholic

Church) were prominent in the two previous volumes of *More Than Concrete Blocks*, it is notable that no buildings of this type are included in this volume after the early 1980s (Liam McCormick's beautiful Artane Oratory, completed in 1984, is the last religious building included in the book). The work of only a single woman architect was included in Volumes 1 and 2 (Mairin Hope's design on behalf of the Civics Institute), whereas women architects are far more prominent in Volume 3 particularly from the 1990s (Group 91 included Yvonne Farrell, Shelley McNamara, Sheila O'Donnell, Valerie Mulvin, Siobhán Ní Éannaigh and Rachael Chidlow for instance). Gay rights and social justice campaigns also feature more broadly in this book, whereas these issues were largely absent from the previous volumes.

However, the challenge of meeting the housing needs of Dubliners, particularly of low-income households, is just as prominent in this book as it was in the volumes that examined the early- and mid-20th century. This book covers the period that followed the loss of faith in inner-city flats complexes as an appropriate built form for social housing in Dublin. It brings forth fascinating accounts of experiments with alternative designs including the largely unsuccessful experimental housing estate designs used in Darndale in Dublin's northern suburbs (completed in 1976); and the far more successful efforts to reflect local residents' preferences and the traditional streetscape in the design of Ash Grove in the Liberties by James Pike (completed in 1978). Notably the latter followed the Liberties' residents successful campaign against the demolition of their community to facilitate the construction of an inner relief road.

It is sad to note that several of the landmark buildings examined in this book have been demolished or reworked so radically that they are unrecognisable (for examples, Molyneux House and the AIB Bankcentre). The Outline Survey that informed the selection of Case Studies for the book identified several other well-designed buildings of this period that have also been demolished or are under threat of demolition. This situation testifies to the widespread and long-term undervaluing of built heritage in Dublin but most especially of architecture from our recent history.

I hope that this wonderful book will help to rectify this situation by educating readers about the value of our recent built heritage.

Michelle Norris
Professor of Social Policy
Director, Geary Institute for Public Policy, UCD
July 2023

Preface: How to use this book

This is Volume 3 of a three-part series telling stories about Dublin while keeping the city's buildings as the central players. Volume 1 covered the period 1900 to 1940 and Volume 2, the period 1940 to 1972. This present volume examines buildings conceived of or constructed between 1973 and 1999.

The book opens with three introductory historical essays covering the building culture in Dublin and Ireland of the 1970s (by Carole Pollard), the 1980s (by Ellen Rowley) and the 1990s (by Merlo Kelly). These overview essays set the scene, in general architectural terms, bringing in key political events and referencing popular culture along the way. They throw up related or contrasting contemporary building projects, outside of Dublin City. The scene-setting is followed by 31 studies ranging from iconic situations such as the Poolbeg Chimneys (1971–78) by Merlo Kelly, the Papal Cross (Phoenix Park, 1979) by Ellen Rowley, or the Central Bank (1980) on Dame Street by Carole Pollard; to lesser-known structures like the AnCO Training Centre (1981) in Finglas by Aoibheann Ní Mhearáin or the Artane Oratory (1984) by Natalie de Róiste. Capturing the growth in conservation and adaptive reuse projects during the period, the book includes a case study on Trinity College's Dining Hall and Atrium scheme (1987) by Aoife O'Halloran, while the case study on St James's Energy Centre (1984) by Carole Pollard throws light on the contemporary interest in industrial architectures. Each study is framed according to the building's social purpose and its original commissioning, raising issues around architectural technology and materials, economic histories and urban development.

For Volume 3, the series editor is joined by Dr Carole Pollard as co-editor. The volume deviates from the model of previous volumes by bringing in the research team's voices and pens more fully. In this way, the case study essays are directly authored by the research team and are not shaped by the series editor, Ellen Rowley. There is a much lighter editorial filter and resultingly, a less uniform voice through the volume, compared to Volumes 1 and 2. Instead, Volume 3 complies with standard edited collections, presenting varied writing styles while also bringing Carole Pollard's PhD research around 1970s and early 1980s Dublin (see 'About the Editors') to bear. Throughout, the research is punctuated and enlivened by Paul Tierney's photography. And in turn, the new photography is supplemented atmospherically by architects' drawings, practice pamphlets, contemporaneous photographs.

As with the previous volumes, this book is a hybrid thing, and its final section is a succinctly designed guidebook of Dublin City's buildings of the period 1973–99. Guided by Shane O'Toole's deep knowledge of the subject, on to which Paul Tierney and Charles Duggan's research was laid, the Outline Survey grew. Shane's archive research – carried out through 2020 – concentrated on the holdings of the Irish Architectural Archive (IAA) and namely contemporary publications and award schemes from the RIAI, the AAI, *Plan* Magazine and more. This process identified published projects and award-winning buildings which may have escaped the research team's initial gathering in 2011–12. The Outline Survey was then compounded by further research and fact-checking by recent UCD Architecture graduates, Lily O'Donnell (through 2020–21) and Cara Jordan (through 2021). In all, the Outline Survey for this Volume 3 has grown to *c.*140 sites.

The principal content of this Volume is of course the 31 case studies which unpack about 34 sites, representing a wonderfully inconsistent built environment. Carried out over a number of years, these Case Studies inevitably vary in relation to how the information is presented. The sources shift according to repositories, personal archives and official accounts. Markedly, this Volume is influenced by living histories: inevitably so. Some might even argue that the buildings being explored and discussed are so recent that the discourse doesn't constitute 'history'. As with previous Volumes, the research relies on contemporary newspapers and the architectural press, but much of the richness of this Volume comes from architectural practices and the original users of the buildings. This is living history after all and the oral testimonies of two generations of architects were possible to capture. Key collections included the IAA's Stephenson Gibney Associates (SGA), de Blacam & Meagher and Group 91 papers, as well as the practice archives of Scott Tallon Walker (STW) and Robinson Keefe & Devane (RKD).

Volume 3 covers the decades of the end of the twentieth century, as Ireland joined the European Commission and Dublin city grew confident enough to reimagine Temple Bar. So, much of this history captures the growth and subsequent architectural framing of social infrastructure during this period. All of the desk research was compiled and understood in the context of building visits and secondary reading around this history, including readings of Irish politics, economic and social history, and of international architectural histories.

The Case Studies and indeed the Outline Survey at the book's end are neither definitive nor exhaustive records of the architecture of the period. Instead, these are authoritative and, importantly, *representative* of the architecture of the period. Organised to present something of the breadth and typicality of Dublin's built stock from 1973 through to the end of the century, the sites discussed are definitively *not* a 'best of'. The reader may therefore be surprised at some omissions. For instance, where are the experimental or excellent community schools and the innovative factory campuses? Quite simply these buildings are not in the Dublin city jurisdiction. So, within that more limited definition of 'Dublin', the team compiled a representation of architectural production and culture, 1973–1999. From that base, Case Studies were chosen for more extensive research. Those deeper studies represent the places which frame the different patterns of life: places for dwelling, places for worship, places for labour, places for resort, places for learning, and so on, in Dublin city: 1973–1999.

For the curious reader, the original and in most instances longer versions of the Case Studies can be read at the IAA, where the '20th-Century Architecture in Dublin City' project is on deposit.

Ellen Rowley and Carole Pollard (Editors)

Note to the reader: Measurements are provided in a mixture of feet and metres, depending on the original architects' approaches. Where the economics of projects is relevant, we provide the original IR£ (IEP) amounts, leaving the reader to their own calculations; as the essays move through the decades, the reader will get their own sense of construction costs and values. When Ireland switched from IR£ to €, the rate was €1.27 (€1.2697) to IR£1.00, or EUR 1.00 to IEP 0.787564 (1 Jan. 1999-9 Feb. 2002).

We have worked hard to source interesting and atmospheric visual material from the archives. Some are straightforwardly by photographers like John Donat and sourced from the RIBA collections, for instance, but in some instances the images come from construction pamphlets or practice portfolios. Where possible, we acknowledge and attribute images therefore we apologise for any photographers or authors we have missed.

Acknowledgements

This book is the third volume in a three-part series which is based on a pioneering survey and research-based study into the architecture of the twentieth century in Dublin City. It is an action of the Dublin City Heritage Plan supported with grant assistance from the Heritage Council of Ireland.

First and foremost, the research team would like to acknowledge the support of Charles Duggan (as Heritage Officer, Dublin City Council). Charles commissioned the research from 2011, consistently supporting the project ever since and through his professional tenacity has brought Volume 1 (2016), Volume 2 (2019) and this present Volume 3 to fruition. We also wish to acknowledge the support of Dublin City Council's Acting Chief Executive, Richard Shakespeare; Deirdre Scully, Acting City Planner; Máire Igoe, Acting Executive Manager; Sheila Hennessy, Senior Executive Officer. Thank you to Abigail O'Reilly, Graduate Heritage Officer, and colleagues from the Conservation Office: Paraic Fallon, Niamh Kiernan, Mary McDonald, Aislinn Collins, Mary-Liz McCarthy, Sinéad Hughes, and former colleagues Sarah Halpin, Carl Raftery, and John Beattie.

Deep-felt thanks are due to mega talented and conscientious book designer, Peter Maybury; to Noelle Moran and Orla Carr at UCD Press, for helping the editors get this volume over the line; and to our two anonymous readers for their astute comments and advice towards improving the essays.

We are very grateful to all the archives and libraries which facilitated our research especially the staff at the Irish Architectural Archive (IAA): Colum O'Riordan, Eve McAulay, Aisling Dunne, Simon Lincoln, Anne Henderson and Julia Barrett. This Volume and the whole series could not have been made without the IAA's extensive collections or without the IAA's expert and generous staff.

Thank you to the staff of Dublin City Archive and Library, Gilbert Library and Dublin City Council Planning Counter; the staff at Richview Architectural Library, UCD, namely Nessa Collinge, Emily Doherty and Helen Layton Morgan; to Sandra Collins, Arlene Healy, Audrey Drohan, Andrew Clinch and James Molloy of UCD Library; the staff at the National Library of Ireland; the staff at National College of Art and Design (NCAD) Library and NIVAL, NCAD; Noelle Dowling, Peter Sobolewski (Dublin Diocesan Archives); Karen Johnson (Christian Brothers Province Centre); Gerard Crowley, Brendan Delany, Gerry Hampson, Tanya Keyes, Pat Yeates (ESB Archive); Frederick Gilbert Watson (McLaughlin & Harvey Archive).

The following people and architectural practices have greatly assisted in the making of this book, from enabling access to buildings and archive materials, to supporting and encouraging the researchers and photographer: Marcus Donaghy, Miriam Delaney, James Pike (Ash Grove); Tony Cotter, John Fleming, Rachel Moore, Niall Lennon Day (Molyneux House); Malcolm Hughes, Gillian Morgan, Sarah Fortune (Merrion Hall); Ronan Phelan, Paul Hadfield, Niall Scott, Michael Tallon, Kamila Synak, Sarah Jane Lee (PMPA, Papal Cross, Bank of Ireland, Port/Dock HQ – Scott Tallon Walker Architects); David Torpey (Miesian Plaza); Gerry Barry (Port/Docks HQ); Robert Byrne (AnCo); John Meagher (d.2021), Shane de Blacam, Nicci Brock, Trevor Dobbyn, Andy Richardson (de Blacam & Meagher); Mathew Hand (Donaghmede); David Lanigan (A & D Wejchert); Joan O'Connor, John de Vere White (Herbert Mews); David Browne, Vincent Delany, Martin Donnelly, Philip O'Reilly, Maura Butler, Barra Heavey, Fergus Dowd, Deirdre Hayes (Irish Life, AIB HQ, Poolbeg Chimneys – RKD); Brian Moran (Hines); Kay Mooney, Brian Ferns (Central Bank); Jean O'Sullivan (Poolbeg); Sheila O'Donnell, John Tuomey, Willie Carey, Joan Whelan, Monika Hinz, Will Dimond (IFI, Juvenile Court, Multi-Denominational School – ODT); Noel Collins, Eugene Dudley (Dublin District Children's Court); Mathew Barry (IDA); Penny Storey, Martin Donnelly, Orla Sweeney, Carlos Gonzalez Diez, Moira O'Brien, Lisa Mc Caffrey, Michael Murray, Edward McParland, Éilis O'Donnell, John Monaghan (Trinity Buildings Office, Trinity Enterprise Centre/IDA, Dining Hall, Arts Building, Parsons); Jim O'Beirne, David Clarke, Carole O'Riordan, Kim Fetherstone, John Purcell (SJH Energy Centre); Mary Daly (Treasury Building); Eamonn Duffy (City Architects); Thaddeus Breen (Wordwell Press); Derek Byrne, Brian Dempsey (Henry J. Lyons); Sunniva O'Flynn, Sarah Glennie, Bert Donlon (IFI); Maeve Dowling, Christina Maurice (Allies and Morrison); Tom Ryan, David Ebbs, Peter Cook, Sophia Gibb (British Embassy Dublin); Thomas Glendon, Serbian Orthodox Church Parish of Saint George (Artane Oratory); Aisling White, Caroline Kennedy PR (Castle Street); Tony Horan (Horan Rainsfort Architects); Mary O'Brien (Willow Field); Shelley McNamara, Yvonne Farrell, Paula Stone (Grafton Architects); Derek Tynan, Niall Rowan, Stefany Georgieva (DTA); Kate O'Carroll (Printworks); Paul Keogh, Rachael Chidlow (PKA); Valerie Mulvin, Niall McCullough (d.2021), Ruth O'Herlihy, Caoimhe McAndrew (McCullough Mulvin); Cliodhna Shaffrey, Michael Hill, Órla Goodwin, Niamh O'Malley, Ruairí Ó Cuív, Tanad Williams, Andreas V. K. Kindler, Brian

Fay (Temple Bar Gallery + Studios); Ray Dinh, Michael Hayes (Darndale); Matt Carroll, Susan Roundtree, Cian Neville (Fitzgibbon Court); Gerry Cahill, Robert McManus (Gerry Cahill Architects); Jan Mingle, Sr Stanislaus Kennedy, Emma Moore, Nieve White, Sr Sile Wall, Therese Towey (Stanhope Green/Focus Ireland); maintenance and management of Dublin City Council housing department, including Eileen Martin, Eamon Griffith, Brian Curran, Peter Murphy and Kay Noonan Cork; Joe Lawrence, Pierre Long; Hugh Campbell; Grainne Shaffrey; Loughlin Kealy; Michael Pike; Barbara Ennis; Jane Mitchell; Barry Kelly; Freddie Penco; Brian O'Shaughnessy, Lilu Savage (MArch UCD 2021); Haylee Derrickson, Aisling Ward (MArch UCD 2023); Una McQuillan; Jonathan Makepeace (RIBApix).

The editors apologise to their patient husbands and families for missing spring and summer days together. Ellen Rowley thanks Stephen, Lillian, Essie and Joan. Carole Pollard thanks Ray, Ellen, Luke, Harry and Charlie.

This Volume is dedicated to architect, writer and Dubliner, Niall McCullough.

Ellen, Carole, Merlo, Aoibheann, Aoife, Natalie, Paul and Shane
Summer 2023

About the Authors

About the editors

Ellen Rowley (PhD) is an architectural humanities teacher and writer on twentieth-century Irish architecture. She is Lecturer in Modern Irish Architecture in UCD's School of Architecture, Planning and Environmental Policy, where she teaches architectural history and culture programmes. Her research into Modernism and Irish architecture focuses on themes of Catholic patronage and suburban development, obsolescence and mid-century buildings today, housing and everyday architecture in Ireland, 1940–80. Ellen's collaborative research project, *Evolving Legacies* (with Philip Crowe, since 2021), focuses on the adaptive reuse of Catholic buildings in Ireland, most particularly convent buildings and post-1940 parish churches. Her work with artist Fiona Hallinan and the Department of Ultimology on the demolition of Finglas Church has culminated in a film, *Making Dust* (2023, director Fiona Hallinan). Ellen continues to publish extensively in international and local contexts including her housing monograph, *Housing, Architecture and the Edge Condition: Dublin is Building, 1930s–1970s* (Routledge, 2018). Ellen co-edited the Yale University Press/Royal Irish Academy series *Architecture 1600–2000,* Volume IV of *Art and Architecture of Ireland* (Yale, RIA, 2014) and more recently (with Finola O'Kane), *Making Belfield. Space and Place at UCD* (UCD Press, 2020).

Since 2011, Ellen has led this Dublin City Council and Heritage Council of Ireland research project on the 20th-century architecture of Dublin City. To date the project has produced this book series; *More Than Concrete Blocks: Dublin City's 20th-Century Buildings and their Stories*; Volume 1, 1900–1940 (FCP, 2016) and Volume 2, 1940–1972 (FCP, 2019), as well as architectural tours and talks. She was consulting curator at No. 14 Henrietta Street, tenement house and museum for Dublin City Council (DCC), and consulting curator of UCD's jubilee celebration of its 1960s campus. In 2019–20, Ellen was guest editor on RTE Radio One DAVIS NOW radio lecture series on 'Making Home' (producer/director, Clíodhna Ní Anluain). In 2017, she was awarded Honorary Membership of the Royal Institute of the Architects of Ireland (RIAI) for her services to Irish architecture.

Carole Pollard (PhD) is an architect and architectural historian and a Fellow of the Royal Institute of the Architects of Ireland (RIAI). Her practice comprises conservation consultancy (specialising in twentieth-century architecture), writing and teaching. She recently completed a PhD at the School of Architecture in UCD where her thesis topic was Irish architect Andrew Devane (1917–2000) and his office block architecture in 1960s/70s Dublin. Carole's MA thesis (NCAD) on architect Liam McCormick (1916–1997) resulted in the publication: *Liam McCormick, Seven Donegal Churches* (Gandon Editions, 2011).

Carole is a past president of the RIAI and recently chaired the RIAI Conservation Accreditation Taskforce which developed new RIAI Conservation Standards and a new accreditation system for architects in conservation practice. Carole joined the Dublin City Council '20th-Century Architecture in Dublin City' research team in 2014, contributing to the two volumes to date of *More Than Concrete Blocks* (FCP, 2016 and 2019). Carole teaches at Dublin School of Architecture at TU Dublin where she is Programme Chair for the Professional Diploma in Architectural Practice post-graduate course. Recent publications include 'Letters from America: Andrew Devane 1945–1956', in *Building Material 23* (AAI, 2020); 'Bord na Móna settlements in the 1950s', in *Out of the Ordinary – Irish Housing Design 1950–1980* (Routledge, 2020); and 'A lifelong affair – Liam McCormick and Imogen Stuart', in *Modern Religious Architecture in Germany, Ireland and Beyond* (Bloomsbury, 2019).

About the authors

Natalie de Róiste is an architectural historian and a town planner with extensive inventorying experience with the National Inventory of Architectural Heritage (NIAH). She has been working on the 20th-Century Architecture project for DCC since 2011, and managed and developed the Outline Survey from its inception to its publication through *More Than Concrete Blocks* Volumes 1 and 2(FCP, 2016 and 2019). Natalie also managed the archive illustrations for the first two volumes. Natalie wrote several entries to *Architecture 1600–2000*, Vol. IV of the *Art and Architecture of Ireland* series (Yale, RIA, 2014).

Merlo Kelly is a Grade 1 Conservation Architect with Lotts Architecture & Urbanism, a Design Fellow in Architecture and a PhD candidate at University College Dublin. She is a member of the Irish Architectural Archive, ICOMOS, An Taisce, and is a Peer Assessor for the Arts Council of Ireland. In 2012, she was awarded the ICOMOS Rachel MacRory Award for her MA in Urban and Building Conservation (MUBC) thesis on Luke Gardiner and the development of north Dublin. This research led to her book *An Introduction to the Architectural Heritage of Dublin North City* (Dept. of Arts, Heritage and the Gaeltacht, 2015).

Research forms an integral part of Merlo's teaching and practice, and she has disseminated her research in several publications and public lectures, contributing chapters to *Portraits of the City – Dublin & the Wider World* (FCP, 2012); *More than Concrete Blocks* Volume 1 (FCP, 2016) & Volume 2 (FCP, 2019), *Malton's Views of Dublin* (Martello, 2021), *States of Entanglement* (Actar D, 2021) and *James Hoban: Designer and Builder of the White House* (White House Historical Association, 2021). Merlo has written extensively for the 20th-Century Architecture project since the project commenced in 2011.

Aoibheann Ní Mhearáin graduated from UCD School of Architecture in 2001 and was awarded an MArch from Princeton University in 2008. Practising as an architect she has worked nationally and internationally, including with Grafton Architects, Dublin, OMA, Rotterdam, John McLaughlin Architects, Dublin as well as running her own practice, anima. She has taught in UCD School of Architecture, Cork Centre for Architectural Education and Princeton University. Aoibheann's research has focused on the history of 20th-century architecture in Ireland and includes essays on the community school in Birr, Co. Offaly by Peter and Mary Doyle, in *Infra-Éireann: Infrastructure and the Architectures of Modernity in Ireland 1916–2016*, edited by Gary A. Boyd and John McLaughlin (Routledge, 2016) and on the work of Tyndall; Hogan Hurley in *Irish Housing Design 1950–1980: Out of the Ordinary*, edited by Brian Ward, Michael Pike, Gary A. Boyd (Routledge, 2020). Working with Queen's University Belfast and John McLaughlin Architects, Aoibheann co-ordinated the Getty Foundation funded research project on the conservation of St Brendan's Community School in Birr. She was awarded a research grant in 2018 and she won the RIAI research award in 2021. Aoibheann was a participant in the Close Encounters Exhibition of the Venice Biennale in 2018, with Mary Laheen.

Aoife O'Halloran is a recent architectural graduate working in practice. She holds an MA degree in architecture from University College Dublin (2019). Her final year dissertation was awarded the School of Architecture's Dissertation Prize and was further nominated for the Royal Institute of British Architects President's Award. Her research centred on the 1976 ideas competition, 'A Parish Church' which instigated a building campaign of late-modernist churches around Dublin's periphery. Her research unpicked the competition through the lens of a number of its commissions, namely that of de Blacam & Meagher's Church of Our Lady of Mount Carmel in Firhouse. Aoife works with Lawrence and Long Architects and has completed an award-winning scheme of four contemporary townhouses in Ranelagh, as well as a number of conservation-led projects on a variety of Protected Structures.

Shane O'Toole is an architect, architectural historian and critic, Adjunct Associate Professor at UCD, Honorary Fellow of the RIAI and International Fellow of the Royal Institute of British Architects. He was named *International Building Press* architecture writer of the year in 2008, 2009 and 2010 for his pieces in *The Sunday Times* and *Building Design* (UK). Shane was also the recipient of awards from CICA, the International Committee of Architecture Critics, in 2011, 2014, 2017 and 2020 when he was granted the Perre Vago Award for Journalism for a keynote essay in *The Architectural Review* (UK). He was inaugural Director of the Irish Architecture Foundation and twice Commissioner of the Irish Pavilion at the Venice Biennale. He was a co-founder of DoCoMoMo (Documentation and Conservation of Modern Movement buildings and sites) International at Eindhoven in 1990.

After extensive private research into the architecture of Dublin 1900–1999, Shane originated the 20th-Century Architecture project's Outline Survey in 2011. His most important critical essays from 1989 to 2021 have been collected in two volumes: *One Hundred & One Hosannas for Architecture* (Gandon Editions, 2017) and *Ninety-Nine Tesserae from Architecture* (Karl Krämer Verlag, 2021).

Paul Tierney is an architect, researcher and architectural photographer. He is a lecturer and tutor in TU Dublin and Griffith College Dublin. An architectural photographer since 2002, Paul has vast experience capturing contemporary and modern buildings in Ireland. His photographs have been published annually in *New Irish Architecture*; in international journals such as *The Architects' Journal* and *Japan Architect*; in *Scott Tallon Walker: 100 Projects* (Gandon, 2006), and *Architecture 1600–2000,* Volume IV of *Art and Architecture of Ireland* (Yale, RIA, 2014).

Paul has had a number of solo photographic exhibitions and was chosen for the Royal Hibernian Academy (RHA) annual show in 2004 and 2008. He and his work formed a central part of 'FREE MARKET', the Irish Pavilion at the Venice Architecture Biennale 2018. Since 2011, Paul has been integral to this '20th-Century Architecture in Dublin City' project, as project photographer, technology manager and contributing researcher.

About Dublin City Council Heritage Office

The *More Than Concrete Blocks* book series and the research project on 20th-century architecture in Dublin which fuels it are commissioned and funded through the Dublin City Strategic Heritage Plan 2023–8. This broad-ranging plan was developed in consultation with individuals drawn from the fields of archaeology, architectural heritage and cultural heritage representing individual practitioners, NGO heritage organisations and interest groups, government departments, and third-level educational institutions. There are five strategic goals identified in the plan which recognise the importance, first and foremost, of a community-led and locally focused approach to what we do and what we support, and the need to facilitate greater access to heritage and to make room for diverse voices. Creating knowledge is one of the strategic goals. It underlines Dublin City Council's commitment to continue to add to our existing knowledge by continuing to commission and publish new academic research on aspects of Dublin's cultural, social, archaeological and architectural heritage.

Series Introduction
More Than Concrete Blocks

Ellen Rowley

In the early 1930s, the architect, writer and town planner Manning Robertson composed the curious volume *Cautionary Guide to Dublin*, a miscellany of annotated photographs of Dublin buildings designed to guide the layman through the rights and wrongs of Dublin's contemporary architecture. Contemporary readers may find the punctilious Robertson's calls for 'order and tidiness' and 'restraint and good proportion' rather stuffy and didactic, but his introduction is revealing of the common perception of the 1930s city:

> In natural beauty of situation, in the dignity of its wide streets and Georgian architecture,
> few capitals can vie with Dublin. Only during the past fifty years has the octopus of
> thoughtless development and ill placed and ill designed buildings seriously threatened our city.
> (Robertson, 1934)

Robertson's references to Dublin's Georgian fabric and to the city's geographical position at the mouth of the Irish Sea and at the foot of the Dublin mountains are unsurprising. More notable is how he points negatively to the tentacles of recent ribbon development; the trickle of building seeping through the townships of Pembroke, Rathmines, Drumcondra and Clontarf, all enabled by the mid-to-late nineteenth-century transport networks of suburban railways and trams. Increasingly, as Robertson saw it, new buildings were 'threatening' the integrity of the traditional city.

What is most interesting in all this is the reality that by the 1930s, the abiding architectural feature of Dublin remained its Georgian building stock, set onto the eighteenth-century city-centre plan of the Wide Streets Commissioners and the speculation of such developers as Luke Gardiner. Indeed, this Georgian fabric remained remarkably unaltered until the 1960s, a situation that stood in contrast to the 20th-century urban development of other European capitals. In sketching the character of Dublin's architecture through the 20th century, we cannot forget that the city remained small, with its so-called traditional form relatively intact certainly for the first decades of the century. By 1914, its population had crept up to the modest figure of approximately 300,000, but the 1930s witnessed a surge in population, and from then until the early 1960s, Dublin grew by 30 per cent and was transformed from city to city-region. During this period, the city underwent an idiosyncratic process of urbanisation which necessarily influenced the shape, look and the overall tendencies of its 20th-century architecture.

More Than Concrete Blocks Volume 3

What we cannot forget in trying to understand what was built in Dublin during the 20th century is the relationship between the physical artefact and social and cultural histories. Fact: there was a relentless 'drift from the countryside' (the Irish euphemism for rural depopulation), representing the shift from rural to urban, ostensibly from the 1930s onwards. The city swelled and mushroomed; urbanisation was rapid and intense, leading to the emergence of an urban centre that became defined by its slums for at least the first half of the century. In the ongoing attempts to clear the slums, the city was turned inside out: we might note that paradoxically, urbanisation brought about the unravelling of the traditional city fabric and the development of masses of public and private housing at the city edge.

Therefore, we could assert that one dominating feature of Dublin's 20th-century architectural history was the fairly uninhibited growth of suburbia. Unlike equivalent development in Western metropolises from the 1920s through the 1950s, however, the rash of low-lying suburban residences in Dublin was not accompanied by the erection of iconic structures or plazas or skyscrapers at a regenerating commercial city-centre. Of course, impressive buildings did appear, and this overview of Dublin's 20th-century architecture respectively addresses those important contributions. However, until the great shifts in economic policy in the early 1960s which brought about a generation of American-inspired corporate and semi-state buildings, Dublin's architectural development was mostly confined to modest buildings. This may be termed the making of a 'middle landscape' which was overseen and largely designed by Dublin Corporation (the forerunner to Dublin City Council) and private speculative development. This landscape took the form of housing estates, small-scale commercial terraces, mass-produced edifices of religious authority (Catholic churches and schools), local health clinics and occasional large hospitals, vocational colleges and public libraries, some significant transport structures, as well as a sprinkling of factories, petrol stations and cinemas.

While the story is not so neat and straightforward, taking dramatic turns here and there, this tale of belated urbanisation forms the central narrative within the greater adventure that is Irish Modernism. Importantly, regardless of attempts following independence towards decentralisation, Dublin continued as the country's primary urban centre. The city's 20th-century pre-eminence was largely down to physical and geographical circumstances. By 1951, Dublin contained almost one-fifth of the Republic's total population, at 569,000, while the combined populations of the regional urban centres of Cork, Limerick and Waterford was just 154,000. Nevertheless, Dublin's stature was always partly symbolic. As the Free State's first minister for Local Government Ernest Blythe stated in 1923, 'the character of the capital will have a very important influence upon the progress and development of the State.'

So, in a chicken-and-egg scenario, Dublin was thrust into the role of Ireland's leading urban place while actively embracing its place at the vanguard, growing physically and culturally throughout the 20th-century. So it was that the city's architecture continuously expressed this leading role. Dublin was always the incubator of foreign ideas and technologies. And such incubation, in architectural terms, may have reached its zenith following a historic sequence of firsts, namely: Ireland joining the European Economic Community (EEC) in 1973; then an international and sustained local economic recession coming out of the 1970s oil crisis; and ultimately, the migratory experience. Migration of Irish architects was enforced – the so-called brain drain – and while away, they read, studied under, and met new heroes of international architectural Modernism. Pointedly, many of these architects returned, freshly armed. By the end of the century, with the lessons of Modernism having been absorbed, its architects found themselves at the heart of the most significant building boom in the history of the State.

This overview recounts that story.

Ellen Rowley (Series Editor)

1970s: Architectural Culture

Carole Pollard

Road widening scheme at the junction of North King Street and Church Street, photograph by Pat Langan in *Hands Off Dublin*, Deirdre Kelly, 1976 (Private collection)

The Turning Point

Despite a recent orgy of destruction, [Dublin] has been much less pulled about than other cities of comparable size and importance. This is true of the fabric of the city, but it is also true of the community: the process of segregating interests and classes has not got so far; there still remains in Dublin a traditional urban sense to which we can appeal; she is still – just – a living city.
(*The Architectural Review*, 1974)

In 1974, the November edition of the British journal *Architectural Review* was titled 'A Future for Dublin'. There was no question mark placed at the end of the title, but the content raised significant questions about what Dublin might look like in the future if current development trends continued. Importantly, the authors – including *Architectural Review* editor Lance Wright who knew Dublin well – believed that it was not too late to preserve the city's unique character. The article described the challenges Dublin was likely to face in the coming years and presented advice on how to avoid the mistakes that had been made in many British cities. Essentially, it was a strongly argued plea to the city's decision-makers, architects, and citizens to avoid poorly considered planning decisions that would further decimate Dublin's architectural and historical integrity.

This volume of *More Than Concrete Blocks* begins at this very point in Dublin's history, when the city's architectural legacy was tottering on the brink of irreversible change. As it turned out, no one – not least the editors of *Architectural Review* – could stand in the way of the significant political, social, and developmental changes that would be imposed on the city during the tumultuous days of the 1970s. As the 1970s essays in this volume of *More Than Concrete Blocks* show, the dominant force in the shaping of the city during the decade was the ongoing demand for office buildings accompanied, to a lesser extent, by efforts from Dublin Corporation to improve and consolidate pockets of community housing.

This volume starts in 1973, a watershed for Ireland in terms of social and economic progression. After 60 years in public life, the country's most prominent political leader, Eamon de Valera stepped down as President of Ireland. The year also marked the death of John Charles McQuaid, ending his 32-year reign as Archbishop of Dublin. Since the foundation of the State, those two men had been primarily responsible for the direction of Ireland's cultural expression: a unique blend of Catholicism, insularity, and myopic nationalism which flourished from the 1940s and lingered into the 1970s and beyond. Their influence extended into every facet of Irish life including, it can be deduced, public opinion about architecture and the evolution of Dublin city: de Valera through his rural equals good / urban equals bad rhetoric; and McQuaid through his patronage of a prolific number of schools, churches, and hospital buildings designed and built during his reign. While sharing a culture – as most church and statesmen did at this time in Ireland – McQuaid and DeValera did not always agree. There were nuanced differences in their approaches, but generally speaking their influence seeped into perceptions that the city centre was not a wholly suitable place to raise a family, and that the historic city, because of its myriad colonial associations, was not representative of an independent Irish state. Arguably, their view that the city had dubious societal value permeated the minds of many who held the fate of the city within their gift.

Despite the decline in the city centre, over the decade of the 1970s the population of greater Dublin expanded by 17 per cent reaching 903,000 in 1980. Population growth was primarily driven by employment opportunities because of the expansion of the city's industrial base and an increase in jobs in the services sector, particularly banking, insurance, and finance. However, during the same period, there was a sharp hollowing out of city's core as the resident population within the canal ring continued to drop (from 270,000 in 1926) to a new low of 70,000 in 1979. Most of the city's populace lived in the ever-expanding suburbs that ringed the city beyond Dublin Corporation boundaries.

In 1973, a coalition government, comprising the second largest political party, Fine Gael and the Labour Party, was in power and full of optimism for continuing economic growth and social progress. The same year, Ireland joined the European Economic Community (EEC) opening the country to the ideological and cultural pluralism of Western Europe. However, optimism was dampened when the Yom Kippur War in October 1973 led to an oil crisis that forced an economic slowdown and a set-back in the pace of Dublin's development. Major building projects that were underway were reduced in ambition and scale, and others were abandoned. There was a short-lived economic pick-up in 1976 but a second oil crisis in 1979 once again stalled progress. At the same time, escalating violence in Northern Ireland threatened peace on the island and preoccupied political debate. By 1974, inflation was running at 20 per cent and during 1975 the Government had to increase

Office interior at Bank of Ireland HQ, Baggot Street, 1975 photographed by John Donat (Courtesy of Scott Tallon Walker image collection)

social welfare payments and introduce food subsidies while unemployment rates escalated.

Despite the economic uncertainty however, development in Dublin continued through the 1970s, most notably on the southside of the city where sites for office buildings were in huge demand. Significant developments included Irish Shipping headquarters at Merrion Hall on the city's south-eastern boundary, the lavish Bank of Ireland headquarters on Baggot Street Lower, and Dublin's first private corporate campus, AIB Bankcentre in Ballsbridge. There were two main factors driving the demand for offices on the southside: the historically prosperous southeast quarter retained its elegant demeanour (thanks largely to the ongoing influence of the Pembroke Estate) and most of the city's workforce lived in the expanding middle-class southside suburbs. In the meantime, however, other parts of the city deteriorated because of slum demolitions, road widening schemes and general neglect. The development of the Irish Life Centre on Lower Abbey Street was an important exception, and a rare example of urban regeneration on the north side of the city.

As our series overview discusses, suburban expansion drove ever-increasing reliance on the motor car so that traffic congestion became a serious problem. State-commissioned reports on traffic management recommended solutions such as turning the Grand Canal into a motorway or building a northside ring road on top of the Royal Canal with a four-lane flyover at the Liffey river. Although none of the more ambitious (i.e., costly) road schemes were built, Dublin Corporation proceeded with localised demolitions of streets with apparently little consideration of where the traffic was actually going. During the 1970s many streets, including major

More Than Concrete Blocks Volume 3

Frances Quillinan
Senior Architect
Limerick City Council,
1971 (Courtesy of Archive
of The Limerick Leader)

thoroughfares like Clanbrassil Street and Cork Street on the southside and Parnell Street and North King Street on the north side, were allowed to decay as their buildings were demolished to make way for road widening. This led to the unintended consequence of an abundance of surface carparks on razed and derelict sites which in turn induced more cars into the city.

Social unrest, borne out of tensions over social progress and economic hardship, led to a series of public demonstrations on the streets of Dublin. Socially-driven protests that were witnessed in other parts of the western world during the 1960s eventually came to Dublin in the 1970s. During the early years of the decade, students at the National College of Art on Kildare Street held protests demanding a democratically-controlled college that would contribute to the cultural wealth of the city and country. Feminism increasingly became a political issue, as witnessed when the Irish branch of the Women's Liberation Movement (IWLM), established in 1970, held a meeting of 1,000 women in the Mansion House in 1971. Later that year the IWLM organised a trip from Connolly Station to Belfast to buy contraceptives in protest at their prohibition in the Republic. At the forefront of the IWLM's demands was equality in the workplace through the abolition of the Marriage Bar which, under Section 16 of the Local Government Act of 1955, placed a ban on employing married women across the public sector. The ban extended to many other institutions too and meant single women had to resign from their job upon getting married and married women were disqualified from applying for vacancies.

One of the cases the IWLM championed was that of Frances Quillinan, a mother of four who had worked as an architect on a temporary contract in

The Hirschfield Centre, Fownes Street Upper after a fire in November 1987. (Courtesy of Derek Speirs)

Limerick Corporation for eleven years. When she applied for a permanent post that was advertised in 1971, she was not even granted an interview because she was married and therefore automatically ineligible for the position. While precluded from the permanent post in 1971, Frances Quillinan was able to pursue secure tenure following the lifting of the Marriage Bar. Though lifted in 1973, due largely to conditions attached to Ireland's membership of the EEC, the Marriage Bar endured for most of the 1970s when there were few women architects in practice except for those who were unmarried or those who continued to practice with their architect husbands.

Through this period, international events influenced the tenor of protests on Dublin's streets. The first of many anti-apartheid protests took place marching from O'Connell Street to Leinster House in 1970. A sit-down protest against war in Vietnam was held at the US Embassy in Ballsbridge the same year. Support for the Stonewall riots in New York led to Dublin's first public gay rights demonstration in 1974 when 10 people marched from St Stephen's Green to Merrion Square. The National Gay Federation was founded in 1979 and opened their headquarters, the Hirschfield Centre, in Fownes Street in April that year. Dublin's first Pride Week was held that June.

Tragically, violence also visited Dublin's streets. Catholic unrest in Northern Ireland escalated in the aftermath of Bloody Sunday on 30 January 1972 when British soldiers shot unarmed citizens during a civil rights protest in Derry. This event marked a turning point in the Troubles in Northern Ireland, spilling over the border into the Republic. As described further in our British Embassy essay, February 1972 saw Dublin's British Embassy on Merrion Square petrol bombed and destroyed. In 1974, three bombs exploded in Dublin, killing 27 people.

Industrial strikes and demonstrations were a familiar scene throughout the decade with two bank strikes, the first in 1970 which lasted six months and a second in 1976; a

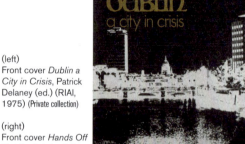
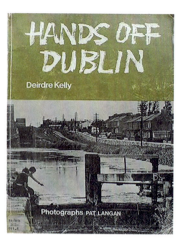

(left)
Front cover *Dublin a City in Crisis*, Patrick Delaney (ed.) (RIAI, 1975) (Private collection)

(right)
Front cover *Hands Off Dublin*, Deirdre Kelly (1976) (Private collection)

string of ESB (Electricity Supply Board) strikes started in 1972; a Dublin bus strike in 1974; and a four-month postal strike in 1979. Also in 1979, almost 300,000 people – 10 per cent of the national population – took to Dublin's streets protesting about the PAYE tax system. The biggest gathering of the decade, however, took place when 1,250,000 people flocked to the Phoenix Park in September 1979 to hear Pope John Paul II say mass at the newly inaugurated Papal Cross.

More explicitly relevant to the stories held in this volume, some of the biggest protests of the decade revolved around the destruction of the city's built heritage and the loss of city communities. The first major campaign, known as the 'Battle of Hume Street', began in 1969 and lasted into 1970. Also in 1970, activist Deirdre Kelly established the Living City Group whose purpose was to sustain urban communities within the city rather than dispersal to distant suburbs. In 1976 Kelly published *Hands off Dublin* (O'Brien Press), a stark portrait of the destruction of the city. Dublin Corporation investment in housing in the city included the large suburban-style development at Darndale or more exceptionally, small city regeneration housing developments including Ash Grove in the Coombe which consolidated an existing community. Máirín de Burca, of the IWLM and Sinn Féin, was also a strong advocate for the protection of existing communities in the city centre. In 1976, Friends of Medieval Dublin was established by Revd F. X. Martin to halt the development of new headquarter offices for Dublin Corporation on the site of Dublin's first Viking settlement at Wood Quay. The 'Save Wood Quay' campaign drew thousands of supporters from as far afield as Scandinavia, with several colourful and noisy marches over subsequent years. Despite designation of the site as a national monument in 1978 and occupation by the protesters, the campaign failed.

1970s: Architectural Culture

The Catholic Church continued to be a major player in the development of churches, schools, healthcare buildings and the ongoing development of University College Dublin at Belfield. Churches and schools were built primarily in the new suburban parishes that surrounded the city, including the church of the Holy Trinity, Donaghmede by A. & D. Wejchert Architects. Church bodies were also involved in the relocation of schools from city centre sites to greenfield suburban campuses including Wesley College which moved from St Stephens Green to Ballinteer (1969, Robin Walker of Scott Tallon Walker), St Andrews College which moved from St Stephen's Green to Booterstown (1973, Ahrends Burton Koralek), and Alexandra College which moved from Earlsfort Terrace to Milltown (1972, Ryan & Hogan) (Outline Survey, More Than Concrete Blocks (*MTCB*), Volume 2). The appeal of the pastoral campus also influenced the location and design of new headquarters for RTÉ at Montrose (1973, Scott Tallon Walker) (Outline Survey, *MTCB* Volume 2) and AIB Bankcentre, Ballsbridge (1979 & 1980, Robinson Keefe & Devane).

Throughout the decade, as more women remained in professional practice, their influence began to shape the city's architecture. Polish architect Danuta Kornaus-Wejchert worked in Robinson Keefe & Devane from the mid-1960s until she established a practice with her husband Andrzej Wejchert in 1974; while Mary O'Grady Doyle, who had previously worked with Michael Scott & Partners, established a practice with her husband Peter Doyle in 1973 (see Women's Refuge, Rathmines, Outline Survey). Maura Shaffrey who practised with her husband, Patrick Shaffrey, built a reputation as one of Ireland's finest conservation architects. Meanwhile, at Stephenson Gibney & Associates, by 1975 two of the eighteen associates were women: Aine Lawlor, an interior designer, and Judy Neligan, a graduate of the DIT School of Architecture. Deirdre O'Connor, who graduated from DIT in 1973 worked with Robinson Keefe & Devane until 1976, and subsequently joined Arthur Gibney & Partners becoming the only female of six co-directors in 1981.

The rise in the dominance of banks and finance houses is an important part of the story of Dublin's architecture of the 1970s. Each of the country's main banks built new headquarters buildings in the city: Allied Irish Banks at Ballsbridge (1979, Robinson Keefe & Devane); Bank of Ireland at Baggot Street (1972 and 1975, Scott Tallon Walker); and Ulster Bank at College Green (1976, Boyle + Delaney). As touched upon in the 1980s

Architects at work in Diamond Redfern Anderson offices, Dublin, mid-1970s (Courtesy of Denis Anderson collection at Irish Architectural Archive)

essay, it was during the same period that the State commissioned the new Central Bank headquarters on Dame Street (1980, Stephenson Gibney & Associates) and the Currency Centre at Sandyford, in Co. Dublin (1974, Stephenson Gibney & Associates). Insurance companies continued to provide capital for the development of offices blocks, and by the end of the decade, Irish Life Assurance Co. had consolidated its position as the largest property investment company in the country. It financed many commercial developments accommodating the city's growing office workforce and was a notable pioneer in the development of the city's northside where it developed a new headquarters at Lower Abbey Street within the larger Irish Life Centre (completed in two phases in 1979 and 1985).

Also in the mid-1970s, Irish Life embarked on a second, even more ambitious northside scheme, which, if it had been completed, would have been the biggest development project of the decade in the city. Irish Life partnered with Dublin Corporation to redevelop the Moore Street/Henry Street/Parnell Street area with a multi-use scheme including a shopping centre, offices, a multi-level carpark, a hotel, and an entertainment centre, with a theatre, cinemas, bars, and restaurants. In the end, the only part of that scheme to be built was the ILAC Centre, designed by David Keane & Partners and completed in 1981. Dublin Corporation's grand ambitions, and those of many other developers, were ultimately thwarted by the deep recession that engulfed Ireland in the closing years of the 1970s, with as we will read, detrimental economic consequences for the subsequent decade.

Against the tide of widespread demolition and prolific commercial development, the alarm bells rung by Lance Wright and his colleagues in *Architectural Review* special Dublin edition of 1974 were not ignored by Irish architects. The following year, the RIAI published *Dublin: A City in Crisis* (RIAI, 1975), a collection of essays by the country's leading architects expressing concerns and proposing solutions that they felt would facilitate new development without destroying of the city's character. Some contributions were tokenistic, however others set down fundamental principles which, notwithstanding the economic recession that ensued, might have set Dublin's development on a different course. This is particularly true of the urban housing ambitions of James Pike's essay, 'City Housing Development' in *A City in Crisis*, as discussed in '1970s Housing'; Andy Devane's essay 'Space About Buildings' which laid down the urban rationales for his design of Stephen Court, AIB Bankcentre and the Irish Life Centre; and Robin Walker and Stephen Woulfe Flanagan's essay 'Street Infill', discussed in the PMPA essa.

Dublin: A City in Crisis was a forerunner to efforts by Irish architects to draw upon international design theories to influence and drive change in Dublin's development pattern; the evolution of these efforts is explored the 1980s and 1990s essays that follow.

Save Wood Quay protest on Fishamble Street, 1978, photograph by Thaddeus Breen
(Courtesy of History Ireland)

1980s: Architectural Culture

Ellen Rowley

> The deterioration of the physical environment of Dublin city centre has passed beyond the point of concern. For years it has been evident that the centre has become less a place to live and work, and more a place of blighted streets, empty houses and deserted workplaces. Dublin's streets show less the pace and order of a capital, and more the squalor and dereliction of a city with an uncertain future. (Gerry Cahill + Loughlin Kealy, *UCD Projects for City Quays* (School of Architecture, UCD, 1987)

Derelict Quays, Inner City Survey, 1985 (Courtesy of Irish Architectural Archive)

The desolate tone of this 1987 commentary came in the face of plans for a huge transport hub (designed by US firm, Skidmore Owings Merrill) which would span the River Liffey from Ormond Quay to Temple Bar. The plans pointed to a crisis for Dublin city centre; a deeply-rooted and seemingly insoluble crisis around the architectural history, everyday design and pedestrian experience of 1980s Dublin. In an attempt to generate some critical discourse, the School of Architecture at University College Dublin hosted a symposium focusing on the future of the city's quays. Through very specific design proposals, the radicalising of the quays could work to salvage the greater city. And nowhere was Dublin's gap-toothedness and neglect more visually pronounced than at its river.

In the end, as we know from our 1990s essays and explorations of Temple Bar, the behemoth transport hub never happened in Dublin, and the quays' decay continued apace. But the riverine experiment, as published in Cahill and Kealy's collection of essays *UCD Projects for City Quays* introduced above, showcased the frustration and rising fear within Dublin's architecture community. What was to become of the city? How could local government's finances and policy-making better fuel architectural design and community-making?

The city quays proposals were some of many reactionary theoretical or blueprint architectural projects which swirled in the ether during these years. Afterall, in such a maelstrom of economic recession and unemployment, emigration and political tensions, it's not surprising that a rich architectural culture would emerge: creativity in the eye of the storm. Dubbed the 'Irish Renaissance' in *The Architects' Journal* of October 1984, a vocal younger generation of architects, back in Ireland between stints working or studying abroad were intent upon changing design approaches to the historic fabric of Dublin. Although their tools were exhibition and publication – opening an architecture gallery (Blue Studio) in Dublin, for instance – their reach grew, and their ambition deepened.

More Than Concrete Blocks Volume 3

1980s Streets,
Inner City Survey,
1985 (Courtesy of Irish
Architectural Archive)

36

Beginning at the start of the decade with an exhibition in February 1980 in London, *Traditions and Directions: The Evolution of Irish Architecture* (curated by Yvonne Farrell of Grafton Architects), it was clear that these younger architects were looking at and understanding Irish architecture differently. The built environment of the past – from city quays and Georgian squares, to bawns and demesne walls – was to be valued, adapted, added to. By the end of the decade, they had established a new architecture award scheme (New Irish Architecture, NIA est. 1985/86 by John Tuomey and others) as part of a reinvigorated Architectural Association of Ireland. And some of these architects were coming to the attention of Irish Prime-Minister or Taoiseach, Charles Haughey, with their 'Pillar Project' ideas competition for a replacement for Nelson's Column on O'Connell Street of 1988 and then, by 1991 for their 'Making a Modern Street' proposal to redesign a terrace in Dublin's Liberties neighbourhood.

Thus emerges a bucolic portrait of 1980s Dublin (and Irish) architecture: we find an almost arcadian landscape of heritage value, exhibitions, award schemes and ideas competitions. Further enforcing this view were the many interesting building projects coming to fruition in the early 1980s, which were the results of 1970s competitions. For instances, as signposted in the 1970s essay, the Dublin Diocesan Church Competition (1976) and the Community Schools competition (1974) yielded considered new buildings

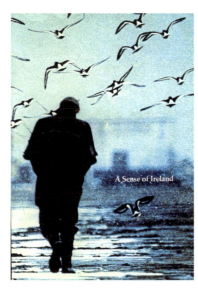

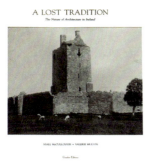

Collage of book covers: *A Sense of Ireland*, RCA, 1980; Dublin City Quays Project, UCD, 1986; *New Irish Architecture*, AAI Awards, 1987; *A Lost Tradition*, Niall McCullough and Valerie Mulvin, 1989

through the 1980s that consistently pushed the boundaries of their types. The churches were conceived as modest low-budget multifunctional buildings, part community centres, with innovative centralised floor plans and technologies. One younger architectural practice to come out of this process (having gained two new church commissions, at Firhouse [1979] and Rowlagh [1982]) was de Blacam & Meagher, and in 1989, that practice won another church competition with their quasi-subterranean Chapel of Reconciliation in Knock, Co. Mayo.

More Than Concrete Blocks Volume 3

St Thomas Community College, Bray, 1981, Val Byrne (Courtesy of Val Byrne, Gleeson Whelan Byrne image collection)

Just so, some of the community schools emerging out of the 1974 competition repositioned Ireland's architecture of education through the 1980s. Again, the type was reconceived and stretched, here bringing community amenity into the secondary school building or exploiting alien technologies and materials. At Birr Community School (1979–81), the architects Peter and Mary Doyle employed pre-cast concrete shed frames to make 5,300 square metres of educational and communal spaces, mostly one storey and arranged around six courtyards and an internal street. Another wife and husband team, also forming in the 1970s, Andrzej and Danuta Wejchert were busy with school buildings through the 1980s on foot of their success in the 1974 competition. Most radical in their educational repertoire was the pioneering Dalkey School Project of 1984 – an early iteration of the multidenominational Educate Together – where interior flexibility allowed for temporary uses by different learners.

These Dalkey and Birr schools remain beloved by their school communities today. Seemingly the 1980s world of Irish education was more than ready for innovative design. Shortly after its completion, by 1982, Birr was awarded the RIAI Triennale Gold Medal (1980–2) with the

COMMUNITY COLLEGE at BRAY co wicklow ireland 1981
VAL BYRNE architect

Derelict Dublin, in the shadow of Central Bank, Inner City Survey, 1985 (Courtesy of Irish Architectural Archive)

assessors celebrating its 'imaginative' use of an industrial technology and the 'disciplined resolution of many functional and organisational problems' (RIAI citation, 1982). And in 1981, another community school, this time for the growing satellite community at Leixlip, Co. Kildare won *Plan Magazine* building of the year in 1981. Its asbestos-cement and steel-framed mono-pitch roofs were big and bold, different or new, and definitely assertive.

The Leixlip Community School was designed by Arthur Gibney Architects. Stephenson Gibney Associates (SGA, see Molyneaux House, Merrion Hall and Central Bank essays in this volume) disbanded as the 1970s closed, so that this Leixlip school was one of the earliest of Gibney's solo schemes. But SGA still had joint projects on site or nearing completion as the new decade dawned, such as the Central Bank, rising on Dame Street and the Irish Mint or Currency Centre, ground-scraping in the south Dublin suburb of Sandyford. Architectural transposals of the contradictions of 1980s Irish culture, these two buildings were yin and yang, emotionally.

Where the mint and its financial workings were secure, integral, and actually invisible to the public, the Central Bank became an architectural platform for public outrage, especially in economic terms. By the time the seven-storey monolith was complete, it had cost £10 million. This coincided with the spiralling of national debt: in 1979 net foreign debt exceeded £1,000 million, which had grown by 1983 net foreign debt to £6,703 million! If ever a new building could encapsulate a national mood of at best, bewilderment and animosity, at worst, outrage and anger, it was the Central Bank. Its immense scale was alienating and defiant, while its immense cost appeared feckless. It signalled architectural 'notions', pitching the Dublin public against contemporary architecture. This was 1980s iconoclasm.

Mounting debt was matched by growing queues at unemployment (dole) offices – 126,000 people were unemployed in 1982, 11.4 per cent of the working population, rising to 17.6 per cent by 1987 – and ultimately to increased emigration. For architecture graduates, over half would emigrate within months of graduating (HEA Report, 1987). And so, to counter those earlier glimpses of a bucolic 1980s Irish architectural culture, come the jaundiced flashes. As the floors of the Central Bank filled up with its bank bureaucrats, in February 1981, 48 young people died in a fire at the Stardust Ballroom disco in north Dublin, leading to significant reform of Ireland's Building Regulation legislation.

That same year, in May, the hunger strikes by Republican prisoners in Northern Ireland's Maze prison, saw the death by hunger strike of Bobby Sands. Political tensions in Northern Ireland were reaching an impasse, while in the Republic political scandals, government coalitions, social activism and moral fundamentalism were the main stay in the early-mid 1980s. In 1983 for instance, there was an abortion referendum, which introduced the Eighth Amendment to the Irish Constitution, acknowledging the right to life of the unborn child (repealed by referendum in 2018). The murder of a gay man in a park in the north of the city in 1983 led to street protests organised by the gay community. Homosexuality was not decriminalised in Ireland until 1993 but the seedbed for LGBT+ rights, as discussed in the 1970s essay grew strongly during the 1980s. In 1986 then, the Divorce Referendum was defeated by 25 per cent.

Seemingly the population was not ready for too much change: change to the traditional Irish family structure; or indeed (as per public outcry around the Central Bank), change in terms of scale in the city. Property rights were probably at the heart of the public's rejection of the 1986 Divorce Referendum. Was change afoot? Yes, but change was happening haltingly, jerkily even. If the architectonics of Dublin's public housing programme of the 1980s, with their nostalgia for the artisan dwelling cottage, are anything to go by, this was a time to retreat, to recover from the bombast, the certainty and the steadfastness of Modernism which had brought recession and had housed people in unserviceable technocratic housing blocks.

Much about Ireland at this time was still firmly locked up, entrenched in the ways of previous orders. Hidden histories were coming to light and for instance, the death of a teenager, Ann Lovett, in secret childbirth (beside a grotto) in the Midlands in 1984, showed just how repressive and damaging this order could be. At the same time, the role and perception of women, as described in our 1970s essay with the lifting of the marriage ban, the introduction of unmarried mother's allowance and the general swell of feminist activism, had been changing. By the mid-1980s then, according to Ailbhe Smith (Irish feminist, academic and LGBT activist), there was unprecedented cultural expression by Irish women. Indeed, from this juncture and forever more, women began to lead the way in Irish architectural culture. Key figures included: Sheila O'Donnell, Siobhán Ní Éanaigh, Shelley McNamara, Valerie Mulvin, Rachael Chidlow, Yvonne Farrell, Mary Laheen and Anne Fletcher. Their designs and projections appeared in the New Irish Architecture awards, while their writings and teachings amplified the plight of Irish architectural design. Though missing from the directors' tables at the bigger and more commercial practices – and this is still the case in 2023 – women architects like Angela Rolfe, Nancy Strahan, Maeve Molloy, and Mary McKenna took their place in the Office of Public Works and local government sections, as never before. And key voices in conservation activism, like Maura Shaffrey and Deirdre O'Connor, were those of women.

As the decade marched on, the fate of the Dublin street loomed large. The rise in conservation awareness, coming again from the combative 1970s and exacerbated by the controversy over the height of the Central Bank, led to a maturing of respect for the Georgian fabric of the city. As one commentator wistfully noted in the *Irish Architect*: 'Georgian Dublin represents a form of urban structure balanced in a quiet equilibrium between all its elements' (George Mitchell, Irish Architect, June/Aug 1988, p. 39). Such discourse was echoed on the ground, with important adaptations to older buildings. There was the conversion of part of the former UCD buildings into the

Forticrete
Advertisement, 1984

National Concert Hall (Michael O'Doherty, OPW, 1981, see essay in *MTCB* Volume 1).

There was de Blacam & Meagher's insertion of a new atrium and zany bar when restoring Trinity College's Dining Hall after a devastating fire (1987). There were the plans to refurbish significant historic structures for the new Irish Museum of Modern Art, to be sited either in the dockland tobacco factories (of CHQ) or at the Royal Hospital Kilmainham. And looking at the list of books being reviewed by the architectural press for Christmas, 1984 (*PLAN*), from Patrick & Maura Shaffrey's *The Buildings of Irish Towns* (O'Brien Press, 1983) to John Bradley's *Viking Dublin Exposed* (O'Brien Press, 1984), one would be forgiven for believing that contemporary Irish architecture was all about its past.

The reality though was less about heritage values and more about commercial viability. While those charged with managing the city sought to atone for their 'Modernist sins' through the Metropolitan Streets Commission (est. 1986, report 1987), their objective through this commission and elsewhere, was to champion Dublin city centre context once more, but for commercial gain. As the Commission closely studied the city's commercial quarter from Grafton Street to the top of O'Connell Street, it prescribed more multi-storey carparks at the edges of this quarter, to get the shoppers in to town and proposed more pedestrian zones for those shoppers to shop at ease.

Architecturally, the shopping experience motivated one of the most significant redevelopments on Dawson Street since its 18th-century layout – that is, the demolition of the Hibernian Hotel and its replacement with a deep block of offices, an indoor shopping street and apartments (Friends Provident Centre, Costello, Murray & Beaumont, 1983–8). At about the same time came the adapted Powerscourt Townhouse Centre (James Toomey, Power Design, 1981) followed by the Stephen's Green Centre. The latter opened in time for Dublin's Millennium celebrations of 1988 and was hailed 'the greatest thing that has ever happened in the history of retailing in Ireland.' (*Irish Architect*, Nov/Dec 1988, p. 9). It was also compared to

Moscow's Gum Centre, without the gloom or the sensitivity. Unlike the Hibernian development which at least tried to reckon with the scale of the neighbouring city, the Stephen's Green Centre dwarfed its surroundings from the eponymous historic park with its Fusilier's Arch gateway, to the Art Deco Noblett's Corner (for essays on both, see *MTCB* Volume 1). It stampeded over the archaeology of Dublin's beloved Dandelion Market, and in this, was certainly the city's southside counterpart to the ILAC Centre (1981, David Keane & Partners) which had landed smack bang on top of the north inner city, obliterating a warren of historic lanes and streets in the process.

These retail developments announced the true priorities of the time. They signalled the arrival of the shopping mall to Dublin centre; vying with their suburban siblings which had been sprouting up, through the decade, with alarming consistency. Many such complexes were published in the architectural press, from Blackrock Shopping Centre (Keane Murphy Duff, 1984) and Frascati Centre (Newenham Mulligan, 1985) both in the suburb of Blackrock, to the massive Nutgrove Shopping Centre (Ambrose F. Kelly Partnership, 1984) with its 1,000-space carpark and Ireland's first McDonald's drive-through restaurant. Aside from Nutgrove's nod to High-Tech architectonics through its steel lattice frame structure – something we see little of in Irish architecture compared to 1980s British architecture

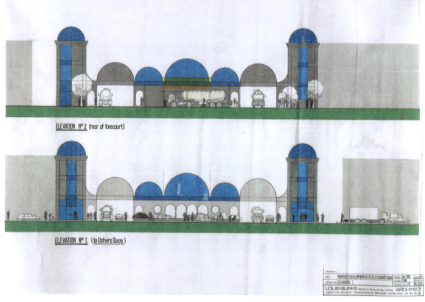

Usher's Island Petrol Station, Louis Burke, 1986 (Courtesy of Louis Burke Architect image collection)

(see AnCO essay in this volume) – these largescale developments chimed with the escalating suburbanisation of the Irish built environment during the period. That direction was reinforced by the contemporary closure of central hospitals and the attendant Tallaght Hospital competition (1985, won by RKD). While other public architectures continued apace in the suburbs such as industrial campuses generally or the UCD Campus at Belfield.

Is it possible to close out the 1980s on a positive note for Dublin's architectural culture? Through a series of crises and consequent responses, attention was being brought to the crumbling centre: An Taisce published its 1985 report on Temple Bar, coining the name of this culturally thriving quarter (see Temple Bar essays in this volume), while tax incentives were introduced for the Custom House Docks area through the 1986 Finance Act. There was the 1988 Housing Act which attempted to tackle homelessness in earnest. Meanwhile, the 1988 Millennium celebrations heralded the pedestrianisation of Grafton and Henry Streets, as well as a series of questionable but enduring public sculpture for the city (such as Molly Malone by Jeanne Rynhart or Anna Livia by Éamonn O'Doherty). Symbolically, one of the few developments on the western stretches of the city quays was a Post-Modernist petrol station on Usher's Quay (Louis Burke Architects, 1986). All were attempts to either sanitise or commercialise or simply, to call out this long-neglected place – Dublin city. But by the end of the decade there were still very few people living there and its quays continued to fall down, choked by the fumes from cars chugging by.

AIB Bankcentre,
Ballsbridge, c.1986
(Courtesy of RKD image collection)

1990s: Architectural Culture

Merlo Kelly

The Irish soccer team is welcomed home, July 1990 (Courtesy of INPHO Photography)

Still in 1990, Dublin was a bedraggled city, riddled with derelict structures and vacant lots. Alan Parker's 1991 film *The Commitments* captures the decrepit streetscape and pervasive social ennui that characterised the city at the start of the decade. The economy was at a low ebb, but despite bleak prospects, a sense of excitement and resurgence of confidence began to emerge in the early years of the decade. Amidst the urban decay, an irrepressible street culture that thrived in the 1980s continued to enliven the city centre, with music and art taking centre stage. Mary Robinson was elected as the first female President of Ireland in 1990. The Irish football team's successes in the Italia 90 World Cup prompted a joyous homecoming through the city which is captured in Tony O'Shea's photographs of the event. And Irish musicians such as Sinéad O'Connor, U2 and the Cranberries began to take the world by storm.

As the 1980s essay described, that decade was marred by economic recession and stagnant growth, with few opportunities in construction. Like so many at the time, young architects had been forced to emigrate and seek opportunities and experience overseas. A dearth of construction meant that many who remained invested time and energy in developing theories on the urban condition, and proposals for its regeneration. Emerging from this period of reflective design and study, at home and abroad, architects were brimming with ideas and poised to build. Returning émigrés and international influences in the field of architecture and urban studies meant that change was already underway as the decade opened. The spotlight was firmly placed on Dublin following the European City of Culture designation in 1991, marking a distinct turning point in the city's fortunes.

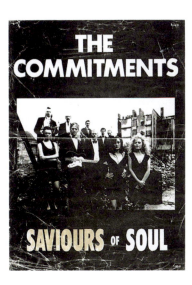

Poster for the film *The Commitments*, 1991 (Private collection)

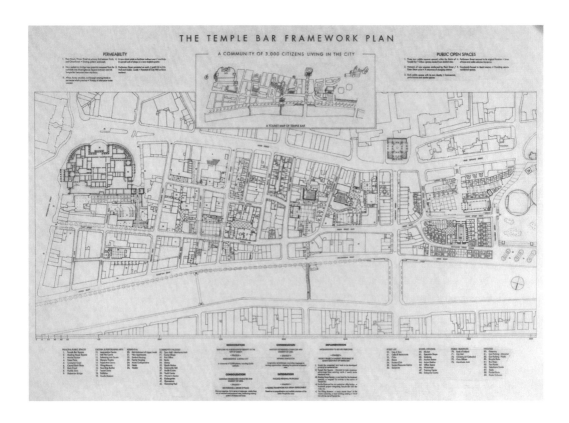

Temple Bar Framework plan by Group 91, 1991 (Courtesy of Group 91 collection at Irish Architectural Archive)

New thinking had begun to change perceptions and treatment of the historic city, with urban studies and writings such as Italian architect and theorist Aldo Rossi's *The Architecture of the City* (MIT Press, 1966), and US architectural historian Colin Rowe's *Collage City* (MIT Press, 1978) representing this shift. Closer to home, architect Niall McCullough's *Dublin – An Urban History* (Lilliput Press, 1989), and historian Maurice Craig's *Dublin 1660–1860* (Cresset Press, 1952), shone a light on Dublin's unique architectural legacy and historic urban patterns. These new ideas began to unfold in 1990s developments. In 1991, the National Inventory of Architectural Heritage (NIAH) was established to record post-1700 built heritage, and the Dublin Civic Trust came into being in 1992. And critically, as the decade closed, the Local Government (Planning & Development) Act in 1999, saw legislation put in place to list historic structures for protection.

With this new lens through which to examine the historic city, the Temple Bar area on the south bank of the Liffey became a focus of scrutiny. As mentioned at the outset in the 1980s essay, there was an increasing threat to the area posed by the proposal for a CIE transportation hub spanning across Ormond Quay, Wellington Quay, and many of the historic streets in the quarter between the Liffey quays and Dame Street. An Taisce's 1985 report 'The Temple Bar Area – A policy for its future', had highlighted growing concerns and called for urgent action. This was reputedly the first reference to the 'Temple Bar Area', a name borrowed from the historic street running parallel to the river. The plight of Temple Bar, which had been dubbed Dublin's 'Latin Quarter', attracted political attention having gained traction in the press. Attitudes began to slowly shift. Public outcry and economic constraints meant that plans for the transport depot were eventually abandoned in 1987. Taoiseach Charles Haughey was impressed by French President Mitterand's *grand travaux* in Paris – the Louvre Pyramid, Grand Arche de la Defense and Bibliothèque Nationale among others. He fancied Temple Bar as his own *grand projet*, and thus focused his attentions on the area.

A state agency Temple Bar Properties was established following the Temple Bar Renewal and Development Act (1991) to manage the reinvention of this area and to create a new 'Cultural Quarter' for the city. A competition to develop an 'Architectural Framework Plan for Temple Bar' was announced; 12 practices were invited to enter, and Group 91 submitted the winning entry. Comprising 13 architects from eight small architectural practices, Group 91 had come together to mark Dublin's

The reimagined courtyard at IMMA on Opening Day, May 1991, the signature event of Dublin's tenure that year as European City of Culture (Courtesy of Shay Cleary Architects image collection)

designation as European City of Culture. Many of them had collaborated on urban proposals and exhibitions in the 1980s, which could now be tested. Just prior to the competition, in May 1991, Group 91 had staged 'Making a Modern Street', an architectural exhibition exploring new ideas for urban living. Central to their Temple Bar strategy was the establishment of 'a community of 3,000 citizens living in the city' (Group 91, Temple Bar Framework Competition entry). Their design strategy prioritised a holistic overview of the historic area involving the conservation and regeneration of existing structures and streets, rather than a *tabula rasa* approach.

As part of their scheme, pedestrian routes and public spaces were designed to connect a series of 'cultural clusters' dotted through Temple Bar, opening up new streets and spaces within what were predominantly derelict urban blocks. In many ways O'Donnell + Tuomey's Irish Film Centre (1992), was a precursor to this design approach – a cultural centre housed within a collection of historic structures, criss-crossed with pedestrian routes. While conscious of urban developments in London, Group 91 also looked to Europe for precedents in the design of public space and infrastructure. Contemporary developments in Barcelona were undoubtedly a source of inspiration, where the emphasis was on small-scale intervention rather than the implementation of a rigid masterplan. In Barcelona, public spaces and 'surgical' urban interventions by firms such as Bach & Mora and MBM Arquitectes were designed to stimulate urban renewal, encouraging an incremental approach to urban design. Rather fittingly, David Mackay of MBM Arquitectes was an assessor in the Temple Bar Competition.

Implementation of the framework plan was relatively swift, with 21 planning permission applications lodged in July 1992. The works to Temple Bar were transformative, connecting buildings and streets that had been marked by urban decay. Meeting House Square (Paul Keogh Architects and others, 1996) was one such 'cultural cluster', accommodating Shane O'Toole and Michael Kelly's Ark Cultural Centre for Children in the former Meeting House, alongside O'Donnell + Tuomey's Gallery of Photography and National Photographic Archive. The square itself was designed by Paul Keogh Architects and was defined by overlapping pedestrian routes. Nearby,

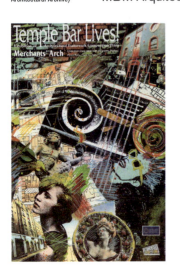

Invitation to Exhibition of Temple Bar Framework competition plans, 1991 (Courtesy of Group 91 collection at Irish Architectural Archive)

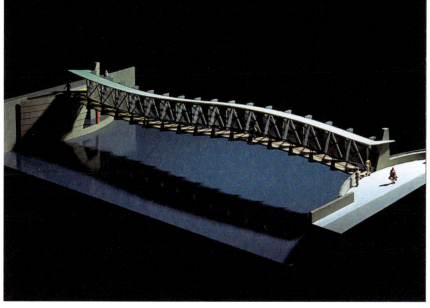

Model of proposed Poddle Bridge over River Liffey, designed by McGarry ní Eanaigh Architects, made by Unit Twenty Two Architectural Model Makers (London) and photographed by Bill Hastings (Courtesy of McGarry ní Éanaigh Architects image collection)

the industrial elegance of McCullough Mulvin's Black Church Print Studio (1996) and Temple Bar Gallery & Studios (1994) enlivened the historic street of Temple Bar. McGarry Ní Éanaigh Architects' Poddle Bridge never materialised, however their Liffey Boardwalk brought footfall to the north quayside as the decade closed. Other developments in Temple Bar include Murray Ó Laoire's Green Building (1994), an early testbed for sustainable design in the city and Arthur Gibney & Partners' restoration of an important early 18th-century house at 25 Eustace Street (1998).

    The middle of the decade ushered in an economic boom, the start of the 'Celtic Tiger' if you will, and with it a renewed sense of optimism and an explosion of urban growth. The expansion of the Irish economy between 1995 and 2000, at an average rate of 9.4 per cent, was remarkable. The 1998 Good Friday Agreement brought long-awaited peace to the island of Ireland and a sense of stability that was felt nationwide. A proliferation of new cultural venues across the city brought new life to old streets, with music venues and nightclubs dotted throughout the centre attracting locals and tourists alike. City-centre rents were still affordable, allowing smaller businesses to thrive – cafés, restaurants, and independent shops. Developments in Temple Bar were trailed by plans for the regeneration of the east docklands. On foot of 1987 legislation to establish an International Financial Services Centre (IFSC) in Dublin, the Custom House Docks Authority was set up to oversee the redevelopment of the north city docks between the years 1987 and 1997. An international architectural competition for the first phase of urban renewal on a 27-acre site was won by Dublin-based Burke-Kennedy Doyle Architects and completed in 1991. Eastward expansion of the city's docklands, on both the north and south banks of the river, was later overseen by the Dublin Docklands Development Authority, established in 1997. The resurgence in activity in commercial sector – not seen since the heady early years of the 1970s – saw changes in architectural practice, including the arrival of the 'project manager'; one of the most successful being architect Joan O'Connor who became the first woman president of the RIAI in 1996.

The re-inhabitation of the city centre was a recurring theme throughout the decade and was reflected in the city centre population rise from 916,000 in 1990 to 980,000 in 1999, quite a remarkable turn-around from the all-time inner-city low of 70,000 in 1979 as discussed in the 1970s essay. The emphasis on the creation of a 'living city' was largely a reaction to the suburban exodus prompted by city development plans in previous decades. This occupation of the city came in various forms and was not without its downsides. Tax breaks for developers resulted in a plethora of pastiche Georgian-style housing developments dotted around the city – along Bachelor's Walk, Mountjoy Square, Francis Street, Portobello Harbour and other prominent streets, housing 'shoe-box' apartments behind plain brick façades. Without adequate legislation in place to protect historic structures many were sacrificed in the dash to develop prime city centre plots. The

Competition model for Custom House Docks Development (International Financial Services Centre) (Courtesy of BKD Architects image collection)

Bride Street / Golden Lane housing, hand-drawn perspective (Courtesy of Eugene Gribben, Dublin City Architects)

illegal demolition of Archer's Garage (1946, Kaye Parry Ross Hendy) on Fenian Street in 1999 was a particular low, though it marked a turning point as the developer in question was obliged to reinstate the building (see essay in *MTCB* Volume 2).

On a higher plane, projects such as Derek Tynan Architects' Printworks (1994), and de Blacam & Meagher's Mixed Development at Castle Street (1999) raised the bar for housing design standards, taking their cues from historic proportions and materials, while introducing contemporary forms to the streetscape. There was also an investment in social housing projects, for example, Gerry Cahill Architects' New Street Housing (1995) which formed a new street edge in Dublin 8.

Exciting developments in the Dublin suburbs included London-based Allies and Morrison's British Embassy (1995) on Merrion Road, reinterpreting the country house typology with a minimal palette of materials and slick detailing, and O'Donnell + Tuomey's rhythmic brick Ranelagh Multidenominational School (1999) which cleverly navigates a tight sloped site between busy street and Georgian terraces. The surge in population and demand for housing led to creative solutions in suburban laneways. FKL's Three Houses in Rathmines (1999) and de Blacam & Meagher's Heytesbury Lane Mews (1998) are notable examples which redefined the mews typology. Innovative commercial developments also began to occupy city laneways, with Grafton Architects' Denzille Lane Cinema and Apartments (1999), and their industrial Office Building on Strand Street Little (1999) bringing life to the back streets.

More Than Concrete Blocks Volume 3

Green Building
Temple Bar, 1995
(Courtesy of MOLA
Architecture image
collection)

Regeneration and adaptive reuse of existing building stock continued through the 1990s, with considerable state investment in the conservation of historic public buildings. This included the completion of works which had begun in the 1980s to Dublin Castle, the Royal Hospital Kilmainham and the former UCD School of Engineering on Merrion Street (now Government Buildings). The 17th-century Royal Hospital Kilmainham was sensitively adapted by Shay Cleary Architects to accommodate the Irish Museum of Modern Art (IMMA) in 1991. Extensive renovation works to James Gandon's Custom House were completed by the OPW in time for its bicentenary celebrations in 1991. Restoration work to Thomas Cooley's City Hall (1779) commenced towards the end of the decade in 1998. Thomas Burgh's Royal Barracks (1707), now Collins' Barracks, were restored, adapted, and extended by the OPW and Gilroy McMahon Architects to house the Decorative Arts and History collection of the National Museum of Ireland.

This investment in cultural projects continued with de Blacam & Meagher's Beckett Theatre, a timber-clad playhouse tower which quietly dominates a narrow passageway in Trinity College. Elsewhere in the college grounds, Grafton Architects' sculptural Parsons Laboratory (1995) deftly introduced a new landscape to its historic setting, while ABK Architects' adjacent Dublin Dental Hospital (1998) is juxtaposed with the historic terrace at Lincoln Place.

New civic projects included Scott Tallon Walker's riverside Dublin Civic Offices (1994) on Wood Quay, which neatly conceal and connect to Sam Stephenson's controversial 'bunkers' and frame a public amphitheatre and garden. Scott Tallon Walker was also responsible for the low-lying planar Dublin Zoo Entrance Pavilion, which announced the zoo enclosure in its leafy Phoenix Park setting.

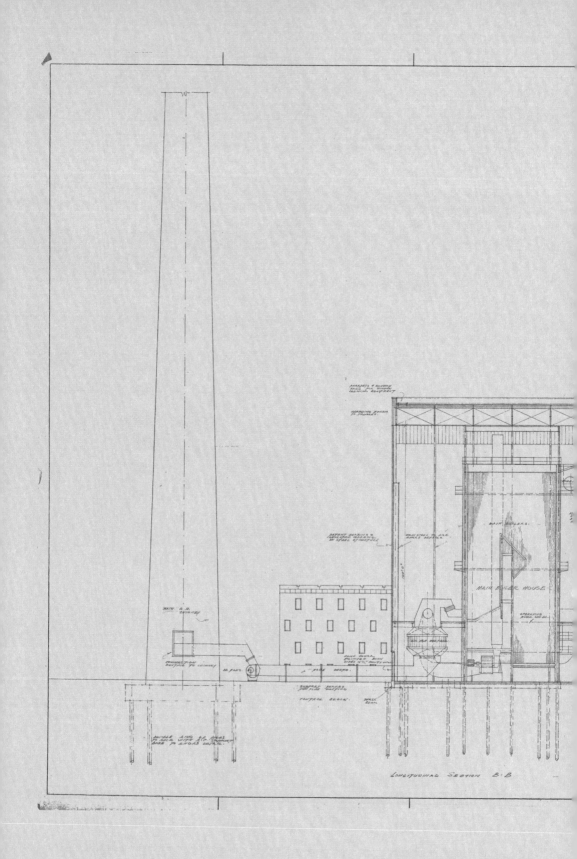

Case Studies

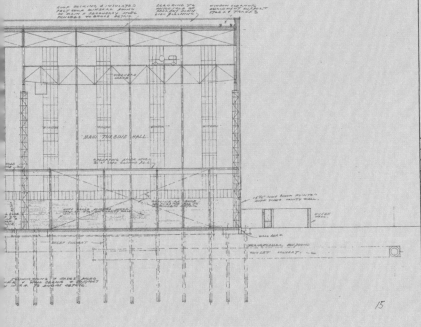

Case Study
Molyneux House, Bride Street, Dublin 2, 1973
Carole Pollard

05 [DEMOLISHED]

In 1971, architects Sam Stephenson and Arthur Gibney, partners in one of Dublin's busiest practices, purchased the former Jacob's Biscuit Factory recreational hall on Bride Street for £60,000. Originally built as a chapel for the Molyneux Asylum for Blind Females (1815) the building presented Stephenson and Gibney with the opportunity to create a bespoke architecture studio for their expanding practice. Their decision to convert an existing building was revolutionary in Dublin at a time when the predominant approach to development was to demolish and build anew. The conversion retained the original structure of the former chapel behind a new brick façade onto Bride Street; its unconventional design a visual declaration of Stephenson and Gibney's standing as Ireland's most avant-garde architectural duo at the time.

Indeed, the façade of Molyneux House remains one of the most distinctive in the city today. On its street edge, the building presents as a cluster of brick towers of varying proportions. Chamfered edges create deep shadows between the towers, the tallest of which has a projecting fourth floor with a flush floor-to-ceiling window, not unlike a periscope. The building's unusual fortress-like form is both perturbing and intriguing. Reflective glass in the windows denies any opportunity to spy activity within, while the periscope window and deeply recessed balcony on the fourth floor suggest covert surveillance of the street below. The prevailing sense of fortification is emphasised by the dark brown colour palette of brick, bronze window frames and dark bronze-tinted glazing. The building's relationship with St Patrick's Cathedral across the road is tempered by refracted reflections of the Cathedral's stonework in its windows. This is particularly so in the evening when the façade of Molyneux House transforms into a shimmering tapestry made with the colours and shadows of the setting sun.

Molyneux House was one of very few purpose-built architectural studios in Dublin in the 1970s. It remained as Stephenson's studio and *pied-à-terre* in Dublin after the dissolution of Stephenson Gibney in 1976 and Stephenson's subsequent move to London in the 1980s. In 2003, new owners extended the building, removed a section of the front boundary wall and the entrance gate, and paved over the original entrance courtyard. The open-plan interior studio spaces were altered and sub-divided. In 2023, following the grant of planning permission (in 2022) to build a hotel on the site, the entire structure was demolished except for the brick façade that stands on Bride Street. Stephenson was one of Ireland's most public, and prolific, architects during his lifetime: the discombobulated skeletal remains of his idiosyncratic Molyneux House façade remind us of the fragility of the city's 1970s architectural legacy.

More Than Concrete Blocks Volume 3

Model for early larger development at Molyneux House (*Build*, June 1975)

A Showcase for Success (and a White Canary)

Molyneux House was named after the original home of Thomas Molyneux (1641–1733) which stood on nearby Peter Street. In 1815 the house became Molyneux Asylum for Blind Females, and an Anglican chapel was built on Bride Street. Molyneux House stands on the site of the chapel. In 1862 the Home for Blind Females moved to Leeson Park, but the chapel remained in use until the 1920s. In 1943 it was bought by Jacob's Biscuit Factory (at that time located on Bishop Street), and used as a recreational facility for workers. When Stephenson and Gibney bought the premises in 1971 it retained all the characteristics of a chapel, being predominantly a single large volume with a tripartite Victorian façade.

Stephenson Gibney & Associates (SGA) was founded by Sam Stephenson and Arthur Gibney in the late 1950s as a two-man partnership. By 1972 the company had grown to be one of the largest in Ireland with 18 associates and close to 100 staff. At its peak, their offices at Molyneux House accommodated 130 architectural staff. According to the company brochure of 1975, the firm had commissions in Ireland, Belgium, France, Greece, USA, Japan, and the West Indies. From the earliest days of their practice, Stephenson and Gibney placed importance on the quality of their office environment as an indication of the high-level design skills they could offer to clients. Their first office premises was on the top floor of Dublin's most exclusive department store, Brown Thomas, and was fitted out with a Japanese-inspired decorative scheme including shoji screens and rush matting. Both Stephenson and Gibney considered interior design to be a fundamental part of their design practice and regularly undertook interiors projects for both domestic and commercial clients. One of their earliest and most famous interiors is the Horseshoe Bar in the Shelbourne Hotel (1959) which is still intact.

Case Study: Molyneux House

The decision to build a bespoke architectural studio was made on foot of several considerations, including the fact that they had outgrown their existing premises. Both men had become increasingly involved in property development and they recognised the economic advantages of purchasing a site where they could design and build a premises that would showcase their skills. Not only were they the architects for Molyneux House, but they also took on the role of main contractors, sub-contracting the various trade packages, and using the project as a pilot scheme for potential new practice ventures including complete design management contract services.

When they moved into their new offices in the spring of 1973, Stephenson and Gibney were at the peak of their careers, but their relationship within the partnership was beginning to falter. Stephenson was the primary designer of their Molyneux House studios, and his increasing dominance in the firm is evidenced by the fact that he retained the best part of the building for his own use. He designed a personal suite of rooms, including living accommodation, on the fourth floor of the building with views towards St Patrick's Cathedral and its park.

Molyneux House shortly after completion, 1973, (John Donat / RIBA Collections)

View across reception area to main entrance with brick-lined courtyard beyond (John Donat / RIBA Collection)

Entrance to Molyneux House marked by brick 'pyramids' on footpath. (John Donat / RIBA Collections)

Stephenson and Gibney were faithful Dubliners with the city's best interests at heart. They hoped that their development on Bride Street, on the edge of the city's historic Liberties area, would encourage others to invest in this run-down and neglected part of the city. Stephenson's affinity with his native city is exemplified in his accommodation of the Dublin Bird Market traders who had for many years traditionally held their bird market in Bride Street. The Bird Market is one of Dublin's oldest extant markets, some say dating back 900 years. The yard where the market took place was demolished in the 1960s as part of a road-widening scheme and the traders moved to the empty area beside the Jacob's Biscuit Factory recreational centre. When Stephenson and Gibney bought the site, they agreed to design their building around the needs of the Bird Market. They created a paved and lushly planted entrance courtyard which doubled as the perfect environment for bird sellers to display their wares in bird boxes suspended on the wall. As a gesture of thanks to Stephenson, the bird traders presented him with a white cock canary as a gift for providing them with a new home.

The Idiosyncratic Façade

Prior to the Stephenson Gibney intervention, Molyneux Chapel comprised a large, double-height volume over ground floor ancillary rooms. The front façade had three equal bays, each with a tall round-headed window at the first floor with square-headed windows to the floor below. The bays were separated by raised pilasters with classical plaster mouldings and the central bay projected above the parapet line of its two companions with a plasterwork inscription panel and decorative frieze. The large first floor space had rows of round-headed windows along each side elevation, and the roof was supported by a Queen's post timber roof truss which spanned the full width. Stephenson removed everything except the external walls and the Queen's post truss and inserted a free-standing concrete frame containing four storeys of office accommodation within the existing volume. The internal circulation was located within an internal void that rose from the entrance lobby. An elegant open-shaft lift opened onto a bridge which served as a landing for the main staircase and a connection point between the offices on either side.

Stephenson placed the main entrance on the north side of the building, facing the courtyard. A tall, narrow opening in the brick boundary wall was

denoted by a brick paved entrance apron flanked by two low-lying brick pyramids which led to entrance courtyard (where the Bird Market was held). The building was entered via a large revolving door set within deep brick walls, and the brick ground finish continued as far as the reception desk. The contrast between the dark, shadowy courtyard and the reception lobby was startling: the vertical circulation void revealed bright, open studio spaces, with trailing plants overhanging the concrete-framed transoms and views of architects busy at sloping drawing boards in the spaces beyond. Stephenson Gibney's offices were the epitome of architecture-studio cool, with white-painted concrete, exposed cabling, bespoke timber box-like hanging light fittings, free-standing screen partitions, and large graphic art posters. Natural light poured in through new windows fitted in the old chapel window openings and from the rooflight over the stairwell void. The drawing studios were on the second and third floors, with office administration and meeting rooms on the ground floor. Gibney and Stephenson, and their personal secretaries, occupied the fourth floor. An annex built to the rear of the entrance courtyard contained a caretaker's flat and staff canteen.

Stephenson retained the original façade of the chapel for structural reasons but put his own stamp on the building by constructing a second outer layer that occupied the space between the existing structure and the street edge. This innovative move was characteristic of Stephenson's ability to solve a problem with an inventive solution and a certain amount of irony. Stephenson was a vociferous opponent of Georgian pastiche, a trend favoured by planners and developers in Dublin in the 1970s when many modern office blocks were built behind mock-Georgian façades. Pastiche was seen as an easy way of appeasing the preservationist lobby however, here, Stephenson turned that approach on its head; he applied a Modernist façade to an historic building. In contrast to the classical symmetry of the 19th-century façade, Stephenson's intervention breaks forward from the old in an irregular manner so that a series of uniquely different spaces are created between the old and new skins. Those new spaces provided several functions: on the ground floor they held plant and WC facilities, and on the second and third floors they acted as meeting room nooks. At fourth floor, Stephenson created a self-contained apartment with private kitchen, bathroom and living space tucked into the inter-wall space and with a balcony overlooking St Patrick's Cathedral. After the practice was dissolved in 1974, Stephenson retained Molyneux House and continued to

Case Study: Molyneux House

use the apartment during the 1980s when he was mostly based in London. He eventually sold the building in 1991 when his practice Stone Toms Stephenson was wound up. Subsequently, in the 1990s, a four-storey extension was added to the rear, Stephenson's interiors were mostly ripped out, the courtyard and caretaker's flat were demolished, and the boundary wall taken away to allow for on-site parking.

In 2023, the 1990s office building and the chapel building were demolished to make way for a new hotel development which will also occupy the adjoining site on the corner of Peter Street. All that remains is Stephenson's unique Brutalist brick façade.

Interior view showing concrete frame structure inserted into body of former church (John Donat / RIBA Collections)

Sam Stephenson
in his office suite
in Molyneux House
(John Donat / RIBA
Collection)

Case Study: Molyneux House

Facts and Figures

Sam Stephenson and Arthur Gibney bought the Jacobs Recreational Hall in 1971 and construction commenced in 1972. They moved into the building in 1973, renaming it Molyneux House. In 2003 the building was extensively altered, and a five-storey office building was built to the side and rear. In January 2022, planning permission was granted to demolish the existing buildings except for Stephenson's front façade. The new development, which includes the adjoining corner site at Peter Street, will comprise of a 247-bedroom hotel rising from four to nine storeys.

Architects: Stephenson Gibney & Associates
Sam Stephenson (1934–2006) was the principal architect on this project. He was educated at Belvedere College and studied architecture at the Dublin Institute of Technology (DIT) Bolton Street (now TU Dublin), but never graduated. While a student, he won the RIAI Travelling Scholarship in 1956 which later exempted him from the RIAI's Associateship examination. After a period in private practice, he established Stephenson Gibney & Associates with Arthur Gibney in 1960. The partnership was dissolved in 1975 when he established Stephenson Associates. He was awarded an Honorary Diploma in Architecture by DIT in 1972, was elected a Fellow of the RIAI in 1975 and won the RIAI Triennial Gold Medal for the period 1977–9 for the Central Bank Currency Centre in Sandyford. He moved his practice to London in the 1980s, forming Stone Toms Stephenson, and returned to Dublin a decade or so later.

Arthur Gibney's biography can be found in the Merrion Hall essay

Structural Engineers: J. McCullough & Partners
Quantity Surveyor: W. O'Sullivan
Landscape Architect: Niall Hyde
Main Contractors: Stephenson and Gibney acted in the role of main contractor, awarding sub-contracts (approximately 36) for the various trades and stages of construction, including:
Labour only contractor: Kirwan Bros Ltd
Demolition contractor: Matthew O'Dowd Ltd
Electrical: P Lynch & Co.
Heating and ventilation: Climate Engineering Ltd
Plumbing: H. A.. O'Neill & Co.
Lift installation: Pickerings Ltd
Telephone installation: Sound Systems Ltd
Window installation: Aluminium Systems Ltd
Ceilings: P. J. Clinton & Co.
Bowrock ceilings: P. Kelly
Decoration: J. Treacy & Co.
Glazing: Dublin Glass & Paint Co.
Structural steel: H. May & Co.
Reinforcing steel: T. Pearson & Co.
Concrete: Readymix (Eire) Ltd
Mortar: Roadstone
Marble reception desk: Stone Developments Ltd
Stainless steel reception desk: T. Kealy & Sons Ltd

Joinery (doors): Carey & Clarke Ltd and C. Roche & Son
Roofing: T. C. Walsh & Co.
Ceramic tiling: D. D. O'Brien & Co.
Bricks: Kingscourt Brick Co.
Furniture: Joinwood Ltd
Steel fittings: Structural Welders
Rainwater goods: Marley Ltd
WC partitions: Allied Building Agencies
Sanitaryware: Davies Ltd
Asphalt roofing: Briggs Amasco
Lift shaft bore hole: Cementation Co. (I) Ltd
Light fittings: ECI (Lighting) Ltd
Flooring: M. Cronin
Carpets: The Carpet Centre
Ironmongery: Brooks Thomas Ltd
Kitchen equipment: Hammond Refrigeration and Catering

Sources
Unpublished:
Stephenson Gibney archive at the Irish Architectural Archive, Merrion Square
Tony Cotter, interviewed by Carole Pollard, August 2018
Fallon, Paraic, 'Addition of Former Central Bank including restaurant annexe, Public Plaza including 'Crann an Óir' sculpture, Dame Street, Dublin 2 to the Record of Protected Structures in accordance with Section 54 and 55 of the Planning and Development Act, 2000.' (Presented to Dublin City Council, undated)
O'Toole, Shane, 'Central Bank of Ireland' in 'Documentation Project and Pilot Survey of the Architecture of the 20thCentury – Book 3: Case Studies' (Presented to Dublin City Council & the Heritage Council, 2011)

Published:
Anon., 'Stephenson Gibney & Associates' brochure (*Stephenson Gibney Associates*, undated), Box No. 9, Stephenson Gibney archive at the Irish Architectural Archive.
Anon., 'Only a Little Hiccup', *Plan* (Vol. 5, No. 9, Dec. 1974)
Anon., 'Stephenson Gibney – A Home in the Liberties', *Build* (Vol. 11, No. 8, June 1975)
Magee, Noel, 'Molyneux House: Flight from Calais to Peter Street and Leeson Park', (ULSARA, www.ulsara.ie/molyneux-house/4591206964, accessed 5 Oct. 2019)
McDonald, Frank, *The Destruction of Dublin* (Gill & MacMillan, 1985)
Wright, Lance, 'New Use in Dublin', *Architectural Review* (Vol. CLVII, No. 936, Feb. 1975)

Case Study
Merrion Hall, Merrion, Dublin 4, 1973
Carole Pollard

Merrion Hall sits low on its site on Strand Road, close to the Merrion Gates rail crossing on the Strand Road/Merrion Road coastal route. The three-storey, concrete framed building is positioned midway between two neighbouring residential properties with generous space on either side. The ground level is low so that when viewed from the road the building gives the impression of being only two-storeys. At ground floor level, a courtyard opens on the front façade so that the second floor reads partly as a bridge, and a long rectangular pool emerges from the internal courtyard under the bridge and out into the building forecourt. The shallow pool is fitted with a fountain. Recessed lights in the soffit of the second-floor bridge enhance the textural and reflective effect of the water on the white concrete frame when lit at night.

The expression of the structure is the building's defining feature. A precast concrete frame of square columns and beams sits proud of aluminium-framed, dark tinted glass. Each floor of offices enjoys floor to ceiling glazing which slides behind the square-edged concrete frame, independent of the structure. There is a very definite crispness about the external expression of columns and beams seen against the background of recessed, tinted glass walling, and emphasised by the clean, sharp corners of the white pre-cast concrete. At the same time, the building is modest: it is kept purposely low and unobtrusive, partially hidden behind the concrete boundary wall, and its material expression is simple and unadorned.

Since the building passed from the hands of the semi-state organisations who were its original occupants, the condition of the building has deteriorated. Now owned by a property investment company and let on long lease to its current tenants, there is not the same impetus for maintenance. Although the office spaces have been recently upgraded, the concrete frame is showing signs of (repairable) stress, and generally the external envelope of the building and its landscaping are suffering from neglect. The reflecting pool is empty, there are cracks and poorly executed repairs in the concrete paving and the lawns are unkempt. As a result, Gibney's intended integration of the building into its designed landscape is presently lost.

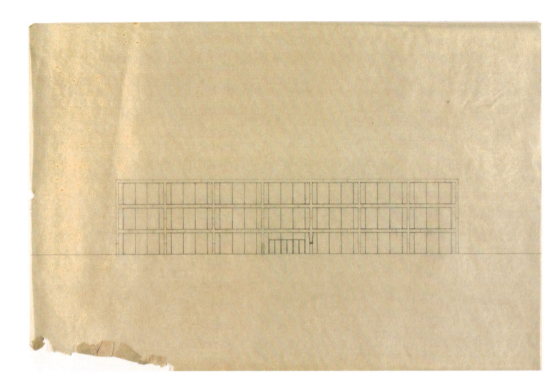

Sketch of elevation showing concrete frame joints (Courtesy of Stephenson Gibney collection at Irish Architectural Archive)

Irish Shipping on Dublin Bay

By the 1960s Dublin office block development was firmly anchored on the prosperous southside of the city, putting increasing pressure on the suburbs of Ballsbridge, Sandymount and Donnybrook in the postal district of Dublin 4. Office developers sought big sites to facilitate large floor plates and flexibility on height, and those sites had become increasingly more difficult to assemble in the city centre. As a result, Dublin 4, which had an abundance of spacious houses in extensive gardens, and several underdeveloped green-field sites, became an attractive alternative. Dublin 4's leafy prosperity provided the ideal environment for commercial developments that aspired to the American trend of locating corporate headquarters buildings in suburban rather than downtown locations.

The site at Merrion Road, which is technically in the district of Merrion not Sandymount, was for many years a horse-riding stable. Horses were exercised on the sandy strand that gives the area its name and runs along the south-eastern edge of Dublin Bay. The rear of the site (its western edge) is bounded by the Dublin to Wexford railway line and there is a right of way through the site from Strand Road, over a railway pedestrian bridge to the grounds of Merrion Church to the west. The site had a history of being prone

Case Study: Merrion Hall

to flooding and prior to its development, concerns were expressed about its suitability for building. However, preparatory works, including pumping of the site prior to construction and the use of pile foundations, have kept the site relatively dry despite being lower than Strand Road and the local high tide mark. A two-storey house sits on the seaward side of Strand Road opposite Merrion Hall but does not obstruct views of Dublin Bay from the upper two floors. The views are particularly spectacular from the north-east corner of the third floor, looking towards Howth Head.

In 1965, having acquired the site, the Property Corporation of Ireland, appointed architects Stephenson Gibney & Associates to design a headquarters building for Irish Shipping Ltd. Earlier that year an outline planning permission for an office block was refused by Dublin Corporation (architect unknown) and it is likely that lack of success led the Property Corporation to seek the services of Stephenson Gibney & Associates, an architectural firm well known for their bullish approach and ability to obtain planning permissions even in difficult circumstances. The project was designed and led by Gibney, whose architecture was more restrained in style than that of his business partner, Stephenson.

Irish Shipping was a semi-state body in ownership of an associate company, the Insurance Corporation of Ireland. The Property Corporation of Ireland was established by Irish Shipping for the sole purpose of developing the headquarters building using funds provided by the insurance company reserves. Irish Shipping, a deep-sea shipping company, was established during World War II to secure and supply the country's import needs. In the post-war years the company continued to operate as a commercial strategic reserve but was forced into liquidation in 1984 because of losses of almost £200 million. However, during the 1950s and 1960s the company was at peak activity, investing heavily in expanding and improving its fleet which was named after trees. One of the ships from this period, the Irish Elm, built in Verolme Dockyard in Cork in 1969, provided each crew member with their own cabin and boasted an officers' bar and a crew bar. It also had a swimming pool. No doubt the luxurious high-specification finish of the shipping fleet influenced Irish Shipping's architectural brief for their new headquarters. In 1974, the year they moved into Merrion Hall, the company announced profits of more than £2 million with revenues also coming from its associated companies, Irish Continental Line passenger ferries and the Insurance Corporation of Ireland.

More Than Concrete Blocks Volume 3

View along the front façade, 1973 (Courtesy of Stephenson Gibney collection at Irish Architectural Archive)

The Merrion Road site offered the potential to build a building far greater in size than the needs of Irish Shipping and so the brief stipulated that the development would provide additional lettable office space to the maximum allowed by the site's plot ratio (a device used by planners to determine the size of building permitted on a site). A planning application for offices and an apartment building was made by Stephenson Gibney in 1968. It was granted permission in February 1972, after a protracted appeals period. Construction of the office block was completed in 1974 but the apartment building was never built. This omission is not uncommon: often planning permission for commercial developments in residential neighbourhoods like Sandymount were granted based on the provision of a residential component – primarily to assuage concerns of local residents. This omission was not uncommon; often planning permissions for commercial developments in residential neighbourhoods like Sandymount were granted based on the provision of a residential component – primarily to assuage concerns of local residents – but there was no enforcement to ensure those residential units were built.

Central Courtyard with reflecting pool (John Donat / RIBA Collections)

Office interior overlooking central courtyard and 'bridge' over pool (John Donat / RIBA Collections)

The completed building comprised of 4,700 square metres of floor space over three floors, of which Irish Shipping only required 1,700 square metres. Another semi-state body, Córas Tráchtála (CTT) and its sister company, the Irish Goods Council, occupied much of the remainder of the building. CTT was founded in 1959 to market Irish goods abroad and the Irish Goods Council was founded in 1974 to promote the sale of Irish goods in Ireland. The Irish government, in 1960, had granted CTT administrative responsibility for improving standards of industrial design, leading to the publication of a report 'Design in Ireland' in 1962. Bill Walsh, former chief executive of CTT and later chief executive of the Kilkenny Design Workshops, was a great admirer of Mies van der Rohe, saying his buildings were 'monuments to calm' (O'Toole, 2017, unpaginated). That appreciation of Mies may well have sealed the deal for CTT's move to Gibney's Miesian pavilion on Sandymount Strand. Irish Shipping occupied the first floor of the building while CTT and the Irish Goods Council occupied the second floor. The companies maintained individual entrance foyers on opposite sides of the building, one in the south wing and one in the north wing, but shared restaurant facilities on the ground floor (south side). The remainder of the ground floor was leased to other companies. The letting agent, Finnegan Menton, advertised the site as 'ideally located for businesses drawing staff from the south side of the city' and a 'rare opportunity for tenants to secure accommodation on Dublin's first marine office site' (Finnegan Menton advertisement, *Build*, 1974). When Irish Shipping went into liquidation in 1984, CTT, which later became An Bórd Tráchtála, took over the lease of the entire building which was sold in 1987 to development company, British Land. In 1996 British Land sold Merrion Hall to a private investment firm for £5.1 million. A short time later the building's primary occupancy by semi-state bodies came to an end. In 1998, An Bórd Tráchtála and Forbairt (whose role was to make industrial development grants) were merged to form Enterprise Ireland; they vacated the building in 2000. In 2021 it changed hands for €25 million.

Modular geometry

By the late 1960s, Stephenson Gibney & Associates had become the dominant architectural practice in Ireland. The two partners were quite different in both their personalities and their architectural style. Stephenson's architecture tends to be more dramatic, bold, and often contentious. Gibney's architecture on the other hand, is more studied, considered and even restrained. Two other Stephenson Gibney projects featured in this volume – Molyneux House (1973) and Central Bank (1980) – characterise Stephenson's architectural style, while Merrion Hall, on the other hand, is clearly the work of Gibney; it exemplifies his trademark application of sensibility melded with strong, sculptural forms. Gibney was an accomplished watercolour artist, and the delicacy and precision of his painting style is repeated in his architecture. Like most architects of his generation, he was influenced by the work of the Modernist masters, Le Corbusier and Mies van der Rohe and certainly the ideals of both – free floor plans with flexible spaces and crafted with elegant simplicity, respectively, can be seen in Merrion Hall.

The later years of the 1970s saw Gibney re-evaluate his relationship with Modernism, particularly its more rigid and purist ideologies which he believed 'had failed to address fundamental functional, social, and psychological issues' (White and Lunney, 2012). In a 1973 interview, however, he defended his reluctance 'to depart from simple architecture, from the rectangle' (*Plan*, 1973, p. 12) and said that he strove to design buildings in which the user felt 'important' (citing Kevin Roche's Ford Foundation building in New York as an exemplar) rather than 'anonymous' (citing Mies van der Rohe's Seagram Building in the same city) (White and Lunney, 2012). Merrion Hall is considered to be one of Gibney's finest works, a building he himself described as 'an exercise in the geometry of the module' (*Plan*, 1973, p. 13). The building was commended in the RIAI Gold Medal triennial awards for 1971–3.

Described in a review as 'a beautiful example of simple design' (*Plan*, 1974, p. 7). Merrion Hall is a perfect square with a central courtyard, built on a grid of 7.2 metres and set in a 1.8 metre module. Floor to ceiling heights are 3.6 metres. The external frame was constructed in precast concrete columns and beams using Ballybrew white aggregate to produce the light colour. All the internal columns and floor slabs were cast in-situ concrete, as was the flat roof which was finished with asphalt. Despite the fact that the site had a history of flooding and that the ground floor was excavated to reduce the impact of the building on the site, a basement area was excavated to house all the plant equipment.

The defining feature of the building is the expression of the external concrete frame which sits a half module proud of the floor to ceiling glazing that runs in a continuous band around the building. The dark tint of the glass contrasts strongly with the white concrete, emphasising the sharp corners of the concrete frame whose columns appear to sink like stakes into the ground. This effect is particularly strong where the central columns on the front elevation plunge into the water pool. Despite the dark colour of the glass, the frame casts shadows which are amplified by the depth of the structural recess, and further heightened at ground floor where there is a deep undercroft at the front of the building.

On plan, the building is square with an elongated internal courtyard which opens to the east (front) side on the ground level. The main entrances are located on the outside of the square, one on the north side and one on the south side, and there are secondary doors into the internal courtyard. The lack of active access to the courtyard means that it is mostly empty and fails to invigorate the building, particularly when viewed from the office floors above. Originally, a staff restaurant at the south-eastern corner ensured activity along the building's frontage which is laid out in square concrete slab paving and rectangular lawns. The central pool feature at one time contained active fountains. As well as serving a decorative function, the pool acts as a receptacle for rainwater channelled from the building's roof and the pebble-filled troughs that line the upper surfaces of the external concrete beams, through pipes embedded in the concrete columns. The absence of gutters and downpipes on the building's façades ensures no disruption of the clean sharp lines of the structure.

Unlike many other architectural practices of the period, Stephenson Gibney & Associates provided interior design services as part of their architectural services. Merrion Hall presented Gibney with the ideal opportunity to introduce his clients to the *Burolandschaft*: the office interior design concept that was prevalent throughout Europe. *Burolandschaft* – which translates as 'office landscape' – was developed in Germany in the late 1950s with the purpose of integrating managers and workers in open-plan areas separated by plants and moveable screens. Gibney's large open floor plates, flooded with natural light, were ideally suited to the open-plan model. However, following client reluctance to move away from traditional cellular arrangements, Gibney produced a solution which could facilitate both office layout typologies. He deliberately placed the internal courtyard off centre, giving more depth (28.6 metres or 16 modules) on the west side and a slightly narrower (14.4 metres or 8 modules) space on the east side. He intended that the east side, which benefits from views towards Dublin Bay would be divided into executive offices and meeting rooms, while the west side would be modelled entirely on *Burolandschaft* principles. However, in the end, both Irish Shipping and CTT refused to concede on traditional hierarchical layouts and Gibney's subsequent interior design plans show the west side laid out with traditional cellular executive offices adjacent to secretarial pools.

The controlled symmetry of the building is extended to the provision of services: there are two service cores, one in the north wing and the other in the south wing, containing lifts and services and with a granite lined reception area on each ground floor. Clad externally in ribbed granite slabs, and with internal walls plastered, the service cores have staircases, lavatories, and tea rooms. The finishes in the cores include terrazzo flooring and stainless-steel handrails, both beautifully detailed. Several original flush-fitting stainless steel light switches remain.

At the time of its completion, Merrion Hall was considered to be excellent value for money. One commentator declared:

> This fully air-conditioned high-quality building at a cost of £12.48 per square foot must represent one of the finest developments completed in this period, where high rates of inflation applied. The budget cost of £775,000 was adhered to by closely monitoring the decision-making process and the flow of information to the site. Probably because SGA's buildings consistently display very high quality; it is commonly assumed that their buildings are of equally hight cost. Merrion Hall clearly shows that this is a mistaken view and that the firm has a remarkable capability of producing high quality buildings at costs which are comparable with other developments of much less quality (*Build*, 1975, p. 26).

Nonetheless, over time the building has developed structural defects due to weathering and wear-and-tear on the concrete. Those defects have been largely remedied and in recent years upgrading works have been carried out on the building's services. Unfortunately, the floor space on the ground floor has been insensitively subdivided and some of the external spaces have been fenced off. The landscaping is in poor condition. Merrion Hall deserves better: the proportions of the office spaces are conducive to modern office demands, unlike many office blocks of the period which cannot meet current workplace standards. It is one of the most enduring Irish office blocks of its age.

Case Study: Merrion Hall

Facts and Figures

Merrion Hall is a three-storey office block on a site extending to 1.82 hectares. The building was commissioned by Property Corporation of Ireland in July 1965 and went to tender in February 1972. Construction began in July 1972 and was completed in December 1973. The total floor area was 4770 square metres, and the cost of construction was £775,000.

Architects: Stephenson Gibney & Associates. The partner in charge was Arthur Gibney, assisted by Aidan Murray, John Bloomer, Tony O'Hara and Klaus Unger. The contact supervisor was David Johnston.

Arthur Gibney graduated from the School of Architecture, Bolton Street in the late 1950s and in 1960 established his practice with his college classmate Sam Stephenson. In 1962 they won the international architectural competition for a new headquarters building for the ESB on Fitzwilliam Street, Dublin. This project propelled both Gibney and Stephenson into the limelight where they remained for the rest of their careers. After the dissolution of Stephenson Gibney & Associates in 1974, Gibney established Arthur Gibney & Partners. In 1974 he won the RIAI Triennial Gold Medal for the Irish Management Institute at Sandyford, Dublin. In 1989 he was elected president of the RIAI and in 1990 was elected president of the Royal Hibernian Academy (RHA) where he remained in post until shortly before his death in 2006. Gibney was considered one of the greatest men of his generation in the world of the arts in Ireland. In addition to his architectural skill, he was an accomplished painter, sculptor, historian and academic. His long tenure as president of the RHA is reflective of that position. His doctoral thesis on Irish Georgian buildings was posthumously published in 2017.

Structural Engineers: Ove Arup & Partners
Mechanical Engineers: Varming Mulcahy Reilly Associates
Quantity Surveyors: Desmond MacGreevy & Partners
Main contractors: John Sisk & Sons Ltd
Electrical Contractors: ESB

McGrattan & Kenny Ltd Mechanical Services installed the air-conditioning system.
T. G. Kealy & Sons supplied and erected the stainless-steel elements.
Stone Developments installed marble wall cladding, fascias and floors.
Ballybrew Quarries in Enniskerry, Co. Wicklow supplied the stone
Crystal Glass Co. Ltd, Dublin 1 supplied the glass and glazing system
Booth Concrete Ltd, Northern Ireland supplied the precast concrete columns and beams

Sources

Unpublished
Stephenson Gibney & Associates archive at the Irish Architectural Archive

Published
Anon, 'Is Less More', *Build* (Vol. 10, No. 10, April 1974)
Anon, 'CTT / Irish Shipping Joint HQ', *Build* (Vol. 11, No. 8, June 1975)
Anon, 'Squaring up to Dublin Bay', *Building* (4 Oct. 1974)
Anon, 'Merrion Hall, 1972', *Irish Architect* (June/July/Aug. 1988)
Anon, 'Arthur Gibney, Leading Architect and Gifted Man of the Arts', *Irish Times*, 27 May 2006
Fagan, Jack, 'Office Blocks Make £6.5m', *Irish Times*, 21 Feb. 1996
Hurley, Livia and McParland, Edward (eds), *The Building Site in Eighteenth-Century Ireland* (Four Courts Press, 2017)
O'Toole, Shane, 'When Mies Was Asked to Build in Ireland' in Shane O'Toole, *101 Hosannas* (Gandon Editions, 2017)
White, Laurence William and Linde Lunney, 'Arthur Gibney', *Dictionary of Irish Biography* (RIA and Cambridge University Press, 2012) online version

Case Study
Bank of Ireland HQ, Baggot Street, Dublin 2, 1972–5

Carole Pollard

13

The former Bank of Ireland headquarters is situated on Baggot Street Lower in the heart of Dublin's south Georgian quarter. Located midway between the junction with Fitzwilliam Street and the bridge over the Grand Canal, it occupies a sedate stretch of the street, with large trees on a central median between two wide carriageways. Although predominantly lined with four-storey Georgian houses, the site of the Bank of Ireland HQ previously contained a single-storey industrial facility. As a result, the development did not involve the demolition of historic Georgian houses, meaning it did not attract the same level of controversy as many of its contemporaries built nearby. When Bank of Ireland purchased the site in 1968, it already had planning permission for two office blocks, a five-storey block facing onto Baggot Street (Block B) and an eight-storey block on a podium at the rear of the site (Block A). The Bank retained the architects who had designed that scheme, Michael Scott & Partners, but instructed them to make significant changes in terms of the quality of the specification and generosity of space within the buildings. Later, in 1973, Bank of Ireland acquired four adjacent Georgian houses on the street which were demolished to make way for the four-storey block that turns the corner from Baggot Street into James Street East (Block C). This was the final piece in the carefully calibrated composition of three blocks arranged around a T-shaped double-level plaza that is known today as Miesian Plaza.

Described by architecture critic Lance Wright as 'almost certainly the purest example of [Miesian] style in Europe's offshore islands' the building, as its current name implies, is regarded as an homage to Mies van der Rohe, a world-famous architect of the 20th century (Wright, 1975, p. 96). The Bank of Ireland headquarters was designed by Ronald Tallon of Michael Scott & Partners who admitted that the Miesian references were probably overstated and that the building in fact marked the end of the practice's devotion to Mies' philosophies. Nonetheless, the building is often compared to Mies' Seagram Building in New York, mostly because of the similarity between the glass curtain façades constructed in bronze. In form, however, the buildings are very different: the Seagram building is a single-block skyscraper, whereas the bank headquarters is an assembly of three buildings, four-, five- and eight-storeys high arranged around two plazas. The mathematical rigour of Tallon's architectural composition, which is generated from a 1.63 metre (5ft 4in) grid, resulted in a taut and restrained modernist insertion into Dublin's sober Georgian streetscape. It has always been considered one of Dublin's finest examples of modern office buildings of the period.

In 2010, Bank of Ireland relocated their headquarters to Mespil Road. A short time later, knowing that when the bank vacated their Baggot Street premises it would be at serious risk of demolition, Dublin City Council undertook the process of assessment that led to the addition of 50–58 Lower Baggot Street to the Dublin City Council Record of Protected

Ground floor plan
(Courtesy of STW image collection)

Structures (RPS). Considered by the Council's conservation department to be 'Dublin's finest example of the restrained and elegant Miesian style' (*Irish Times*, 8 April 2015), the building complex was one of only a handful of Dublin's 20th-century structures to hold protective status at that time. In 2012, Bank of Ireland sold the buildings to a developer, and in 2015 planning permission was granted for a major refurbishment. The works, under the supervision of the original architects, Scott Tallon Walker, successfully upgraded the building complex to a Leadership in Energy and Environmental Design (LEED) Platinum rating, the highest level of accreditation. It is currently the headquarters of the Department of Health.

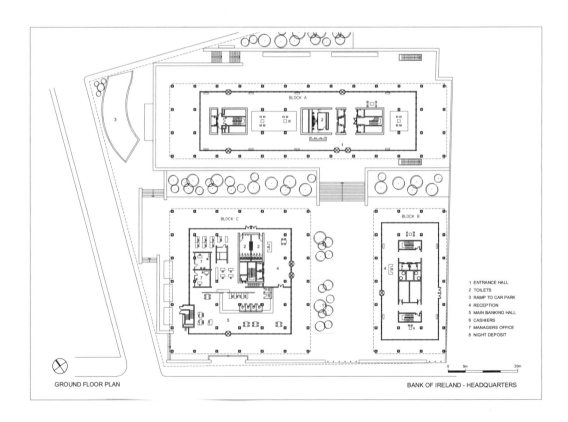

Bank of Ireland HQ model (Courtesy of STW image collection)

A Manifestation of Banking Ambition

The Bank of Ireland was established in 1783, making it Ireland's oldest bank in continuous operation. In 1803, the bank purchased the former Irish Parliament building on College Green as their headquarters. The building, one of Dublin's most striking landmarks located in the very heart of the city opposite the front gate of Trinity College, was designed by architects, Edward Lovett Pearce, James Gandon, Robert Parke, and Francis Johnston, and built between 1729 and 1796. Bank of Ireland purchased the illustrious premises after the Act of Union (Ireland) in 1800 transferred parliamentary power back to London. The company's status as the country's premiere bank was reinforced in 1922 when it was appointed official banker to the Irish Government. Throughout the 20th century Bank of Ireland continued to expand and, like all of Ireland's financial institutions, enjoyed a period of major expansion from the late 1950s. The bank acquired the Hibernian Bank in 1958 and the National Bank in 1965, and a short time later established

View of headquarters building shortly after completion of Block C by John Donat (Courtesy of Scott Tallon Walker image collection)

investment and asset management subsidiaries. In 1969, the Bank of Ireland Group was incorporated.

In 1968, the Bank commissioned a new, modern headquarters building on Lower Baggot Street, approximately two kilometres from College Green and the city's traditional commercial centre. The physical expansion of its property assets was part of the bank's long-term business strategy; the brief for the new headquarters building would reflect both national and international ambitions. The decision was also influenced by the shifting pattern of development in the city arising from the preference to locate modern office blocks within the city's south-east Georgian core. In fact, Bank of Ireland were leaders in the trend that saw all of Ireland's major financial institutions develop new headquarters during a period of intense property development in the city, including the Irish Life Centre for Irish Life Assurance Co. and AIB Bankcentre for Allied Irish Banks. The bank retained the College Green premises, but the company's principal functions transferred to Baggot Street.

Bank of Ireland paid £1.5 million for the 1.5-acre Baggot Street site. The deal was described as 'one of the biggest in the Dublin property world for some time' (*Irish Times*, 10 May 1968). Formerly occupied by Lincoln & Nolan car assembly plant, the site had planning permission, granted in 1967, for two office blocks designed by Michael Scott & Partners. At the time of the purchase, demolitions were complete, and works had commenced on the foundations.

Michael Scott & Partners was probably the most highly regarded architectural practice in Ireland at the time with a reputation for high-quality,

Case Study: Bank of Ireland HQ

high-specification modern buildings. The offices of Scott and his partners, Robin Walker and Ronald Tallon, were described as 'the cockpit of Irish architecture' (O'Toole, 2017, Essay no. 69, unpaginated). Their appointment by Bank of Ireland was not surprising; in addition to their professional reputation, the practice had an established connection to the site through Scott's existing planning permission. Also, Robin Walker, one of Scott's practice partners had designed the National Bank of Ireland (a subsidiary of Bank of Ireland) offices on Suffolk Street/College Green, completed in 1965, now demolished (see Outline Survey in *MTCB* Volume 2).

The brief for the Baggot Street project was to provide a new administration headquarters which would incorporate departments previously housed in different buildings around the city. Ronald Tallon was assigned the task of amending and refining Scott's earlier scheme. Tallon retained the building heights stipulated by the 1967 planning permission – five storeys on Baggot Street and nine storeys to the rear – but omitted a floor in the taller block, reducing its capacity to eight storeys in favour of increased internal floor to ceiling heights. Tallon's decision had a great and long-lasting impact on the building. In aesthetic terms, the increased height of the windows emphasised the building's verticality and improved the quality of the interior spaces; however, in terms of practicality and longevity, the increased floor to ceiling heights (which exceeded those generally found in office blocks of the period) meant that the building was suitable for upgrading works carried out 50 years later. In 1973 Bank of Ireland acquired four adjacent Georgian houses on the street which were demolished to make way for a third, four-storey block, which completed the urban composition of the entrance plaza and turned the corner into James Street East.

Tallon upgraded the specification standard for finishes throughout the building, and as a result, the building was one of the most opulent of its time. A critique written shortly after the building was occupied noted that 'in the field of commercial patronage [Bank of Ireland HQ] provides a shining example of building quality' (Wright, 1973, p. 97). Indeed, Wright's article in *Architectural Review* considered the new Bank of Ireland Headquarters one of the most advanced building complexes in Europe, providing a standard of environmental comfort far above the norm.

The external façade of the buildings was particularly innovative, employing a bronze manganese curtain walling system that gave the building its distinctive appearance. Robin Walker had designed Ireland's first purpose-

Central plaza with Michael Bulfin sculpture *Reflections* (John Donat / RIBA Collections)

made curtain wall at the recently completed National Bank, Suffolk Street, and he worked with Tallon on the design of the façade at Baggot Street. Their innovation was challenging for Irish builders who had not employed such construction methods before, but Tallon's meticulous detailing in drawings and written specifications ensured a successful outcome. The amount of bronze manganese used in the construction of the façades sparked rumours that the Bank of Ireland headquarters affected world prices for the material.

In addition to the quality of its building specification, the Bank of Ireland headquarters was remarkable for its generosity in handing over its outdoor spaces, and almost all its ground floor spaces to the public. Tallon was aware of the civic opportunity the building complex presented and later declared that Bank of Ireland were 'the only clients we've ever had who wanted to hand something back to the city' (*Building*, 1972, p. 28). On behalf of the bank, Tallon commissioned the two large pieces of sculpture for the plaza spaces and assembled a very important collection of contemporary artworks, predominantly by Irish artists, which were hung in the ground floor exhibition spaces. Bank of Ireland headquarters benefitted hugely from Tallon's exceptional taste, building an important collection of Irish art. Tallon's total control over the design process ensured a universally harmonious composition, both internally and externally. His exceptional aesthetic ability gifted Bank of Ireland with an important collection of Irish art.

Case Study: Bank of Ireland HQ

Richness and Restraint

From 1960 onwards, Michael Scott & Partners was very much the domain of Robin Walker and Ronald Tallon, although Scott remained in the practice until the mid-1970s. Tallon joined the practice in 1956 and a short time later, Walker (who had worked with Scott since 1948) left to work with Mies van der Rohe in Chicago. He returned to Dublin in 1958 and his commitment to Mies' design philosophy greatly influenced Tallon 'so there was a natural blending of [their] interests' (O'Toole, 2017, Essay no. 94, unpaginated). Tallon was also greatly influenced by Japanese architecture and modular coordination, and his architecture has an immediately identifiable idiom.

His architectural expression was grounded in mathematics, using strict geometries, with a strong reliance on the square. Late in his career, Tallon admitted that he was 'obsessed with the simplicity of the square' and that it had been the principal controlling mechanism for his architecture (O'Toole, 2017, Essay no. 94, unpaginated). The square is certainly the defining element at Baggot Street: the proportions of the three blocks are a square (Block C), a double square (Block B) and a quadruple square (Block A). The rigour of the composition is further compounded by the mathematical rhythm of the structural grid. Block A is set out on a 12 x 4 grid, Block B on a 6 x 4 grid, and Block C on a 6 x 6 grid of columns.

Tallon's composition at Baggot Street began with his consideration of the extant planning permission: a five-storey block that maintained the existing street line on Baggot Street (Block B), and a nine-storey building at the rear of the site (Block A) at right angles to the smaller building. Working within those confines, he greatly enhanced the architectural quality of the buildings in terms of their relationship to each other, in his consideration of the plaza spaces that intersected the site, and in the level of specification both internally and externally.

He amended the taller building so that it provided eight floors of offices on a raised podium over three levels of basements, two for car parking and the third for the mechanical plant and storage. Blocks A and B were completed in 1972, and a third four-storey building on the corner of Baggot Street and James Street East (Block C) was constructed in 1975. Each building was planned based on having a maximum floor area in relation to windows, with compact central vertical service cores containing stairs, lifts, mechanical distribution ducts and toilet facilities. The services installation was sophisticated with an automatic sprinkler system in the event of fire, a

Ground floor exhibition space (Courtesy of Scott Tallon Walker image collection)

carbon monoxide build-up warning system, complete extract ventilation, and numerous electrical and mechanical services outlets. Natural ventilation was provided by means of air shafts at the ends of the building and fluorescent lighting with automatic time control gave a high level of illumination. The plant room was designed and fitted out to provide 'the most desirable temperature and humidity conditions under any outside climatic conditions' (*Build*, 1972, p. 24).

Tallon's composition created a hierarchy between the buildings that overrode the homogony of their external appearance. The plaza between Block B and Block C was entered on grade from Baggot Street and paved with Ballybrew granite slabs laid on the lines of the building's modular grid. A large yellow steel sculpture by Michael Bulfin was placed outside Block B, on the axis of the reception desk, while two flush planter beds (one a 3 x 1 module and the other a 1 x 1 module) balanced the composition along the edge of Block C. The podium entrance to Block A was reached via a flight of granite steps to a pair of revolving door drums inset in double-height recessed glazing. A second large sculpture by John Burke, this time in primary red, was placed on the lower podium which formed the edge along James Street East. The bright colours and distinctive forms of the sculptures made a striking contrast against the monochromatic backdrop of the building façades. In addition, rows of slender birch trees generated flickering shadows across the façades.

Case Study: Bank of Ireland HQ

The building was constructed with reinforced concrete flat slabs supported on reinforced concrete columns. The bronze curtain wall had floor to ceilings double glazing, with a special bronze tinted sun resistant glass on the outside and clear glass on the inside. The ground floor of each building was fully glazed and fitted with several sets of revolving doors. All internal partitions abutted window mullions so that the clarity of the structure was maintained at all times. The granite used to pave the plazas was carried into the interiors to clad the service cores. All the interior elements of the building related to the module defined by the façade glazing panels with ceilings and internal partitions set out on the same grid. Internal demountable partitions were purpose made in brown oak, and natural materials were used throughout the building including undyed wool carpets. The architects were given complete control of the design of the interiors, designing the desks and other furniture. Significantly, Tallon personally selected and sited the paintings and sculptures which both assimilate and augment the aesthetic pleasure of the building.

In his critique in *Architectural Review*, Wright observed that the headquarters was 'almost certainly the purest example of [Miesian] style in Europe's offshore islands', but he criticised the siting of such an overtly Modernist building in the city's Georgian quarter. He identified the Bank's willingness to spend money on their headquarters as the building's salvation; in contrast to the many poor-quality speculative office developments that were being built on prime sites in the city at the time, he noted that: 'Bank of Ireland is a blessed exception, and it is a pleasure to see an adequate amount of money so beautifully spent.' (Wright, 1973, p. 97)

A lengthy review in the Irish publication, *Build*, praised the quality of the building in terms of its generous specification. The review commended the limited palette of materials employed, drawing similarity with the discipline of good historical architecture. Just as Georgian architecture mainly displayed brick and glass, the Bank of Ireland's external expression was predominately bronze and glass. By granting Tallon a building budget that exceeded most contemporary office buildings in Dublin, the Bank acquired a building that mirrored the aesthetic frugality of its historic neighbours, but transcended the mediocrity associated with many contemporaneous office buildings in Dublin.

Facts and Figures

Planning permission for two office blocks on the site was granted in 1967 to a developer who subsequently sold the site to Bank of Ireland. The architects, Michael Scott & Partners, were re-appointed by the bank in May 1968 and works started on site in August 1968. Bocks A and B were completed in July 1972. Planning permission for Block C was granted in February 1973, and works were completed in 1975. The first phase of development (Block A and Block B) comprised 25,342 square metres of office space including: offices, ground floor exhibition areas, dining, kitchen and ancillary spaces, service cores, and parking spaces. The total cost of the building was £4,600,000.

Architects: Michael Scott & Partners. Partner-in-charge, Ronald Tallon assisted by Peter Doyle, Frank Fahy, Mary Doyle, Gerald Palmer and Lawrence Kyne

Dr Ronald Tallon (1927–2014) graduated from University College Dublin in 1950. He worked with the OPW before joining Michael Scott in 1956. He formed a partnership with Michael Scott and Robin Walker in 1960. Between 1955 and 1970, the practice won three of the six RIAI Gold Medals awarded during that period. In 1980 Tallon was awarded a papal knighthood for designing the setting of the 1979 papal visit to the Phoenix Park. In 1990 he was conferred with an honorary doctorate from UCD for his contribution to architecture. His enormous talent and contribution to the Irish architecture was acknowledged in 2010 when he was the recipient of the inaugural RIAI James Gandon Medal for his lifetime achievement in the profession.

Consultant architect: Kenneth Kiersey, Chief Architect, Bank of Ireland
Planning Consultants: Becker & Becker
Quantity Surveyors: Seamus Monahan & Partners
Structural Engineers: Ove Arup & Partners
Building Contractors: Wimpey & Co. in association with G&T Crampton Ltd

Artists:
Michael Bulfin, sculptor, *Reflections* (1978)
Bulfin (born 1939) is an Irish sculptor and artist based in Dublin. He was educated at UCD and Yale University, USA. In 1965 he was awarded a German Government scholarship to study in Hamburg. He was chairman of the Project Arts Centre and is a member of Aosdána.
John Burke, sculptor, *Red Cardinal* (1978)
Burke (1946–2006) studied at the Crawford School of Art & Design in Cork and at the Royal Academy of London. He later taught at the Crawford School of Art & Design. He was a founding member of Aosdána in 1981.

Patrick Scott, *Eroica* tapestry (1979), *Blaze* tapestry (1979), *Aubusson* tapestry (1979)
Scott (1921–2014) trained as an architect and worked for 15 years for Michael Scott & Partners before concentrating on a career as an artist. His paintings are in several important international collections. He was a founding member of Aosdána and in 2007 was conferred with the title of Saoi, the highest honour that can be bestowed on an Irish artist. In 2021, to mark the centenary of his birth, An Post issued a special stamp featuring Scott's work.

Paintings purchased by Tallon on behalf of the bank were executed by the following artists: Tim Goulding (two felt banners), Alexandra Wejchert (three paintings), Michael Farrell (painting), Anne Madden, Gerda Fromel, Michael Farrell, Cecil King, Roy Johnston, Robert Costelloe, Barrie Cooke, Robert Ballagh, George Campbell, Maurice McGonigal, Louis le Brocquy, Colin Middleton, T. P. Flanagan, Gianfranco Pardi, James Coleman, Brian Henderson, Norah McGuinness, Alexander Calder, Emil Schumacher, Victor Vasarely, William Scott, Brian King, Derrick Hirs and Derrick Greaves.

Sources
Unpublished
Tallon, Ronald, *Report on Bank of Ireland HQ, Baggot Street* (September 1972)
Published
Anon., 'Bank of Ireland Headquarters, Dublin', *Build* (Vol. 9, No. 9, Dec. 1972)
Cairns, Frank, 'Bank of Ireland acquires site for new HQ', *Irish Times*, 10 May 1968
Kelly, Olivia, 'Refurbishment of former bank HQ to go ahead', *Irish Times*, 8 Apr. 2015
O'Regan, John (ed.), *Scott Tallon Walker Architects: 100 Buildings and Projects, 1960–2005* (Gandon Editions, 2006)
O'Toole, Shane, 'When Mies Was Asked to Build in Ireland', *Architecture Ireland* (No. 170, Sept. 2001)
O'Toole, Shane, 'Interview with Ronald Tallon', *Scott Tallon Walker Architects: 100 Buildings and Projects, 1960–2005* (Gandon Editions, 2006)
O'Toole, Shane, 'The Cockpit of Irish Architecture', *101 Hosannas for Architecture* (Gandon Editions, 2017)
O'Toole, Shane, 'Why Four?', Architecture Ireland (No. 271, Sept./Oct. 2013)
Wright, Lance, 'Bank of Ireland Headquarters, Dublin', *Architectural Review* (Feb. 1973)

Case Study
Darndale Housing Estate, Coolock, Dublin 17, 1976

Ellen Rowley

In 1974, while Darndale estate was mid-construction, an architectural journalist hailed it Dublin's 'most interesting housing project to date'; stating that Darndale was 'a radical departure from the standard layout and has separated pedestrians from the motor car' (*Street*, Dec. 1974, p. 8). Her comments point to the estate's experimental nature in terms of its layout and the houses' original building technology, based on a dry-lined concrete block module. This two-storey pitched-roof and concrete module world was at once recognisable and different for Dubliners. While the houses looked familiar in their terraces, their façades were starker than Dublin Corporation houses at nearby Coolock and elsewhere. Their windows were smaller and fewer, their walls were less textured. But least familiar of all were the network of narrow lanes, feeding from semi-private courts and leading out to half developed fields and the ring road beyond.

Sure enough, the experimental architecture of Darndale was influenced by the late 1960s and early 1970s studies at the Greater London Council (GLC), in their quest to make community-friendly new housing on a large scale. The Dublin architects, Arthur Lardner and Partners, engaged in the GLC's developments in such places as Andover, Bletchley and Newmarket where low-rise housing was situated at a higher density, in the hope to resettle communities at edge sites. So it went at Darndale which was yet another slum-clearance rehousing colony, pitching people out to Dublin's green-field edge. If Darndale's concrete module and higher density were experimental, the geography of the periphery certainly was not. In an attempt to place-make before the cement dust had time to settle, Lardner and Partners designed Darndale Estate as a series of smaller housing estates, clustered around 'courts' and named Marigold Court, Buttercup Park, Tulip Court, Primrose Grove and Snowdrop Walk. Given the lack of flowers and dominance of concrete for the estates' first 20 years, these aspirational street names were disingenuous at best.

The estate has captivated the literary and photographic imagination around neglect and poverty. It has been written about in novel and film as a late 20th-century slum, most particularly in the otherwise joyous 1991 film, *The Commitments*, and in the stark Magnum photographic series by Martine Franck (1993). Beginning soon after the estate's full occupation, residents and community groups began to question the built fabric and layout. Through the 1980s, the estate became notorious for anti-social behaviour with houses becoming vacant and many original residents moving on. Social amenity was absent, and the estate had the highest unemployment rate in Ireland. Its curious morphology was blamed for the incessantly high crime rates on the estate, and by the end of the 1980s, a major refurbishment programme was initiated which refurbished Darndale Estate, phase by phase.

The primary act in this refurbishment was the reversal of houses – moving their front door to the back and so on. This reversing of houses had a huge impact on the scheme's layout because alleyways were blocked off and pedestrian malls, semi-private semi-communal spaces previously at the front of houses, were now incorporated into back yards. In many phases, pairs of new houses were built, to enclose communal areas and vistas and to terminate new access roads. The original plan to keep cars out of the estate was overturned in this early 1990s refurbishment and in response to residents' requests and needs, car parking overtook courtyards (Marigold). Though physically improved, the estate's maligned reputation continues to a lesser extent in the 21st century. Community thrives and the houses are all actively occupied in 2023, with little vacancy or dereliction.

Aerial view of Darndale Estate upon completion (Courtesy of G. & T. Crampton, UCD Digital Library and Joseph Brady)

Case Study: Darndale Housing Estate

Origins and Ideals: Low-Rise, High-Density, Segregation
According to the Dublin Corporation Housing Committee, Darndale was approved already in late 1968, and at that point, it was to be another sub/exurban scheme of about 3,000 units. Arguably the brief was to make something less 'open' and at higher density than the recent Ballymun Estate and Dublin's other older formidable suburban housing colonies. Certainly, the architects (Arthur Lardner and Partners) studied recent London City Council (LCC) and Greater London Council (GLC) developments which were turning away from low-density and mid to high-rise towards high-density and low-rise schemes. In many ways, Darndale Estate was the architects' attempt at remaking a slice of traditional city housing, but in a new greenfield site.

In the end, the estate was broken up into five areas which were constructed in three phases and made up of 921 houses rather than the proposed 3,000. It was modelled on a recent precedent in Hampshire, England for new 1960s housing at Andover. Like at Andover's Cricketer Way, Darndale's homes were to be higher density, two storey and set into a pedestrianised context. The architects distanced their designs from the Dublin Corporation standard while keeping them low cost and at a density of 16 houses per acre.

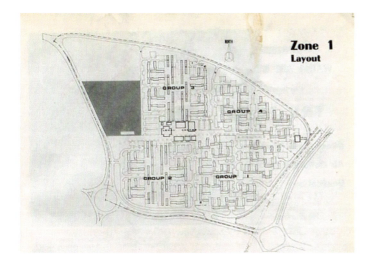

Site Layout of Darndale Estate
(Courtesy of Arthur Lardner & Partners image collection)

More Than Concrete Blocks Volume 3

Street view
(Courtesy of G. & T. Crampton, UCD Digital Library and Joseph Brady)

A series of interconnected squares generated the estate's layout. One of its quirkier features were the network of narrow streets – only nine feet wide in some instances – which were marked by archways housing bedrooms. Though there were over 20 house plan variations in the original Darndale Estate, derived from eight different house types, 90 per cent of the houses were three-bedroomed; 7 per cent were four-bedroomed and only 3 per cent were two-bedroomed. The extra bedroom was usually an addition placed in the archway or flyover.

The overall layout was idiosyncratic and related to a system adapted from Radburn of segregating vehicles from pedestrians: cars were kept to the periphery, encircling the estate via a ring road, entering only as far as the parking bays; there were larger pedestrian malls, smaller pedestrian streets and then courtyards, to be shared by (up to) nine households. Architect and former Darndale resident, Raymond Dinh analyses the houses and reads their links and public realms in terms of varying thresholds: from the courtyards to the semi-public outdoor spaces of the narrow pedestrian streets, often covered by archway or flyover bedrooms and most usually overlooked by the house's small kitchen windows. Dinh describes how the 'small patch would be tended to by the occupant, giving further variety to the collective and a sense of ownership to the individual' and emphasises

Case Study: Darndale Housing Estate

Houses under construction, c.1973, construction pamphlet (Courtesy of Irish Architectural Archive)

the hope and aspiration of the estate; that the tight layout aimed to be more conducive to community living (Dinh, 2012, p. 8).

Terraces comprise from four to eight houses, with central houses or those book-ending a terrace projecting beyond the terrace plane. Each house had its own front door, articulated by a small canopy and a pattern of small window openings. Houses' rear elevations mostly had large picture windows. The floor plans were pretty staid with ground floors comprising a small hall feeding into a kitchen to the front and living room to the rear; first floors mostly contained three bedrooms and a bathroom arranged around a neat landing.

The Darndale houses are both traditional and radical in their conception: traditional in form and radical in material. They are composed of tiled pitched roofs and cavity walling, but at their basis is a radical modular block which was developed by Clondalkin Concrete. This block is a dense masonry unit or module, measuring 200m x 400m and due to its waterproof fair-faced surface, it did not need any treatment. Inside walls were dry lined which was another radical aspect in that no wet trades (plastering) were required on site during construction. Without cutting any blocks, the dimensions of the module dictated the scheme from the front elevations' small windows to the large picture windows overlooking each house's small yard.

Construction was difficult in the inner parts of the estate once the archways were constructed. They, and the complex street layouts generally, became obstacles for the builders. This aspect, as well as the varied house plans, meant that the Darndale Estate was particularly difficult to construct, despite the promise of its dense concrete modular unit. This general difficulty was further compounded by the fact that three different contractors built the estate: G&T Crampton (groups 1 and 4); Thomas McInerney (group 2); and MFN Construction Co. Ltd (group 3).

The Reality of Darndale
The very particular layout of the estate, as per the example of Cricketer's Way and the adoption of the Radburn system of vehicular segregation, led to the original design's undoing. One of Darndale's initial claims was that it was designed so that anyone could walk from one part of the estate to another without having to cross a road. Theoretically the layout involved parking spaces at the rear of houses and communal spaces to the front, in the hope

to champion pedestrians and to stimulate encounters and relations. This type of layout replaced the more common grid-iron street pattern, where access is perhaps more even and democratic, with a type of intricate superblock, where a large piece or block of land containing the houses and the arteries for pedestrians is surrounded by main roads; in this case, access is more exclusive and selective. In reality, the separation created an island effect, leading to a lack of efficient surveillance and passive supervision at Darndale, which in turn bolstered crime and fed anti-social behaviour. Pedestrian walkways and arteries enabled criminals' quick escape while *culs-de-sacs* trapped Gardaí.

While this behaviour began to unfold, the estate was coming under the national political lens. As early as 1978, it was the topic of a Dáil questions and answers with Independent TD Dr Noel Browne questioning Minister of the Environment Sylvester (Sylvie) Barrett as to whether he was aware of the 'long-standing grievances of the residents… regarding conditions on the estate?' Browne also asked, 'How is it that a group of houses of this size, which is quite considerable, can be built without provision for serious recreation facilities, shopping facilities and proper maintenance?' (Dáil questions, 1978). The Minister responded by outlining the complaints around the houses' dampness, more prevalent in houses without fireplaces, and around litter stating that the 'high density layout makes this scheme very prone to litter'. Focusing on vandalised gullies and the accumulation of rubble, the Minister had nothing to say about the lack of social amenity.

Seemingly, no matter how the architecture tried to emulate the traditional city, the new estate in Ireland would always fall at the social infrastructure hurdle. At Darndale, as a marked improvement upon Ballymun Estate for instance, the Catholic church and community hall were designed as a single (prefabricated) structure and were finished in December 1974, at the same time as the first houses. But other than the primary school, nothing tangible followed for 25 years until the 1999 international architectural competition for a new community centre (complete 2001, DMOD Architects).

The hopelessness coming out of the lack of amenity was exacerbated by a profound shift in Darndale's population brought about by the introduction in 1985 of the £5,000 Surrender Grant. The grant enabled the more economically mobile tenants to give up their council houses and receive £5,000 to buy their own house privately, elsewhere. At Darndale, units became vacant, and the Corporation's most problem tenants were allocated homes there; the Surrender Grant had caused what Anne Power called 'an avalanche of moves off the worst estates and hastening their social collapse' (Power, 1993, p. 79).

Darndale's community groups became more vocal and active. Either because of the extremity of its plight or because of its extraordinary architectonics, the estate had been visited by An Taoiseach, Garret FitzGerald, coinciding with the 1985 community survey, 'Image Changers'. By January 1986 the Government confirmed its commitment to rehabilitate the estate through a process of deep refurbishment. A major survey was carried out (Dyer, 1988) which identified community needs arising from lived experiences, in order to compliment and influence Dublin Corporation Architects Department. Funded by the Remedial Works Scheme, in operation since 1985, the remedial programme sought to address the following: reduce the amount of undefined surface area; provide enclosed front gardens; provide curtilage car parking where possible; incorporate back alleys into private back alleys; develop courtyards into communal space; provide a fireplace and chimney into each house; provide a new elevation treatment to houses, with a distinct architectural character for each section; select an area as a pilot scheme and establish a local architectural office.

Architect Sean Ó'Laoire critiqued the remedial works in an article for *Irish Architect* 1991, as they were happening, over eight phases. He described the process of phasing the rehabilitation – under the guidance of a local steering committee – as a process which would be underpinned by the same design objectives, but which would be adaptive enough, with each subsequent phase, to react to the challenges and outcomes of the preceding phase. Community consulting continued throughout the process and residents' opinions on what they did and did not like in the refurbishment were taken on board. For instance, fireplaces and enclosed porches were very popular and communal gardens were not.

The primary design move by the City Architects was the complex reversal of the houses' fronts and backs. Houses which were reversed were typically given a porch while the other unreversed houses retained the canopies over their front doors. Dinh summarises the effect of this bold move, which minimised undefined open space and closed alleyways, and effectively undermined Darndale's original planning concept:

Case Study: Darndale Housing Estate

This had a defining effect on the character of the spaces, and in many cases contradicted the original design intentions. In addition to changing the orientation of the houses and their relationship to the public realm, the houses themselves were given a 'facelift', as it was expressed by the residents that a new elevation treatment was very important for the perceived image of their homes. (Dinh, 2012, p. 15)

Earlier phases of refurbishment (phases 1–4) saw courtyards transformed into enclosed communal gardens, but these were not looked after and were not repeated thereafter. The last phase of refurbishment, at Tulip Court, was the most extensive and considered the most successful. Costing £1.82million for 80 houses, compared to phase 1's £0.94million for 29 houses (Primrose Grove), Tulip Court's houses were given fully enclosed porches, brick cobble-lock paving and extensive landscaping. As a result, Primrose Grove was refurbished again, in an eighth phase.

Case Study: Darndale Housing Estate

Facts and Figures

Darndale Estate is located to the north-east of Dublin city, just three kilometres from Dublin Airport. It is bordered to the east by the Malahide Road, to the west by Priorswood, to the north by the R139 (old Clonshaugh Road), and to the south by the Riverside housing estate in Coolock. It sits, low-rise, apparently marooned or at least isolated and cut off from the busy ring roads, surrounded by green wasteland. Its streets are named as Buttercup Park, Marigold Court, Primrose Grove, Snowdrop Walk and Tulip Court. It was commissioned in 1969 by Dublin Corporation as client, but construction did not begin until 1973 and was complete in phases from December 1974, through to 1976.

Architects: Arthur Lardner and Partners with Reginald McGovern acting as partner in charge of the estate while Seamus Ruddy, Paddy MacNeill and Boyd Jones were the project architects.

Arthur Lardner graduated along with 11 others from the UCD School of Architecture in 1946. He is listed as having worked at Michael Scott's office (Michael Scott & Associates becoming Scott Tallon Walker) but this is not substantiated. He had established quite a practice during the 1960s to have gained the Darndale Estate commission by 1969. Before Darndale, the practice designed the textured and richly decorated Catholic church at Cooleragh, Co. Laois (1963–5) where the architect in charge was Andre Zakrzewski. This church is typical of pre-conciliar Modernism and is notable for its figurative stained glass by Murphy Devitt studios. At about the same time, 1964, Lardner and Partners were designing Hume House in Ballsbridge and were clearly committed to modernism in scale and materials. The practice was most active during the 1970s and important projects, all of which made new city blocks in Dublin, include Norwich Corner (1975) for Norwich Union insurance on Dawson/Nassau Streets and Norfin House, Wilton Place (1973), both of which are now demolished.

Landscape design: Shipman Brady Martin are landscape and urban design specialists who were established in 1968 by Philip Shipman, Hugh Brady, and Arthur Martin. The latter two were Irish architects while Shipman was an English architect who studied at the Regent Street Polytechnic in London and with famed landscape architect Ian McHarg in the University of Pennsylvania. The three met through UCD's Professor of Planning, Jim Fehily, establishing their firm by making a national coastline study for An Foras Forbatha. Early in their practice they became consultants for the Northern Irish Housing Executive and the Craigavon Commission, which likely brought them to the fore for Darndale's planning and landscape development.

Quantity Surveyors: Boyd & Creed
Civil Engineers: McCarthy & Partners
Contractors, for Groups 1 and 4: G& T Crampton
Contractors for Group 2: Thomas McInerney
Contractors for Group 3: MFN Construction Co. Ltd
Electrical Installations: Power Electrical Co., Abbeyfield, Killester
Glazing and glass contractors: Crystal Glass Co. Ltd, 1 Lower Dorset Street
Prefabricated timber roof trusses: Jack O'Keefe, East Wall
Roof tiling: A. Fitzpatrick & Sons., Newry
Floor tiles: D. J. Kelly & Co. Ltd, Cabra Road
Plastering on metal stud partitions: William Power
The refurbishment from the late 1980s into 1990s was undertaken by William Neville + Sons, and Terence Harvey Contract Services

Sources

Unpublished
Dail Eireann Debate, Questions and Answers, 12 Feb. 1978 https://www.oireachtas.ie/en/debates/debate/dail/1978-02-16/5/ (accessed through 2012–18)
Dail Eireann Debate, Questions and Answers, 8 July 1987 https://www.oireachtas.ie/en/debates/debate/seanad/1987-07-08/9/ (accessed through 2012–18)
Dinh, Raymond, 'Renewing Darndale: Problems and potential' (Unpublished MArch dissertation, UCD School of Architecture, 2012)
Housing Committee No. 164, *Reports and Printed Documents of the Corporation of Dublin* (Nov. 1968)

Published
Anon., 'Local Authority Housing, Andover: Development of Cricketers' Way, Admirals' Way and Area 7', *Building* (Vol. 216, No. 22, 1969)
Anon., 'Residents Beat the Odds', *Evening Herald*, 2 Oct 1991
Anon., 'Darndale: Focusing on the positive', *The Voice of Northside Centre for the Unemployed* (Issue No. 49, May 1996)
Blowers, A. T., 'Council Housing: The Social Implications of Layout and Design in an Urban Estate', *The Town Planning Review* (Liverpool University Press, 1970)
Brady, Joseph, *Dublin 1950–70: Houses, Flats and High-rise* (Four Courts Press, 2017)
Dinh, Raymond, 'Darndale: The Building and Rebuilding of a Twentieth-Century Housing Estate', *2Ha* (No. 4, 2017)
McArtain, Donagh, *Darndale Belcamp Community Survey* (Dublin, 2007)
McCafferty, Nell, 'Minister Opens New Flats Scheme', *Irish Times*, 5 June 1971
McManus, Ruth, *Crampton Built* (Gill & MacMillan, 2008)
O Laoire, Sean, 'Darndale Refurbishment', *Irish Architect* (Vol. 1, 1991)
Power, Anne, *Hovels to Highrise: State Housing in Europe since 1850* (Routledge, 1993)
Rowley, Ellen, *Housing, Architecture and the Edge Condition: Dublin is Building, 1935– 1975* (Routledge, 2019)
Street, Clara, 'Darndale', *Plan* (Vol. 5, No. 9, Dec. 1974)

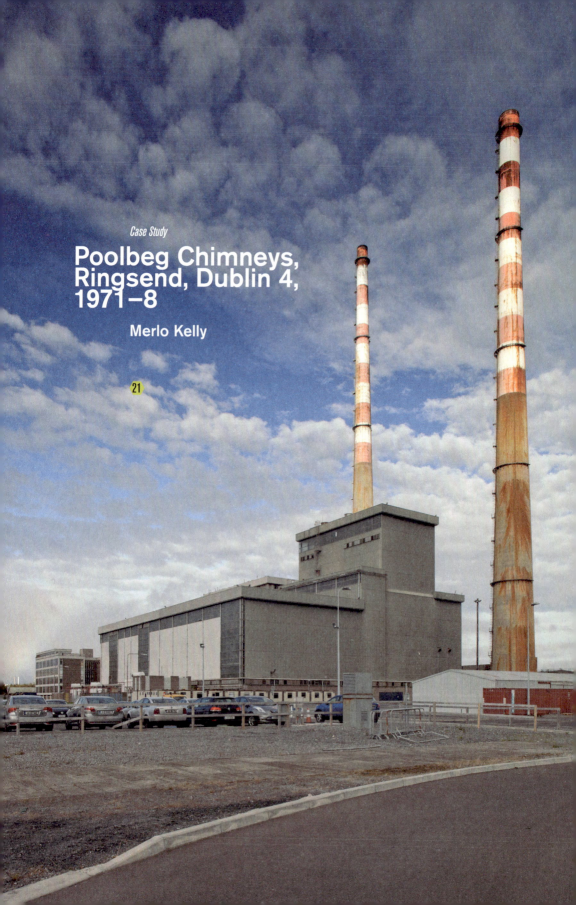

Case Study
Poolbeg Chimneys, Ringsend, Dublin 4, 1971–8

Merlo Kelly

The distinctive red-and-white-striped Poolbeg chimneys were constructed as part of the ESB Poolbeg Generating Station (formerly known as Pigeon House B), which took its name from the Poolbeg Lighthouse at the entrance to the Liffey estuary in Dublin Bay. Poolbeg is a gas-fuelled power station known as a thermal generating station, and its operations convert chemical energy into electricity by burning gas. It was originally designed as an oil-fuelled power station. The chimney stacks and their associated buildings and large-scale infrastructural elements are amassed within an enclosed complex on a peninsula of reclaimed land within the south docklands area of Dublin Bay. The first chimney was completed in December 1971, when Poolbeg Units 1 & 2 were commissioned. The second chimney was completed in November 1978, coinciding with the commissioning of Poolbeg Unit 3.

The twin stacks at Poolbeg form part of our industrial heritage, and perhaps more surprisingly, the 'candy-striped towers' have become part of our cultural heritage, and a representation of Dublin city. For many emigrants travelling back to Ireland by boat or plane, the towering chimneys are landmarks representing the first sight of home. In an *Irish Times* article in February 1970, Lionel Fleming reports a light-hearted quote from one of the ESB officials on site: 'This chimney is going to be so high that they'll be able to see it from Holyhead. We're thinking of putting a notice for them on top, "Irish workers, come home".' In recent times, the chimneys have appeared in a diverse array of artistic representations rendering them synonymous with our image of the Dublin skyline. Featuring in paintings, photography, postcards, advertisements, music videos, graphic design and theatrical performances, our perception of the chimneys and their significance in the urban context are by now inextricably intertwined with such representations.

In 1984 the station was converted to burn natural gas from the Kinsale gas field and subsequently underwent upgrading with the introduction of new gas turbines. The chimneys were adaptable to these alterations. In 2000, Poolbeg was further upgraded to use Combined Gas Cycle Technology (CCGT), and in 2010 this system superseded the original phases of development leaving Units 1, 2 & 3 defunct. It was at this point that the chimneys and Turbine Hall were finally decommissioned. The chimneys were capped in 2015 to prevent internal deterioration. While functioning, the emissions protected the chimney interior from damp and moisture ingress. In recent years, moisture levels have built up and so the access doors at the base of each chimney have been opened in an effort to dry out the chimney interiors. Views inside the chimney voids show that some of the brick lining is in need of repair. The external surface of the concrete has not been painted in recent years and the strong red-and-white stripes are fading while small sections of the concrete surface have become dislodged.

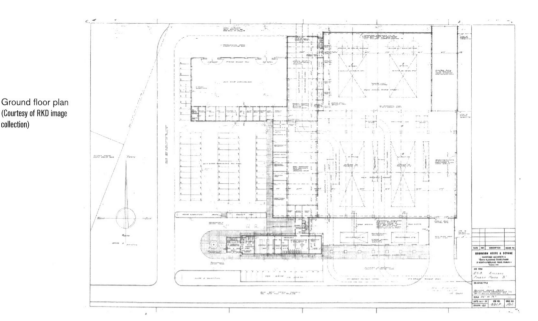

Ground floor plan
(Courtesy of RKD image collection)

Layered Industrial Landscape

The site for the Poolbeg Generating Station sits north of Irishtown Nature Park and is accessed by Pigeon House Road which contains remnants of the former Pigeon House Fort. The station is located beside the Pigeon House Hotel (1793), and the red-brick Pigeon House Generating Station (1903), which remains a prominent Dublin landmark. The Pigeon House Power Station was founded by the City of Dublin Electricity Works in 1903 and took over from the power station at Fleet Street supplying most of Dublin city's electricity until the 1950s. The Electricity Supply Board (ESB) was established as a semi-state body by the Irish Free State government under the Electricity Supply Board Act in 1927, to oversee the provision of electricity across Ireland. In 1929, ESB took over the running of the Pigeon House station from the Dublin Corporation Electricity Department. An extensive new wing was added to the original station in the 1930s. The Pigeon House continued to produce electricity, feeding into the national grid until it was decommissioned in 1976.

During the Second World War (1939–45) – known locally as 'The Emergency' – the Pigeon House station and Ardnacrusha hydroelectric station on the Shannon (completed in 1929) strived to meet electricity needs nationwide, but an increased demand for electricity in the 1960s called for a new generating station. A site adjacent to the Pigeon House was selected because of its proximity to Dublin city and its ready supply of cooling

Case Study: Poolbeg Chimneys, Ringsend

water from the river Liffey. Consequently, a land reclamation process was embarked upon and the South Wall, which dates from the late-18th century, was partially broken to accommodate the new station which was known as 'Pigeon House B'. ESB reports estimate that 750,000 tons of sand were dredged from Dublin Harbour for use on the Poolbeg site.

Work commenced on the project in 1966, with construction on the 90-acre site beginning in 1969. Poolbeg Units 1 & 2, including Chimney A, were completed for a cost of £20 million, and commissioned in 1971. Each unit contained 120 MW Brown Boveri steam turbines and generators. According to Fleischmann's film, Chimney A cost £350,000 to construct. On completion of this first phase, the Poolbeg complex had a capacity which was four times that of the original Shannon scheme at Ardnacrusha.

The two striped tapering chimneys, built in 1971 and 1978, dominate the industrial site and the surrounding urban landscape. The red and white stripes were designed to maximise the visibility of the chimneys, further to a requirement given by the Aviation Authority. At the time of construction, the chimneys were the highest structures in the country, both measuring c.207 metres in height. They have since become Dublin landmarks, defining the city skyline.

To understand the chimneys, it is important to examine the architectural assemblage of the site. The Poolbeg Generating Station also accommodates a number of related industrial and office buildings, among them the Generating Hall, the Water Pumping Station, the Gas Installation building and the Administration Block. The first phases of the project saw development clustered to the west of the reclaimed peninsula, but later phases of building gravitated to the east as the systems were upgraded to Combined Gas Cycle Technology (CCGT).

The Generating Hall, or Turbine Hall (now decommissioned), is a steel-frame structure clad in grey steel incorporating large expanses of aluminium curtain wall glazing, situated directly south of the chimneys. This spacious hall is connected internally to the six-storey Administration Block, or Control Building, a concrete-frame building clad in brown brick and featuring advanced glazed bays to the north and south elevations. A row of double-height workshops with a monitor roof profile and clerestory lighting flank the western façade of the Turbine Hall. High-voltage substations are located to the south of the site, including air space sheds and insulated gas space sheds.

The immense steel frame structure of the Turbine Hall measures 43 metres in height and is set out on a concrete substructure. The reinforced concrete base was constructed above ground and then sunk to a depth of 12 metres below ground level. According to Fleischmann's 1973 film, skilled divers were employed in the construction process. The roof structure is supported on the steel trusses of the main structural frame.

The Administration Block was designed specifically for the Poolbeg context according to architect Fred Browne, who was one of the project architects for the Poolbeg complex. It is an elegant brick-clad office block, with lancet windows and projecting glazed bays. The recessed ground floor allows the articulation of a columnar structure supporting the upper levels. The interior features a marble-clad entrance area, terrazzo staircase and finely detailed handrails and ironmongery.

The sensitive natural landscape in which the generating station is located is home to diverse forms of wildlife, and the complex is adjacent to the Irishtown Nature Park. A key consideration in the design of the two chimney stacks was the minimisation of atmospheric pollution. Advancements in concrete construction and new calculations regarding heights allowed the design of efficient chimney structures which adhered to environmental recommendations. Modestly landscaped grounds in the complex attempt to enhance the natural setting, and Brent geese have been known to feed and rest on the site during winter months. An amenity area was established at nearby Shelly Banks, with a swimming area and car park provided along the sandy shore. The historic South Wall to the east of the complex remains an established promenade for city dwellers, terminating at the picturesque Poolbeg Lighthouse (1767) and home to the Half Moon Swimming Club which was founded in 1898.

Tapered Shells and Concrete Corbels

The ESB embarked on a number of ambitious projects in the 1960s and 1970s, breaking new ground in construction terms. They organised international research trips for design teams, and these led to the establishment of professional and trade connections across Europe and the USA. This exploration of new technologies and consequent advances in construction methodologies brought with it a new confidence. Turlough Hill in Co. Wicklow (1974) and Poolbeg Generating Station date from this pivotal time, and both display the employment of new building techniques

Aerial view of ESB Pigeon House and Poolbeg chimneys looking towards the city, c.2003 (Courtesy of ESB Archives)

on a grand scale. In terms of energy efficiency, Poolbeg broke new ground internationally at the time:

> It has surpassed the efficiencies achieved by any other station of its size in Europe and North America and has set a new standard in availability and performance. (Fleischmann, film, 1977)

The intention was to provide a series of tall chimney stacks on the Poolbeg site but these plans were hampered by the 1973 oil crisis as documented in an *Irish Times* article:

> Original proposals provided for a number of stacks over 600 feet high, but it is not immediately clear whether the world energy situation will encourage the ESB to go ahead with these long-term plans for oil-fired stations in this part of Dublin (*Irish Times*, 27 Feb. 1974).

The article goes on to report that despite the fact that 'as many as half-a-dozen of these 600 ft plus generator chimneys' were planned for Dublin shores, only one further chimney had been approved for construction.

Opening Ceremony
(Private collection)

The heights of the chimney stacks were based on an optimum of not less than two and a half times the height of the boiler house. This was designed to prevent gases being drawn down, which would result in turbulence around the adjacent buildings. Chimney A measures 207.48 metres in height and Chimney B measures 207.8 metres. The chimney structures are tapered, comprising a painted concrete outer shell, varying in thickness from 800mm at the base to a mere 180mm at the top. A cavity of approximately 100mm separates the outer concrete layer from the brick inner lining which varies in thickness from 230mm at the base to 115mm at the top.

According to steeplejack Brian Segar, who worked on the maintenance of the chimneys, each chimney was constructed using a 'slip form' system. This novel method entailed making a circular mould into which the concrete was poured. When the concrete had dried, the mould was repeatedly moved upwards and filled accordingly with concrete. The consequent series of concrete rings eventually formed the chimney.

The outer reinforced concrete shell tapers as it rises and incorporates a series of concrete corbels, at 30-foot intervals, which support the inner brick lining. Chimney A ranges in diameter from 13.8 metres at the base to 4.9 metres at the top, whereas Chimney B is wider measuring 15.6 metres at the base and 7 metres at the top. Both the inner and outer faces of the concrete shell are painted. The inner lining is composed of acid-resistant brick and comprises a series of stepped brick sections supported on corbels which are incorporated into the concrete outer shell. An additional 115mm of Moler brick (brick with a higher insulating capacity) lines the inner lower levels of the chimney. The floor is composed of acid-resistant brick laid on Moler brick over a hollow concrete block base. A reinforced concrete pad foundation is supported on a series of reinforced concrete cylindrical piles,

Case Study: Poolbeg Chimneys, Ringsend

each measuring one metre in diameter, and extending 30 metres below ground surface.

Each chimney features an access door at ground level and a series of steel service platforms, rest platforms and continuous ladders for ease of maintenance. Vent holes within the walls of the chimneys incorporate bird guards. Aircraft warning lights were located at regular vertical intervals and lightening conductors were placed at the tops of the chimneys. Leaching of the concrete has occurred in recent years, with secretions through vent holes in the outer layer of the chimney resulting in discolouration and heavy rust staining. The metal guarding, ladders and screens have deteriorated and show evidence of rust.

Twin Chimneys as Cultural Icons

The ESB expansion in the 1950s was driven by an increased demand for electricity nationwide and prompted investment in the construction of new power stations. This marked a period of industrialisation which left its legacy across the Irish landscape in the form of large-scale structures and associated infrastructure. The social impact of this phase of industrialisation across Ireland was significant. In addition to the Rural Electrification Scheme, the construction process and operation of these centres were a substantial boost for local economies, generating employment and the establishment of associated housing for the workers. In many ways the twin chimneys

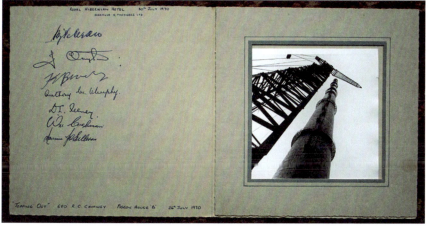

Invitation card for Topping Out ceremony (Private collection)

More Than Concrete Blocks Volume 3

became symbols of hope, marking a new and prosperous industrial phase in Irish history. The ESB 'Power for Progress' document published in the early 1970s reports that the ESB at that time provided employment for 12,000 people nationally. The Poolbeg Station and the former Ringsend Power Station on an adjacent site, now an ESB training centre, benefitted from a city centre location and created an abundance of job opportunities. Housing developments followed, bringing the densification of existing communities.

The construction of the station resulted in the emergence of unexpected cultural connections. ESB engineers on site recollect tales of a curious goods exchange between far-flung countries during the original building phase. Chief Executive of ESB from 1981 to 1991, Paddy Moriarty, reputedly supplied turbines to Vietnam, thus establishing firm links there, and in turn Vietnam supplied fish to Australia, who then provided Ireland with coal.

In 2022, the Poolbeg chimneys are acknowledged as an integral part of the Dublin skyline, and feature in diverse depictions of the city. Their iconic status has been celebrated in numerous artistic and commercial representations, as prominent features or serving as an identifiable urban backdrop. Over the decades the twin chimneys have become objects of affection for the majority of Dublin residents, earning them a variety of nicknames such as 'The Barber Poles', 'Laurel & Hardy' and the 'Witch's Legs'. Poolbeg provided the inspiration for Olwen Fouere and Roger Doyle's 1983 production of *Ignotum per Ignotius*, a music and dance performance staged by their company Operating Theatre in the Douglas Hyde Gallery and financed by the ESB. U2's music video for their 1984 song *Pride (In the Name of Love)* was filmed in the Dublin docklands, and features the Poolbeg site as a backdrop, bringing the two chimneys to an international audience. The chimneys appeared in a Guinness advertisement, sporting the Dublin colours of blue and white, and provided the focus for Tony Kenny's poetic film *Columbarium* (2006). More recently, perhaps prompted by debate regarding their possible demolition, the iconic structures have featured in a proliferation of graphic representations of Dublin, among them artworks by Annie Atkins, Chris Judge and Snow Design. In 2014 Skypixels Ireland used aerial drones to record the chimney interiors, pulling away to reveal their dramatic setting on Dublin Bay. In 2020 the chimneys were the subject of an IAF site specific short film for Dublin Open House.

However, it must be noted that the arrival of the chimneys was not initially welcomed by all and was subject to criticism from some quarters. In 1970, writer Benedict Kiely referred to

> the monstrous ESB chimney stack' and proceeded to elaborate: 'There it stands, slender, grey, red and white, sinister, like a fearful rocket on the launching pad, and just across the water from the mooring-place of the car-ferry for Liverpool... (*Irish Times*, 3 Sept. 1970).

The ESB commissioned an extensive study of their projects throughout Ireland which was published in 2004. The book comprised detailed descriptions of the relevant buildings and an assessment based on the National Inventory of Architectural Heritage (NIAH) system. The power station at Poolbeg was deemed to be of national importance, and its categories of special interest were recorded as artistic, historical, scientific, social, and technical. Following the decommissioning of Poolbeg Units 1, 2 and 3 in 2010, the prospect of demolition became a discussion topic, provoking public outcry which came to a head in the summer of 2014. Petitions were circulated in an effort to save the chimneys and a campaign was led by Dublin City Councillor Dermot Lacey to have the chimneys listed on the Record of Protected Structures.

In 2017, the ESB committed to maintaining of the chimneys for ten years (*Irish Times*, 9 Mar. 2021), and in March 2021, following ongoing requests for the chimneys to be placed on the Record of Protected Structures, proposals to encase the chimneys in fibreglass or concrete were floated.

> These interventions are likely to alter the appearance and integrity of the structures as originally designed. ESB is concerned that adding the chimneys to the Record of Protected Structures will not provide any additional security to that provided under the maintenance programme and may actively impede any ongoing structural interventions or necessary external cladding in the future. (*Irish Times*, 9 Mar. 2021)

Facts and Figures

The Poolbeg Chimneys are part of the Poolbeg Generating Station, Pigeon House Harbour, Ringsend, Dublin 4. The first chimney (A) was completed in 1971 (commissioning of Units 1 & 2 of Generating Station) and second in 1978 (commissioning of Unit 3 of Generating Station). They were commissioned by the Civil Works Department of Electricity Supply Board (ESB).

Architects: Robinson Keefe & Devane

The RKD project architect was Fred Browne and the team included Noel Gilleece, John Cody, Mick Hillery, and Lorcan Lyons. Fred Browne joined Robinson, Keefe & Devane in 1954, and went on to become a partner in the firm. Having travelled on a number of architectural research trips to USA, Browne was introduced to the notion of project management and a 'one-stop shop' approach to industrial projects. This practice, which involved the architect taking the lead from inception to completion, was one which he subsequently engaged in the Irish context.

Engineers: ESB Engineering Department

The engineering team included Maurice O'Sullivan and Anthony Murphy (Head of Civil Works 1970-81) and J. A. O'Riordan, Assistant Chief Civil Engineer at the ESB.

Maurice O'Sullivan, BE, BSc, CEng, MIEI, graduated from University College Dublin in 1945. He was employed as an engineer with Nicholas O'Dwyer Consultancy Engineer (1945–6), Michael Scott Architect (1946–7), and Ove Arup & Partners (1947–9), before joining the ESB Civil Works Department in 1949. O'Sullivan worked on designs for North Wall, Ringsend, and Rhode Stations prior to his involvement in the Poolbeg Generating Station. He went on to manage the Rifaa Training School in Bahrain and a series of major ESB works, among them the upgrade of Marina Power Station. During this period, he was manager in charge of all structural steelwork design and procurement for ESB structures. O'Sullivan was a founder member of CICIND, the International Committee on Industrial Chimneys.

Main Civil Engineering Contractors: Ascon Ltd
Chimney Structure: Bierrum & Partners Ltd, Harrow, England
Chimney Foundations: Irish Engineering and Harbour Construction Co. Ltd
Structural steelwork (Turbine Hall): Dublin Erection Co.

Sources

Unpublished
ESB Archive, Dublin
Robinson Keefe & Devane (RKD) archives
Shaffrey & Associates, *Pigeon House Precinct. Conservation Plan and Re-use Study, Draft E* (Dublin City Council, 2011)
Maurice O'Sullivan, private archives (with thanks to Jean O'Sullivan)
Fred Browne, interviewed by Merlo Kelly, Feb. 2015
Jean O'Sullivan, interviewed by Merlo Kelly, Oct. 2014

Published
Anon., *Power for Progress* (ESB information pamphlet, undated)
Anon., 'Pigeon House B', *Plan Magazine* (Vol. 1, No. 9 June 1970)
Anon., 'Second Giant ESB Tower for Ringsend', *Irish Times*, 27 Feb. 1974
Anon., 'Tall Chimneys are no Answer to Air Pollution', *Irish Independent*, 6 Feb. 1976
Anon., 'Times Past: The Pigeon House', *Irish Times*, 17 Oct 1989
Bielenberg, Andy, *The Shannon Scheme and the Electrification of the Irish Free State* (Lilliput Press, 2002)
Cox, Ron and Philip Donald, *Ireland's Civil Engineering Heritage* (Collins Press, 2013)
De Courcy, J. W., *The Liffey in Dublin* (Gill & MacMillan, 1996)
Delaney B., Carroll P. and Doherty J., *A Heritage Inventory of ESB Buildings in Ireland* (ESB, 2005)
Dunn, Miriam, 'Power stations', in Loeber et al. (eds), *Architecture 1600–2000, Volume IV, Art and Architecture of Ireland* (RIA, Yale University Press, 2014)
ESB, *Poolbeg Generating Station Dublin* (ESB, 1980s)
ESB, *A Profile and History of the Poolbeg Generating Station* (ESB, 1992)
Fleischmann, George (Director and narrator), 'Poolbeg: The story of a generating station' (Film, 1977)
Hogan, Senan, 'Plea to Save Iconic Twin Stacks', *Irish Independent*, 7 July 2007
Kiely, Benedict, 'Sailing, Sailing, Swiftly Through the Smog', *Irish Times*, 3 Sept. 1970
Manning, Maurice & McDowell, Moore, *Electricity Supply in Ireland: The History of the ESB* (Gill & MacMillan, 1984)
McDonald, Frank, 'Odd Couple Have Become Markers of our Capital City', *Irish Times*, 12 July 2014
Murphy, Cormac, 'Poolbeg's Chimneys Puff their Last Plumes', *Evening Herald*, 31 Mar. 2010
O'Sullivan, Maurice, 'Chimneys', *ESB Journal* (July 1966)
O'Sullivan, Maurice, 'Ireland's Tallest Structure', *Irish Builder & Engineer* (May 1976)
Shiel, Michael, *The Quiet Revolution – the Electrification of Rural Ireland* (O'Brien Press, 2003)

More Than Concrete Blocks Volume 3

Case Study
PMPA (later AXA Insurance), Wolfe Tone Square, Dublin 1, 1978
Ellen Rowley

Our sixth building study, the headquarters for the insurance company PMPA is another 1970s office building made for Dublin city centre. Sharing the common purpose with Molyneux House and Baggot Street's Bank of Ireland, of bringing (late) Modernist office architecture into the historic city and street, this PMPA HQ goes a step further by being an infill building. By infill, we refer to a building which has been inserted into an older terrace or context. In this case the infill nature of PMPA carries its resonance or essence, architecturally.

Simply put, PMPA is a three-storey office block with a penthouse level set back from the building line (on the roof) and an unseen basement plant area. Its more mute dark glass façade was enlivened by its large red columns which stood as a screen between the building interior and the city pavement. Designed by the leading Modernist architect of the period, Robin Walker, PMPA displayed all of Walker's urban and architectural preoccupations such as introducing architectural Modernism to the city without ignoring the context, or making a meticulous façade from glass and steel. Importantly, the PMPA building was infill architecture for 1970s Dublin without resorting to pastiche or Georgian copyism. Walker was deeply influenced by the practice of German-American architect Ludwig Mies Van der Rohe (Mies and Miesian design) and, here, the Irish architect pays homage to the Miesian module; that is a module of measurement used to determine the overall design (and grid) of the building.

PMPA's façade, hewn from glass and steel, was always the building's dominant aspect. While it continues to read like a disciplined gridded thing, with glass tightly wrapping around its volume, the glazing panels have been replaced and the ground floor treatment is unrecognisable. Walker's idiosyncratic red columns and his deliberately open arcade have now been enclosed. The building is in continuous use as office space.

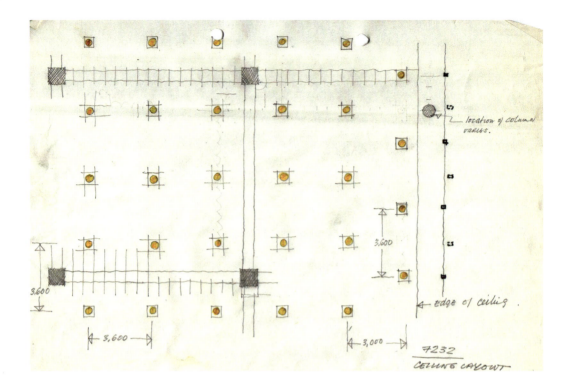

Drawing the Grid, Robin Walker sketch, c.1973 (Courtesy of Scott Tallon Walker image collection)

Infill Office Architecture for 1970s Dublin

The new HQ for this insurance company was commissioned because of fire damage to a building on the site in Wolfe tone Street (known as 'old PMPA'). Scott Tallon Walker Architects were approached in July 1971 to evaluate the damage and propose either the refurbishment of the fire-damaged block, the extension over roof of existing blocks (referred to as block A and B of 'old PMPA') or a new build alongside block A. The architects then commissioned engineers Ove Arup to investigate structural and other aspects of the existing building.

Having established the extent of the damage – timbers and electrics were to be gutted while the existing steel was fine – Robin Walker set to designing 'new PMPA' from 1973. Of the three proposed options, PMPA decided on a new building, to be set alongside the older structures. It was to have two street frontages: the principal front overlooking a small railed urban park on Wolfe Tone Street, and the rear façade looking on to an industrial lane, Jervis Lane Lower which would contain company parking.

As an office building, to fit into the existing PMPA accommodational needs as well as to accommodate the projected growth of PMPA as an insurance company in 1970s Ireland, Walker's design reflected the ongoing shift towards American work patterns. In 1975 Walker requested

Case Study: PMPA

in-depth 'dossiers' from PMPA outlining the contemporary and proposed work structures of the company. The three dossiers broke the workforce down according to gender and grades – for example, we learn that the total number of staff including those working at branch offices was 854, of which 504 were male staff and 350 were female staff – with the third dossier comprising a series of diagrams of workflows, showing the functional divisions of insurance, accounts, personnel, and computer departments. This third dossier highlighted the desired linkages between these departments.

Such corporate enquiry was reflective of the general shift, during the mid-century decades in urban Ireland, towards white-collar office working which was contemporaneously being studied in the fields of social geography and planning. Michael Bannon's research revealed that between 1946 and 1972 Dublin's office population doubled from 45,000 to 90,000, showing that under a national lens, the situation was centralised on central Dublin with, by 1975, over half the office jobs in Ireland based there. The growth in office building in fact was so drastic during a 15-year period that in a contemporary guide to Dublin's architecture by Tomás Ó Beirne, published by the RIAI in 1978 (same year that PMPA was finished), 44 out of 109 buildings shown were office buildings.

At the time of Walker's commission for PMPA and for most of the 1960s leading up to PMPA, the issue of inserting new architectural fabric into the largely intact, still by then, Georgian and to a lesser extent medieval city, troubled the architectural community. 'Infill' became a considerable theoretical preoccupation, and so PMPA presents a practical manifestation of that thought. With his colleague Stephen Woulfe Flanagan, Walker wrote an essay in 1975 on old and new architecture in the city:

> If Dublin has in general a distinctive architectural character it does not result from a superficial similarity in its buildings, but from an essential fibre running through the art of all its periods. Whether the buildings of the city are in brick, stone, steel or concrete, it is the understanding and expression of this essential fibre that will maintain harmony and ensure the retention for the future of the established architectural character of Dublin. (Walker/Woulfe Flanagan, 1975, p. 45)

Clearly PMPA sought to acknowledge the character or 'essential fibre' of its city quarter, as we will see, in terms of roofline and façade rhythm. Also, and perhaps more intangibly, PMPA might be read as a Dublin 'oil

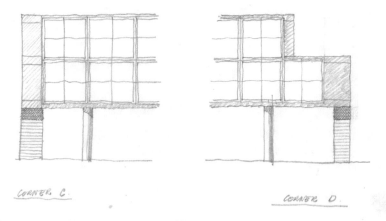

CORNER C.   CORNER D.

crisis building'. In the correspondence between the architects and the quantity surveyor, Seamus Monahan in April 1976, Monahan points out that PMPA's call for an increase in floor space would mean an increase in cost for mechanical services to over £300,000. Monahan highlights that this increase comes primarily from escalating costs in American-sourced air conditioning and refrigeration equipment.

Glass and Steel

Walker's building ultimately responds to its site. As such, the main body of the building is a two-storeyed floating office complex, sheathed in a tight glass skin and importantly, these two storeys of offices at first and second levels relate to the position of the offices in the existing older adjoining PMPA buildings. This main body is expressed by a curtain wall made of mild steel, in turn framing panels of grey-tinted glass – 6mm thick Pilkington Antisun Float grey glass – and was so meticulously detailed by Walker and so beautifully made by Dublin company, Smith and Pearson that it hardly seems to have aged since 1978. Its conception is rooted in a Miesian abstraction of wall and structure. It is composed of two storeys vertically and 14 bays horizontally, with each bay being broken up into four square modules, two over two.

The repetitive squares of glass, stacked symmetrically and amazingly flush with the metal frames, create an unforeseen planarity for Dublin's city centre building stock. The impression of an ordered (gridded) and floating glazed building is ultimately delivered by the set-background floor dominated by five red columns. The columns appear to support the curtain wall at the first and second floors. Book-ending the glazed ground floor and reinforcing the impression of support, solidity and even the conception of this level as a podium for the curtain wall, are two bays of granite cladding. This material is smartly echoed throughout the interior in the granite slabs flooring the entrance foyer as well as the granite cladding the service cores.

In plan, the interior was laid out as open office spaces around two service cores. While the five cylindrical columns ran along the building's two long perimeters, eight square internal columns rationalised interior open plan and structure alike. The important penthouse level, which originally housed the Data Processing Department – due to special air conditioning and false floor requirements – was not visible from the street as it was dramatically set back; however, it emerged, floatingly, as a rectilinear cap on the building only from a position presently occupied by the Jervis Shopping Centre, across the small urban space of Wolfe Tone Square.

Above all, Robin Walker intended to create a 'lightness' at PMPA. For this, the architect turned away from a reinforced concrete substructure,

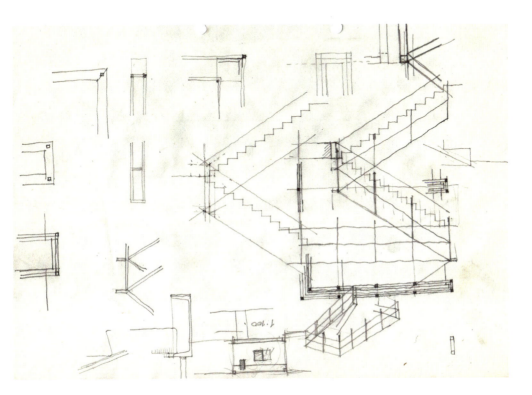

(below)
Making the Stairs,
Robin Walker
sketch, c.1973
(Courtesy of Scott Tallon
Walker image collection)

Floor plan as built
(Courtesy of Scott Tallon
Walker image collection)

124

towards steel and glass. Just before Walker began working out the design for PMPA from 1973, he spoke of steel and the influence of Mies Van der Rohe:

> Steel. I love it, it's so difficult. It's very hard to work with and most rewarding for just that reason. There again Mies gave us the clue how to deal with it, an extraordinary achievement of his in a way. See what has happened since, this great interest in precast concrete and so on … it looks so awful all around the city here. It's extraordinary how much heavier, even with quite a lot of glass, a building of precast concrete looks than a brick building with relatively small windows. The Georgian façade is so graceful (Walker/Cooke, 1972, p. 17).

So much of the building's integrity within the city and for the user is derived from this so-called lightness; described by Walker as, 'a lightness complemented by glazed curtain walling which provides the occupants of buildings with the pleasures of both natural light and external space.' (*Plan*, 1979, p. 9). Then in 1985, Walker reflected on the materiality of glass, calling forth the example of his PMPA project:

> The aim, in designing the façade of this building was to achieve a 100% glass wall as the building has a very deep section. The grid of the building is 900 mm square – the grid of the coffers in the floor slab. The main structural columns and beams occur in the first 900 mm wide strip immediately inside the glass façade […] The glass façade, being free of partitions, was not

Case Study: PMPA

limited to the 900mm grid and is made of 3.6m square panels. The glass is slightly tinted and although this has advantages in controlling solar gain, I believe the building might have been better with untinted glass (Walker, 1985, p. 21).

According to Robin Walker's son, architect Simon Walker, PMPA's façade makes a very keen contribution to the city, almost speaking to his father's design maturation at this late-1970s junction:

The glass façade reflects the trees and above them the sky, seeming to extend the space of the park. At the same time the recessed ground floor and penthouse levels model the building and greatly reduce its impact on the elevation of the street, dematerializing, if you will, the building's mass into proportions more sympathetic to its surroundings (Simon Walker lecture, Jan. 2011).

At work – interior view (Courtesy of Scott Tallon Walker image collection)

Facts and Figures

This office headquarters for insurance company, PMPA – Private Motorists Protection Association – sits on Wolfe tone Square, bridging Wolfe tone Street, and Jervis Lane Lower. The new building was commissioned in 1973 following investigations (1971) into fire damage in the 'old PMPA' 1940s block. The design for this new building was finished by 1975, and the contractors, Sisk, signed the contract in June 1976. The architects were Scott Tallon Walker and the project architect and partner in charge was Robin Walker who was assisted by Seamus Byrne. Christine Casey rightly pitches PMPA together with the much-lauded Baggot Street Bank of Ireland where both are 'elegantly conceived and impeccably made buildings which observe the rigorous proportionality of Mies [van der Rohe]' (Casey, 2005, p. 77).

Robin Walker (1924–91) is arguably the seminal figure, in theoretical and intellectual terms, of Irish architecture during mid to late 20th century. He won the RIAI Triennial Gold Medal (during the 1967–70 period) for the UCD Restaurant Building and the RIAI Medal for Housing for the O'Flaherty Weekend House in Summercove, Kinsale, Co. Cork. He taught at the two Dublin schools of architecture (UCD and Bolton Street), and for three decades he was at the forefront of Irish architectural culture through his contributions to architectural writing (e.g., the Dublin Building Centre's journal *Forgnán*), his lectures to the Architectural Association of Ireland, and as a frequent keynote speaker at the RIAI annual conferences.

Having spent the decade after his graduation from UCD in 1946 between Michael Scott's office and significant stints abroad – one year in famous Swiss architect, Le Corbusier's atelier in Paris; an episode of post-war reconstruction experience with the Danish architect Erhardt Lawrence in Rhodesia; and then, postgraduate study from 1956/7 at IIT under Ludwig Hilberseimer's supervision, before and after which he worked in the office of Skidmore Owings Merrill – Walker had assimilated many influences which were brought to bear on his design practice in Ireland. His key contribution was his pursuit of Modernist architecture, as appropriate to the native situation. In this way, Walker cited the foreign example but always through local means, materials, and burgeoning technologies. For example, he reputedly designed Ireland's first complete curtain wall system (for the National Bank façade on Dublin's Suffolk Street, now demolished) with the local iron/steel firm Smith and Pearson.

Within the nurturing context of Michael Scott's practice, Robin Walker thrived. He worked closely with Ronald Tallon who, like Walker at the end of the 1950s, had become a committed disciple of the Miesian principle of 'building-as-structure'. By 1961 Walker and Tallon were made partners of Scott's firm which in the early 1970s became Scott Tallon Walker. From 1960 to *c.*1975 Tallon and Walker between them were responsible for a huge body of very successful modernist buildings such as the Bord Failte HQ (see *MTCB* Volume 2), RTÉ campus (see *MTCB* Volume 2), Carrolls Factory (now Dundalk IT),

Wesley College, Knockanure RC Parish Church (Co. Kerry), the O'Flaherty and Goulding Houses, and the Bank of Ireland Headquarters.

Structural Engineers: Ove Arup & Partners, led by Gerry Dunne
Contractors: J. Sisk and Sons. Emmett Russell, foreman and O Harrington, contracts manager
Quantity Surveyors: Seamus Monahan & Partners, led by Clifford Campbell
Mechanical and Electrical services: Scott Tallon Walker in consultation with Leo Lynch & Co.

Sources

Unpublished
Walker, Simon, 'Robin Walker –Seven Apollonian Trails. Robin Walker: the quest for the spiritual in architecture', unpublished conference paper, DoCoMoMo Ireland/IMMA, Jan. 2011)
Scott Tallon Walker Archives (Job No.7232), Merrion Square, Dublin

Published
Anon., 'Michael Scott and Partners', *Architectural Design* (Mar. 1968)
Anon., 'Inner City Infill by Scott Tallon Walker', *Plan* (Aug./Sept. 1979)
Bannon, Michael, *Office Location in Ireland: The Role of Central Dublin* (An Foras Forbatha, 1972)
Casey, Christine, *Dublin: The Buildings of Ireland Pevsner Guide* (Yale University Press, 2005),
Cooke, Harriet in conversation with Robin Walker, 'Plan Profile', *Plan* (Nov. 1972)
Long, Patrick, 'Robin Walker 1924–91', in James McGuire and James Quinn (eds), *Dictionary of Irish Biography Cambridge* (RIA and Cambridge University Press, 2010)
O'Connell, Dermot, 'The Irish Architectural Scene', *Building* (9 Sept.1966)
O'Regan, John (ed.), *Scott Tallon Walker Architects: 100 Buildings and Projects, 1960–2005* (Gandon Editions, 2006)
O'Regan, John (ed.), 'Robin Walker, 1924–91', in *Portfolio: architecture, painting and time-based media in Ireland* (Gandon Editions, 1991)
Rowley, Ellen, 'From Dublin to Chicago and Back Again', in Linda King/Elaine Sisson (eds), *Ireland, Design and Visual Culture* (Cork University Press, 2010)
Walker, Robin and Stephen Woulfe Flanagan, 'Street Infill', in *Dublin: A City in Crisis* (RIAI, 1975)
Walker, Robin, 'Notes on Glass', *RIAI Bulletin* (No. 50, Feb. 1985), pp. 20–2
Walker, Simon (ed.), *Change is the Reality: The Work of Robin Walker Architects* (Canalside Press, 2022)

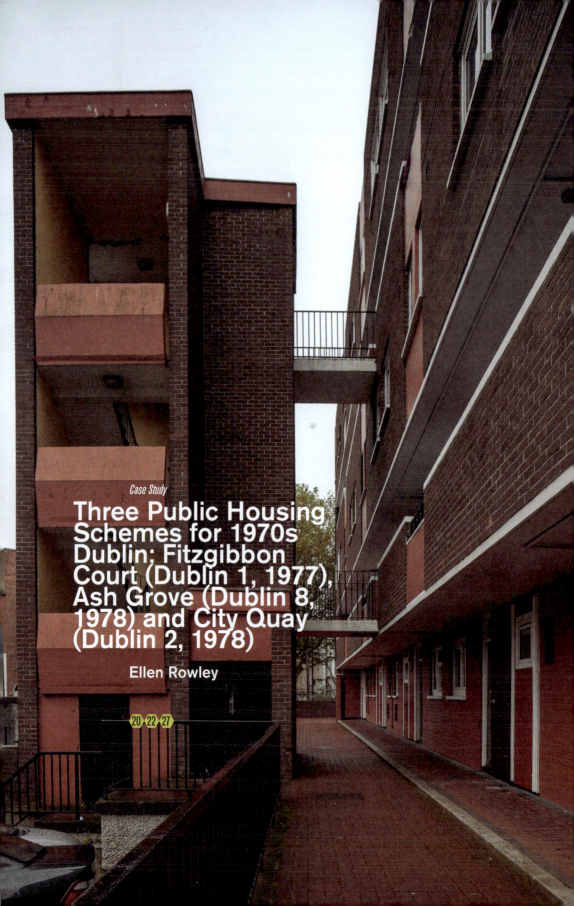

Case Study

Three Public Housing Schemes for 1970s Dublin: Fitzgibbon Court (Dublin 1, 1977), Ash Grove (Dublin 8, 1978) and City Quay (Dublin 2, 1978)

Ellen Rowley

Taking three housing schemes as examples, this seventh essay presents an overview of the architecture of Dublin's city-centre public housing in the 1970s. The three schemes – Fitzgibbon Court, Ash Grove (also known as Coombe North) and City Quay – form a pattern of rejected housing type, activist housing type and new housing type. Fitzgibbon Court near Mountjoy Square represents the last of the city's mid-century maisonette flat blocks (see *MTCB* Volume 2); Ash Grove represents an alternative housing type, in brown brick and modernist design, generated by a community in the Liberties; while the City Quay scheme, coming out of a Dublin Corporation housing competition of 1975, represents a new type of redbrick housing in response to Ash Grove, which goes on to proliferate in Dublin through the 1980s.

Importantly, Ash Grove in the Liberties may be understood as the catalyst or main character in this story, book-ended by Fitzgibbon Court at the start and City Quay (and its type) as the so-called 'happily ever after', at the end. And the story's arc is formed by the rejection of flat blocks for city-centre public housing. The five-storey blocks which contained duplexes or maisonettes had been fulfilling Dublin Corporation's remit to supply working-class housing in the city since the late 1950s. By the early 1970s, these blocks had become architectural pariah. And in the space of Dublin's oldest city quarter, the Liberties, the flat block was rejected by the community for a new high-density but low-rise model of brick housing which was reminiscent of Dublin's late 19th-century artisan dwellings or row-houses. A high-level residents' activist group, the Liberties Residents Association (LRA) was formed through which the community procured the Ash Grove or Coombe North housing project. Meanwhile the City Quay scheme was borne out of a municipal housing competition predicated on the need for change. Both represent short-lived radicalization of Dublin's otherwise staid 20th-century public housing processes.

All three housing schemes are fully inhabited today and are in good condition, due in the main to each scheme's popularity. Coming out of each scheme's solid design credentials, we find consequent consistency of residents and tenancy. As part of city-wide flat improvement schemes, Fitzgibbon Court's windows were changed to uPVC windows in the early 2000s, while the outdoor precinct has undergone adaptation for children's play areas and parking. In 2008, the water tanks in each unit were updated. Ash Grove and City Quay are essentially unchanged – in terms of complex layout, relation to neighbouring streets and brick aesthetic – yet both, at the level of individual units, continue to undergo significant decorative adaptations. In both estates, the tenant purchase scheme encouraged residents to buy their homes and as such, there is a mix of ownership and tenancy. Throughout both – but more immediately visible in the closer confines of Ash Grove where the robust brown brick is so dominant – window types, front doors and gates or railings are varied, with individual households having changed original fittings according to trends and occupants' taste.

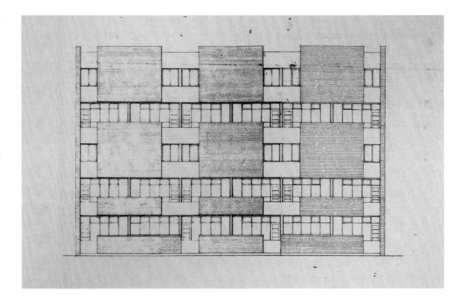

Fitzgibbon Court, elevation drawing, c.1975, City Architects (Courtesy of Dublin City Library and Archive)

Threshold Treatments: Sites and Floor Plans

The best way to understand and then, by extension, compare a set of housing schemes is to consider how many people or units are housed at each site (i.e., the density of occupation); how tall the buildings rise; and, how we access the buildings. This last point is most interesting as it points to the biggest difference between the Fitzgibbon Court scheme and its contemporaries at the Coombe and City Quay. That difference is in what the architectural profession might term, 'threshold treatment': how the buildings touch their ground or sit in relation to their neighbourhoods and how they make, enhance or ignore streetscapes.

This term also refers to how residents enter and move through the buildings, from public city to private individual home. At Fitzgibbon Court, three related five-storey blocks, with the two longer blocks (six-flat wide and ten-flat wide) fronting Fitzgibbon Street and the smallest four-block wide block sitting perpendicular, hinged as such, to the back of the scheme. Significantly, this scheme comes as the last in a portfolio of Dublin Corporation flat blocks, a type described in Volume 2 of this series (see *MTCB* Vol. 2), which were designed from 1958 and developed and built across the city over the following two decades. It contained 53 homes at the time of its completion in 1977, as against its two nearest schemes – Matt Talbot House (on neighbouring Charles Street), complete in 1971 which contained 72 units and Mountainview Court (on Summerhill) of 1974 which contained 102 units (demolished).

With just 53 homes, Fitzgibbon Court would have been a middle to smaller-sized scheme and yet, its site was generous. Originally, when

Case Study: Fitzgibbon Court, Ash Grove, and City Quay

Ash Grove in development: residents engaging with design, as published in Liberties Magazine, December 1975

Aerial view of the redevelopment area to the south of the Coombe showing the Guinness Dispensary and 'The Weavers' bar in the top left hand corner. The site is bordered at the lower end by the Dublin Corporation's new motorway proposals.

Children taking a close look at what may be their future home.

Mr Turlough O'Donnell (Delany, McVeigh & Pike, Architects) explaining the model to an interested audience.

being developed, these blocks aimed at 50 to 60 habitable rooms. Usually, schemes were made up of three blocks on a one and half acre site, thus providing a density of just over 100 people per acre. By the time of Fitzgibbon Court, this formula may have become tired, and the city architects were, arguably, aiming for greater site sensitivity. Unlike precedent schemes where blocks occupied their sites in parallel formation, irrespective of the surrounding urban grain, Fitzgibbon Court sought to address its primary

More Than Concrete Blocks Volume 3

street, Fitzgibbon Street more directly and more thoughtfully. Set back from the path and at a lower level than the sloping street, in an attempt to also address the perpendicular North Circular Road, this scheme is entered in a deliberate way, across a raised path and into the back of the blocks, where flats can be accessed. In this way, there are clear zones of private and public space. The sequence brings the pedestrian from street via a 'prolonged entrance' (Neville, 2016) to the blocks' stairs and areas of circulation. The sequence is transformational, in so far as the pedestrian is aware, through shift in level and path, that they are somewhere different, somewhere private.

Constructed from 1973, each of the scheme's three blocks contains ground floor two-room flats; first to second floor two-storeyed three-room maisonette units with interior staircase; and third to fourth floor two-storeyed three-room maisonette units, again with interior staircase. In the maisonettes the lower level contains the entrance stair hall, beyond which sits the main living space leading to a private balcony and the small kitchen. The upper level presents an easier layout of landing, serving two or three bedrooms and a bathroom. Like its precedent and sibling maisonette schemes, and unlike recently completed radical flat blocks at Ballymun in north Dublin, Fitzgibbon

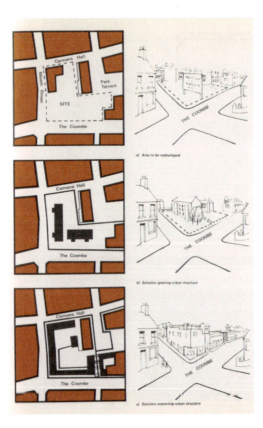

James Pike, Urban Context Scenarios, 1975 (as published in Delany [ed.], *Dublin a City in Crisis* [RIAI, 1975])

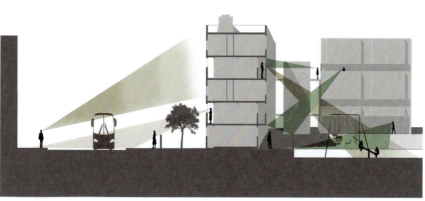

Fitzgibbon Court, threshold study drawing by Cian Neville, MArch UCD Architecture, 2016 (Courtesy of Cian Neville)

Court was technologically traditional, comprising a system of reinforced concrete load-bearing columns and floor slabs which were cast in situ. Party walls were load bearing and no structural elements were prefabricated.

The constancy of the floor plan, from the earliest maisonette schemes and through their 1960s proliferation, points to the underlying condition of Fitzgibbon Court's architecture as being at once part of a typology which then tries to strike out, improve or streamline that typology. For instance, though Fitzgibbon Court deviated from the usual parallel block layout of these schemes, by placing a smaller rear block at a right angle to the primary blocks, the circulation schema of independent stair tower, bridges and deck access remained the same. This solution, amounting to only two bridges and two access decks per block (at first and third levels) endured due to the economics of its rudimentary nature.

Many of the earlier schemes' decorative idiosyncrasies – from overburnt brick gable ends and the characteristic gull-wing roofs or circular pebble-dash stair towers, to mosaic friezes and lozenge-shaped openings – had disappeared at this 1970s juncture. Instead, the later blocks sported only a monochrome mosaic tile and dark machined brick. At Fitzgibbon Court, while the quirky mosaic friezes had gone and as such, the public façades had minimal depth, the usual texture and delight was brought to the blocks through the balcony ironwork. In the same way, while the round-tower stairwell of earlier schemes was also gone, effort was made to restore some sense of architectural adventure with Fitzgibbon Court's rectilinear brick stair-towers whose storeys were marked by splayed concrete slabs.

In terms of threshold treatment, Fitzgibbon Court went far to improve upon the ill-considered siting of other maisonette schemes which, being mostly concerned with their north/south orientation, tended to ignore the historic pattern of their neighbouring streets. However, an ambivalent

Ash Grove mid-construction, c.1976 (Courtesy of James Pike, Delany McVeigh Pike image collection)

duality between private (access and circulation) and public (balcony) fronts remained at Fitzgibbon Court, nonetheless. And residents continued to live in a stacked-up vertical manner, sharing public stairwells. The reaction against this ambivalence came, as we'll see, with the Ash Grove commission in the Liberties. The key motivation for change was, indeed, the desire for an alternative threshold treatment. First off, the Liberties residents did not want their homes to be stacked and as such, tall (five-storey) and bulky blocks were replaced with mostly three-storey buildings, as various combinations of single and two-storey homes. Secondly, Ash Grove arose in a completely bespoke manner, responding to the particularities of the Liberties streetscape.

Ash Grove drew from and was shaped by the surrounding neighbourhood. It formed climbing and descending terraces, wrapping itself along the street edges and making two courtyards. In the end, the 35 homes, one community centre (today, a creche) and five shops combined to create a new city block. But unlike other new public housing, from previous decades in Dublin, this scheme came out of the existing streets and so the block could be read and accessed as a (new) small chunk of the historic city. Front doors were placed variously through Ash Grove so that residents accessed their homes by ground floor porches on the streets or off a wide upper street in the courtyard. Visitors and neighbours could also come in and through the estate: either into Ash Grove's courtyards or through a large, stepped cut, making a pedestrian link, from the busy street of the Coombe up to Carman's Hall.

Because the site slopes down from Carman's Hall to the Coombe, the housing scheme feels almost like a traditional hilltop development;

Case Study: Fitzgibbon Court, Ash Grove, and City Quay

alien for modern Dublin yet familiar somehow. This experience or feeling also emanates from how the scheme is a continuous terrace which folds around corners, holding the perimeter of three streets and enclosing, almost defensively and defiantly, the private open spaces of the courtyards. Certainly, the dense dark-brown brick walls contribute to the sense of defensiveness. Upon closer examination, the scheme's walls, though unbroken, are full of sculptural and visual interest. The ground level, either marked by shops or one-storey units, is consistently eaten into with deep cuts housing porches. When we learn how the architects approached the Coombe site and their overall motivation, coming from the residents, which was about providing an alternative to flats, we understand why Ash Grove behaves as it did originally and still does today in 2023. And it all comes down to threshold; in other words, how each home is entered or how each home touches the ground. About this motivation, architect James Pike wrote in the 1970s:

> In respecting the pattern of existing streets, the precise relationship of the street to the dwelling becomes of major importance. Is the ground floor raised 2 or 3 steps above the pavement? Is there a small front garden? [...] Can raised pavements be used for further separation? Considerable natural changes in level can be used to give access to upper storeys while maintaining contact with the ground [...] The proximity of a development area of the Coombe to the busy Meath Street shopping area provides immediate contact with the bustle of city life. (Pike, 1975, p. 73)

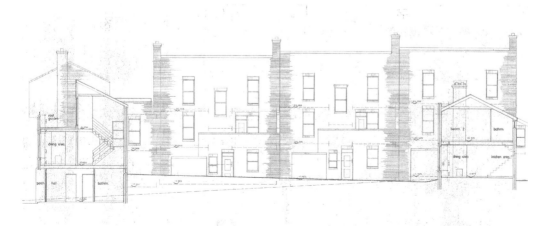

Ash Grove section, through Meath Street showing rear elevation to Carman's Hall (Courtesy of James Pike, Delany McVeigh Pike image collection)

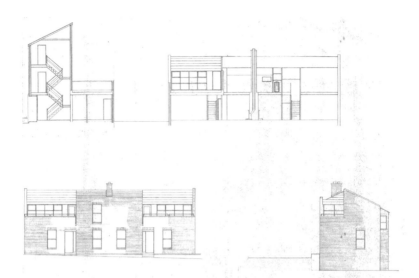

Ash Grove long section (Courtesy of James Pike, Delany McVeigh Pike image collection)

At Ash Grove, the dominant house types were the two-storey house and the single-storey unit under a duplex. And for our third housing scheme example, City Quay, we find it following a similar mould. However, unlike at Ash Grove where access was from a combination of street and courtyard, the City Quay houses were more uniform in behaviour. Gone was the varied threshold treatment though the scheme was still driven by the key relationship of street to individual home. At City Quay, the scheme comprised 48 homes as a mix of three and two-storey buildings. Laid out in three discrete blocks, the terraced housing subtly snaked through the site, from the river quay to Townsend Street. The overall site was cut by an ever-busy traffic route, Lombard Street East, bringing cars from the river into the heart of the South Georgian city. And while two of the scheme's taller terraces fronted the river, most of the housing addressed and was accessed from Lombard Street East, running perpendicular to the river.

The material expression at City Quay was red-brick. The houses were all terraced, with pitched or mono-pitched roofs and with their own front doors and fanlights. Though variety was limited compared to Ash Grove, there were five different house types (aside from anomalous corner houses) and of these, the most memorable and enduring was the three-storey type, with an interesting ground floor composed of projecting living room and a deeply cut front door, fronted by a pocket garden, wall and railing. Generally, the City Quay houses and those that followed across the city, opted for narrow and deep footprints. Due to many being three storeys, the houses were dominated by stairs and circulation space; their design has been criticised for this, as well as for their small window openings.

Over time and with the continuing ownership of homes, each of the

Case Study: Fitzgibbon Court, Ash Grove, and City Quay

View of Ash Grove housing upon completion, c.1978, Delany McVeigh Pike (Courtesy of James Pike, Delany McVeigh Pike image collection)

various terraces across the City Quay scheme carried its own character, despite the consistency of material and detail and mostly, of entry level. The hard landscaping and edge of the small streets created in the interior of the scheme were ameliorated by colourfully-rendered façades. Otherwise, the City Quay estate was markedly green and soft in its landscaping, for such an urban scheme. Well-maintained pocket gardens and grassy open spaces contributed positively to the high-density low-rise city housing estate, to the extent that the City Quay housing was awarded the 1979-81 RIAI Silver Medal for Residential Architecture. The RIAI citation remarked:

> The actual existence of the housing is a tribute to the indomitable spirit of an inner-city community who refused to be 'deported' to suburbia. In the millennium year the City Quay Housing is a symbol of hope for the revitalization of Dublin's inner city. (Silver Medal for Housing Citation, 1979–81)

Indeed, the suburban-versus-urban message in this citation raises the big questions around 'why' City Quay was developed as it was. In the same

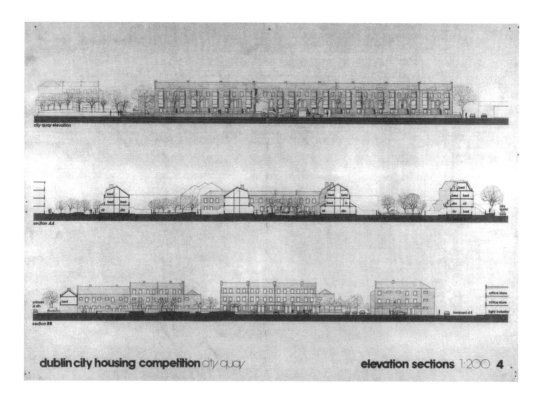

City Quay Competition drawing, BKD (Published in Competition Assessment, Dublin Corporation, 1976-8)

breath, we might ask 'how' Ash Grove came about in the climate of late 1960s modernising Dublin and its ever-Modernist urban planning interests. For more, let's go 'Back to the Streets' and specifically to the market streets around Dublin's Liberties area in the south inner city.

Back to the Streets

As we have seen in Volume 2's analysis of the Charleville Mall flat block scheme, Dublin Corporation used the model of a five-storey maisonette block for urban housing through the 1960s and for the first half of the 1970s. At the end of the 1960s, there was growing antipathy towards all flats though the catalyst for this was Ballymun Estate and its high-rise element, rather than the maisonette blocks. Through the early 1970s, the media was continually reporting on Ballymun, pointing to the broken-down lifts and the lack of support infrastructure in the neighbourhood. There were student sociological and medical studies investigating public health at Ballymun, most especially around the mental well-being and incidence of upper respiratory tract illness in the tower-block residents. In a Dublin Corporation Housing Committee Report of 1976, Ballymun was even posited as a 'questionable environment'. Already in October 1973, the Minister of Local Government (from the new coalition government) James Tully stated that

Case Study: Fitzgibbon Court, Ash Grove, and City Quay

he would not allow any high-rise local authority housing; or rather, he would not sanction any local authority housing over three storeys, except in streetscapes where it was necessary. Clearly high-rise housing, and flats generally, had become 'the baddies' of this 1970s story. And Fitzgibbon Court was to be the last of its kind for Dublin.

In fairness to the maisonette blocks, they were Dublin Corporation's attempt to provide a cottage within a flat-block framework. While this quasi-traditional approach was well sensed by the Corporation, when the flats were presented by the end of the 1960s, they were increasingly unpopular with prospective residents. The enduring presence of the Dublin artisan cottage on the other hand was leading to a renewed interest in its potential. All of these housing choices and other contemporary debates around urban heritage and conservation were played out at the time in the medieval neighbourhood around Christ Church Cathedral and the Liberties. Like much of the city centre, this area was in a prolonged state of desecration. Contemporary activist architect Deirdre O'Connor identified how, between 1936 and 1971, the population of central Dublin had halved (from 266,000 to 132,000) and that the Liberties had the highest percentage of elderly people.

This community drain was exacerbated by the 1965–71 Dublin Corporation plans to plough through the neighbourhood with a motorway. Planned as part of a series of traffic initiatives coming out of Karl Schaechterle's traffic-flow study of Dublin (1965) and Myles Wright's 1967

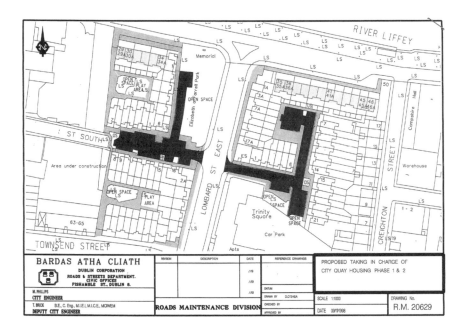

City Quay site plan
(Courtesy of City Architects, Dublin City Council)

(above left) View of City Quay housing, 3-storey type (2-storeys over ground floor flat), 1978, BKD (Courtesy of G. & T. Crampton Photograph Archive, UCD Digital Library and Prof Joseph Brady)

(above right) View of City Quay housing, c.1980, BKD (Courtesy of Burke-Kennedy Doyle image collection)

expansion plan, central Dublin was to have three-lane dual carriageways, inner relief roads and flyover bridge roads. But the residents of the Liberties, having enough of these plans to demolish whole sections of their neighbourhood, mobilised themselves into the Liberties Residents Association (LRA). In an unprecedented move for working-class urban Ireland, this group, the LRA, appointed a new architectural and urban design practice – Delany McVeigh Pike – to help them. The residents did not want to be rehoused outside of the city – no relocation to 'Ballyfarouts'; they did not want flat block housing; they did not want multi-lane fast roads; but they did want artisan dwelling patterns that spoke to the traditional squares and streets of the area.

Maybe it was inevitable that the process was protracted but ultimately, the residents got their way, through their hard work and advocacy and the quite brilliant design talent of the young architect, James Pike. Pike studied the area and key to his evolving housing design – what was to become Ash Grove – was his rejection of the Fitzgibbon Court model of five-storey flat blocks. Clearly Pike, listening to his clients and valuing the historic urban terrain, came up with new cuts and courtyards, making and shaping the 35 housing units according to level change and according to existing streets.

Case Study: Fitzgibbon Court, Ash Grove, and City Quay

The project went to site by 1975 and was complete by 1978. In the end, the designed scheme was like a perimeter block in that it held tight to the surrounding street edges and actually made those edges, most publicly along Meath Street and at The Coombe.

In terms of achieving high densities at lower heights and bringing in courtyard prototypes, Ash Grove might read as an urban counterpart to that earlier case study, Darndale Estate. At least, much of what Darndale was trying to do in the green fields of north Dublin, the Ash Grove scheme managed to achieve in this beleaguered pocket of the historic city. As discussed elsewhere (Rowley, 2019) many of the design ideas for these Dublin schemes came from the architects at the Greater London Co. Council. For Ash Grove, with its robust brick forms and stepped landscaping, Miriam Delaney discusses the influence of schemes such as Lillington Gardens, Pimlico (Darbourne + Darke, 1961–80) and Odham's Walk, Covent Garden (Donald Ball, GLC, 1973-9).

In terms of community activism in procuring housing, the Ash Grove example remains remarkable. Though the LRA with Delany McVeigh Pike were unable to overturn the Corporation's road plans completely, those plans were vaguely tempered. Critically, a whole new housing model was devised; tantalising enough to motivate Dublin Corporation to make changes. Arguably on foot of Ash Grove, the Corporation, in June 1975, announced the only significant housing architectural competition in the modern history of the state.

> The Dublin Corporation is at present embarked on an extensive housing programme both in the Co. and City Centre Areas and the schemes range from single-storey to medium rise housing in high density sites [...] this competition is promoted to stimulate new thinking in centre city housing which will create a good overall environment for family living. (Competition Conditions, 1975, p. 7)

A Housing Competition

Aside from a small country cottage competition (1944) and a couple of hypothetical Ideal Home competitions through the 1940s and 1950s, there had been no state-sponsored design competition for housing in the history of independent Ireland. As such, the competition announced in 1975 by Dublin Corporation, for an explicit area on the southside of the river near to dockland activity, was big news for the architectural community. There were

(opposite above)
City Quay

(below)
Ash Grove

85 submissions and the four winning schemes responded closely to the competition conditions. After all, the competition very specifically sought to address the city again; particularly sites which were central, neglected and in a dilapidated state with a stock of traditional (for which read artisan late-19th century) housing. As the competition announced:

> It is the Corporation's policy to preserve as much as possible of the housing stock and rehabilitate a certain proportion of the existing houses within a site together with infilling of the balance with new housing [...] The Corporation proposes to draw up a new panel of Architectural firms... (Competition Conditions, 1975, p. 7)

In reality, Dublin Corporation needed help to turn back towards the city; to embrace the city as a valid context for residential life, once more. Compulsory purchase orders (CPOs) were complex, expensive and prolonged and as such, if the Corporation had some good housing designs 'in the bag', the process of reclaiming the city through CPOs could run smoother. Therefore the competition site had to be a typically complicated urban place. City Quay was by the River Liffey, meaning it had been home to light industry which was by the 1970s becoming redundant. City Quay was also at the edge of the commercial city meaning it needed to be connected with a new through-road. And City Quay contained some older housing stock, to be maintained.

The competition brief outlined that the housing – an undetermined quantity – should rise to no higher than three storeys and that the density would be at 150 people per acre, maximum. Emphasis was laid on the supporting social infrastructure such as playgrounds and a pub, as well community facilities. Provision was to be made for mixed housing types: 70 per cent larger family homes and an amount of single-person units. This last point reflected the growing interest, through the 1970s, in Irish social patterns and anthropological and economic studies thereof. The Labour Minister of Local Government, Jim Tully was aware that the nuclear family three-bedroomed house, at the heart of Irish housing policy since the dawn of independence (and before) was not responsive to contemporary needs. In a similar way, the flats proliferating around the city up until this point, were too small for Dublin families.

In fact, we could argue that the competition was a reaction to the cultures and technologies underpinning Irish housing at that mid–1970s point: from the return to the cottage in the city to the championing of traditional technology of chimney and load-bearing brick-clad walls. The rise in industrialised systems, then in currency for social housing, had brought swathes of not-fit-for-purpose housing on stream. But the international oil crisis from 1973, with the peak in energy costs, rendered all of the experimental housing – that is, houses built without hearths and chimneys – redundant. And shortly after construction, many of these houses had to be retrofitted with chimney infrastructure. Understandably then, there was a suspicion of technologies like fan heaters and such, and a retreat towards tradition ensued. Much of the language pervading the competition, from the 85 submissions and the assessors' reports reflected this mood. The submissions and the assessors evoked the 'local' and 'characterful', stressing the need to make a so-called 'Dublin urban vernacular'. Referring to simplicity in form, one entrant wrote that the new City Quay houses should be of a 'built form which could immediately be identified as Dublin and Dublin alone' (Assessors' Report, 1976, p. 17).

The reality was that the new called-for typology, and what was built, was influenced, as per usual, by Britain. All the room dimensions and details which were outlined in the competition conditions came from the important British 'Parker Morris Report' of 1961. Indeed, the primary architectural assessor for the competition was the British architect, JW Darbourne of Surrey-based practice, Darbourne + Drake. The other assessors were a mixture of UCD academics and Dublin Corporation officials and architects. But the centrality of the British 'voice' in the assessment process and competition conditions could not be denied. The four schemes which were shortlisted – by Kidney Burke-Kennedy Doyle, Diamond Redfern Anderson, P Don Henihan and Campbell Conroy Hickey – were chosen because apparently their designs had made the greatest effort with recreation and communal facilities. According to the assessors, these proposed schemes also worked hard to integrate the roads with the houses, and they incorporated varying house plans and types. Markedly, there were no flats in any of the winning proposals.

Of the four practices, Kidney Burke-Kennedy Doyle were awarded the City Quay commission. They designed 35 homes as a mix of three-storey types but mostly, two-storey family houses and also, on the river front two-storey over single-person units at street level. Overall, some would say there is a lack of variety through the City Quay scheme, compared to say Ash

Grove. But the repetition and strong street presence inherent in the terrace housing idiom were welcome traits, worthy of emulation. And this emulation happened to differing extents. While City Quay was being built, other forms of this new housing type were being planned for different pockets in the city; for instance, at the former Cattle Market site in Stoneybatter, the Drumalee Estate was being laid out (City Architects, 1979) or the New Street Scheme (1980) near St Patrick's Cathedral, by Delany McVeigh Pike.

These brick schemes were to become the next urban housing type to proliferate across the city and as such, they joined the barrack block, the artisan dwelling, the Simms' flat block and the maisonette blocks to take their place in Dublin Corporation's 20th-century urban housing portfolio. While window openings were often small and scant, and the three-storey family homes were dominated by circulation, these housing projects were popular and they have endured. As I have stated elsewhere 'the schemes tried to overlay, rather than erase tenement memory and in so doing they began to reframe, perceptually at least, Dublin's scarred urban communities: from high-density slums to medium-density homes.' (Rowley, 2019, p. 245).

Facts and Figures

Fitzgibbon Court is situated on the west side of Fitzgibbon Street opposite Fitzgibbon Garda Station (OPW, 1912). The 1790s street is significantly sloped between Mountjoy Square and North Circular Road and as such, the site brings an awkward shift in levels as well as the wedged backland form. The flat scheme was designed as part of a portfolio of public housing flat blocks through the 1960s in Dublin Corporation. Drawings for the scheme date from 1973 while it was under construction in 1976 and finished and occupied by 1977.

Architects: City Architects in Dublin Corporation.
The Coombe North/Ash Grove scheme is complexly set around two courtyards, making a trapezoid site between and addressing three streets: Meath Street, The Coombe and Ash Square. The scheme was commissioned in 1968 and designed over a period of four years. It was under construction by 1975 and complete by 1978.
Architects: Delany McVeigh Pike Architects.
The planning and architectural practice was founded in 1964 by Patrick Delany, Eoin McVeigh and the younger English architect, James Pike. Pike led the Ash Grove design having come to Dublin from London in 1964. He was educated at Regent Street Polytechnic (now University of Westminster), and went on to specialise in housing and, especially, apartment design throughout his career in Dublin. This began with the Coombe work and in 1975, he published the scheme in the Delany-edited RIAI publication *Dublin: A City in Crisis*. In 1992, Pike established O'Mahony Pike (OMP) Architects, continuing his interest in high-density housing and designing exemplary (private) schemes such as Mount St Anne's (Milltown, Dublin), as well as new towns for Dublin like Adamstown. In 2006, OMP won the RIAI Silver Medal in Housing for Hanover Quay, Dublin. Pike was awarded the RIAI James Gandon Medal for Lifetime Achievement in Architecture in 2017.
Commissioners: The Liberties Residents Association, led in part by community activist Larry Dillon.
Contractor: G&T Crampton Ltd

City Quay housing scheme occupies a considerable southside site (reputedly 10.5 acres) between the River Liffey and Townsend Street (parallel to Pearse Street). The housing competition was launched in June 1975 and results were published in March 1976. Kidney Burke-Kennedy Doyle won the competition along with three other teams and they were awarded the commission for the City Quay scheme which was built and complete in 1978. The other winners were Diamond Redfern Anderson, P. Don Henihan and Campbell Conroy Hickey. All premiated schemes were awarded £1,000 and were placed on a panel to be engaged in housing commissions.
The assessors for the competition were J. W. Darbourne, British architect of Surrey-based practice Darbourne + Drake, Surrey; Professor H. C. Higgins (UCD, School of Architecture); Dr Cyril White (UCD, Department of Social Sciences); J. F. Maguire (DCC, Chief Housing Architect); C. Dardis (DCC, Chief Civic and Amenities Architect); E. G. McCarron (DCC, Department of Planning Officer).

Architects: (Kidney) Burke-Kennedy Doyle (BKD) Architects
BKD Architects was founded in 1959. After winning the housing competition in 1976, for which City Quay won an RIAI Silver Medal for Housing 1979–81, the practice gained the housing commission at Sean Moore Rd, Ringsend, before moving on to commercial buildings, finishing The Square at Tallaght in 1990. BKD are best known for their design of the first phase of the Irish Financial Services Centre (1991) and later, the Dundrum Shopping Centre (winner of European Shopping Centre, 2007).
Main Contractor: G&T Crampton Ltd

Sources
Unpublished
Department of Local Government, 'Programme and Other Information for Study Tour of Housing Committee Economic Commission for Europe to Ireland, 7–12 June 1962'
Dublin City Library and Archive files: Kevin Street/Bishop Street flats – drawings (layout plan dating 1961); B1/05/02 – Kevin St/Bishop Street flats – external and urban context; R1/01/03 Dublin City Council Flat Schemes 1850–1977
Dublin Corporation, *Dublin City Housing Competition: General Conditions and Brief* (Dublin, 1975)
Dublin City Council, *Dublin City Housing Competition: Assessors' Report* (Dublin, Mar. 1976)
Neville, Cian, 'Fitzgibbon Court Flats' (Unpublished Research Seminar Paper, Situating Dublin's Flats, UCD Architecture, 2016)
Ruairi Quinn, interviewed by Ellen Rowley, Mar. 2018

Published
Anon., 'Coombe: Newmarket Housing Scheme', in *The Liberties Magazine* (Dec. 1975/Jan. 1976)
Anon., 'NBA Housing at Coombe South', in *Construction* (Dec./Jan. 1981)
Boland, Kevin TD, 'Review of Housing' Dáil presentation, reprinted in *Building Survey* (1969/70)
Delaney, Miriam, 'The Coombe North', in Gary Boyd, Michael Pike and Brian Ward (eds), *Out of the Ordinary. Irish Housing Design 1955–1980* (Routledge, 2019)
Department of Local Government, *Housing in Ireland*, pamphlet series (Dublin: Stationery Office, 1962 and 1969)
Department of Local Government, *White Paper: Housing – Progress and Prospects* (Dublin

Stationery Office, 1964)
Department of Local Government, Housing in the Seventies (Dublin Stationery Office, 1969)
Kilfeather, Frank, 'A New City: a New Dubliner?', *Irish Times* (3 Feb. 1978)
McLaran, Andrew and Paul McNulty, 'High-Density, Low-Rise Housing in Inner Dublin', in *Irish Geography* (Vol. 18, 1985)
McLaran, Andrew, *Dublin: The Shaping of a Capital* (Belhaven Press, 1993)
McManus, Ruth, *Crampton Built* (Gill & MacMillan, 2008)
Ó Beirne, Tomás, *Family Size in Ireland* (An Foras Forbatha, July 1971)
O'Connor, Deirdre, *Housing in the Dublin's Inner City* (UCD Research Unit, 1979)
Ó hUiginn, Pádraig, 'Some Social and Economic Aspects of Housing: An International Comparison', *Administration* (Spring 1960)
Rowley, Ellen, *Housing, Architecture and the Edge Condition: Dublin is Building, 1935–75* (Routledge, 2019)
Royal Institute of Architects of Ireland, Silver Medal for Housing Citation, 1979–1981, http://www.irisharchitectureawards.ie/silver-housing-medal/winner/city-quay-housing
Schaechterle, Karl-Heinz, *Part I General Traffic Plan. Traffic Investigation Concerning the Future Main Road Network* (Ulm/Donau, 1965)
Wright, Myles, *The Dublin Region: Advisory Plan and Final Report* (Government Publications, 1967)

Case Study
Church of the Holy Trinity, Donaghmede, Dublin 9, 1978

Ellen Rowley

25

The Church of the Holy Trinity squats like a triangular decommissioned spaceship on an open green space opposite the contemporaneous Donaghmede Shopping Centre (1973). Built in response to the growing Catholic population of this new north Dublin suburb of Grangemore or Donaghmede, the quirky and instantly recognizable form of the late–1970s church was the outcome of an architectural competition held by the Dublin Diocese. In part a response to the international oil crisis and the crippling debt in which the diocese found itself by the early 1970s, the aim of the 1976 competition, hosted by the Dublin Archbishop, Dermot Ryan, was to encourage innovative and affordable church designs for new ever-spreading Dublin suburbs. Budgetary concerns were primary and this Donaghmede parish church should be understood as a strategic move away from Ireland's large, monumental revivalist Catholic churches of the previous decades.

Designed by the practice A. & D. Wejchert Architects, the Church of the Holy Trinity is marked out by its remarkable geometric sculptural form. The lead designer was Polish architect (and practice partner), Danuta Kornaus-Wejchert. Her interests in geometry, spirituality and communality are all brought to bear in the church's impressive cruciform plan, carved out of four intersecting angled roof plates. Here, the roofs are the walls. They enclose the crucifix plan which in turn organises the church's functions: three arms of the crucifix contain the congregational seating, all directed towards the centrally-placed altar, while the fourth is screened off, behind the altar, to house a smaller chapel and sacristy, store and toilet, as well as the parish office at first floor level.

The Church of the Holy Trinity continues to function as a parish church, celebrating daily mass, two Sunday masses, funerals and other sacraments. Despite declining numbers in mass attendance across the Dublin Diocese and the Irish Catholic church generally, this church maintains its role as a vibrant community-focused public building, as well as a sacred space open for reflection. At its northern edge, the parish takes in the neighbouring and seemingly ever-growing housing areas of Balgriffin and Clongriffin.

During the 1990s the church was closed for an extended period due to significant redecoration and a deep refurbishment of the roof. Reopening in 1999, the church's signature roofline remained the same while glazing was updated. Internally, the roof structure was covered and changes were made to the flooring and the sanctuary including the incorporation of stone from the nearby ruin of the 12th-century Grange Abbey. Timber screen-like partitions were added to distinguish nave from entrances and also, the entrance doors were realigned. While some would maintain that these changes have undermined the church's structural integrity or specifically, the roofs' impact, the interior of this church continues to present itself as a wonderfully light-filled and geometric volume. Other material changes to the building include the placement of railings around the church, outside, cutting it off somewhat from the green and differentiating it from the profane space of the surrounding suburb.

Architect's perspective drawing of interior (Courtesy of A & D Wejchert image collection)

'All of the priests and most of the people feel a Church is now an urgent need'
(Donaghmede parish memo, 1976)

As new housing was built and more estates developed through the early 1970s in the area of Grangemore and Donaghmede, demand for social infrastructure inevitably increased. The first structure to be built, as the schemes of two-storey pitched roof pebble-dashed and brick houses grew and spread, was a primary school which opened in June 1973. Shortly after, in October 1973, the first phase of the new suburban Donaghmede Shopping Centre was opened. Donaghmede was constituted as a parish in 1974 and then the second school was completed in June 1975.

During this time, there was a temporary mass hall erected for the emerging parish, but it was quickly overtaken by the school children's needs and was put to use as a third school for 360 pupils. The hall was divided by partitions into four teaching spaces for the eight classes, with each teacher charged with 40 to 50 children. Daily mass then was said in the corridors while Sunday masses entailed the moving out of all the school furniture so that seating for 560 parishioners and standing room for 100 more could be

Case Study: Church of the Holy Trinity, Donaghmede

Ground floor plan
(Courtesy of A & D Wejchert image collection)

accommodated. Before long the parish needed a fourth school. Growth was tremendous and unyielding, and it was taken for granted that this growth and expansion was Catholic in nature.

A 1976 planning document, compiled by the new Donaghmede parish priests outlined present and immediate future needs: in July 1976 there were 2,350 families or households, expected to climb to 2,500 by the following summer of 1977. While the parish was struggling to accommodate the children in schools – the Office of Public Works promised a fourth school – the four priests were housed in an assortment of dwellings along the primary spine of the area, Grange Road. The biggest issue was the lack of a permanent church, despite the fact that a site had been purchased (for £24,000) opposite the shopping centre site from the same developer, the Gallagher Group, as early as 1972. By 1976, the situation was getting urgent. The priests called on the Dublin Diocesan administration to approve the parish's plan to replace the temporary mass centre with a church. By their assessment, their proposed church would need to seat 1,000 parishioners with standing room for a further few hundred. It would all come down to money.

Meanwhile, similar housing and communities were being built at Dublin's southern and western fringes, at places like Tallaght and Firhouse. Understanding this incessant suburban expansion, the Dublin Archbishop,

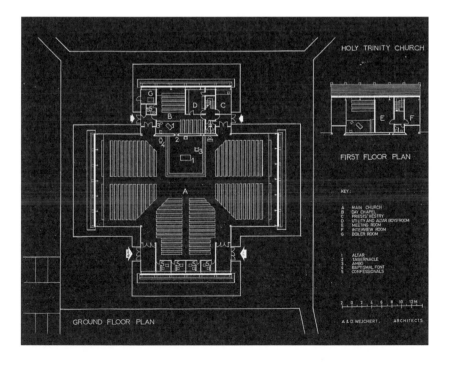

Dermot Ryan held an ideas competition, 'A Parish Church', in 1976 to promote more interesting, even experimental Catholic church designs on a restricted budget. In this, the point of the competition was three-fold: firstly, all new churches must be affordable; secondly, new designs should be innovative in plan, in form and even in materials; and thirdly, the ideas competition meant that the designs could be built in any of the emerging suburban parishes of the 1970s Dublin Diocesan landscape.

From the correspondence between the Donaghmede parish and the Dublin Diocese – primarily from parish priest, Fr Joe Collins to the Vicar Episcopal of Pastoral and Financial Development, Fr Des Williams – it is clear that 'A Parish Church' competition was the only show in town. Donaghmede immediately cited the competition and associated exhibition – which was on display in the Red House (Clonliffe) – in its July 1976 proposal for a new church, even specifying which design they would prefer: 'From an examination of the exhibits at the Church Design Competition we feel that the Hope, Cuffe & Associates design would be best suited to our requirements and would fit in very well with our site.' (Parish projection/memo, 1976). The Donaghmede priests reasoned that the Hope/Cuffe design was similar

to their popular temporary mass centre and as such, would bring some continuity to the ever-changing, growing community. In the end though, by October 1976, the diocese offered the parish the choice of the four prize-winning architects from which the parish chose A. & D. Wejchert:

> Many thanks for your letter of 18th Oct 1976 and for giving us the choice of four architects for a possible church in the parish. Having consulted with the other priests, some architect friends and another eminent personality, I am about to commission A. & D. Wejchert for the work. (Fr Collins, Donaghmede Parish File, 1976)

It is interesting to see the parish priest having agency over the church design at this juncture, with the happy appointment of Wejchert Architects. Danuta Kornaus-Wejchert took over as the project architect in charge, ably assisted by Paul Roche. Evidently wasting no time, the practice had drawn up designs and compiled all the tender documents by the summer of 1977. They were set to have a completed and open church by Easter 1978.

Having worked with John Sisk & Sons builders on the extensive University College Dublin campus at Belfield, the Wejcherts were keen to work with Sisk at Donaghmede. The bank loan for the church was secured in March 1977 and the summer was spent streamlining the design so that Wejcherts' and Fr Collins' plans could fit into the extremely restricted diocesan budget. In July that year, some concrete beams and internal steelwork, screens and suspended ceilings were stripped from the design, while changes were made to the floor finishes, internal doors, external planting and carparking areas all bringing considerable savings to the project. Once again, it was coming down to money. For instance, while the Wejcherts wanted concrete tiles for the building's significant roofs, corresponding to the neighbouring housing, the Archbishop's office prescribed cheaper asbestos tiles.

The building contract was settled at £198,250 by September 1977 but it is not clear if this included key elements such as seating, confessionals, and altar furniture. For the former, the priest was back battling for more budget in October 1977; for 1,066 seats, stating that there was by then 2,540 houses in the parish, with a further 190 houses being occupied by the following year. For the latter, the architects designed the altar, ambo, chair and baptismal font. And for the Stations of the Cross, altar candles, tabernacle door and other essential church elements, Fr Collins

commissioned the sculptor, Alexandra Wejchert (the architect's sister), in April 1978. He had received a large donation from two parishioners and used the gift for this more decorative purpose. Wejchert's Stations – of aluminium fitted to Perspex – were approved by the Diocesan Commission for Sacred Art and Architecture and by December 1978, Donaghmede's Church of the Holy Trinity was opened. Snagging around the building's details and defects seems to have continued into 1980, by which time the patron priest, Fr Joe Collins had died. His successor, Fr O'Sullivan was clearly less enamoured by Wejchert's experimental roofs, outlining a litany of problems, from poor lighting to leaking, in an angry letter:

> I have just come from the Church where rainwater has once again soaked seats and carpeting in the main aisle. The roof of the Church is a disaster. Will it ever be put right? (Fr O'Sullivan, Donaghmede Parish File, 1980)

Case Study: Church of the Holy Trinity, Donaghmede

Interiors with roof details (Courtesy of Wejchert Architects image collection)

Designing for Faith in 1970s Dublin: Influences and Inspiration

Donaghmede's Church of the Holy Trinity, along with Beaumont's Nativity of Our Lord (Robert Kingston, 1977) and Firhouse's Our Lady of Mount Carmel (John Meagher, 1979), was an explicit translation into built form of 'A Parish Church' competition-winning design. The Wejcherts' design was one of five commended submissions to the competition. The assessors commented on its 'striking form [...] a clear expression of the unique structural system used to roof a cruciform plan. The arrangement of voids and solids provides excellent high-level lighting to the church.' (Assessors' Report, 1976, p. 20). And undoubtedly, it was the same structural system of roof-as-wall enclosing and enabling the cruciform plan which was, in the end, built for the Catholic population of Donaghmede.

The close relationship between the finished building and the competition design clearly expedited the process of making this new church. The rigours of the competition meant that all commended designs had met the brief for a liturgically- and spatially-reformed Catholic parish church. Furthermore, as we know from the Donaghmede correspondence, budgetary concerns were primary. The test, as one critic put it, was to design a church for approximately 800 people at the mandatory cost limit of £100,000. This then grew to a church for 1,100 people at a cost of no higher than £110,000. According to the assessors, many of the 193 submissions ignored this aspect but those five commended designs responded realistically to the cost requirement. Of the competition, Archbishop Ryan explained:

> ...in these new areas (of Dublin) the new houses are built around a centre which, while providing the various Community needs, also serves to knit together the Community who live in the area. The Diocese is called on to provide in this setting and within strict financial limits, a place of prayer, a House of God. The purpose behind this Competition is to stimulate thinking about the design and construction of these churches and how best they can fulfil their role in these new parishes. (Competition Report, 1976, p. 3)

As such, the designs were all to sit in any suburban context: they were not neighbourhood specific. Different forms of construction, the placelessness of new suburbia and the strict financial limits were the driving forces. In these, the Wejchert design excelled. But probably more than anything, the Church of the Holy Trinity-as-built enclosed a 'place of prayer' becoming a 'House of God', thereby profoundly honouring the competition brief. Mathew

Hand has established Danuta Kornaus-Wejchert's authorship of the entry to the church competition, and subsequently, her design of the Donaghmede and slightly later Blessington parish Church of Our Lady (1982). Hand associates the success of both parish churches to, among other things, Wejchert's own spirituality. Aoife O'Halloran, writing about the Donaghmede church in comparison with another competition church, Our Lady of Mount Carmel in Firhouse, emphasises the Church of the Holy Trinity's beautiful quality of light. Certainly, Wejchert's design, from the cruciform floor plan to the sloping wall-roofs and the high-level glazing, created a successful space, from liturgical and by extension, spiritual perspectives.

The liturgical perspective was important at this point in the life of the Irish Catholic church. It was ten years since the meetings of the Second Vatican Council (Vatican II, 1965) and the reform of aspects of the church – namely encouraging more participation from laypeople through greater dialogue between laypeople and the clergy – was finally being felt on the ground, across Ireland's parishes. One material manifestation of this dialogue was the newly imagined church; the church as a humble room, with the removal of physical and then psychological barriers between the sanctuary and the congregation. Increasingly churches were built in circular, octagonal and fan shapes precisely because these shapes made for centralised and less hierarchical plans than the traditional basilica or Latin Cross form.

At Donaghmede, Kornaus-Wejchert adopted the Greek Cross – that is, a cross with four arms of equal length. She then dissimulated the cross plan through screens and pews. The seating, placed across two, almost three of the crucifix arms became fanned seating which as we have discussed, focused on the centrally-placed altar, itself on a rectilinear platform. Without knowing or outwardly sensing it, the barrier between the sanctuary and nave areas disappeared. It was in this sense of communion, between people and the altar, that the interior of the Church of the Holy Trinity subscribed to the progressive reformed liturgy.

While much of the liturgical reform enabled by the church's architecture comes out of the floor plan and its organisation, Donaghmede church went further still with its interior volume: its height, its light-filled air. The signature sloping roofs, holding the windows high above eye-level converge over the centre of the cross plan. Hard to read at first, the four mono-pitched roof-walls climb diagonally from the consecrated ground, intersecting and making

Case Study: Church of the Holy Trinity, Donaghmede

a disruptive dramatic space. Two things happen inside this building. Firstly, we focus on the sanctuary which is framed by a rectangular screen in which a crucifix is cut; and secondly, we look up. As Lance Wright observed about the church, 'It gives intimacy round the edges and uplift in the middle' (Wright, 1978, p. 22).

This marriage of the intimate and the uplifting, almost like conflicting scales of experience, was unusual and likely derived from the idiosyncratic geometrical biases of Kornaus-Wejchert's design. Her triangles and rectangles. Indeed, she was known for her mathematical skills and interests. From the outset the practice was unafraid to let geometric form dominate and ultimately guide a design. And at this Church of the Holy Trinity, the triangle reigns supreme: stable, straight and grounded as it touches the earth; pointed and dynamic as it reaches the sky. Externally, the triangle was arguably more powerful, as the triangles of roof stretching from ground to sky made a memorable visual image. As Wright stated, 'it provides the topographical advantages of a tower at much less than a tower's cost.' (Wright, 1978, p. 22).

Just when a monument was needed, for a community neither able nor willing to build on a monumental scale, Wejchert brought this memorable triangular monument of sorts to the windswept greens of Grangemore. Did Wejchert always know what a community needed? Putting the architect's geometric tendencies to the side, it is interesting to note the practice's general success with competitions. To win or have a submission commended in an architectural competition points to a pre-emptive empathy on the part of the designer; pointing, that is, to an innate understanding of what a community will need, moving past the present needs and addressing those needs to come. Andrzej Wejchert was brought to Ireland due to his winning of the University College Dublin campus masterplan competition for a new campus at Belfield (Co. Dublin, 1962). And a decade or so later, coinciding with the establishment of A. & D. Wejchert Architects, the practice was awarded second place in the 1974 (Community) Schools competition. Then the practice's entry to the Tallaght General Hospital in 1985 brought commissions at Naas General Hospital (Co. Kildare) and at Connolly Hospital, Blanchardstown (Co. Dublin).

Not forgetting the practice's success in 'A Parish Church' competition in 1976, all of the above competitions and subsequent commissions insinuate a deep humanity, as well as an interest in well-being, in communality, in learning, and in the sacred. As the Church of the Holy Trinity fills up and empties on Sundays and every day, it is continuously realising its initial brief to be a 'House of God'. Remarkably, and like some of its (1970s/80s) contemporaries but unlike almost all earlier Catholic parish churches across Dublin, it does not need to contract. Still, almost 50 years after its design, it serves its community comfortably.

Facts and Figures

The Church of the Holy Trinity sits in Grangemore Park, to the north of Grange Road and opposite the Donaghmede Inn, as part of Donaghmede Shopping Centre.

Architect: Danuta Kornaus-Wejchert of A. & D. Wejchert Architects was the designer and project architect of the Donaghmede church. Born in 1938 in Lwow/Lviv (now Ukraine), Danuta Kornaus studied architecture at the Warsaw Polytechnic School where she met Andrzej Wejchert. Wejchert was born in Gdansk in 1937. Upon graduating in 1962, Kornaus and Wejchert worked in state architecture jobs where Kornaus designed healthcare buildings. While Kornaus was in Paris, from 1963 studying at l'École Nationale Supérieure des Beaux-Arts, Wejchert submitted a design for a new campus for University College Dublin and won. He moved to Ireland in 1964 and Danuta Kornaus followed, where she worked in Robinson Keefe & Devane Architects (the practice which Wejchert associated with the UCD campus job), working with Andy Devane on projects such as Turlough Hill ESB power station (1974). Kornaus-Wejchert (by then married to Andrzej Wejchert) learned much about Ireland's burgeoning building regulations and planning legislation. In 1974, the two architects established A. & D. Wejchert Architects becoming known through the 1970s and 1980s for educational and health buildings such as the pioneering Dalkey School project national school (1984). Their 1979 Ailwee Caves Visitor Centre, Co. Clare won critical acclaim with commendation from the RIAI Gold Medal jury (1977–79) and a Europa Nostra award (1980). Danuta's interest in church design brought commissions at Donaghmede, soon after at Blessington (1982) and later, their Chapel of Apparition (1992) at Knock. Danuta Kornaus-Wejchert died in Dublin in 2014, five years after Andrzej. Having won many awards, A. & D. Wejchert Architects continue to thrive today, despite the passing of the founding partners.
Artist: Alexandra Wejchert was born in Krakow, Poland in 1921. Though ultimately practising as a sculptor, Alexandra first studied architecture at the Warsaw University before art at the Academy of Fine Arts, Warsaw. She moved to Dublin in 1965 after her brother, Andrzej won the UCD competition. Her sculptural work is best known for its large scale, bright colours and interesting 1970s synthetic materials of plexiglass and Perspex. Most of her work may be termed 'public art', most usually commissioned by corporate and university clients, however she made smaller-scale work for churches and other contexts. Her Stations of the Cross, tabernacle door and series of candles for Donaghmede were admired by the Commission for Sacred Art and Architecture (Patrick Pye and Dr James Whyte) who deemed the pieces to be of better value and quality than most ecclesiastic art at the time. She died in Dublin in 1995, having become an Irish citizen in 1979 and a member of Aosdána in 1981.
Commissioner/patron: Fr Collins was the parish priest at Donaghmede from 1975 until his untimely death due to illness in 1979. During this time, he reputedly established much of the community's social infrastructure including the building of several schools, the church, the Trinity Gael's GAA club and more. In 2008, a landmark public park, in sustainable terms, was opened and named after Fr. Collins, in honour of the work he did in securing the public lands for recreational purposes.
Competition: The competition, 'A Parish Church' was launched in February 1976 and the results were announced in June 1976. The jury comprised two priests and three architects: Reverend Patrick Dowling, Reverend Joseph Dunn, Raymond McDonnell, Cathal O'Neill and Oscar Richardson. The commended architects were Hope Cuffe and Associates; Robert Kingston; Kidney Burke-Kennedy Doyle; Robin Walker; and John Meagher. All five prize-winners were awarded £700 each.

Engineer: Thomas Garland & Partners
Quantity Surveyor: Boyd & Creed
Contractors: John Sisk & Sons
Structural steel work: Smith & Pearson
Mechanical Services: A Johnson & Son
Electrical Installation: C. J. Ryder & Co.
Roof materials: Ferroklith woodwool slabs, Gypsum Industries.

Sources
Unpublished
Archdiocese of Dublin, *A Parish Church: Single Stage Competition for the Design of a Parish Church*, Final Assessors' Report (Archbishop's House, Mar. 1977)
Donaghmede Parish File, Archbishop Ryan Papers (uncatalogued, including 1976 parish memo), Dublin Diocesan Archives (DDA), Drumcondra, Dublin
Donaghmede Press Cuttings File, Irish Architectural Archive (IAA), Dublin
Hand, Mathew, 'A Church in the Town: A Documentation and Analysis of the Architectural Conception and Subsequent Life of The Church of Our Lady of the Most Holy Sacrament at Blessington, Co. Wicklow (1982)' (Unpublished MArch dissertation, UCD Architecture, 2019)
O'Halloran, Aoife, 'The Work of Human Hands: A Discussion of the 1976 Archdiocese of Dublin Parish Church Competition with a Focus on de Blacam & Meagher's Church of Our Lady of Mount Carmel' (Unpublished MArch dissertation, UCD Architecture, 2019)

Published
Anon., 'Five Tie in Church Design Competition' in *Irish Times*, 24 June 1976
Anon, 'Higher Planes – Holy Trinity Parish Church, Grangemore, Dublin 13', in *Concrete Quarterly* (1980)

Cantrell, Wilfred, 'Ecclesiastical Architecture', in *Irish Architect* (Vol. 82, 1991)

Concannon, Maureen, P. Fletcher and A. Wejchert-Pearson , 'Remembering Danuta Wejchert', in *Architecture Ireland* (Vol. 275, No. 3, Jun./Jul. 2014)

Cooke, Harriet, 'Plan Profile: Andrzej Wejchert', in *Plan* (Vol. 6/4, 1975)

DeBlacam, Shane, 'Church Form', in *Introspect: An Annual Review of the Visual Arts* (1976)

Glancey, Jonathan, 'Trinity Triangles', in *The Architects' Journal* (Vol. 169, 1979)

O'Connell, Dermot, 'Lord, Who Shall be Admitted to your Tent', in *Introspect: An Annual Review of the Visual Arts* (1976)

O'Neill, Cathal, 'A Strategic Portfolio', in *Irish Arts Review* (Vol. 25, No. 3, 2008)

Ryan, Raymund, 'Eclectic Geometries', in *Irish Architect* (Vol. 183, Jan. 2003)

Steedman, Neil, 'Dublin Churches', in *Plan* (Vol. 10, No. 1, 1979)

O'Regan, John (ed.) for Andrzej Wejchert, *A&D Wejchert and Partners* (Gandon Editions, 2008)

White, Laurence William, 'Andrzej and Danuta Wejchert', in *Dictionary of Irish Biography* (RIA and Cambridge University Press, 2016), online version

Wright, Lance, 'Dublin Angles: Church, Grangemore, Dublin', in *Architectural Review* (Vol. CLIXVIII, 1978)

Ceiling detail
(Courtesy of Wejchert Architects image collection)

Case Study
Herbert Mews, Ballsbridge, Dublin 4, 1979

Carole Pollard

The terrace of six houses known as Herbert Mews is barely visible from Herbert Road, in leafy Ballsbridge, one of Dublin's oldest suburbs. Tucked away behind trees and accessible from a private road, these are not traditional mews houses in that they do not form a street edge along a laneway in place of former stables or outbuildings. Instead, the terrace occupies a carved off piece of the garden that once belonged to the adjacent Victorian villa. The garden location ensures a tranquil setting: the houses are surrounded by lawns planted with birch trees and a variety of shrubs. In addition, a rowan tree has been planted in front of each house, following an ancient Celtic traditional belief that the rowan tree symbolises courage, wisdom and protection.

The six two-storey houses form a single block with long elevations oriented north to the front and south to the rear. They are constructed in grey concrete brick, tempered by the natural timber finish of the hardwood windows, glazed screens and doors. An open colonnade runs along the length of the front elevation of the terrace, providing shelter at each of the entrance doors. At the back, each house has a small, south-facing enclosed courtyard with a gate opening onto a communal private garden bounded by mature trees and hedging. The interior layout of each house is identical with a central double-height space, lit from above, flooding the interiors with natural light. This means that even the mid-terrace houses are bright. The abundance of natural light compensates for the tight dimensions of some of the rooms.

Despite its strong Modernist form and the incongruity of its building materials – grey machined concrete brick and natural timber joinery – Herbert Mews nestles comfortably amongst its older, more traditional neighbours. Modest scale and thoughtful landscaping help the terrace assimilate into its environment, but such humility conceals the innovation behind the design. Built in 1979, these houses were the vanguard for future mews-type developments that now line the back-lanes of Dublin's Georgian and Victorian terraces. With their extremely efficient internal planning and innate modesty, they set the standard for a new housing typology that remains relevant, innovative and popular 40 years later.

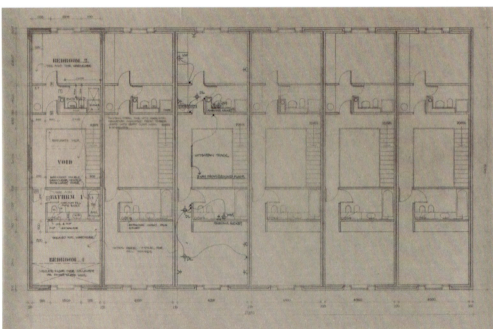

(above)
Site plan (Courtesy of de Blacam & Meagher collection at Irish Architectural Archive)

(below)
First floor plan (Courtesy of de Blacam & Meagher collection at Irish Architectural Archive)

To be a Mews or Not to be a Mews

The decision to name the terrace 'Herbert Mews' arose from a marketing strategy devised by the estate agent, John de Vere White who felt in late 1970s Dublin that the word 'mews' attracted a more discerning purchaser. The houses are essentially suburban maisonettes, but their design is radically different to the standard type of suburban housing development built in Dublin, and throughout Ireland. Since the 1950s, the majority of suburban houses were built in large repetitively planned estates of semi-detached two-storey houses designed by speculative builders who used the same house plans over and over again. Certainly, Herbert Mews offered an antidote to that development model.

The developer, J. J. Costello, took a risk in doing something different. Costello was a small-scale developer and the scheme at Herbert Road was the biggest project he had ever undertaken. In 1975 he obtained outline planning permission for five three-storey maisonettes on the site, but taking site and construction costs into account, knew that he needed a more cost-efficient design solution. His agent, de Vere White introduced him to young architect John Meagher of de Blacam & Meagher in late 1976. The practice of de Blacam & Meagher had been established the same year on foot of success in an architectural competition for new Catholic churches, out of which they designed a church at Firhouse in south Dublin. Herbert Mews and the Church of Our Lady of Mount Carmel, Firhouse (1979) were the practice's inaugural projects in a long and successful design partnership.

According to John Meagher the budget for the job was very tight. This dictated the efficient internal planning as well as the selection of materials, including the decision to use concrete brick for the elevations. Through frugal management of space and materials, Meagher managed to fit six houses, rather than five on the site, and also reduced the houses from three to two storeys, further cutting costs. De Vere White recalls that the developer, Costello, responded enthusiastically to his architect's proposals. Drawings in the de Blacam & Meagher archive show early sketch proposals with the concept for a compact terrace of six identical houses emerging quickly. There are several different options for the massing and elevational treatments, including one which proposes continuous clerestory glazing on the front façade and tall boiler house chimneys lined along the rear of the houses. The final scheme has reduced window sizes to front and rear and eliminates the tall boiler house chimneys.

More Than Concrete Blocks Volume 3

Front and rear elevations (Courtesy of de Blacam & Meagher collection at Irish Architectural Archive)

Initially, de Vere White had reservations about the overall size of the houses but there was a positive response when they were put on the market; they sold within months of completion. The price even increased. When the houses went on the market in November 1979, they were £62,500 each, by May 1980, when the last two were sold, the price was £64,500. Coverage of the mews houses in the property press was magnanimous. One property editor described the development as 'the best townhouse alternative to an apartment which I have seen' (*Irish Independent*, 3 Nov. 1979). Recognising how the efficient internal planning did not compromise on the quality of the interior spaces, the article notes:

> inches out and the concept would have been ruined. The layout of the houses is strikingly different. That bit is easily achieved. The hard bit is that it must work. And it does. A narrow area is made to look spacious. Virtually concealing the stairs and exposing the landing were a masterstroke. (*Irish Independent*, 3 Nov. 1979)

Another newspaper article described the scheme as Dublin's most exciting townhouse design citing such features as a walled patio and a dream kitchen.

The speed of the sale of the houses and the strong prices achieved were all the more remarkable for the fact that Ireland was on the verge of a severe economic recession as a result of the 1979 global energy crisis. A 'Review of the Building Industry' reported that 'output in the industry reached a record level in 1979... due principally to exceptionally high levels of activity in housing' but this peak was short-lived and the 1980s saw a significant drop in house building (*RIAI Bulletin*, 28 Sept. 1980, p. 6). The sharp and sudden downturn in residential construction is probably the primary reason why Meagher's architectural innovations at Herbert Mews did not spawn imitators across urban Ireland until many years later.

An Antidote to the Typical Irish Suburban House Model

As an antidote to the dreariness of contemporary Irish suburban housing, Herbert Mews is successful on many levels. Its architecture rejects pastiche, particularly any reference to popular neo-Georgian idioms. The houses reflect modern lifestyles, with the living rooms at the heart of the building and an easy flow between all the rooms. The houses function both as open-plan – when all the pocket doors are open – and as a series of discrete spaces

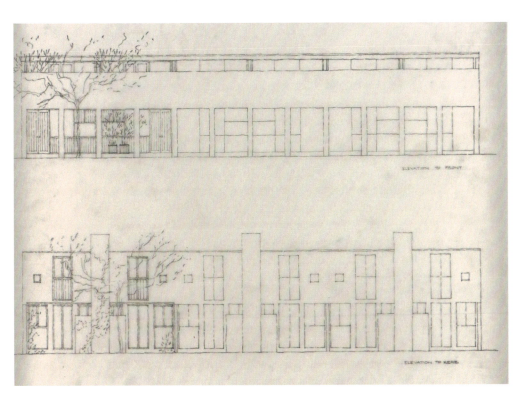

when those doors are closed. Thoughtful arrangement of both internal and external spaces brings a harmony to how the houses function individually, and how neighbouring houses respond to each other. The orientation of the houses and pioneering handling of natural light means that the interiors are light-filled all day long.

The internal floor is just 84 square metres, taking the form of one room wide and three rooms deep. To the front there is an entrance hall and kitchen; the central third of the house is a double-height dining area lit from above by a square roof light; the rear part of the house accommodates the south-facing living room. The dining area and living room are separated by a central fireplace and chimney breast, but the visual connection is maintained through an open hearth. The partially concealed staircase leads to an open landing area overlooking the dining area below. At first floor, the master bedroom is located to the front and includes an ensuite bathroom lit by a roof light. A second double bedroom is located to the rear, as is the family bathroom also roof-lit.

There is no unnecessary circulation space. What is lost in floor space at first floor level, coming from the double-height volume, is more than

(opposite)
Elevation study 1
(Courtesy of de Blacam & Meagher collection at Irish Architectural Archive)

Elevation study 2
(Courtesy of de Blacam & Meagher collection at Irish Architectural Archive)

regained in the spatial qualities and abundance of natural light. Similarly, any discomfort arising from minimum floor to ceiling heights in the secondary rooms is offset by the luxury of that bright, soaring space. Storage is cleverly designed into alcoves and recesses, while glazed internal doors at ground floor give unimpeded views through to the south-facing courtyard. The houses benefit enormously from passive solar house design, a precursor to *Passivhaus* building standards. Orientated north-south, the large areas of glazing on the south elevation overlook sheltered courtyards. The four inner houses have minimal external surfaces reducing heat loss. The north-facing front ground floor colonnade provides shelter from wind and rain at the entrances, while at first floor there is only one window to the master bedroom.

The interior surface finishes are modern – shadow gaps between the flush plaster and architrave joints, and recessed skirtings. Herbert Mews is an early essay in an architectural language that de Blacam & Meagher developed to great fluency in their later projects, and one which has influenced a generation of Irish architects after them.

Meagher, in his role as a teacher and as a practitioner, was part of a movement of Irish architects of the late 1970s and early 1980s who sought to establish an Irish architectural identity. As discussed in our 1980s Architectural Culture essay, in 1980, an exhibition entitled 'Traditions and Directions – the evolution of Irish Architecture' was held as part of the

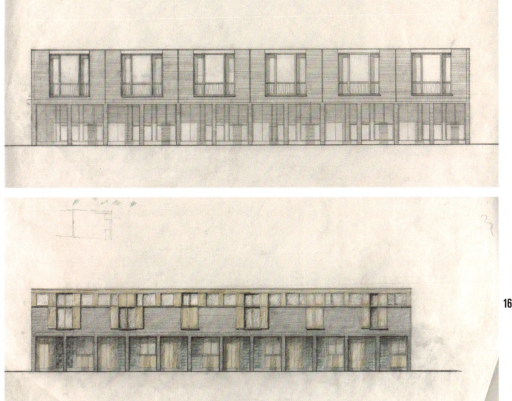

'Sense of Ireland' Festival of Irish Arts and Culture at the Royal College of Art in London. The curator, Irish architect Yvonne Farrell, circulated 500 architects working in Ireland with an invitation to exhibit their work however the response was poor, and fewer than 50 architects responded. The exhibition had a strong focus on domestic architecture – often the only commissions open to young architects – and the work of de Blacam & Meagher featured strongly. Among their projects selected for exhibition was Herbert Mews, of which Farrell wrote:

> The study of the group of houses concerns itself with the modern problems of numbers and the need to harness modern urbanism. A new attitude to complex urban forms is necessary to absorb modern needs. Increasingly, suburbia is being questioned for its lack of complexity of function, for its complete lack of place, its isolation, which further separates people from each other in terms of distance, time and community. (Farrell, 1980, p. 1).

More Than Concrete Blocks Volume 3

There is nothing overtly 'Irish' about the design of Herbert Mews, but its architecture is a direct response to both the opportunities and the constraints of the brief and the site. The philosophy behind the design stems from de Blacam & Meagher's ethos of exploring how landscape and buildings interact; in how the terrace of houses is set within the historic Victorian garden and in how each house contains its own garden as a private outside roofless room.

While the only architectural publication of the Herbert Mews scheme was in the 'Traditions and Directions' exhibition catalogue, the ideas explored at Herbert Mews are clearly evident in later de Blacam & Meagher mews designs, including the much-published Mews House Heytesbury Lane (see Outline Survey), which was constructed 20 years later in 1997, winning both RIAI and AAI awards.

Facts and Figures

de Blacam & Meagher Architects were commissioned by J. J. Costello in 1976. The works commenced on site in 1978 and the houses were completed and ready for sale in 1979.

Architect: John Meagher (1947–2021) was described in his obituary as an 'architect of considerable craft and taste' (Keogh, Obituary, 2021). He was born in Dublin and educated at Dublin Institute of Technology (now TU Dublin) where he graduated in 1971. He was awarded a scholarship to the School of Architecture, Helsinki University of Technology, Otaniemi, Finland 1971–72. He worked for Robert Venturi in the practice Venturi & Rauch in Philadelphia, Pennsylvania, USA where he was involved in producing drawings for Venturi's book *Learning from Las Vegas: the Forgotten Symbolism of Architectural Form* (MIT Press, 1972). Meagher established the practice de Blacam & Meagher with Shane de Blacam in Dublin in 1976. As a partner in the practice, Meagher went on to win several architectural awards, including the RIAI Silver Medal for Housing 2003 for 1 Castle Street, and RIAI Regional Awards for 1 Grand Canal Quay (2001), Martha's Vineyard private house Dalkey, House at Strand Road Dublin, and Mews House at Heytesbury Lane Dublin. The work of the practice has been widely published in international architectural journals. Meagher was president of the Architectural Association of Ireland 1977–1980. In 2004 Meagher and de Blacam were ranked by *Architects Today* as 'the godfathers of contemporary Irish architecture'. Their work featured in the Irish pavilion at the Venice Biennale in 2010 and 2018. In 2021, de Blacam and the late Meagher were awarded the RIAI James Gandon Medal for their Lifetime Achievement in Architecture.

Developer: J. J. (James) Costello
Consulting Engineer: Frank Lee, Lee McCullough Consulting Engineers
Quantity Surveyor: John Skelly & Associates
Main Contractors: Cooney & Jennings, Glenageary, Co. Dublin

Sources

Unpublished

de Blacam, Shane, 'The Practice of de Blacam & Meagher' at AA School of Architecture, London, 30 Jan. 2001, see https://www.youtube.com/watch?v=I3o2LnswiVk
John Meagher, interviewed by Carole Pollard, 2014
Joan O'Connor (resident of Herbert Mews), interviewed by Carole Pollard, 2014
Drawing files in de Blacam & Meagher archive at the Irish Architectural Archive (IAA)
Planning files relating to Herbert Mews at Dublin City Council

Published

Anon., 'Review of the Building Industry', in *RIAI Bulletin* (27 Jun. 1980)
Cairns, Frank, 'Splendid Design Concept for Herbert Mews', *Irish Independent*, 3 Nov. 1979
Farrell, Yvonne, 'Introduction', in *Traditions and Directions: The Evolution of Irish Architecture* (RCA, 1980)
Jones, Edward, 'Notes on Contemporary Irish Architecture', in *Traditions and Directions: The Evolution of Irish Architecture* (RCA, 1980)
Keogh, Paul, 'John Meagher obituary: An architect of considerable craft and taste', *Irish Times*, 10 Apr. 2021
McCullough, Niall, 'Irish Renaissance', in *The Architect's Journal* (No. 44, Vol. 180, 31 Oct. 1984)

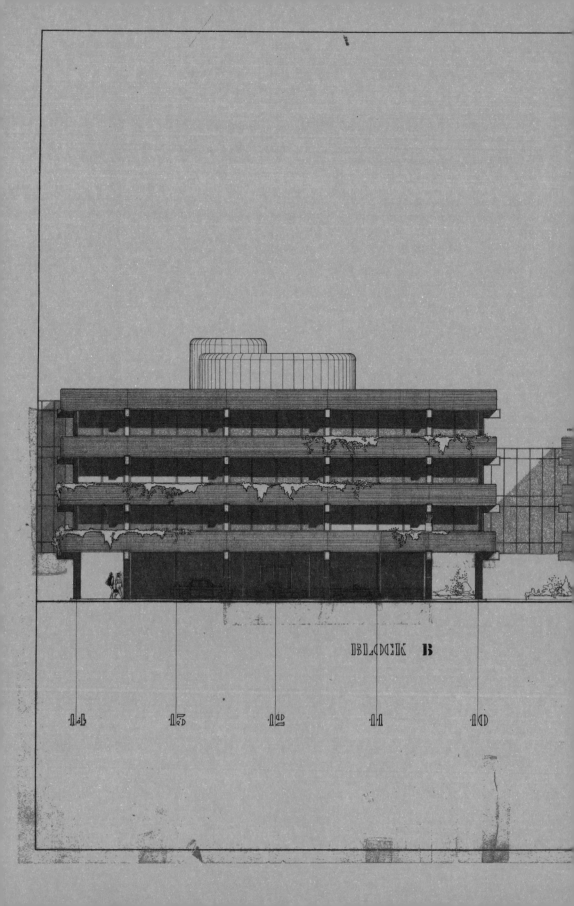

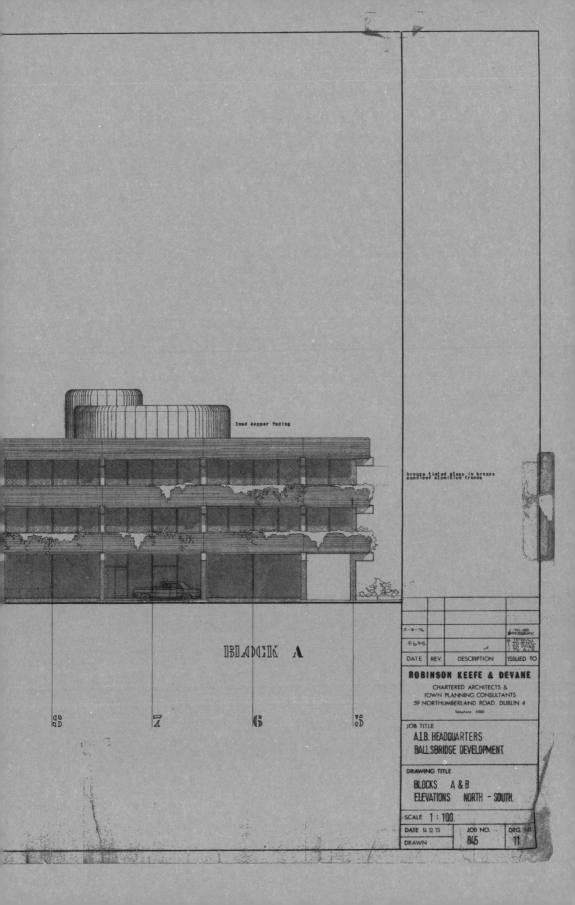

Case Study
AIB Bankcentre, Ballsbridge, Dublin 4, 1979

Carole Pollard

31 [DEMOLISHED]

Situated on Merrion Road, the main artery that runs through Ballsbridge, AIB Bankcentre represented a high point in Irish office block architecture and an eloquent counterpoint to the prolific mundanity of office blocks that had recently begun to populate the Dublin 4 postal district. Composed to compliment the classical architectural language of the Royal Dublin Society (RDS) complex across the road, the buildings were integrated into a bespoke landscaped garden and were accentuated with carefully selected artworks. Described at its official opening as 'the hanging gardens of Ballsbridge' (*Irish Times*, 20 Feb. 1980), Bankcentre brought a vision of corporate America to Dublin. Draped with trailing vines and sitting on manicured lawns, the offices were arranged as a series of pavilions, stepping in height from four to six storeys, well set back from the Merrion Road edge. Conceived by the newly formed Allied Irish Banks conglomerate which became known as AIB, Bankcentre was ultimately designed to project the banking group's financial prowess. The ambitious brief given to the architects addressed the desire to establish 'an environmental design principle… [that] should not only fulfil the Group's functional needs but also make a contribution to the physical environment of Dublin' (Fitzpatrick, 1979, p. 111).

AIB Bankcentre was designed and built as a corporate campus, an American typology that became increasingly popular in Europe in the 1960s. AIB was not the first institution to adopt the suburban campus model in Dublin – see the RTÉ Campus at Montrose from 1960–73 (see *MTCB* Vol. 2) for example – but it was the first private commercial enterprise to do so. Designed by architect Andrew Devane of Robinson Keefe & Devane, the original scheme comprised 15 pavilions arranged in a symmetrical composition, nine of which were built. Distinctive for its horizontal emphasis, the structure was expressed as continuous concrete bands alternating with recessed, glazing strips which created deep shadows. The ground floor was similarly recessed so that the buildings appeared to float over the landscaped surfaces below. The dominant feature of the landscape design was a long central axis that ran as a pedestrian boulevard from pedestrian gates on Merrion Road to the Bankcentre's main entrance, with a long, linear pool and a dramatic sculpture set in a fountain at its termination point.

In 2008, Robinson Keefe & Devane Architects undertook extensive refurbishment works on the campus, primarily involving the extension of the larger blocks at the rear. Substantial changes were also made to the landscaping, including the removal of the lawns and the linear pool on the central boulevard. The entire front area of the site was paved over and Alexandra Wejchert's sculpture, *Freedom* was relocated closer to the building's main entrance. The refurbishment works were funded by the 2007 sale of the four front-facing pavilions which were subsequently sold on a number of times to different developers. In 2019, planning permission was granted to demolish the four pavilions and over succeeding years, a series of further planning permissions facilitated the development of high-density office accommodation on the site. In 2021, the developer acquired AIB's retained headquarters buildings on the rear portion of the site. The new development, called Fibonacci Square, was let to Facebook on a 25 year lease. In 2022 the property, which no longer contains any of Devane's original buildings, was put on the market for €1.3 billion.

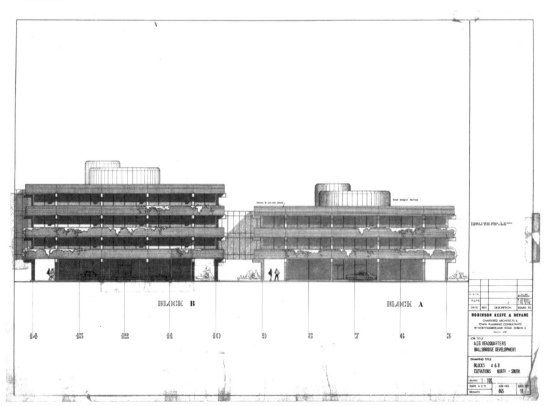

Elevations of three- and four-storey pavilions (Courtesy of Robinson Keefe & Devane image collection)

Block model
(Courtesy of Robinson Keefe & Devane image collection)

Corporate Campus

There were several reasons why the board of AIB decided to locate its headquarters on the outskirts of Dublin city, among them the Edenic promise of the corporate campus. In the latter years of the 1960s, when this project was first conceived, improvements in the Irish economy saw frenetic activity in commercial property development, none more so than in the development of headquarters buildings for the nation's financial institutions, including the major banks and insurance companies. In the early years of the 1970s, Bank of Ireland built their headquarters on Baggot Street and Irish Life Assurance Ltd announced plans to build at Abbey Street. Construction work on the Central Bank in Dame Street began in 1973.

AIB's headquarters was located in the far reaches of Dublin's prosperous suburb of Ballsbridge. AIB claimed that it was forced to locate to a site outside the city centre because it could not find a site in the city of suitable size. However, this claim could be more accurately interpreted to mean that they could not find a site of suitable size in a suitable part of the city. In fact, there were many large sites available, particularly on the north and west edges of the city centre, but none matched the allure of Dublin 4.

AIB was incorporated in September 1966 through the amalgamation of three Irish banks – Munster & Leinster Bank (founded 1885), the Provincial Bank of Ireland (founded 1825), and the Royal Bank of Ireland (founded

Site Plan with block layout and landscaping (Courtesy of Robinson Keefe & Devane image collection)

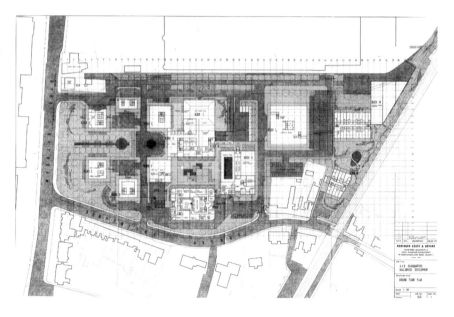

1836). The merger arose from strategic thinking at both commercial and political levels about the future of the Irish economy and growing competitiveness within the Irish banking sector. Foreign direct investment in industrial development in Ireland, particularly from the United States, was an important factor, and AIB specifically targeted that market. It incorporated discrete subsidiary companies including an investment bank (AIIB) and a finance wing (AIF) which themselves became the fifth and sixth largest banks in Ireland respectively. During the period 1966 to 1978 the staff of AIB grew from 2,700 to nearly 8,200.

The idea of a corporate campus in a parkland setting was attractive for many reasons: it would appeal to the bank's growing international client base; it would make an appropriate statement about AIB's ambitions; and it would facilitate the construction of several buildings with discrete functions on one site. This last factor arose from the desire to retain autonomy within AIB's different activities, particularly in relation to AIF and AIIB. While innovative, the idea of a corporate campus was not entirely new in Ireland by that time. As mentioned above, RTÉ had relocated to a campus at Montrose. Institutions such as UCD, moved from Earlsfort Terrace to Belfield (from 1960), St Vincent's Hospital moved from St Stephen's Green to Elm Park (1970) and secondary schools such as St Andrew's College, Alexandra College, and Wesley College all left their city centre locations for greener, more spacious, and healthier environments.

The search for a site for Bankcentre began in 1971 when AIB acquired

Case Study: AIB Bankcentre, Ballsbridge

Bankcentre with trailing planting on balconies in Architecture Ireland, May/June 1994 (Courtesy of Robinson Keefe & Devane image collection)

a site of a formed Carmelite convent on Northbrook Road in Ranelagh which, although not far from the central business district – which by this time occupied the southeast quadrant of the city from Dame Street to Ballsbridge – was in a predominantly residential area. Architect Andrew Devane was appointed and instructed to prepare schematic designs. He proposed a series of individual low-rise pavilions, set amongst the mature trees on the site. However, even before any planning application had been made, the local residents' group, the Upper Leeson Street Area Residents' Association (ULSARA), had made their opposition clear. The site would require re-zoning from residential to commercial use before any planning application could be made, and Devane warned that they were unlikely to achieve permission for a large office development on this site.

The decision to abandon the Ranelagh scheme was sealed when AIB were presented with the opportunity to buy a site in a much better location. In 1972, the bank entered negotiations to purchase the former RDS Bloodstock Sales Paddocks on Merrion Road. Although this site would also require re-zoning, the proceeds of the sale would go towards the consolidation of RDS activities in Ballsbridge. The RDS had special status under the 1963 Planning Act which meant the planning authority would be favourably disposed towards any development that enabled the RDS to expand and/or improve its facilities.

The site presented AIB with the opportunity to build a high-profile headquarters with an unrivalled level of public visibility. Additionally, the

location was ideal because of its proximity to the city's expanding southside suburbs where many bank employees lived. The purchase of the site was completed in December 1973 by which time Devane had lodged a planning application for a 46,500 square metres (500,000 square feet) development including 'offices, residential (two blocks containing 69 apartments), educational facilities, recreational facilities, branch bank, workshop and stores, [and] basement parking' (RKD file note, 1973). The inclusion of an 'experimental theatre' in an earlier proposal was indicative of AIB's intention to contribute to the community and the arts, however it was omitted in the final scheme. Despite an appeal by third parties to the Minister of Local Government, planning permission was granted in December 1974. Works began on site in April 1975.

The planning permission included the provision of 90 apartments to be located to the rear of the site with access from Serpentine Avenue. AIB sold this portion of the site to developer Finbarr Holland who redesigned the apartment blocks. On completion in 1976, he sold the apartments to a 'good cross-section of business and professional life, including stockbrokers, solicitors and (inevitably) bankers.' *(Irish Independent,* 24 Sep. 1976). Because of Ireland's deteriorating economic conditions during the 1970s, AIB's ambitions for their new headquarters were curtailed and Devane's original

Case Study: AIB Bankcentre, Ballsbridge

scheme was reduced. Six of the proposed blocks, or pavilions, were not built. Facilities omitted included the recreational centre (which was intended for use by the public as well as AIB staff) and the educational component which included dormitory accommodation for staff undergoing training.

The poor economic conditions also affected the construction programme. Works were held up by various industrial strikes, causing supply delays, and the financial management of the project caused problems for all parties concerned. One of the aspects of the project which suffered most was the landscaping design which had to be severely curtailed when it was discovered that the contract sum was three times the original estimate. Nonetheless, Devane and landscape architect, Jim Fehily, worked hard to ensure the spirit of the original landscape design concept was not lost, however there were some casualties. The original irrigation system for the window planters was downgraded and, as a result, the trailing vines which gave the building its distinctive appearance became difficult and expensive to maintain over time.

Despite financial constraints, AIB remained committed to commissioning original art works for their headquarters, and Devane played an important role in ensuring that this final segment of his vision was fulfilled even after the construction works had been completed. Indeed, Devane's role in commissioning artwork for Bankcentre was recognised when AIB was awarded 'Most Outstanding Contribution to Art in the Work Environment' in 1987 (Ruane, 1988, p. 157).

Pastural Pavilions

Devane began design work for the Ballsbridge scheme in April 1973, starting with a detailed survey of the site and the production of measured hand drawings of existing neighbouring buildings including the RDS. The careful attention to the detail of the surrounding buildings, their scale, materiality, and component parts informed the design of the new structures and influenced the selection materials and the nature of the construction details. The warm grey hues of the granite and limestone finishes at the RDS inspired Devane's selection of concrete with granite chip aggregate as the primary building material, blended with soft grey-hued mosaic tiles to enrich the building's tectonic quality.

The concept of designing a collection of discrete pavilion-type office buildings had originated in Devane's scheme for the Ranelagh site, however,

(left)
Alexandra Wejchert sculpture *Freedom* at main entrance (Courtesy of Robinson Keefe & Devane image collection)

(right)
John Behan sculpture *Megalithic Memories* (Courtesy of Robinson Keefe & Devane image collection)

the Ballsbridge solution is far more successful and aesthetically pleasing. At Ballsbridge, Devane controlled the design by imposing a 7.2 metre grid that allowed him to manage the composition. The hierarchy of the individual pavilions was dictated by the relationships with neighbouring buildings including the RDS, residences on Serpentine Road, and the adjoining Irish Hospitals Sweepstakes building which was demolished in 1990. The grid in turn controlled the arrangement of the pavilions in relation to each other and dictated how the landscape design mediated the surrounding site and perimeter edge. It also informed how the building interiors were divided and how and where vertical elements such as stairs, lifts and service ducts occurred.

All structures were built using in-situ reinforced concrete flat-slab construction with precast cladding panels. The volume of work was considerable, but the construction methodology was simple and repetitive, and therefore relatively economical. All buildings were generated off the 7.2 metre grid, each made up of three bays plus two half bays, one at each end. This rational system changed in the central, tallest blocks G and H which were two buildings joined together to form a single structure. Blocks A, B, C and D were located to the front of the main block, stepping in formation like a guard of honour to the main entrance. These four pavilions accommodated AIF, AIIB and a local bank branch. Each had their own entrances, receptions areas and meeting rooms but were interlinked with walkways at upper levels.

Case Study: AIB Bankcentre, Ballsbridge

A single-storey building to the north of Block G/H housed the staff canteen accommodating 400 people, and other ancillary services.

Perimeter beams were designed with brackets cast into the columns to carry the cladding panels. A total of 612 uniform panels were cast on site by the main contractor. A specialist tiling contractor was installed on site to apply the mosaic tile finish. All the columns at ground floor level and all the protruding brackets had a bush hammered finish. Bronze tinted glazing was recessed behind the lateral cladding panels. A curtain wall finish on the façade of the main building was a focal point of the development. All mechanical equipment on the roofs was concealed in timber-built circular plant rooms clad in lead. Bankcentre showcased Devane's design skills and was the ultimate evocation of his longstanding philosophy of creating an architecture that responded to the human need for sensory harmony with nature. As a young architect, Devane had studied under Frank Lloyd Wright and the architecture at Bankcentre evoked Wright's 'organic architecture' ethos. The buildings were designed so that employees enjoyed naturally lit office spaces and pleasant green vistas from their desks. Workers and visitor alike experienced an office environment like no other in Dublin, with the background murmur of running water, sunlight glinting on mosaic tile and stainless steel, and the ever-changing colours of nature.

Devane and Fehily worked together to design a landscape that enhanced the massing and horizontal emphasis of the buildings. The central three bays of each façade were planted with cascading veils of green vines, while the corner bays were plant free. The buildings were all about their exposed angular corners which jutted out like sharp elbows, creating an optical rhythm that underlined the visual success of the central boulevard. Deep concrete slabs, clad in shimmering white mosaic tiles, cast deep shadows on the alternating bands of recessed glazing, accentuating the contrast between the hard lines of the structure and softness of the planting and lawns.

The landscaping of the site was an integral part of its architectural success and provided inspiration for the artists that were commissioned to create works to complement the development. Artist Alexandra Wejchert eloquently described her reaction to walking the site with Devane in 1978, some months before it was complete:

> I react so strongly to architecture as well as to any art, and so really can I see something I like. But the day when you showed me the AIB will remain in my memory: the pleasure of feeling

the scale here again so different, sensing the relationship of the layout to the three dimensions, the airy and spatial way of interlacing the garden areas with the buildings, the strong spine of the water line with the adherent fountains merging with surrounding gardens… it is such a rich design… full of grandeur, wisdom and it has a poise of eternity which I haven't seen in any other modern building. (Wejchert letter, 1978)

AIB shared Weichert's enthusiasm for the scheme, organising a special event on the new campus for senior members of its workforce in November 1979. A ceremony to officially open the building was presided over by the Taoiseach, Charles Haughey in February 1980. Despite extensive coverage in the press, the building did not feature in the Irish architectural journals and did not receive any architectural awards. The lack of architectural coverage was primarily down to Devane's decision not to permit reviews – he declined invitations from both *Plan* magazine and the RIAI journal *Architecture in Ireland* to feature the building. Interestingly, Bankcentre is one of only a scant few office buildings of the era that is praised by Frank McDonald in his 1985 polemic, *The Destruction of Dublin.*

Bankcentre was Devane's last major project in Ireland. From 1980 onwards he lived abroad, first in Rome and later in Calcutta (now Kolkata), although he continued to be involved in projects from afar. He returned to Dublin to oversee the installation of artworks at Bankcentre and was present in 1985 when Alexandra Wejchert's magnificent stainless-steel sculpture, *Freedom*, was erected in the circular pond at the end of the central boulevard.

Despite the sculptor, Wejchert's opinion that Bankcentre had the 'poise of eternity' (Wejchert letter, 1978) and Devane's assertion in a letter to his client, Jim Fitzpatrick, that the project was 'the greatest in my life' (Devane letter, 1979), AIB Bankcentre was substantially demolished in 2019 with later radical alterations and additions to the site in the early years of the 2020s. None of Devane's original scheme remains.

Case Study: AIB Bankcentre, Ballsbridge

(above)
Drawing of proposed interior at entrance lobby. (Courtesy of Robinson Keefe & Devane image collection)

(below)
Main entrance lobby. (Courtesy of Robinson Keefe & Devane image collection)

Facts and Figures

AIB bought the site in Ballsbridge in 1973. The re-zoning of the site was approved in June 1974 and planning permission for the development was granted in December 1974. Works commenced on site in April 1975. The complex was occupied by AIB from March 1979 and officially opened by Taoiseach, Charles Haughey, in February 1980.

Architects: Robinson Keefe & Devane Architects (RKD)
Lead designer and project architect Andrew (Andy) Devane assisted by Roddy McCaffrey and Martin Donnelly. Devane (1917–2000) was born in Limerick and studied architecture at University College Dublin where he graduated in 1941. In 1943 he sat examinations to become a town planning consultant. In 1946 he travelled to Frank Lloyd Wright's Taliesin Fellowship where he spent 14 months. On his return to Ireland, he re-joined the practice of Robinson Keefe. In 1948 he became a partner and the practice was renamed Robinson Keefe & Devane (later RKD Architects). Devane was a prolific and versatile designer. His early works include the Mortuary Chapel at Naas (1948) and the GI Unit at the Meath Hospital (1954) (see *MTCB* Vol. 2). His portfolio of buildings includes churches, hospitals, primary schools and technical schools. He is probably best known for his house at Howth, Journey's End Lodge (1961), St Fintan's Church at Sutton (1973) and his major campus developments including St Patrick's College, Drumcondra (1964) (see *MTCB* Vol. 2), the Irish Life Centre on Abbey Street (1978 and 1982). Devane was awarded a RIAI Silver Medal for his contribution to Irish architecture in 1989.

Roddy McCaffrey, a nephew of Robinson Keefe & Devane founding partner, Cyril Keefe, studied architecture at UCD. On graduation in 1953 he spent a short time at RKD before travelling to work in the United States. He returned to the practice in 1962 and worked there until his retirement. McCaffrey was Devane's right-hand man, working closely with him on all his projects. Martin Donnelly joined RKD in 1970 and worked closely with Devane on many projects, including Stephen Court, AIB Bankcentre, the Irish Life Centre and Tallaght Hospital. He retired in 2017.

Landscape architect: James Fehily & Associates
James (Jim) Fehily (1930–2020) studied architecture at University College Dublin from 1949–54. One of his earliest and best-known works is the Church of Our Lady of the Assumption in Killyon, Co. Meath (1957). Fehily went on to undertake postgraduate studies in landscape architecture with Ian McHarg at the University of Pennsylvania and worked thereafter for the well-known landscape architect, Dan Kiely. Fehily was a co-founder of the Society of Landscape Architects in Ireland in 1966 and later Professor of Planning at UCD.

Services Engineers: Varming Mulcahy Reilly Associates
Structural Engineers: Joseph McCullough & Partners
Quantity Surveyors: Grellan Shortall of Seamus Monahan & Partners
Main Contractors: G&T Crampton. Contracts Manager Bobby Fotheringham
Piling Contractors: Murphy International
Mosaic Tiling Sub-Contractor: Ernest Verso
Glazing Sub-Contractor: Sean Billings
Main contractors: G&T Crampton

The original contract sum was for £8.9 million. The completed contract amount was somewhere between £20 and £30 million.

Artists: Alexandra Wejchert (1921–95): *Freedom* sculpture in the entrance fountain and a suspended sculpture in the main entrance lobby (both 1985). (See Wejchert's biography in Donaghmede Church essay in this volume, p. x)
John Behan (*b*.1938): *Megalithic Memories* sculpture in garden (1982)
Desmond Kinney (1934–2019): mosaics including a four-part external mosaic mounted on the wall in the gardens outside the dining hall (1980)
Anne Price-Owen: interior ceramic relief sculpture (1980)

Sources

Unpublished
Vincent Delaney, interviewed by Carole Pollard, Apr. 2018
Martin Donnelly, interviewed by Carole Pollard, Apr. 2018
Roddy McCaffrey, interviewed by Carole Pollard, June 2018
Pollard, Carole, 'Andy Devane and the Architecture of the Modern Irish Office Block, 1963–1989' (unpublished PhD thesis, UCD School of Architecture, 2022)
RKD Archive files, Project Ref. No. 845
Letter from Alexandra Wejchert to Andy Devane, 24 Sept. 1978, RKD Archive 845/35-B
Letter from Andy Devane to Jim Fitzpatrick, 8 Mar. 1979, RKD Archive 845/1A

Published
Anon., 'Holland Gives Bank Dutch Courage!', *Irish Independent*, 24 Sept. 1976
Anon., 'Taoiseach Opens AIB's New Bankcentre in Ballsbridge', *Irish Times*, 20 Feb. 1980
Anon., New HQ for AIB in Ballsbridge, RTÉ online archives (accessed 7 Mar. 2019)
Devane, Andrew, 'Space About Buildings', in Patrick Delany (ed.), *Dublin: A City in Crisis* (RIAI, 1975)
Fitzpatrick, J. E., *Root and Branch: Allied Irish Banks Yesterday, Today and Tomorrow* (AIB, 1979)
Jones, Karl, 'AIB Details Plans for £5m Ballsbridge Site', *Irish Times*, 15 Dec.1973
Jones, Karl, 'New AIB Headquarters to be Formally Topped Out Today', *Irish Times*, 1 Jun. 1977

McDonald, Frank, *The Destruction of Dublin* (Gill & MacMillan, 1985)

Mozingo, Louise, *Pastoral Capitalism: A History of Suburban Corporate Landscapes* (MIT Press, 2011)

Murray, Cormac, 'Garden Bank: The AIB Bankcentre', in *Architecture Ireland AI Extra Building Review* (16 Nov. 2015)

Ruane, Frances, 'The Allied Irish Bank Art Collection', *The GPA Irish Arts Review Yearbook* (1988)

Case Study
Papal Cross, Acres Road, Phoenix Park, Dublin 8, 1979

Ellen Rowley

Today in the early 21st century, the 1979 Papal visit is marked by the soaring 35m high white steel cross, set atop a grassy mound in the middle of Phoenix Park's 'fifteen acres' site. The rest of the original designed landscape, including the 60 altar banners, are no longer at the site; pointing to the ephemeral nature of this commission but also to the cross as a memorial architecture and monument. The original landscape was designed by Scott Tallon Walker Architects and led by partner Ronnie Tallon. While Tallon's design talent was in evidence in the strong vertical (the cross) and horizontal (the banners) frames for Pope John Paul II's mass, the most compelling aspects of this ephemeral architecture were around the logistics and planning of such a massive gathering.

Here was the biggest public event ever experienced in Ireland and following rumours, the Papal visit was only confirmed, and the architects appointed eight weeks before Pope John Paul II was to come, on 29 September 1979. To understand the urgency, from design and fabrication perspectives alone, a normal steel contract in late-1970s Ireland would take 18 weeks: six weeks to deliver the material and 12 weeks for fabrication and construction. But the team had only eight weeks altogether. Also, the architects were appointed by Dublin Diocese's Archbishop Ryan on the eve of the builders' holidays (first Friday of August 1979) and their contractors, Sisk, had to recall many workers back from annual leave. The third great challenge was the precarious lack of knowledge around numbers. Should the architects aim for a congregation of one million or more? Ireland's unpredictable climate and the volatile political situation in Northern Ireland, and subsequent terrorist activity, added further to the diocesan and architectural anxiety. Moreover, a central requirement was that each step of each event was to be televised, to an audience of potentially one thousand-million viewers. As such, televisual technology had to be embedded into the design and organisation from the outset.

In the end, the Pope landed by helicopter in the Phoenix Park shortly after midday, amid blue skies and to a crowd of 1.3 million. While his three-day Irish visit involved public ceremonies at Galway, Knock, Limerick and Drogheda, Dublin was the focal point and the first place, setting the stage and tone of this national and international momentous occasion. It was the first time that the Pope had set foot in Ireland; an Ireland which strongly identified as Roman Catholic but which, by the late 1970s was fast secularising. Ronnie Tallon and his colleagues, with the team of engineers, builders, manufacturers, craftspeople and technical experts, created the most appropriate landscape and architecture to function in both pragmatic and celebratory terms. The elegant cross is all that remains. It acts as a visual marker in the predominantly low-lying green and wooded landscape of the Phoenix Park. In its luminous whiteness, the cross barely shows signs of its 40-plus years as it is innately robust and simple. In 2019, the engineering

Site strategy map
(Courtesy of Scott Tallon Walker image collection)

company Weslin carried out thorough refurbishment works of the lower cross's paint surface and of the stone areas, paving and tarmacadam, as well as restoring the engraving, which reads: 'Moladh go deo le Dia [Praised be God Forever]. Pope John Paul II offered mass at this place on 29th September 1979. Be converted every day'.

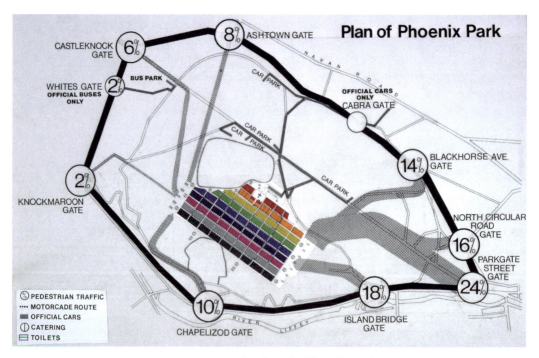

Case Study: Papal Cross, Phoenix Park

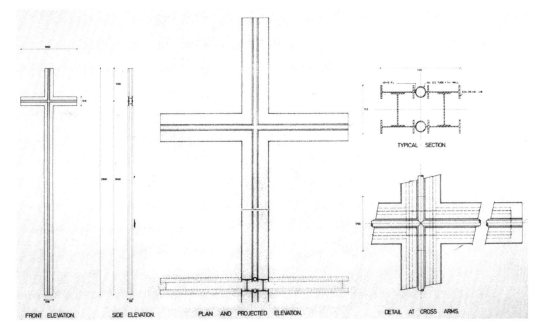

Detail drawing of steel cross (Courtesy of Scott Tallon Walker image collection)

Design Strategy for an Outdoor Cathedral

The Papal Cross's original brief is best described, to paraphrase Scott Tallon Walker and their photographic collaborator John Donat, as a 'design strategy'. And that strategy can be broken down into the needs and elements of visual perspective, sound, personal space, movement and collective facility. The primary architectural design was the altar area which would ultimately frame the Pope and enable the unprecedented gathering of people to visually and spiritually participate in the Papal mass. Ronnie Tallon reputedly sketched this out over a two-day period, settling on a soaring vertical element which would be counterbalanced by a wide horizontal element. These two elements were foregrounded by the third critical element, the altar or ground of the design.

Tallon's vertical element was of course the steel cross and he worked closely with engineers, Ove Arup and the steel workers, J. & C. McGloughlin, so that the most elegant and soaring profile could be achieved, in the shortest possible time. For Tallon, the guiding principle was height and as a committed Dubliner, the precedent of note was the Dublin landmark, bombed some 13 years before the Pope's visit, Nelson's Pillar, which rose to 125 feet high (38 metres). Tallon's cross didn't quite make that; being limited to the power of available cranes – two 100-tonne mobile cranes were used – it rises to 35 metres above ground level and at 5.1 metres from the top, it has 4.5 metre-long arms to either side of the shaft. The cross

Clergy gather at the open-air cathedral (John Donat / RIBA Collection)

comprised six rolled steel joists and 5km of welding was necessary in its construction. For the duration of the mass and assembly, the cross appeared out of a carpeted and stepped podium, constructed from scaffolding and designed to resemble a ziggurat. However, the cross is in fact constructed on a concrete box or chamber, measuring twelve metres long x nine metres wide x five metres high. At the cross's base, it is secured to a socket on the floor of the concrete chamber. Wind was a very real concern and as the daily papers recorded, the steel components' journey from McGloughlin's yard at Inchicore, over the River Liffey and along the quays, had to be aborted on the 13 September due to high winds. The next day, wind being calmer, the 30-ton cross was erected.

For the horizontal counterpoint, Tallon planned for 60 individual banners, measuring 60 feet high, to run in a line behind the cross. Though imagined from the outset, with Tallon turning to artist and former colleague, Pat Scott to design them, their production was one of the last aspects of the original brief. Tall white with gold chevron motifs, the banners were hoisted onto flagpoles, supplied by English firm, Piggott Brothers and they were designed to contribute aurally as well as visually. They flapped and moved in the wind, like a kinetic wall, as per Tallon's prescription and the engineer's calculations, but the day before the mass, more than half of the banners were torn down by winds bringing hundreds of seamstresses to the site to repair them.

The ground on which Pope John Paul II would say the mass was created by means of scaffolding and timber stepping over the concrete chamber

Case Study: Papal Cross, Phoenix Park

Close up of the podium and cross of the open-air cathedral (John Donat / RIBA Collection)

base for the cross, forming what Tallon likened to a ziggurat. Upon this platform or ziggurat stage, Tallon placed a massive altar extending to 20 feet in width and just over three feet high. Seeking liturgical guidance from the Diocesan representative Monsignor Thomas Fehily, Tallon commissioned Thomas (Tom) Glendon (see Artane Oratory carving) to layout and carve the 'Sancti Venite' – a eucharistic hymn about St Patrick – across the altar walls. Above this long low altar was the Papal *baldaccino* comprising a white steel frame and two flanking canopies which sheltered the 250 concelebrants. In the white and red vestments, designed by Joan Merrigan and sewn by women from Sallynoggin, Co. Dublin; in Patrick Scott's banners (made in various convents around the country); in the ciboria (for communion bread) made by 40 potters, the architects determined a 'white' unifying aesthetic.

    Tallon considered all elements together, even bringing in a tapestry for the Pope's robing chamber by a Polish artist, Anna Urbanowicz which the architect had previously seen at a 1979 exhibition of Polish art in Dublin. Tallon's penchant for clarity was everywhere in evidence. He invited two carpet producers Des Kelly and Curragh Carpets to contribute and both companies offered their services and material for free. In the end, over two acres of carpet was employed – grey for the altar ziggurat and red for the nave. This was, after all, an outdoor cathedral and Tallon created a *Gesamtkunstwerk* or a total work of art.

More Than Concrete Blocks Volume 3

Logistical Precision

Having been appointed on the first Friday of August 1979, with eight weeks to design and construct everything, the architects gathered all the consultants necessary to make the event at a meeting in their Merrion Square offices by midday the following Monday. Tallon was clear-sighted and sure-footed throughout the process and for the first and last time in the history of Scott Tallon Walker, the three partners (Ronnie Tallon, Robin Walker and Niall Scott) worked very closely together on the same project. The design strategy meetings were the stuff of legend, taking place most evenings and often running late into the night. RTÉ seconded a staff member, Michael Croke and two nerve centres evolved – the architects' offices on Merrion Square and the Red House, at Clonliffe College.

From the wind bracing of the cross to the baking of 835,000 hosts; from recruiting 2,000 eucharistic ministers to training a 5,000-strong choir, this was a story of logistics and ambition. The chosen site, measuring 180 acres, had no services at all. As such, draining, water supply, toilets, electricity and catering had to be brought in. During the weeks before 29 September 1979, 3.7 miles of ring-main water supply were installed; 1,500 toilet cubicles were provided, draining to soakways and to the miles of installed drains; and 77 catering points were created.

Though unimpeded for the anticipated crowds, such an open space represented a significant amount of wind. Ove Arup conducted major non-linear computer analyses to create the structures of cross, fabric-tensioned dais and *baldaccino*, which would withstand the wind. Before any such analysis was undertaken, the engineers surveyed the site using tacheometry, thereby gaining knowledge of level changes and becoming better able to plan the height for the altar. The architects set out to create an intimate situation for the congregation and they placed altar, ceremonial dais and cross at 40 feet so to maximise visibility for the majority. After surveying the site, earth had to be excavated for the carpark areas and for the cross's base. This base remains today and is a reinforced concrete chamber, set onto foundations and cast on site. The functional and technical ingenuity of the project is clear in the secondary use of the concrete chamber as a vestry and restroom for the Pope on the day.

Another key area of technical and practical concern was movement. Niall Scott studied the park exhaustively, calculating (as is written on the architects' site maps and drawings) that with eight people per minute

Case Study: Papal Cross, Phoenix Park

entering the park, it would take three hours to fill and then empty the park. He designed the Popemobile route following his analysis that '3.295 miles at five miles per hour equals forty-seven minutes' (Scott, Oct. 2019). He also considered that each person needed six square feet of space and set to order the proceedings like a grid city of benches demarcated by routes. Major routes were 40 feet wide, lesser ones were 30 feet. Meanwhile Robin Walker was researching potential marquees and temporary structures for first aid, catering, toilets and even, for mortuary purposes, and settled on a system, the Orbit, which provided 65,000 square feet of accommodation. Reflecting on the push for a single tent system, John Donat wrote that: 'Not least of the problems was to persuade statutory authorities such as health, police and security to accept the marquee provision rather than littering the site with a rag-bag of temporary huts, mobile units and caravans.' (Donat, 1980, p. 136)

In order to accommodate over one million mass-goers, the congregation was split into a series of corrals, with each corral accommodating 1,000 people and having its own colour and code. Upon arrival into the park, every person received a corral number/sticker. The corrals were laid out in a grid pattern and were delineated by timber stakes and rope; in total, 120,000 Department of Forestry thinnings (for stakes) and 40 miles of rope (for barrier) were used.

Scott was also working closely with the OPW to solve the problem of the park's set of historic and relatively narrow gates, temporarily removing them for restoration and painting, and making a new entrance at the park's northern side. It might be said that the original brief moved into the territory of conservation. There certainly was debate about excavating and maintaining the 'fifteen acres' site, as well as the wider Phoenix Park, in the lead up to the Papal visit and the architects were acutely aware and sensitive to the site as the city's green lung and as a profoundly historic place.

The presence of television recording was critical in the subsequent design of the gathering on 29 September 1979. Tallon had to arrange the altar so that it was angled to face the sun during the broadcast. Cameras and commentary structures could not obstruct the views of the congregation, so the architects worked closely with a relatively inexperienced RTÉ: for the mass there were ten commentary booths, each one measuring 20 metres long x two metres high, and seven cameras which were placed at varying distances from the altar. For all of this there had to be stand-by circuits and power facilities in the event of power or circuit failure. And RTÉ, in broadcasting to a potential television audience of a thousand million, had to borrow equipment and circuitry from the BBC.

A special radio-telephone system was established due to the heavy volume of telephone traffic during the organisation period, followed by the extreme broadcasting demands of the three-day visit which amounted to 47 hours of live outside broadcast (OB) radio transmission and 26 hours of live OB television transmission. OB stations had to be established throughout the country and RTÉ reached out internationally for help with this infrastructure which brought the BBC in to set up 15 such OB stations.

Influences
Niall Scott recounts how the 'fifteen acres' site was prescribed to the architects as a result of the successful and comparative 31st Eucharistic Congress, which came to Dublin in 1932. However, the exact position to the south of the American ambassador's residence was dictated in terms of orientation for televising Pope John Paul II's mass. Technology and the compunction to broadcast the event to the Irish diaspora internationally were major factors in the 1979 design strategy. The architects immediately looked to contemporary mass gatherings such as the Rolling Stones concert in London's Hyde Park, and the Wembley Stadium football finals.

This was, after all, the dawn of a new type of event management and architects were to take the helm. It was also an era of oil crisis and the dawn of a stylistic shift in rejection of high Modernism. For Tallon and Walker, these were difficult design times, and the Papal Cross commission provided the perfect opportunity to bring Tallon's usual references of Ludwig Mies Van der Rohe's universal rectilinear formalism and the Imperial Villa in Kyoto (Katsura-Rikyu) to an alternative and more festive manifestation. At the Phoenix Park, we find a white measured gridded design experience, enlivened with colour and movement.

In his analysis of Tallon's impact, when the older architect won his RIAI Lifetime Achievement Award in 2010, Shane O'Toole pointed to the *The Book of Tea* by Kakuzo Okakura (1906) stating that 'the Art of Life' underpinned the best of Tallon's work. O'Toole calls this Tallon's 'Eastern sensibility'. But more potently for the making of the Papal Cross landscape, at a troubled junction in Irish Catholic history, O'Toole situates Tallon's design vision and brilliance in Tallon's belief that tomorrow will be better than today; that progress is a positive force. Indeed, if nothing else, the Papal Mass as a design experience was optimistic.

Facts and Figures

The Papal Cross is situated in the Phoenix Park in the so-called 'fifteen acres' area, though actually the original site extended across 180 acres. This part of the park is to the south of the American ambassador's residence, off Chesterfield Road and on a road called Acres Road. The grid reference is O 113 353, and the cross arms point approximately 35° south of east and north of west (Ove Arup, unpublished engineering report, 1979). While the landscape of the cross today is open green fields, the area immediately approaching the cross was laid with tarmacadam, creating an avenue and a carpark area which is most heavily used at weekends. For the occasion in September 1979, 9,600 square yards of tarmacadam were laid for paths, carpark, helicopter pad and roads, thus forever transforming the ground surface of this wild open and somewhat vast part of Dublin's Phoenix Park. It was commissioned in August 1979 and completed eight weeks later in September 1979.

Architects: Scott Tallon Walker with Ronnie Tallon (1927–2014), as project architect and Robin Walker (1924–91) and Niall Scott as partner architects. The Papal Cross commission gained Ronnie Tallon a Papal Knighthood. For Ronnie Tallon, see Bank of Ireland essay; For Robin Walker, see PMPA HQ essay; For Niall Scott, see Port and Docks HQ essay.

Artist: Patrick Scott, artist and architect (1921–2014), contributed significantly to the aesthetic of the Papal visit with his banner design. He was named in the architects' document outlining the logistics of the event as the project's 'design consultant'. Banners, of which there were 80 – 60 for around the altar area and a further 20 were strategically placed throughout the park – were of white fabric, reputedly woven in Manchester, adorned with gold chevrons towards the top of each banner and the Papal coat of arms at the bottom. Each banner measured ten metres x two metres and they were hung from flagpoles supplied by Essex company, Piggott Brothers. According to accounts, the banners were sewn in convents throughout the country. Scott was born in Kilbrittain, Co. Cork, and studied architecture at UCD from 1939, working from 1945 for Michael Scott. He became a full-time artist in 1960, with his representation of Ireland at the Venice Biennale that year. While painting and making tapestries during the early period of his career, Scott also engaged in design work, working for instance for Signa Design Consultancy making CIÉ's logo and corporate image. He had many tapestry commissions as well as solo exhibitions through Ireland and Britain. By his death in 2014, he had become one of Ireland's primary artists of the second half of the 20th century.

Engineers: Ove Arup and Partners were centrally important to the success of the Papal visit. The partners involved were Frank Lydon, Morgan Sheehy, Ralph McGuckin and others. Arup, who was the son of a Danish consular veterinarian, was born in 1895 in Newcastle-upon-Tyne and educated in Germany. He studied mathematics and philosophy prior to his education as an engineer. He returned to the UK in 1923 and resided there until his death in 1988. Arup worked in London for two Danish engineering firms specialising in concrete before establishing Arup and Arup, a company of civil engineers and contractors, in 1938 with his cousin. This partnership was terminated in 1946 and Arup founded Ove Arup and Partners, a firm that reputedly changed the practice of engineering. He was structural engineer for such international projects as the Sydney Opera House (Australia), the Pompidou Centre (France) and Coventry Cathedral (UK), as well as Irish projects including Busáras and the RTÉ campus. Dundalk-born structural engineer, Peter Rice worked with Arup on many international projects such as the opera house. Known today as Arup, it is one of the leading engineering firms in the world. Morgan Sheehy, a structural engineer and a director of Arup until his premature death in 1992, was the lead engineer on the Papal visit project.

Client: Archbishop Dermot Ryan
Diocesan Directors of Papal Visit: Bishop Joseph Carroll, Fr Thomas Fehily
Contractors: John Sisk & Son Ltd: George H. Sisk, Sean T. McElligott, Peter Crean
Metal Work: J. & C. McGloughlin Ltd
Quantity Surveyor: John Gannon
OPW: Pascal Scanlon, Joan Forde, John Cumming, John Morgan
RTÉ: Michael Croke
Altar Panel: Thomas Glendon, sculptor and letter carver (see Artane Oratory essay)
Altar furniture and Candlesticks: Kilkenny Design Workshops, Waterford Crystal
Flagpoles: Piggott Brothers, Essex
Carpets: Des Kelly Carpets, Ltd, Dublin and Curragh Carpets, Ltd
Sound/Speakers: National Sound Producers, Ltd
Tents: Orbit Structures/Modern Display Artists – Ronald Petrie
Scaffolding: Scafform Ltd

Sources
Unpublished
Archive files, Job Number 7940, Scott Tallon Walker Archive, Merrion Square
Phoenix Park Press Cuttings file, Irish Architectural Archive
Niall Scott, interviewed by Ellen Rowley, Oct. 2019

Published
Anon., 'Papal visit creates discord', *Irish Times*, 24 May 1979
Anon., 'ESB cuts threaten Papal visit', *Irish Times*, 14 Sept. 1979
Anon., 'Irish cuisine for Papal visit', *Irish Times*, 20 Sept. 1979
Anon., 'Spending on Papal visit criticised', *Irish Times*, 28 Sept. 1979

Case Study: Papal Cross, Phoenix Park

Anon., 'Day of Faith and Gaiety. Pope John Paul II in Ireland', *Irish Times*, 1 Oct. 1979

Anon., 'Papal visit had "lasting significance"', *Irish Times*, 1 Nov. 1979

Binchy, Maeve, 'Dawn met by sea of Faces', *Irish Times*, 1 Oct. 1979

Donat, John (ed.), *The Pope in the Park: 29th September 1979. The Pastoral Visit of Pope John Paul II* (Academy Press, 1980).

Ferriter, Diarmaid, *Ambiguous Republic: Ireland in the 1970s* (Profile Books, 2013)

Finlan, Michael, 'Papal visit fittings', *Irish Times*, 29 Oct. 1979

Flanagan, Donal, 'Papal visit leaves a challenge', *Irish Times*, 23 Oct. 1979

Garvin, Tom, *Preventing the Future: Why has Ireland been Poor for so long?* (Gill & MacMillan, 2004)

Girvin, Brian, 'Church, State and Society in Ireland Since 1960', in *Eire Ireland* (Vol. 43, Nos 1 & 2, Spring/Summer 2008)

Humphreys, Joe, 'Church Refused to Surrender Papal Cross', *Irish Times*, 28 Dec. 2012

Kilfeather, Frank, 'Ecstasy over coming Papal visit', *Irish Times*, 30 July 1979

McDonald, Frank, 'No Final Decision on Cross', *Irish Times*, 26 Feb. 1980

Meagher, John, 'Sign of the cross: The designers who planned an "outdoor cathedral" in 8 weeks', *Sunday Independent*, 19 Aug. 2018

Nolan, Patrick, 'Papal visit shortened further', *Irish Times*, 1 Sept. 1979

O'Regan, John (ed.), *Scott Tallon Walker Architects: 100 Buildings and Projects, 1960–2005* (Gandon Editions, 2006)

O'Toole, Shane, Citation on Ronnie Tallon for RIAI Lifetime Achievement Award, 2010, reprinted as 'Remembering Dr Ronnie Tallon (1927–2014), RIAI Obituary of Tallon, 25 Jun. 2014, https://www.riai.ie/news/article/remembering_dr._ronald_tallon (accessed 2019)

Veritas, *The Visit of a Saint: Celebrating the 40th Anniversary of the Visit of Pope John Paul II to Ireland* (Veritas, 2019)

Walsh, Caroline, Interview with Ronnie Tallon, 'Going for a Million', *Irish Times* (special supplement), 22 Sept. 1979

Case Study
Central Bank, Dame Street, Dublin 2, 1979

Carole Pollard

In simple and straightforward terms, the Central Bank is an office building comprising seven floors of offices built over a raised and recessed ground floor reception area with two storeys of car parking in the basement below. However, the process of how the building came about, and the impact that it has had on the city since its inception in the mid–1960s were anything but straightforward. Starting in 1965, it took nine years, numerous planning applications to Dublin Corporation, and much-broadcasted postulations by a variety of architects, politicians and public figures before planning permission was finally achieved in 1974. It took another five years before the Central Bank finally occupied its new headquarters because within months of starting on site, the project erupted into an unprecedented level of controversy when it was discovered that the building was nine metres (30 feet) higher than permitted. This discovery plunged the project into one of the biggest development controversies the country had ever witnessed.

Contrary to the apparent simplicity of the building's brief, the complexity of the building's structure revealed the true genius of the building and, in turn, lay at the heart of the difficulties that Stephenson and his team encountered. The reason that the excessive height was apparent so early in the construction phase was because the building was built from the top down. This meant that even though the building was only a skeleton of its eventual self when the error was discovered, its impact was clear for all to see. Photographs from that time show two slender concrete towers (the service cores) soaring from the chasm of the excavated site below, supporting a heavy concrete slab and latticework of bulky steel perched high above the city. It is not inconceivable that if the building had been built from the bottom up, in the traditional way, the additional height might never have been noticed. Subsequently, the architectural treatment of the roof generated another planning battle and, in fact, continued to be the subject of much debate for decades afterwards.

In the years following its completion, amendments were made to the roof treatment which are discussed later in this essay. In 1991, the Central Bank commissioned architect and sculptor Eamonn O'Doherty to design a piece of sculpture, known as *Crann an Óir* (Tree of Gold), positioned on the plaza. The commission marked Dublin's year as European City of Culture and was unveiled by Taoiseach Charles Haughey. In 1999, further amendments were made to the plaza when the fountain and plant room on the south-west corner of the site was demolished and the steps to the main entrance were railed off.

In 2022, the building was given an entirely new roof by its new owners. They created a rooftop glass pavilion, inspired by I. M. Pei's pyramid at the Louvre in Paris, which will eventually house bars, restaurants, and terraces with unrivalled views across the city. The new owners also remodelled the plaza on Dame Street, excavating it to provide access to shops and

Early model of proposed development
(Courtesy of Stephenson Gibney collection at Irish Architectural Archive

restaurants on the levels below ground which were once used as a carpark. At its edges, the newly arranged plaza has a more accessible interface with the city, however, it remains to be seen whether the reduced space (which is one of only a handful of south-facing civic spaces in Dublin) continues to serve its function as a popular meeting venue for city dwellers and tourists alike. One of the most distinctive groups who gathered there regularly from the 1980s onwards were black-clad teenagers who called themselves 'Bankies'. The plaza was a focal point for civic protests of various hues and in 2011 was the location of the 'Occupy Dame Street' movement which established a camp there. Part of the global Occupy movement, the group took its name from the Occupy Wall Street demonstration in New York City's Wall Street financial district and shared similar aims. The Garda Síochána dismantled the camp during a late-night raid in March 2012. It remains to be seen whether the remodelling efforts of its new owners will have cancelled out the civic significance of the plaza so that it becomes merely another temple of commerce.

Case Study: Central Bank, Dame Street

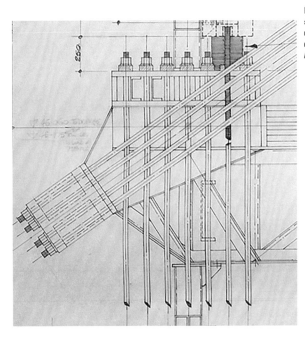

Detail of roof structure (Courtesy of Stephenson Gibney collection at Irish Architectural Archive)

The Hanging Floors of Dame Street

The Central Bank of Ireland emerged from an entity known as the Currency Commission which had offices in Foster Place (1811), an elegant but short street designed by James Gandon adjacent to the Irish Parliament Buildings (later Bank of Ireland headquarters) on College Green. The Central Bank of Ireland, was established in 1943 with particular powers and functions, including the safeguarding of the integrity of the currency and ensuring that 'in what pertains to be the control of credit, the constant and predominant aim shall be the welfare of the people as a whole.' (www.centralbank.ie, 2022)

As a result of the ongoing expansion of its services and growing importance of its role in the administration of the State, in 1965 the Central Bank purchased a site for new, larger offices on nearby on Dame Street. Architect Sam Stephenson of Stephenson Gibney & Associates (SGA) was appointed in 1966. The Bank officially announced their intentions when SGA lodged the planning application for the new building to Dublin Corporation in 1967. Interestingly, around the same time, the Central Bank appointed SGA to design the Central Bank Currency Centre at Sandyford, Co. Dublin, completed in 1974.

Two service cores under construction (Courtesy of Niall Montgomery collection at Irish Architectural Archive)

Stephenson's original scheme provided 13 floors of offices over a double height entrance floor and was topped off with a double height plant (building services) facility at roof level. This equated to a building of 17 storeys – a height that exceeded the city's tallest building at the time, Liberty Hall (1965), which stood at 16 storeys tall (see *MTCB* Vol. 2). Over a series of subsequent planning applications, the design was modified, and the height was reduced to seven storeys of office floors with the double-height entrance level retained but entered at first floor via a flight of steps from the public plaza on Dame Street. The façade was expressed as a series of alternating bands of white concrete and dark-tinted recessed glass. The uppermost floor was expressed as a thick band concealing the building's services.

Stephenson's design concept and construction methodology, developed with the expertise of Ove Arup & Partners, was unique in Ireland at the time: 'pioneering, innovative and satisfying, measured on a world scale' (O'Toole, 2011, unpaginated). Arup engineer, Frank Lydon, was vital to the structural design of Central Bank, a fact that was readily acknowledged by both Stephenson and Gibney. Central Bank was the first building in Ireland to be constructed with

Steel roof frame under construction (Courtesy of Dublin City Library & Archive)

suspended floors and the first office building to use slip-forming technique for the construction of its 45-metre-tall service cores. Each of the seven floors was assembled at ground level and lifted into position. Such was the novelty of the construction method, that the main contractors, Sisk, commissioned filmmakers to record the construction process. The 35-minute film called *The Big Bank* followed the construction of the Central Bank, beginning in 1972 and continued through protests, hold-ups and other events on site until its completion in 1979.

In his technical evaluation of the structure, Shane O'Toole determined that 'the structural system of the Central Bank is pioneering, innovative and satisfying, measured on a world scale. It is the first and only building with suspended floors in this country' (O'Toole, 2011, unpaginated). As we have seen at Poolbeg, slip-form construction was originally used on simple vertical structures, 'but from the 1960s it also came to be used for service cores in office buildings. The Central Bank was the first such Irish application of the technique' (O'Toole, 2011, unpaginated).

The suspension system is visible as cascading steel brackets which descend the building's façade, four each on the front and back and two on the sides. The building's dominant form was emphasised by the scale and depth of the horizontal bands – structure repeating with dark-tinted glass – which bore no relation to the scale of the city either in terms of volumetric

Central Bank shortly after completion in 1980 (Courtesy Stephenson Gibney collection at Irish Architectural Archive)

massing or in how solids (wall surfaces) and voids (windows) were normally dealt with. Indeed, the reconstructed elevations of Commercial Buildings (1798) on the eastern flank of the plaza in front of the building, and the former Crown Life Insurance Company building (1868) on Fownes Street, on the western edge, looked like dolls' houses by comparison with the new imposter.

Architectural Review editor, Lance Wright, described Stephenson's design as 'analogous to a sketch, drawn in a 6B pencil, inserted in the delicate filigree of the 18th-century city' (Wright, 1979, p. 351). For most Dubliners, indeed for everyone who did not have the privilege of working in the Central Bank, its defiant external expression was their only experience of Stephenson's building. In actuality, the interiors revealed a completely different experience. This may not have been immediately evident when stepping into the entrance foyer, a double-height space finished with marble floors and walls and stainless-steel lift doors, but an enormous glass curtain designed by Patrick Scott and created with purple, blue and green glass beads gave a hint of the jaw-dropping experience that lay beyond. Outwardly, the scale of Stephenson's Central Bank dwarfed the city, but on the inside, it functioned as a giant oculus, allowing the raggedy edges of the city skyline to dominate. Dublin in the late 1970s and 1980s was not accustomed to admiration, 'with its untidy roofs, its myriad small felicities,

Case Study: Central Bank, Dame Street

Boardroom with views over city (Courtesy of Stephenson Gibney collection at Irish Architectural Archive)

and its huge disfiguring blotches' (Wright, 1979, p. 352) but nonetheless, the Central Bank windows showcased the city in all its grubby glory.

With uninterrupted bands of floor to ceiling glazing, the building provided unimpeded views of the city, framed by the projecting floor planes. Because the structure was suspended from above, there were no columns to cause obstructions. All the buildings services were accommodated in the deep floor slabs which extended 1.5 metres beyond the glazing, reducing any sense of vertigo when one pressed close to the glass to peer at the city. The framing of the views was emphasised by the sloped window head which angled back to meet the coffered ceiling plane above.

Each of the seven floors provided office accommodation for bank staff, with executive offices and boardroom on the top floor. Staff canteens were located below ground level on the east side of the building – linking the main building to the ancillary offices in the (externally) reconstructed Commercial Buildings. The canteen was lit from above and furnished with bright colours – green and orange – and could be glimpsed by pedestrians passing above on the route from Dame Street through the plaza and under the building's oversailing second floor to Crown Alley and the Liffey beyond.

Aesthetic Agonising

Such was the suspicion generated by the controversy over the height of the Central Bank that *Plan* magazine commissioned an article which examined all the drawings produced for the scheme in an article entitled 'Drawings Intended to Mislead?' (*Plan*, 1974). In some regards, the suspicion was understandable because, at the time, Dublin was experiencing an unprecedented pace of redevelopment against a backdrop of increasing dereliction and loss of historic city fabric. Stephenson was a self-publicist, well known for his outspoken manner and his defence of modern architecture and had, only a few years earlier, been at the centre of the Fitzwilliam Street debacle about the demolition of 16 Georgian houses to make way for the new ESB Headquarters (see *MTCB* Vol. 2).

Wright, who regularly visited Dublin and had by this time become an expert on the city's modern architecture, used the term 'aesthetic agonising' to describe the long and contentious battle over the development of the Central Bank (Wright, 1979, p. 352). The fractious debate which was played out in the public arena can be distilled down to an argument about height – an estimated additional nine metres (30 feet) which, with the benefit of hindsight, made little difference to the impact the building had on its immediate environment, or indeed on the city centre in general. The building was higher than intended because the architects and engineers had not finalised the dimensions for the rooftop 'bridge' structure when the planning application was lodged; nor had they factored in the space requirements for the building's sophisticated air-conditioning equipment located on the uppermost floor.

So, although the building did not vary from its original intention of providing seven floors of offices, the overall height exceeded that permitted. The cost of taking down the structure to its approved height was extortionate and Stephenson refused to consider a flat roof, which in any case would not have been possible because of the structural suspension system. He argued that 'to modify the structural system would destroy this architectural concept and the opportunity of enhancing the urban scene in a unique way will have been lost' (*Irish Times*, 17 Feb. 1974). The solution, finally arrived at through negotiation, was to leave the steel structure of the roof exposed and omit the proposed copper cladding. Unease about the exposed roof profile continued however, and in the 1990s Dublin City Council (formerly Dublin Corporation) granted planning permission to finally allow the roof to be clad in copper.

Case Study: Central Bank, Dame Street

Throughout the years of argument over the building's height, Stephenson remained resolute that its height was appropriate; he never once wavered in that regard. His design concept mitigated against its height and bulk by placing the building at the back of the site, with a large plaza to the Dame Street edge. This placement effectively concealed the building from view from either Trinity College (1759) or the former Parliament Buildings on College Green (1729 and 1796) at the eastern end of Dame Street. Nonetheless, the building had considerable impact on the centre city area, particularly when viewed from the direction of one of Dublin's other major landmarks: the Ha'penny Bridge (1815). From that position, the Central Bank loomed large above Merchant's Arch (1821) and dominated the skyline along the south quays of the Liffey.

Because of the set-back, the impact on Dame Street was less adversarial than objectors had feared. Dame Street was, after all, a commercial street lined with a significant number of imposing 18th and 19th century bank and insurance company buildings (now mostly converted to other uses). Stephenson's decision to reconstruct the Commercial Buildings premises on the eastern edge of the plaza – a decision contentious because only the building's external walls were rebuilt, resulting in the loss of all of the original interiors – tempered the transition from traditional brick and stone-clad Victoriana to hard-nosed Modernism on the street surface.

To counter the views of the conservationists who deplored both the Central Bank building and the unfaithful manipulation of the Commercial Buildings, Stephenson drew on the support of international experts to support his argument. Sir Donald Gibson, former City Officer and Planning Officer of Coventry supported Stephenson's application for permission to retain the additional height, as did Professor Myles Wright, professor of Civic Design at University of Liverpool, who said, 'The difference in height is likely to be imperceptible and … it would therefore be against the public interest to enforce changes in the present design on the Central Bank and its architects' (*Irish Times*, 17 Feb. 1974).

In 1991, Eamonn O'Doherty's sculpture, *Crann an Óir* was erected on the plaza. It was commissioned by the Central Bank to mark Dublin's year as European City of Culture and was unveiled by Taoiseach Charles Haughey. In 1992, planning permission was granted to clad the exposed roof structure in copper. This was completed in 1993. The Central Bank remained at Dame Street until 2017 when they moved to a new headquarters building in the

Case Study: Central Bank, Dame Street

Docklands. The building was bought by Hines, a privately owned global real estate investment company who, in partnership with the Petersen Group, redeveloped it. The architects for this major project, completed in 2022, were Henry J. Lyons with DBFL consulting engineers.

Stephenson's intention from the outset was to design a building that would dominate the city skyline. This was, after all, to be the headquarters of one of the country's most powerful institutions. Height and bulk were appropriate tools to express economic power, particularly at a time when Ireland was flexing its financial muscle. As we have seen with many of the buildings illustrated in this book series, architecture was a primary means of expressing power or intent. Despite the obstacles placed in his way – albeit the greatest obstacle was one of his own making – Stephenson's vision and tenacity delivered a building that both physically and metaphorically fulfilled its purpose. Described by Wright as a 'contained explosion' (Wright, 1979, p. 352), the Central Bank HQ changed Dublin's urban landscape for all time.

Although it is no longer occupied by the Central Bank of Ireland – that entity has relocated to Dublin's new financial district in the Docklands – it retains its position in the national psyche as a defiant symbol of 20th-century Ireland. Now known as Central Plaza, its new owners have reimagined it as a 21st-century temple of commerce, containing offices, shops, and restaurants. In the process, all original internal fixtures and fittings have been removed so that the building is a hollowed-out version of its former self. While the new iteration has been slow to fill with new tenants, the developers promise that when the rooftop bar and restaurant eventually open, all the people of Dublin will be able to experience the magnificent views over the city: that pleasure will no longer be the preserve of a privileged few.

Facts and Figures

The Central Bank acquired the site on Dame Street in 1965 and appointed Stephenson Gibney & Associates as their architects in 1966. Planning permission for a 15-storey tower was refused in 1969. In August 1970, permission was granted for an eight-storey block with 'hung' floors and granted permission in March 1972. According to O'Toole:

The building contract was placed in September 1972 while various planning applications to regularise the situation continued to be lodged. By the time the Corporation decided to refuse planning permission for the changes in November 1973, much of the roof superstructure was already in place. Work was stopped. A public enquiry followed in 1974 and permission was not finally granted until January 1975. It involved a compromise to reduce the height marginally by omitting the proposed copper roof. Completed in 1978, several years behind schedule, the Central Bank ended up costing £10 million – more than five times the original estimate (O'Toole, 2011, unpaginated).

The Central Bank was officially opened on 7 December 1979. In 1980, Sisk's showed a specially commissioned film 'The Big Bank', a 35 minute film that followed the construction of the Central Bank made by Bill St Leger and John Ross.

In 1991, Eamonn O'Doherty's sculpture, *Crann an Óir* was erected on the plaza. It was commissioned by the Central Bank to mark Dublin's year as European City of Culture and was unveiled by Taoiseach Charles Haughey. In 1992, planning permission was granted to clad the exposed roof structure in copper. This was completed in 1993. The Central Bank remained at Dame Street until 2017 when they moved to a new headquarters building in the Docklands. The building was bought by Hines, who, in partnership with the Petersen Group, redeveloped it. The architects for this major project, completed in 2022, were Henry J. Lyons with DBFL consulting engineers.

Architects: Stephenson Gibney & Associates (from 1975, Stephenson Associates) led by Sam Stephenson and assisted by Aidan Murray, Brian Traynor, Gerry Flynn, Paul Richardson, and Bronagh Moriarty. Sam Stephenson's biography can be found in the Molyneux House essay (p.).
Structural engineers: Frank Lydon and team at Ove Arup & Partners
Mechanical Engineers: J. A. Kenny & Partners
Main Contractor: John Sisk & Sons Ltd
The Association of Consulting Engineers of Ireland gave its 1980 Excellence Award for a structural project to the Central Bank.

Sources

Unpublished
Fallon, Paraic, 'Addition of Former Central Bank including restaurant annexe, Public Plaza including *Crann an Óir* sculpture, Dame Street, Dublin 2 to the Record of Protected Structures in accordance with Section 54 and 55 of the Planning and Development Act, 2000'(Presented to Dublin City Council, undated)
O'Toole, Shane, 'Central Bank of Ireland', *Documentation Project and Pilot Survey of the Architecture of the 20th Century – Book 3: Case Studies Presented to the Dublin City Council & the Heritage Council,* (2011)
Stephenson Gibney & Associates archive at the Irish Architectural Archive (IAA), Dublin
St. Leger, Bill and John Ross, *The Big Bank* (35-minute film, 1978)

Published
Anon., 'Bank Building Change Would Cost £1.3m', *Irish Times,* 19 Feb. 1974
Anon., 'Central Bank Building' in *Build* (Vol. 11, No. 8, Jun. 1975)
Anon., 'Architeet laude Central Bank building', *Irish Times,* 16 Jan. 1980
Anon., *Building a Business: 150 years of the Sisk Group* (SISK, Associated Editions Ltd, 2009)
McDonald, Frank, *The Destruction of Dublin* (Gill & MacMillan, 1985)
McDonald, Frank, 'Bright future planned for former Central Bank' (2017) www.frankmcdonald.ie/2017/08/bright-future-planned-for-former-central-bank (accessed 2021)
McSweeney, Finbar, 'Slipforming of Twin Cores for Central Bank Offices, Dame Street', in *Iris* (1 Sept. 1973)
Nowlan, Kevin B., and Edward McParland, 'A Planning Crisis in Dublin', in *Country Life* (17 Jan. 1974)
O'Beirne, Tomás (ed.), 'Central Bank Focus', in *Architecture in Ireland* (No. 2, 1980)
Quinn, Michael, 'Drawings Intended to Mislead? The Strange Sage of the Central Bank', in *Plan* (Vol. 4, No., 14, Dec./Jan. 1974)
Sudjic, Deyan, 'Ireland on the Rise', in *Design Magazine* (Nov. 1980)
Wilkins, Louis, 'A Storey too far', in *Building Design* (17 Nov. 1978)
Wright, Lance (ed.), 'Bank Statement', in *Architectural Review* (Vol. 166, Dec. 1979)

Case Study
AnCO Training Centre, Jamestown Road, Finglas, Dublin 11, 1981

Aoibheann Ní Mhearáin

The AnCO training centre at Finglas was one of many interventions aimed at tackling unemployment in Ireland in the 1970s and 1980s. Built in the recently expanded northside suburb of Finglas in 1981, the training centre sits in the middle of a large greenfield site, surrounded by a landscaped carpark and edged by sweeping roads. Opposite are suburban housing estates of replicated houses interspersed with wide open green spaces; the centre was aimed at serving this community, addressing local needs for training and employment. Identified as a suitable area for housing relocation from the city centre, Finglas was also marked for manufacturing and industrial development. And so, concurrent with major housing construction from the 1950s onwards, investment in industrial development occurred in Finglas, producing a series of industrial estates. Into this mix, the training centre arrived, aimed at upskilling the industrial workforce and offering more rewarding work for the local employee.

Designed by the architects Scott Tallon Walker, the centre consists of a series of discrete, interconnected rectangular buildings; first is the two-storey front of house administration building and, past it, the much larger single volume workshop hall accommodating the industrial training spaces, behind which is a service yard and linear service building. Together these buildings make a composition of low-lying rectangular forms, carefully disposed against each other in the open landscape setting. Punctuating the studied order of the three buildings are seven visually arresting two-metre-high steel portal frames spanning the workshop roof and returning down the sides of the building. Originally painted in a bright red colour, striking against the beige and black of the workshop and administration buildings, these have now faded to a salmon pink.

AnCO was established as a training organisation in 1967 and lasted 21 years until 1988 when it was amalgamated with the National Manpower Service and the Youth Employment Agency to become FÁS. FÁS was dissolved, after much controversy, in 2011 and its activities are now administered by a series of agencies, including SOLAS, Intreo and the Education and Training Boards (ETB). The training centre at Finglas is currently run by the City of Dublin ETB, which works under the auspices of the Department of Education and Skills. Despite the administrative changes, the building is still in use as a training centre, with the workshop largely intact and much of the same training taking place some 40 years after its construction. The administration building continues in its original function as a teaching, canteen and administration area, but has seen a greater change in the curriculum with computer training featuring more and more. A two-bay extension to the north of the administration building and re-cladding of the building's exterior was carried out in 2009 by Scott Tallon Walker Architects.

Detail of wall finishes (Courtesy of Scott Tallon Walker image collection)

Architecture for the Unemployed

An Chomhairle Oiliúna, known as AnCO, the Industrial Training Authority, was established in 1967 under the Industrial Training Act. The organisation's aim was to develop the industrial economy, by supplying the sector with a trained workforce, and also to improve the quality of life of the trainees by providing them with specialist skills and a greater chance of employment. At the time the training centre was planned, in the early 1970s, the industrial sector had become a larger employer than the agricultural sector for the first time in the state's history. Government policies were directed at developing this growing sector and the Industrial Development Authority (IDA) was tasked with generating and implementing the polices that would secure continued industrial growth. The IDA's regional industrial plan of 1973–77 divided the country into nine planning regions and aimed for the creation of 55,000 jobs in the manufacturing sector. AnCO and the IDA worked closely together, with the IDA offering sites and factory space for AnCO's growth, while the European Economic Community (EEC) funded these developments from the European Social Fund. AnCO's role, in turn, was to

Case Study: AnCO Training Centre, Finglas

provide a trained workforce to facilitate the IDA's planned expansion of the industrial economy. In particular, AnCO recognised the lack of women in industry and developed courses targeted at upskilling women and allowing them entry to the industrial workforce.

AnCO's expansion programme of 1974 envisaged an increase in trainees from 3,000 in 1974 to 11,500 in 1978. The development of the training centres was key to achieving this plan and Scott Tallon Walker Architects were commissioned by AnCO to design the Finglas centre in 1978. They concurrently designed and built a second workshop building, of the same design, for AnCO in Ballyfermot. These training centres were designed to emulate the factory or industrial setting, with trainees 'clocking in' and 'clocking out' each day, and the courses on offer in each of the training centres were designed to respond to local industrial need. The National Manpower Agency, a type of recruitment service, found trainees for the courses and helped them find employment following their training. Along with the Finglas and Ballyfermot training facilities, AnCO developed training centres in Baldoyle (1983), Tallaght (extension, 1981) and Loughlinstown (1983, A. & D. Wejchert) during this period. Each of the centres was located in an area suitable for industrial development and with a population of relatively high unemployment, to better reach the potential trainees.

Finglas developed rapidly in the post-war years, beginning as a small village, and expanding to a population of over 40,000 by the time the AnCO training centre was constructed. Early development in the 1950s and 1960s focused on housing development only, without the required social infrastructure to accompany these. Finglas was incorporated into Dublin Corporation in 1953 and at least 60 per cent of the houses built during this rapid expansion were built by the Corporation. In the 1970s development included the establishment of two new industrial estates, one of these on Jamestown Road, the site of the training centre. The centre was aimed at serving the local and surrounding areas of North Dublin where the population was expected to continue its rapid growth through the 1980s, though many of this expanding population were identified by AnCO as un-skilled or semi-skilled workers. Indeed, in 1983, the year the Finglas centre officially opened, the Workers Party TD, Proinsias De Rossa, noted in the Dáil that youth unemployment in Finglas was estimated at 50 per cent.

Steel frame and walkways (Courtesy of Scott Tallon Walker image collection)

Designing for Industrial Training

It was in this context of extreme unemployment that Scott Tallon Walker built the training centre in Finglas for AnCO, an exquisitely detailed industrial architecture, with a striking two-metre-high red superstructure holding up the roof of the training workshop for the apprentices below. Outside the social context of Ireland in the 1980s, in the international sphere of architecture, a shift was taking place towards new ideas of so-called Post-Modernism, away from the dominance of 20th-century modernist architecture. Post-Modernist architecture, and its subset of High-Tech architecture, allowed for greater freedom of expression for architects and was a reaction to the increasingly rigid strictures of modernism as well as its perceived failings. This new movement embraced colour and decoration as a counterpoint to the ordered and sober nature of mid-20th-century modernism.

The training centre at Finglas demonstrates these competing forces in its architectural design, combining as it does sombre ordered façades with the flamboyance of a red truss overhead. But the expressed roof structure of the AnCO Training centre in Finglas is a direct reference to the work of the highly influential German-American modernist architect, Ludwig Mies van der Rohe (Mies) many of whose projects adopt similar external roof trusses providing large open spaces, free of structure for the halls below. Most notable of these is Crown Hall in the Illinois Institute of Technology in Chicago. Scott Tallon Walker had built a reputation adapting Mies' work to the Irish context (see Bank of Ireland HQ, and PMPA HQ essays).

Case Study: AnCO Training Centre, Finglas

These oversized and expressed roof structures, by Mies and Scott Tallon Walker, display a shared commitment to Modernist ideals; the designs embrace the industrial production methods developed through the 19th and 20th centuries, and explore the new structural and formal possibilities that steel and reinforced concrete could offer.

Ronald Tallon, the partner in charge of the training centre, had generated a reputation as a designer for industry, most notably, at the Carroll's Factory, Dundalk, Co. Louth (1967–70). In his work Tallon elevated the ordinary factory building, produced of standardised industrial materials, and treated it as a building of much greater significance; he created 20th-century cathedrals for industry and progress. This interest and care in the methods of industrial production, to create beautiful and significant pieces of architecture, is

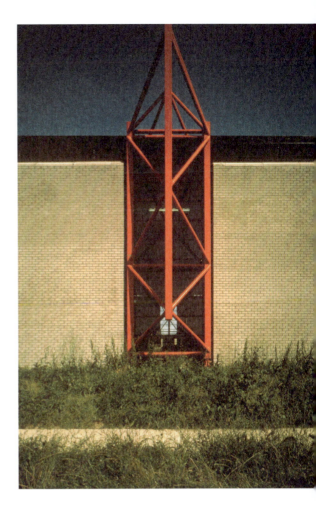

evident in the training centre in Finglas, with the steelwork deployed beyond the purely functional and instead celebrated through its expression in the walls and roof.

The design embraced flexibility and adaptability, a core principle of Tallon's ethos, through the use of a consistent 2.4 metre grid throughout, organising the plans and the elevation. The expressive external lattice portal frame also allows for flexibility of use and future adaptability, as it provides an incredible open space, measuring 36 metres wide, 115 metres long and 7.8 metres high hall uninterrupted by columns. The open 'landscape' of the workshop floor can therefore be endlessly re-configured for new uses or training functions. The workshop floor, in its original design, was populated by training areas demarcated by low blockwork walls, with each trade allocated a dedicated zone on the floor. The training centre was designed to accommodate 408 training places in 1982, the first full year of

More Than Concrete Blocks Volume 3

its operation, a third of these places being allocated to apprentices and the remaining provided in adult education. Training courses ranged in duration from four weeks to 36 weeks across 18 different courses, mostly focused on technical and construction skills and trades, but also included training in office administration and a course dedicated to return-to-work for women. Over time the course offerings have changed, though the workshop building has retained its core architectural concept. Indeed, in 2009, Scott Tallon Walker successfully extended the smaller two-storey administration building, adding an additional two bays, thus proving Tallon's thesis of expandability. Tallon was thinking about the future when he designed the building, allowing it to adapt over time. The architectural methods used to achieve this, include the open plan, the use of the grid and the superstructure, which combined, ensure the continued use of the building 40 years after its construction.

The training centre in Finglas was commissioned in 1978, between the formal establishment of Scott Tallon Walker Architects in 1975 and the departure of Robin Walker in 1982. The lattice portal frame situates the project in the moment of its construction, in the ambit of the emerging High Tech architecture in the UK. Scott Tallon Walker's use of the superstructure here suggests a break from the controlled expression and materials of the modern era for a more High-Tech expression, evident in both the colour chosen and the choice of space frame over truss; it is clear a new direction is emerging in the practice, evolving from its Modernist roots and facing the 21st century.

Case Study: AnCO Training Centre, Finglas

Facts and Figures

The AnCO Training Centre is located in Poppintree Industrial Estate, Jamestown Road, Finglas, Dublin 11. The building was commissioned in 1978 and construction was completed in 1981. The first full year of courses were completed in 1982 and the building was officially opened in March 1983.

Architects: Scott Tallon Walker, led by Ronnie Tallon assisted by Peter de Loughry (project architect) and Brian Roe. Ronald Tallon (1927–2014) (see Tallon's biography in Bank of Ireland HQ essay).

Artist: Patrick Scott (1921–2014) (see Papal Cross essay).
Tallon commissioned a tapestry to be hung in the canteen area. The tapestry was completed for the opening in 1983 and now hangs in the first-floor reception area.

Structural Engineer: Joseph McCullough & Partners
Quantity Surveyor: Desmond MacGreevy & Partners
Mechanical and Electrical Consultants: Varming Mulcahy Reilly
Main Contractor: P. J. Walls
Steel Sub-Contractor: Shannon Foundry
Steel Windows: Anderson & Pearson

Sources

Unpublished
Job files, AnCO, F.0398; F.0391; F.0397 – Scott Tallon Walker Archive, Dublin

Published
Anon., 'Detailed Development Plans for Finglas', *Irish Times*, 25 Mar. 1973
Anon., *The Industrial Training Authority Annual Report & Accounts 1973/74* (The Industrial Training Authority, 1974)
Anon., *Learning for Life* 12-part programme series on education, Radio Telefís Éireann (RTÉ), 29 May 1974, https://www.rte.ie/archives/2014/0306/600492-learning-for-life/
Anon., *Training for Individuals: Expansion Programme 1974/78* (The Industrial Training Authority, 1974)
Anon., *Training Centre Design* (The Industrial Training Authority, Research and Planning Unit, 1975)
Brown, Michael, *Finglas Through the Ages* (Finglas Environmental Heritage Project, 1991)
Hill, J. R. (ed.), *A New History of Ireland, Volume VII, Ireland 1921–84* (Oxford University Press, 2003)
Lee, J. J., *Ireland 1912–1985: Politics and Society* (Cambridge University Press, 1989)
Keogh, Dermot, 'Ireland 1972–84', in J. R. Hill (ed.), *A New History of Ireland, Volume VII, Ireland 1921–84,* (Oxford University Press, 2010)
Johnson, D. S., and Liam Kennedy, 'Two Economies in Ireland in the Twentieth Century', in Colm Keane (ed.), *The Jobs Crisis: The Thomas Davis Lecture Series* (Mercier Press in association with Radio Telefís Éireann (RTÉ), 1993)

Case Study
The Dublin Port Centre Building, Dublin 1, 1981

Carole Pollard

The Dublin Port Centre Building is the headquarters of the Dublin Port Company which administers all the activity of Dublin Port. Located adjacent to the primary deep berthing dock at Alexandra Basin, the building rises six storeys above a concrete podium, surveying the mouth of the River Liffey and the vast industrial expanses of the eastern Docklands. Standing two city blocks back from the Liffey's north bank, the building is still at a remove from recent commercial and residential development advancing eastwards along the north quays. Its location is the frontier point between the city's commercial activity and the industrial flatlands of the port. Looking east from the Port Centre, the R. & H. Hall Grain Silo by Frederick G. Hicks (1920) (see *MTCB* Vol. 1) standing at more than 15 storeys, is the only other vertical structure within view, except for the distant Poolbeg Chimneys standing to the south, and the distinctive red lighthouse on the South Wall.

Prior to significant re-ordering of the site and its boundary in 2017, the Port Centre building was visible only as a top heavy, concrete-framed office building set behind the stone boundary wall on East Wall Road. The glass-clad mass of the building is held deeply within the concrete frame, casting shadows on the glass which vary in accordance with the height and position of the sun and emphasise the building's fortress-like presence. When viewed from a distance, the dominance of the concrete horizontal elements reinforces that planar emphasis but on closer inspection, and especially when experienced at the entrance level podium, the slender vertical elements contribute an elegance not evident from afar. The additional height of the ground (entrance) floor bay contributes further to the subtle but sophisticated proportionality of the building's form.

The skeletal form of the building echoes that of the gantry cranes on the surrounding port sites. Indeed, the industrial context was the inspiration behind the refurbishment works carried out in 2017 which aimed at opening up the Port & Docks HQ site and better integrating it into the city. A refurbished 1960s heritage crane is a new landmark on the site boundary and Corten steel 'turnstiles' (in lieu of solid walls and barrier fencing) give better visibility from East Wall Road. The original ground treatment of square concrete slabs and gravel beds has been removed and replaced with new paving. The soft landscaping has similarly been overhauled includes the installation of a stainless-steel sphere sculpture. The insertion of new artwork is notable because of the demise of the original sculptural piece commissioned by architect Niall Scott in 1980. Michael Warren's large timber sculpture, *Noche Oscura*, designed especially for its place, was removed soon after its installation by the Port Company directors because they did not like it. Its current location is not known.

Model of low-rise scheme, 1977
(Courtesy of Scott Tallon Walker image collection)

An Isolated Oasis

The authorities who have controlled the activities of Dublin Port over the centuries have operated under various names and have headquartered in various locations along the River Liffey. Prior to the construction of Burgh's Customs House at Essex Bridge in 1707, the exact location of the Port Authority is not recorded but presumed to be at Wood Quay where the port was then located. In the late 18th century port activity moved eastwards, closer to the mouth of the Liffey and the Port Authority transferred to James Gandon's Custom House which was completed in 1791. In 1794 the Authority moved to 4–6 Lower Sackville Street (now O'Connell Street), and from 1801 until 1976, was located at the Ballast Office on Westmoreland Street. In 1836 deep-water berths were constructed at the North Wall and these were extended in the 1870s. In the early 1900s the deep-water berth at Alexandra Basin was completed, and in the 1940s Ocean Pier to the south-east of Alexandra Basin came into operation. The 1950s saw the introduction of the first roll-on, roll-off facilities and as a result, container traffic has dominated port business since the 1960s. During the 20th century, activity at Dublin Port grew exponentially and the Port Authority became known as the Dublin Port and Docks Board. In 1953 the Board ran an architectural competition for a new headquarters, but this project did not proceed.

From the 1960s, as Ireland's economic situation improved, city centre property sites became increasingly appealing to speculative developers

Case Study: Dublin Port Centre Building

View of HQ building from across the Liffey (Courtesy of STW image collection / Dublin Port Archives)

who were enjoying an unprecedented boom in office development in Dublin. In 1975, the Board were offered the opportunity of selling the Ballast Office (built 1803, 1866) to Royal Liver Friendly Society, enabling them to cash in and relocate their headquarters closer to the port where their core business activity was based. The Royal Liver Friendly Society controversially demolished the Ballast Office in 1979 and replaced it with a replica building of larger square footage (designed by architects, Scott Tallon Walker). The sale of the Ballast Office provided the Board with the means to build a bespoke headquarters building on land they already owned at the Custom House Docks.

In the 1970s, the eastern part of the city was remote and sparsely developed. Butt Bridge was the most easterly river crossing. Talbot Memorial Bridge (which links Memorial Road and Custom House Quay on the north bank of the river to Moss Street and City Quay on the south bank) was not completed until 1978 and the East Link (Tom Clarke) Bridge, the last bridge on the Liffey before it opens out into Dublin Bay was opened in 1984. On the north side of the river, the lands between the Custom House and the

Entrance podium with Michael Warren sculpture (Courtesy of Scott Tallon Walker image collection)

Alexandra Basin were occupied predominantly by industrial warehouses and storage facilities. The Board owned a 27-acre site surrounding the Custom House Docks and it was here that they planned to build their new offices. Planning permission was granted in 1976 but this plan was abandoned when it became obvious that the Custom House Docks site had greater commercial value as a development site: negotiations between the government and the Port & Docks Board resulted in the establishment of the Custom House Docks Authority under the Urban Renewal Act of 1986. This, in turn, led to the development of the Irish Financial Services Centre (IFSC), the Custom House Docks Quarter and generated future redevelopment of Dublin's Docklands in the decades since. While negotiations over the sale of the Custom House Docks site were underway, the Board rented office space in Gandon House on Amiens Street on a five year lease from 1976.

The Board decided to proceed with developing their headquarters on other lands in their ownership adjacent to Alexandra Basin. They drew up a short list of five architectural firms who they felt had the necessary skills and experience to produce a distinctive landmark building. The list included Robinson Keefe & Devane, A. & D.Wejchert, and Scott Tallon Walker. In 1977, following interviews with each of the shortlisted practices, Scott Tallon Walker were appointed. One of their first tasks was to assist the Board in drawing up a five year development plan aimed at improving port facilities. Permission was then sought and received from the Minister for Environment to re-zone the land at Alexandra Basin from industrial to office use.

Case Study: Dublin Port Centre Building

The new headquarters building, financed by the sale of the Custom House Docks site, was completed in September 1981. Its occupation coincided with the beginning of a deep economic recession that would last for more than a decade, stymying the Board's plans for further port improvement works. From the time of its completion in 1981 until the end of the 20th century, the Port & Docks Board HQ stood as an isolated office block outpost on the eastern reaches of the Liffey, surrounded by dock cranes and shipping containers. In 1997 the authority was renamed the Dublin Port Company. Despite the encroachment of high-specification office blocks and luxury residential developments marching eastwards along the north quays, the Alexandra Dock site remains an isolated oasis surrounded by freight yards and railway sidings and divided from the city by heavy port traffic on East Wall Road.

An Anchor on the Northside Docks

There were very few office developments on the north side of Dublin city during the 1970s: the Irish Life Centre (1978 and 1986) being an obvious exception. With most Dublin Port activity taking place on the north side of the river, going southside was not a realistic option for the Port & Docks Board, and in any case, they owned substantial landholdings on that side of the river. The brief for the project stated that 'the site should have considerable prominence so that the building would be a focal point in the port, dominating the adjacent dockscape and adding to the visual amenity of the area.' (Dublin Port & Docks Board Headquarters report, undated).
A site was selected at Alexandra Road, close to the deep berth at Alexandra Basin, and it presented the architects with a *tabula rasa* or clean slate from which to start. There were no buildings or artefacts to preserve, no adjoining buildings to address, nor any architectural references to acknowledge. Indeed, such was the lack of development in this part of the city that at the time of its completion, the Port & Docks HQ was the tallest office building east of Butt Bridge despite being only six storeys high.

The brief given to Niall Scott of Scott Tallon Walker was to design a landmark building providing 4,000 square metres of offices for the Board's headquarters and 1,500 square metres of separate lettable office space. Initially, Scott and his assistant, Conor Dwyer, developed designs for a building that would sit at the edge of the Alexandra Basin, but this option was turned down by the Board on the basis that the basin quayside was

more valuable as an active piece of port infrastructure. An alternative site was chosen, farther from the basin, on the corner of Alexandra Road and East Wall Road. Scott was disappointed with the alternative site given to him: it was bleak and windswept and, most disappointingly, had no view of the River Liffey or Dublin Bay. In an exercise to ensure that the new building would benefit from views of the water, architect Dwyer was hoisted up in a crane bucket, taking photographs at every three metres in order to establish at what level the building would enjoy views of the port, the sea and the mountains beyond.

Two design schemes were developed for the site – one a vertical solution, maximising the height despite the relatively limited floor area requirement; the other a two-storey horizontal pavilion set in Japanese style gardens. The second option would be cheaper to build but would not have a site presence, nor would it enjoy views over the docks. The board agreed unanimously to proceed with the first option, exploiting the opportunity to create views of the port and its context. Planning permission was lodged on the 1 September 1978. A photograph of the model of the proposal was published in *The Irish Press* on the same day headlining the £2 million development. The main contractor, P. J. Walls, started on site on 29 May 1979, working to a tight programme to ensure that the building would be ready by the time the Port & Docks Board had to vacate their temporary offices at Amiens Street in February 1981. However, despite the efforts of all

Case Study: Dublin Port Centre Building

involved, delays during the construction stage meant that the building was not occupied by the company until November 1981.

The six-storey office building is mounted on a raised podium with a semi-basement below. The above-ground portion of the building is square in plan and sits to the west side of the podium which is half a floor above ground level. The podium is accessed via a wide flight of concrete steps, with an adjacent concrete ramp running down to the lower ground floor level. To the north and south, the ground was excavated to create a landscaped moat that enables natural light to penetrate the office spaces at basement level. Importantly, the sunken area provides a sheltered place for staff to sit at break times. The podium, originally paved in concrete slabs with gravel infill panels, is not sufficiently elevated to afford views of the river and port beyond.

Internally the palette of materials consists of granite, American white oak, white acoustic ceiling panels and grey carpet tiles. These finishes have been replaced on some floors, most notably on the top floor which accommodates the company executives and board room. The architectural order of the building is tempered by Scott Tallon Walker signature gridlines which feature in both the structural elements and in the building linings throughout. The service core, which in the entrance hall is clad with vertically-grooved oak panels, runs the full height of the building and accommodates two passenger lifts, two stair cores, toilets, a tea station and service ducts. On the upper floors the core is clad with smooth butt-jointed American white oak panels and all doors are flush, with flush-fitted ironmongery. The passenger lifts are finished in stainless steel. The uppermost floor of the building is taken up by mechanical and electrical plant equipment, substantially as originally installed. The external expression of this floor is a solid concrete box with flush inset concrete louvre panels. Scott used the requirement for plant equipment to enable an additional floor on the structure; the five glass-clad office floors below, plus the basement floor, satisfied the office accommodation brief but Scott felt that the additional plant room floor would achieve better overall proportions and allow the building to achieve a more dominant presence on the site.

Considering the exposure of the site, the current condition of the building is testament to the quality of the materials used and the refinement of the architectural detailing. The in situ concrete was poured to ensure that all joints are plumb and line through with the precast concrete superstructure. The same concrete mix was used in both precast and in situ concrete, ensuring that the weathering is uniform. With the exception of the plant room floor, all levels have floor to ceiling glazing in a grid-like aluminium frame which mirrors the horizontal emphasis of the outer structure. All the upper floors benefit from panoramic of the city and bay. The deeply recessed glass minimises glare and solar damage to the interior finishes.

The building was not reviewed in the architectural press but, according to Scott, the architects received a letter from the Port & Docks Board thanking them for producing an excellent building which answered their brief. However, from the architects' perspective, one major controversy overshadowed the project. Scott commissioned artist Michael Warren to make a large sculptural piece as a focal point on the entrance podium. Warren, who worked with Scott Tallon Walker on many projects, designed and made a natural oak sculpture, entitled *Noche Obscura* (*The Dark Night of the Soul* from the title of a poem by St John of the Cross). The budget was £12,000. The structure, comprising a series of timbers placed together, was approved by the Port & Docks Board prior to its installation, but the chairman of the Board, Raymond Fay, was critical of the work saying that it was 'like something somebody had left on the sidewalk to take away' (*Irish Independent*, 29 Aug. 1980) and that it had no affinity with the port area. He said he would like to see 'something in remembrance of an old docker or an old schooner which could be identified with the port' (*Irish Independent*, 29 Aug. 1980). Michael Warren defended his piece, claiming that the sculpture would be superb in context when the building was completed. Unfortunately, the chairman of the Board had the support of other Board members, and the sculpture was removed shortly after the building was occupied. The podium space was left empty and desolate as a result, emphasising the exposure of the site rather than mediating the entrance threshold as the architects had originally intended. In 2017, the Dublin Port Company, as it is now known, commissioned Darmody Architecture to undertake works to improve the external realm surrounding their HQ building.

More Than Concrete Blocks Volume 3

Facts and Figures

Architects: Scott Tallon Walker with Niall Scott in charge, assisted by Conor Dwyer.
Scott Tallon Walker were appointed in 1976 following an invited architectural competition. Works started on site in 1979 and were completed in 1981.
Niall Scott was born in 1940 and studied architecture at Dublin Institute of Technology, graduating in 1964 and joining the practice of Scott Tallon Walker the same year. His father was Michael Scott, founding partner of the practice. His first major commission on becoming a partner in the practice was Goffs Bloodstock Sales Complex in Kildare (1976), and his last important building in Ireland before taking up the role as managing director of the STW London Office was the Dublin Port and Docks Board HQ offices in Dublin (1980). He returned to the Dublin office in 1999 and has been involved in the Pavilion Development in Dún Laoghaire and the Mater Hospital Campus in Dublin. He has a particular interest in Irish art and the commissioning of artworks as part of the architectural scheme design.
Conor Dwyer was born in Dublin in 1948 and attended the School of Architecture at UCD graduating in 1971. He worked in London and Dublin before joining Scott Tallon Walker in 1975 where he worked with Niall Scott on the Tretorn Factory, Portlaoise, the Spanish Embassy, Dublin and the Port & Docks Headquarters. He left Scott Tallon Walker in 1981 and went on to work in the computer software business. He moved to France in 1990 and retired from his career in graphic and multimedia design in 2008.

Consulting Engineers: Ove Arup & Partners
Quantity Surveyors: Seamus Monahan Associates
Landscape Architects: Gerry Mitchell & Associates
M&E Consultants: Scott Tallon Walker in-house team
Main Contractor: P. J. Walls Ltd., Dublin, project manager Dan Kavanagh

Sculptor: Michael Warren, *Noche Obscura* (1980)
Warren was born in Dublin in 1950 and trained as an artist at Bath Academy of Art, England and at Accademia di Belle Arti di Milano, Italy. He lives and works near Gorey, Co. Wexford. His oeuvre mainly consists of large-scale, site-specific works, based generally on the precepts of minimalism. His work with Scott Tallon Walker includes pieces at the RTÉ Campus, Donnybrook, at A&L Goodbody HQ, Dublin, and at the Tulach a t'Solais Memorial in Co. Wexford.

Sources

Unpublished
Niall Scott, interviewed by Carole Pollard, 2014

Published
Anon., *Dublin Port and Docks Board Proposed New Headquarters* (Dublin Port & Docks Board, undated)
Anon., *History of the Port Centre Building: Dublin Port Company* (Dublin Port Company, 2013)
Gilligan, H. A., *A History of the Port of Dublin* (Gill & MacMillan, 1988)
O'Regan, John (ed.), *Scott Tallon Walker: 100 Buildings and Projects 1960–2005* (Gandon Editions, 2006)
Rowley, Ellen, 'Office Blocks 1950–2000', in Rolf Loeber, Hugh Campbell, Livia Hurley, John Montague and Ellen Rowley (eds), *Architecture 1600–2000, Volume IV, Art and Architecture of Ireland* (RIA, Yale University Press, 2014)
Warren, Michael, 'Outdoor Works' http://michaelwarren.ie/ (accessed through 2014)

Building shortly after completion in 1980
(Courtesy of Scott Tallon Walker image collection)

Case Study
IDA Enterprise Centre, Pearse Street, Dublin 2, 1978–83

Aoibheann Ní Mhearáin

The Industrial Development Authority (IDA) Enterprise Centre is a campus complex, consisting of single- and two-storey, red-brick buildings accommodating 35 enterprise units, along with a converted industrial 19th-century tower offering an additional eight storeys of accommodation. The 19th-century tower, a disused sugar mill, stands singularly in the middle of the Pearse Street Enterprise Centre. It speaks to the industrial past of the docklands site which was significantly in decline at the time of the construction of the centre in the early 1980s. The Enterprise Centre was an attempt to create a new industrial future for the area, one that was more community based, that supported the development of industry and helped it grow. As part of a wider inner-city plan for Dublin that included the construction of schools and housing, these developments were intended to retain and sustain a vibrant and living community in the city.

When the architect, Matthew Barry of Barry & Associates, made his first site visit in 1978, the 5.2 acre site included the tower and an assortment of old sheds, housing among them the Hammond Lane foundry. The IDA's brief for Barry was to provide a variety of spaces for businesses at different stages of development, from start-up to maturing industries. The challenge was how best to engage with an underdeveloped and hostile urban environment, while also addressing local needs. The architect's response took a different approach to the usual provision of industrial units which typically were housed in large shed-like spaces, set back from the street. Instead, the IDA Enterprise Centre hugs the street edge with two-storey brick enterprise units located all along the site perimeter. Though built directly onto the street edge, the units do not create one long, continuous elevation. Instead, they are expressed as small houses, alternating their orientation along the street, and introducing a domestic appearance to the industrial site.

The site was sold to Trinity College Dublin in 1999 whereafter the Trinity Technology and Enterprise Campus was established there. Alongside this some industrial units remain, while The Lir Academy, the National Academy of Dramatic Art built in 2010, occupies the north-east corner of the site. The Lir comprises a purpose-built structure which connects into and occupies a number of the original industrial units. The buildings are in reasonable condition, with some alterations to glazing and roofing noticeable. A number of the loading bays at first-floor level have been filled in to provide new windows and the lifting infrastructure removed. Many of the units have had new internal fitouts to suit their use now as offices rather than as sites of manufacturing or industrial production. The tower remains as a dedicated craft centre.

Block plan (Courtesy of Barry & Associates collection at Irish Architectural Archive)

A New Enterprise for the City

In 1979 IDA established a special inner city unit to develop industry in the city and identified 34 acres of land for use as Enterprise Centres, in seven sites between the canals and extending west as far as the Phoenix Park. These sites included: Pearse Street (5.2 acres), Prussia Street (0.5 acre), Marrowbone Lane (1.2 acres), The Liberties (1.8 acres), two sites at East Wall (4.5 and 10 acres respectively) and Ringsend (11 acres). The IDA developed these sites in consultation with the local communities, attempting to grow employment through supporting existing local industry and developing new enterprises based in the area. Aimed at small to medium businesses the Enterprise Centres offered units at subsidised rates, with additional incentives including grants towards costs of capital expenditure, centralised administrative services, consultation throughout the set-up process and full support for training costs.

The IDA developed a detailed schedule of accommodation for the site in Pearse Street, specifying the number and sizes of units to be provided. These ranged in size from 100 to 1,950 square feet to accommodate various industries at different stages of development. These units were required to be flexible to allow for different uses. Access for deliveries was a key requirement of the brief and large service delivery openings are provided at

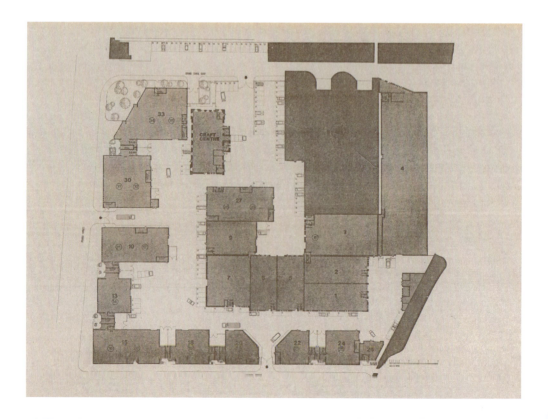

Elevations (Courtesy of Barry & Associates collection at Irish Architectural Archive)

ground and first-floor level, painted in a distinctive green colour. In addition, eight incubator units were provided for first-time entrepreneurs, to support their research and development phase. The tower was identified as a location suitable for craft businesses due to the small scale of the spaces within it. The Enterprise Centre was the first of its kind in Ireland and the largest in Europe at the time of its construction. The centre was expected to produce 700 jobs and its development cost £7 million.

Bringing Industry to Town

Founded in 1949, the IDA was tasked with developing industrial policy in Ireland. Regional distribution of industry was a core aim of industrial policy since the IDA's foundation and in the 1970s the IDA developed a Regional Industrial Plan that divided the country into nine planning regions to manage this distribution. IDA policies offered the greatest subsidies and promotion to the least industrialised areas. Light industry showed a tendency for dispersal with factories established in all sizes of towns in the state and with this a comparative decline of industry in the major centres. This, along with higher job losses in older industries, compounded the problems of unemployment in the city centres, which was estimated in 1981 to be three times the national average and close to 30 per cent in Dublin's inner city.

(above)
Perspective drawing
(Courtesy of Barry & Associates collection at Irish Architectural Archive)

(below)
Street view shortly after completion
(Courtesy G. & T. Crampton Photograph Archive, UCD Digital Library and Prof Joseph Brady)

Growth in the industrial sector in Ireland increased steadily across the 20th century and, for the first time in 1969, surpassed the agriculture sector as an employer. Concurrent with the increased industrial employment was a depopulation of rural areas, with populations moving to urban areas; by 1980, Dublin's population had doubled since the founding of the state. Conversely, however, the city centres saw a fall both in population and industry across this same period with Co. Dublin losing a quarter of its industrial labour force in the decade up to 1983.

The difficulties facing industry in the city included a shortage of industrial sites, high property costs, poor standards of old buildings and difficulty accessing buildings for transport, all of which resulted in a flow of industry out of the city to the industrial estates of the suburbs. This move to sub-urbanisation affected both industry and population in the city centre. To counter the reduction of manufacturing jobs in Dublin's inner city, the IDA developed a special programme in 1979 for inner-city industrial development. This policy was aimed at encouraging the expansion of existing industry to stop the outflow of industry to the suburbs, to secure suitable sites for small industry, to introduce new manufacturing to the inner city and to maintain close contacts with inner city groups interested in the development of the city. It had the aim of creating 4,000 jobs by the end of 1982.

The centre at Pearse Street was one of seven centres envisaged under this policy which offered a total of 34 acres of industrial development in the city centre at a cost of £12 million. The IDA recognised the importance of the community in developing the centres and contributing to job creation. To this end the IDA worked with a community co-operative from the Ringsend, Irishtown and Westland Row area, who operated the canteen, the shop and the secretarial services in the centre. School leavers who had undertaken the AnCO secretarial course were employed in the centre to give them the required experience to gain employment elsewhere. Of the 250 people employed at the opening of the centre, 50 to 60 were from the inner city.

Architecture for Industry

The connection between people, place and industry evident in the early 1980s industrial policy of the IDA was also evident in the architectural design. The architectural language of the Pearse Street Enterprise Centre can be understood as embracing the strictures of industrial programmes –

Case Study: IDA Enterprise Centre, Pearse Street

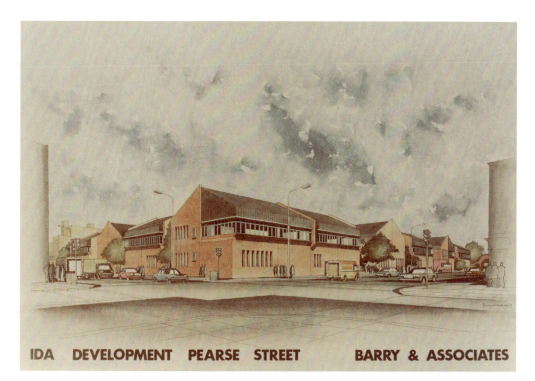

IDA DEVELOPMENT PEARSE STREET   BARRY & ASSOCIATES

large spans and flexibility, built simply with robust materials – while also conveying a more human scale to the development, evident in the form and massing of the perimeter units and the care in the brick detailing that brings scale and variety to the elevations. In its siting, detailing and massing the Enterprise Centre is an essay in connecting industry to its people.

According to the architect, the selection of brick for the Enterprise Centre was in response to the existing context including the adjacent 19th-century St Andrew's National School, now St Andrew's Resource Centre, with its brick and terracotta detailing. Brick is typically associated with domestic architecture in Dublin, and its selection here is part of a series of measures that the architect employs to downplay the institutional or industrial character of the centre, making it more suitable for a city that people live in and use every day. The other key device the architect uses to disguise the factory type is placing the smaller industrial units on the street edge in

Case Study: IDA Enterprise Centre, Pearse Street

Aerial view with Craft Tower (Courtesy G. & T. Crampton Photograph Archive, UCD Digital Library and Prof Joseph Brady)

two-storey buildings that echo domestic architecture, with their pitched roofs and gables, each unit distinguishable from the other. The typical strategy at the time for industrial centres, was to provide a series of large, single-storey shed-like buildings in the centre of the site, with a fenced-off perimeter, but the urban location, and the grounding of this project in community needs, called for a new response to the site. By placing the two-storey enterprise units on the street edge and scaling them like houses, a more sympathetic industrial typology is created, making the centre less alienating to its context. Furthermore, by expressing the scale of the units as individual 'houses', the design at once gives an identity to the businesses with their own front door and separate form, enhanced by the alternating gable fronts to the street along Pearse Street.

While aiming to respond to the low scale, and partially domestic context, the façade at street level was designed with minimal windows, in response to fears about security in the area. Where windows occur at ground floor level in the main units, these are tall, slim windows and much of the street boundary is blank. The exception is the two-storey, flat-roofed link elements between the enterprise units that provide own door access from the street, as well as stairs and connections between the units; these are stepped back from the street and entered through a small, railed garden. The strategy of the smaller units along the perimeter then allowed the larger units to occupy the central areas of the site. The design is balanced between being sympathetic to its surroundings, while also being defensive against it. The centre creates a street edge, but not a street frontage, the units seem like houses, but have no windows on the ground floor. These issues show the architect's desire to humanise the development, while also acknowledging the client's concerns for security.

The Enterprise Centre site is bounded by the railway to the south and with street frontage to Macken Street to the west, Grand Canal Quay to the east, and Pearse Street to the north. There are three vehicle entrances to the campus, one on each of the street façades, giving access to the interior of the site. Once inside the perimeter, there are a number of additional units, mostly single-storey, flat-roofed buildings of larger scale than the units at the perimeter, along with surface car-parking, delivery bays and access to the tower. Units range in size from 100 to 1,950 square feet.

There is great care taken with the brick detailing on the façades of the Enterprise Centre and these details reflect the importance the architect

More Than Concrete Blocks Volume 3

placed on the use of brick in this location. The stepped brick sills at first floor give a distinctive expression to the façade, pushing the first-floor strip windows out beyond the plane of the wall below. Between the two-storey units, brick firebreak walls are apparent, puncturing the roof and appearing in the façade, proud of the wall plane. The functional necessity of the fire break-wall provides additional non-standard brickwork detailing, while also acting to sub-divide the units, so they appear at a smaller scale. The deep brick arch pedestrian entrance shows particular care with detailing which is also visible in the low walls and garden entrances surrounding the buildings.

The simplicity of the building form, including the use of portal frames, exposed structural elements, a clear repeated grid, and economical roofing materials, situates the development in a factory type. The interior was designed to be as flexible and usable as possible, with clear spans provided at first floor and increased head heights provided at ground floor; pragmatic responses to the problem of designing for an unknown future use or user. The loading doors and lifting gear for the upper units provide more expressive elements appearing as figural elements at the doorways, painted in a striking copper green colour, perhaps reflecting Post-Modern influences, though most likely designed to celebrate the functional aspects of the factory.

According to the architect, the retention of the tower on this site was at the insistence of Dublin Corporation's planning department and points to a turn in policy that recognised the significance of existing buildings and required their retention in re-development proposals. The inclusion of the tower in the project is significant on a policy and detail level and identifies this development as one of the earliest to incorporate and value 19th-century industrial architecture within its complex and successfully re-use the spaces. This reflects a changed attitude to existing structures in our city, brought to the fore in projects generated later in the decade, such as the Irish Film Centre (1992) and subsequent development of Temple Bar.

The complex of buildings is still in use, with most of the units occupied, though some vacant. There are a variety of different users, including for academic and research purposes as well as commercial uses. The craft tower has remained occupied by individual craft-based businesses. The most significant change to the site is at the north-eastern corner, at the junction of Pearse Street and Grand Canal Quay, where The Lir Academy was constructed in 2010. Originally the corner buildings had a stepped gable, providing a wide corner for a proposed future road-widening project envisioned by Dublin City Council that never materialised. The construction of the theatre included the partial demolition of units 33 and 34, removing the stepped gables and constructing the theatre building to connect into the existing units. New first-floor glazing has been added to the façade of unit 34, facing Grand Canal Quay. This unit also has a new roof, in keeping with the design of The Lir Theatre. The units were substantially re-configured internally to provide the accommodation for the academy.

The Enterprise Centre can be seen as a pioneer in inner-city development as it marked a turning point where policies addressed the living community of the city. The project also embraced the re-use of existing buildings showing a maturing relationship to our architectural heritage and to the city as a place for living and working; a place that can accommodate both our industries of the future and the heritage of our past. Since the construction of the Enterprise Centre, the docklands area has transformed and is now the home of the 'tech' industry in Dublin. Plans for the site have evolved and presently Trinity College are focused on restoring and refurbishing the original IDA buildings, retaining their original function of supporting industry and entrepreneurship, now incorporating the technological innovations of the 21st century.

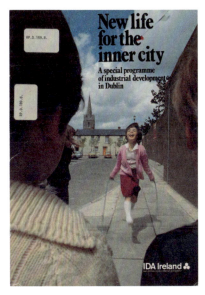

More Than Concrete Blocks Volume 3

Case Study: IDA Enterprise Centre, Pearse Street

Facts and Figures

The Enterprise Centre was the first of its kind in Ireland and the largest in Europe at the time of its construction. The centre was expected to produce 700 jobs and its development cost £7 million. At the time of its opening in 1982, it employed 250 people, 50 to 60 of whom were from the city centre area.

The building was given the Mont Kavanagh Award in 1892 and received the Europa Nostra Diploma of Merit in 1983. The complex was commended in the RIAI Triennial Gold Medal awards for the period 1980/81/82 and won the RIAI Medal for Architectural Conservation for the period 1981/82/83 for the conservation of the 19th century tower.

Architect: Matthew Barry, principal of Barry & Associates.

Barry was educated in DIT in Dublin, graduating in the early 1960s. Following graduation, he worked with Hooper & Mayne in Dublin for a year where he worked on Kevin Street College of Technology (1968) (see Outline Survey in *MTCB* Vol. 2) before joining Michael Scott & Partners the following year. During his three and half years in Michael Scott & Partners, Barry was job architect on the O'Flaherty house in Kinsale, working with Robin Walker, as well as working on the interiors of the National Bank on Suffolk Street (1965) (see Outline Survey in *MTCB* Vol. 2). Barry then went to work for the house building company Wates, working as in an in-house architect for three years. He designed his own house in Dundrum as a prototype for the house builder. Following this, Barry established the practice Barry & Associates.

Quantity Surveyor: T. B. Kennedy & Partners
Structural Engineers: McCabe & Delany
Mechanical and Electrical Engineers: Seamus Honan Associates
Main Contractor: G&T Crampton Ltd

Sources

Unpublished
Anon., 'New Life for the Inner City: A Special Programme of Industrial Development in Dublin' (IDA, 1981)
Barry & Associates archive at the Irish Architectural Archive (IAA), Dublin

Published
Anon., 'The IDA allocated £12 million to Dublin Inner City area', *Irish Times*, 5 Nov. 1981
Anon. 'IDA Pearse Street, Small Industries Enterprise', in *Construction and Property News* (5 Dec. 1981)Gillmor, Desmond A., 'Land and People, c.1983', in J. R. Hill (ed.), *A New History of Ireland, Volume VII, Ireland 1921–84* (Oxford University Press, 2003)
Pearson, Peter, 'Prime Examples of Conversion and Restoration in Dublin', in *Martello* (Spring 1984)
Lee, J. J., *Ireland 1912–1985: Politics and Society* (Cambridge University Press, 1989)
Wren, Maev-Ann, 'IDA offers incentive to Dublin Inner City', *Irish Times*, 15 Jul. 1983

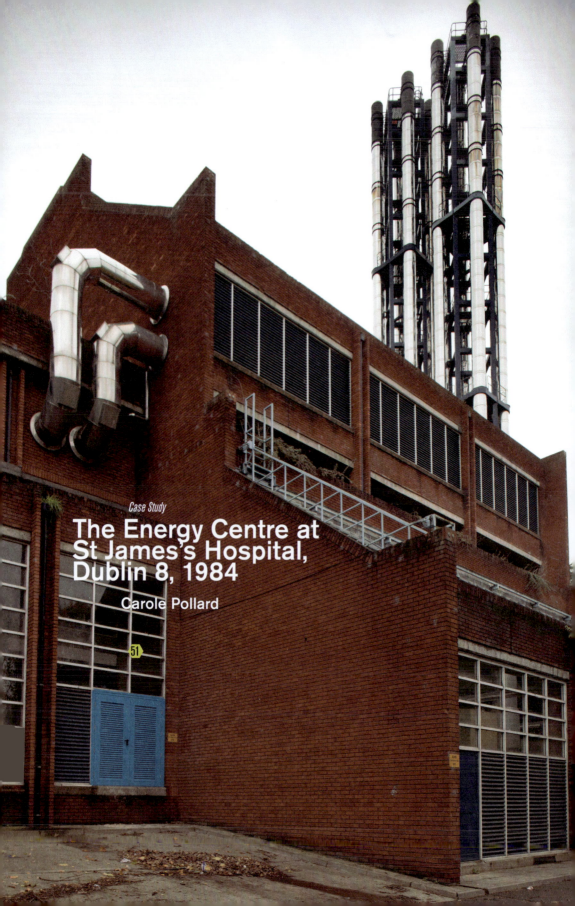

Case Study

The Energy Centre at St James's Hospital, Dublin 8, 1984

Carole Pollard

The Energy Centre at St James's Hospital is tucked away in the northwest corner of the St James's Hospital site, occupying an edge piece of the campus where the ground level drops steeply to meet Mount Brown and Old Kilmainham. As its name implies, the building provides all the power generation, heating and cooling needs for the hospital campus and remains a vital piece of hospital infrastructure despite the evolution in technology since its construction. The building responds to the site level change, appearing as a single-storey structure on the side that faces the hospital, but is three storeys high on the side that faces the neighbouring 1920s Mount Brown housing estate. The manipulation of the site levels to facilitate the building's operational function is the defining move by architect, Jim O'Beirne of Moloney O'Beirne Guy, who, along with British architectural firm Hutchison Locke and Monk (HLM), were the architects for the comprehensive redevelopment of the hospital during the 1980s.

Constructed in red-brick, with blue and white louvered windows, and steeply pitched roofs, the structure is divided into six clearly defined bays. The bays are of varying widths, articulated by raised parapet party walls and projecting double-row brick piers. Primary access to the building is from the hospital campus on the south side. The dominant feature of the original building is a pair of flue stacks, each with four cylindrical stainless-steel flues, which rise 37 metres in open lattice steel towers on the west elevation. Their elegant slender profile reduces their impact on the immediate environment. In addition, the banking of ground on the east side of the building and the planting of trees and shrubs along the south boundary diminishes the building's impact on the two-storey residential terraces that line Mount Brown.

Generally, or in terms of public perception, industrial buildings have held little aesthetic or heritage value in Dublin, hence the small number that feature in this publication. Nevertheless, the Energy Centre represents a unique piece of industrial infrastructure stitched into the urban landscape. Despite rapid and persistent changes to its operating functions – from shortly after its construction to the present day – the building has endured because of its intelligent siting, appropriate scale, and harmonising materials. Most recently, to facilitate the new National Children's Hospital under construction on the campus (since 2016), the Energy Centre has undergone significant technological upgrades and structural changes. Notwithstanding, it remains the centre for energy distribution for the expanding hospital campus, as represented by the new stack of 16 flues which stands alongside the building's original flue stack, albeit stretching several metres higher than the original.

Perspective drawing by Jim O'Beirne
(Courtesy of Maloney O'Beirne image collection)

Powered by Turf

In the second half of the 20th century, plans were made to amalgamate Sir Patrick Dunn's Hospital, Dr Steevens' Hospital, the Royal City of Dublin Hospital, and Mercer's Hospital, in new facilities at St Kevin's. The new hospital entity was partnered with the School of Medicine at Trinity College Dublin and its name was changed to St James's. The redevelopment of St James's Hospital was the largest social infrastructural project undertaken in Dublin in the 1980s.

The history of the hospital dates back to 1667 when a workhouse for the city's poor was built on the site, in the district of Kilmainham. In 1730 a Foundling Hospital to care for abandoned infants was opened and, when the workhouse closed in 1772, the Foundling Hospital remained in operation until 1831. In 1841 the buildings once again became a workhouse, known as the South Dublin Union and that name, and its connotations, still resounds with older generations of Dubliners. The workhouse infirmary took on a primary role as a centre for the treatment and care of the sick and following the formation of the State in 1922 the name was changed to St Kevin's Hospital.

Case Study: Energy Centre, St. James's Hospital

Site plan (Courtesy of Maloney O'Beirne image collection)

In 1975, the Hospital Board advertised for the appointment of architects to lead the future development of the site. A shortlist of suitable firms was drawn up and five teams were interviewed. The architectural team appointed was a collaboration between Dublin-based Guy Moloney & Partners (later Moloney O'Beirne Guy) and the British firm of Hutchison, Locke and Monk (HLM). The latter had significant experience in hospital design and the expertise of David Hutchison, in particular, was key to winning the contract. At its peak, there were 30 architects working on the St James's Hospital scheme.

In 1976, the St James's Hospital Board and the Department of Health published a *Brief for St James's Teaching Hospital, Dublin* which set out the medical and technical parameters for the future development of the hospital. In response, the architects published the *Development Control Plan* for the site in 1978 which included a programme for the phased delivery of buildings on the site. Energy provision was a key component of the design considerations and the existing boiler houses, dating from 1908 and 1912, obviously did not have the capacity to service the much larger and more sophisticated hospital facilities proposed. Priority was given to the construction of a new Energy Centre and it was the first of the new hospital

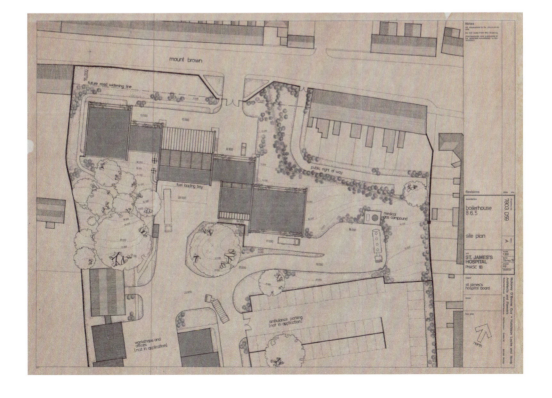

Completed Energy Centre, 1984 (Courtesy of Gilbert Watson, McLoughlin & Harvey archive)

buildings to be completed, coming into operation in 1984.

The design of the building was dictated by the decision to use turf to power the hospital. Two factors played a significant role in this decision. The first was doubt about the future affordability and availability of fuel oil because of two global oil crises in the 1970s; and the second was concern about deteriorating environmental conditions in Dublin caused by smog. Smog, which blighted the city in the 1980s, is a dense mixture of smoke and fog caused by the overuse of bituminous coal. Being detrimental to lung health, the Hospital Board could not be seen to be contributing to the problem of smog, so it readily approved the consultants' recommendations to use turf, the only indigenous source of fuel in Ireland. The 1978 engineer's report for the proposed hospital was prophetic in specifying that 'the plant and its housing will be designed to eliminate, as far as possible, noise and dust nuisance and the flues will be designed in accordance with the rules applying to smokeless zone areas' (*Development Control Plan,* 1978, unpaginated).

The choice of turf was, however, not unique to St James's Hospital. There was a precedent for using turf to power large national institutional establishments, for example, the College of Technology at Kevin Street, Dublin, (1968 dem. 2020), designed by Hooper and Mayne Architects, used turf-fired boilers to provide for its heating requirements, as did Cork Regional Hospital (1973–9) designed by Keppie Henderson & Partners Architects in conjunction with the mechanical and electrical engineers Varming Mulcahy Reilly Associates (VMRA), who were also the engineers at St. James's.

Case Study: Energy Centre, St. James's Hospital

Elevation to hospital campus, c. 1984 (Courtesy of Maloney O'Beirne collection at Irish Architectural Archive)

The Energy Centre's site location was chosen because it fulfilled two important criteria: it was remote from the main hospital buildings and the steep slope allowed for gravity feeding of the boilers. The architects' report observed that 'turf-fired boiler houses are necessarily high buildings', and therefore there was an 'aesthetic advantage to be able to use the sloping site to reduce the physical impact of this building' (*Development Control Plan*, 1978). The original intention was that the six boilers would be fired on a rotation basis, using native Irish turf brickeens to be delivered daily from midland Bord na Móna (formerly the Turf Development Board, est. 1933) facilities and fed into concrete hoppers to the boilers below. However, the continuous flow of turf trucks caused serious disruption to the management of the hospital campus. The quantity of turf required to fulfil the energy needs of the hospital meant that turf was delivered by trucks four times daily, generating a convoy of truck traffic which deposited spoil and created a hazard on the site.

Of course, the decision to use turf – which was classified a smokeless fuel – predated the introduction of the Air Pollution Act of 1987 which banned the use of bituminous or smoky coal in Dublin. And as such, the use of turf was short-lived. Soon, solid fuel was abandoned in favour of natural gas which was fed via the National Gas Grid from the Kinsale Natural Gas Field (Co. Cork). The boilers were adapted accordingly. This 1987 Air Pollution Act included legislation governing the disposal of hospital waste

meaning that the hospital waste incinerator facility had to be shut down for public health reasons. Since then, all hospital waste has been disposed of off-site.

Conversion of the boilers and shutting down of the incinerator changed the operation of the building. The use of natural gas meant much higher fuel efficiency which in turn increased the output of each boiler by 50 per cent, thus eliminating the need to install the planned sixth boiler. The design of the flue towers, each containing four flues, was based on six functioning boilers and two incinerator exhausts. Under the new configuration only one and occasionally two flues were required, however, because the removal of the redundant flues would have had significant cost implications, all eight were left in place.

Standing Tall in a Low-Rise Hospital Campus

From an aesthetic point of view, the pair of towering stainless steel flue stacks act as an architectural feature almost in the same way as a clock-tower or a spire might: a vertical marker. Their continued existence – after they were no longer functional – has contributed to the building's enduring

Under construction, 1982. (Courtesy of Maloney O'Beirne collection at Irish Architectural Archive)

identity in this otherwise residential neighbourhood.

Early in the design process, O'Beirne produced a free-hand sketch perspective of the proposed Energy Centre which was published in the *RIAI Bulletin*, June 1982. The sketch evoked his ambition for the project and featured twin flue stacks soaring into the sky. While the flue stacks that were built were substantially lower than illustrated, they fulfilled O'Beirne's clear intention that they would become a distinctive landmark on the Kilmainham skyline. Indeed, the stacks provided a unique vertical emphasis on the 1980s hospital campus.

The design philosophy adopted by the architects in 1978 was one of 'providing a building [...] intimate in scale' which would 'balance reassurance in atmosphere with function'. It was agreed that 'a low-rise building complex would be most appropriate to these ends, a factor [...] endorsed by a site largely surrounded by residential areas' (*Development Control Plan,* 1978, unpaginated). The first phase of hospital buildings at the St James's campus was handed over in 1988. And the influence of HLM Architects was evident in the architectural language employed, as well as in the building forms and choice of materials: the red-brick, the pitched roofs, the linking glazed walkways and the buildings' domestic scale of two and three storeys, were all echoes of HLM's design interventions at Royal Bournemouth Hospital (1983) and Gatwick Park Hospital (1984), for instances.

Despite its industrial function, the Energy Centre complied with the design philosophy adopted for the entire campus and, as such, belied the nature of the building as an enclosure for large and noisy plant equipment. In addition to accommodating industrial boilers and incinerators, the structure housed water storage tanks, electrical generators, electrical switch rooms and distribution boards, engineering workshops and staff facilities. Contrary to the high-level engineering design of the equipment contained within, the building was constructed using traditional low-tech construction methods: brick-cavity walls, concrete floors, and pitched roofs finished with both concrete tile and glass.

The building form was broken down into bays, with each bay articulated by brick-standing parapets separating a variety of pitched and flat roofs, and projecting brick piers. The building was clad in red-brick, windows were multi-paned with white aluminium frames, and the majority of openings were fitted with blue-painted louvered screens. The louvres served two functions: as a device to break up the scale of the elevations, and to provide ventilation.

For example, the four large circular louvered openings on the west elevation provided ventilation to the boiler room. Care was taken to ensure adequate access space to allow for easy maintenance and subsequent modification of services without undue interference with the operation of the hospital. The services were carried underground in a large corridor-type duct which led from the Energy Centre to all the main hospital buildings.

The landscaping around the building was domestic in character with concrete slab paths, concrete planters, areas of lawn and a row of trees along the Mount Brown edge. By breaking down the building form into a series of elements of different heights, all clearly articulated, O'Beirne produced a building which ameliorated the noise and grime of its interior. It functioned both as a pleasant place for engineering and maintenance staff to work and as a respectful neighbour to the two-storey redbrick terraces that line Mount Brown and Old Kilmainham. In recent times, the setting for the south and west sides of the building has changed considerably because of the construction of an underground carpark for the National Children's Hospital which is accessed at this point.

Steelwork for flues under construction, c.1982 (Courtesy of Maloney O'Beirne collection at Irish Architectural Archive)

Case Study: Energy Centre, St. James's Hospital

Facts and Figures

In 1975, the St James's Hospital Board advertised for an architect-led design team to develop a new hospital on St James's Street in the southwest of the city. In 1977, Irish firm Moloney O'Beirne Guy in association with British firm, Hutchison Locke & Monk (HLM) were appointed architects for the scheme. The St James's Hospital Development Control Plan (or masterplan) was published in 1982 and, the same year, the construction of the Energy Centre commenced on site. Works were completed in 1984.

The building did not receive any architectural awards following its completion, nor was it published in the architectural press. It was, however, a winner of Irish Energy Centre National Boiler Awards in the 'Commercial Boilerhouse' category in 1996, 1997 and 1999.

The master planning of the hospital development was led by David Hutchison (1937–2015) of HLM. Hutchison graduated from the Bartlett School of Architecture in 1960. He started his career at Powell and Moya, working on their Pimlico Library and hospital projects at Wexham Park in Slough (1965) and Princess Margaret Hospital in Swindon. In 1963, he founded a practice with Tony Monk and Graham Locke after winning a competition to design Paisley Civic Centre. The firm built up expertise in healthcare, partly based on contacts made by Hutchison at Powell and Moya. He left HLM in 1991 to set up his own practice.

Jim O'Beirne (1933–2021) of Moloney O'Beirne Guy was the principal architect for the Energy Centre. O'Beirne graduated from the School of Architecture at University College Dublin in 1956. Shortly after graduating he moved to Canada where he worked on Concordia University and the Toronto Dominium Bank, both in Montreal. He returned to Ireland in 1967 and joined the firm of Guy Moloney & Partners, where he became a partner and the name of the firm changed to Moloney O'Beirne Guy. He retired from practice in 2004.

The consulting engineers appointed to undertake the mechanical and electrical design for the overall scheme, including the Energy Centre, were Varming Mulcahy Reilly Associates (VMRA), led by partner Brian Reilly. Reilly was born in 1925 and graduated from University College Dublin in 1947. After some time working in the United Kingdom on major institutional building contracts with leading consulting engineers and contractors, Reilly returned to Ireland in 1952 and joined the practice of J. Varming & S. Mulcahy Consulting Engineers. He retired from this practice in 1993. Within the VMRA practice the project engineers on the Energy Centre were John Doyle (mechanical) and Oscar Gilligan (electrical).

Contractors: McLoughlin & Harvey
Mechanical Contractors: H. A. O'Neil Ltd (Clonskeagh, Dublin)

Sources

Unpublished

St James's Hospital Board and the Department of Health joint project management team chaired by Professor D. I. D. Howie, 'The Brief for St James Teaching Hospital, Dublin' (1976)

Moloney O'Beirne Guy and HLM, 'St James's Teaching Hospital Dublin – Development Control Plan' (June 1978)

Project drawings and photographs from the Moloney O'Beirne Archive

John Purcell (retired partner at Varming Associates Consulting Engineers), interviewed by Carole Pollard, 2014

Published

Anon., 'St James's Hospital Energy Centre' illustration, *RIAI Bulletin* (No. 37, June 1982)

Monk, Tony, *Hospital Builders* (Wiley Academy, 2004)

O'Dwyer, Frederick, *Irish Hospital Architecture: A Pictorial History* (Department of Health and Children, Dublin, 1997)

Case Study
Artane Oratory of the Resurrection, Kilmore Road, Beaumont, Dublin 5, 1982–4

Natalie de Róiste

One of the few Dublin buildings designed by Liam McCormick, the renowned Donegal architect, Artane Oratory of the Resurrection, was commissioned by the Christian Brothers' Northern Province following the closure of St Joseph's Industrial School in 1969 and the sale of the associated farmland to a housing developer in 1972. This part of the land contained the Industrial School graveyard, which had seen burials from 1871 until the closure of the school and beyond. Following vocal criticism of the Christian Brother order's original plans to exhume the remains and re-inter them in another Dublin graveyard, the order bought the site back for a nominal fee and set out to enclose the graveyard and build a memorial oratory. The church is reminiscent of a number of McCormick's Donegal churches, although the suburban site lacks the dramatic setting of much of his oeuvre – that is, the setting of rural Donegal.

The Artane building is in good condition, having been kept in continuous use. Alterations internally include the addition of the stone lectern dedicated to Máirín Uí Mhurchadha (1989) and the redesign of the tabernacle door. Externally, the graveyard wall was increased in height, and a 30-foot cross in the graveyard was removed (as it was proving to be a target for stone throwing). The exterior graveyard walls were originally a deep burgundy colour. This was a departure for McCormick, who normally favoured white roughcast, and was explained as a means to counteract graffiti. The walls were then painted a pale grey but since the new occupation of the oratory by the Serbian Orthodox parish of St George, that congregation instigated the recent repainting of the building – and a return to the original idiosyncratic burnt red colour. The oratory has also welcomed the introduction of a timber iconostasis by this Serbian Orthodox congregation.

The Need for an Oratory

Artane Industrial School was established in 1870 to care for what the Christian Brothers termed 'neglected, orphaned and abandoned children', and was originally licenced to accommodate 825 boys. Numbers declined steadily after the Second World War, and the school closed in 1969, as part of a change in policy at national level. The associated farm (over 350 acres) was sold to a house builder, Abbey Homesteads, who got planning permission for over 700 houses, shops, a community centre, and landscaped open space, before selling the non-residential part of the site to Powers Supermarkets in 1978. The proposed landscaped open space contained two graveyards; the churchyard of the long-ruinous 13th-century manorial church, dedicated to St. Nicholas, associated with Artane Castle, and the graveyard of the Industrial School.

The original plan, following the sale of the site in 1972, was to relocate the remains of the brothers and boys to another Dublin cemetery, as evidenced by a letter to the *Irish Times* by Brother R. Q. O'Driscoll, the Provincial of the Christian Brothers Northern Province, in 1975. O'Driscoll stated that highly complex arrangements for the transfer of the remains had been in progress for two years and were nearing completion. This letter was a response to a highly critical press campaign from the Dublin doctor,

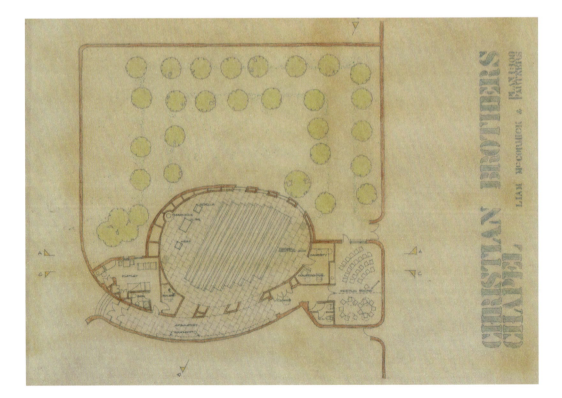

Floor plan, c.1980
(Courtesy of Christian Brother Province Centre Archive)

general practitioner Dr Cyril Daly, regarding the neglect and vandalism of the graveyard. Daly, a campaigner against corporal punishment in schools, and a vocal critic of the Christian Brothers' Industrial Schools – Daly referred to Letterfrack Industrial school as 'St Joseph's Prison for Young Children, Galway' – pointed out that there were no individual grave markers for the boys and claimed that the boys had been buried anonymously with three bodies to a grave; he stated that 'there are dogs who lie buried with more deliberate circumstance' (Letter to the Editor, *Irish Times*, 15 July 1975). Despite the fact that the Christian Brothers had kept records of those interred there, Daly noted the impossibility of individually identifying the remains.

There have been a number of institutional graveyards that have come to national attention across Ireland, as Artane did in 1975, regarding the manner in which the dead are commemorated therein. While grave markers may once have only been the preserve of those who could afford them, an unmarked grave is no longer considered acceptable, and the question of how to address these unmarked burial sites is a live one. In 1993, following the closure of High Park Magdalene Laundry in Dublin's northside, the graveyard associated with it was exhumed, so as to transfer remains to Glasnevin Cemetery. An initial exhumation licence for 133 named women had to be supplemented with a second licence, when the remains of a larger number of women were found. More recently in 2014, Catherine Corless

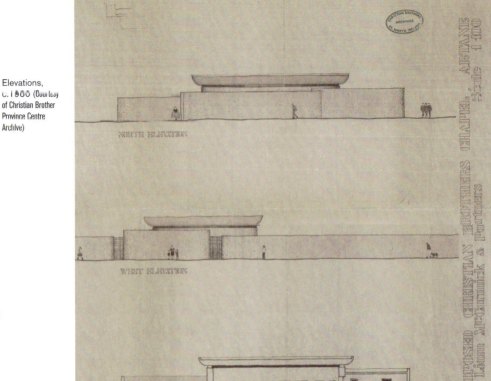

Elevations, c. 1980 (Courtesy of Christian Brother Province Centre Archive)

brought attention to the burial site of a significant number of infants and children in Tuam Mother and Baby Home, which was a decommissioned sewerage tank on an unmarked site.

At Artane, it is not clear at what stage the plans to exhume the remains were abandoned, or whether Dr Daly's campaign had an influence on the decision. Brother Caomhanach wrote that the order had attempted to buy the land back from Abbey Homesteads, prior to its sale to Power Supermarkets, and subsequently entered negotiations with the supermarket group (undated document, Christian Brothers' Archive). In 1978, the Brothers wrote to Archbishop Dermot Ryan regarding the building of a chapel, and in June of the following year, the archbishop instructed Brother T. C. Leonard to appoint Liam McCormick to the design.

McCormick (quoted by Caomhánach) noted the brief as a chapel for 100, with a meeting room, but with the purpose as a memorial chapel for the

Case Study: Artane Oratory

dead of the Artane School being the essence of the project. The drawings in the Christian Brothers' Archive show a slight variation from those dated 1981, which were submitted to Dublin City Council for planning; neither version highlights a memorial wall as a potential or central feature of the chapel brief.

Epigrapher and sculptor, Thomas Glendon, was approached by the architect McCormick to undertake the memorial wall. Working from a list of names supplied by the Christian Brothers, as well as from an introductory inscription and the architectural drawings, Glendon was given free rein in setting out the design of the lettering. The memorial wall had been profiled by the English supplier on the instructions of McCormick, in Whit bed Portland stone. By Glendon's account, he

> 'wanted the feeling that the gentle curve of the ambulatory was like a scroll opened out, so there's the big introductory inscription, then there's the list of names going through, and at the foot of the inscription down near the door there's the prayer from St John's Gospel, and that was more or less the concept of it'. (Glendon, 2019)

Artane Boys Band at official opening ceremony, 1983 (Courtesy of Christian Brothers Province Centre Archive)

Official opening ceremony, 1983 (Courtesy of Christian Brothers Province Archive)

Glendon carried out the stone carving following the opening of the building – 'it was eleven months of work, at 50 hours a week' – with the first three months spent on its design.

> In the background there was an awful lot of preparatory work, each time you wanted to do a design you had to sit down and draw out a list of names, so that was a huge amount of work before you ever got in here.

The inscription of the names was designed to fill the rectangle exactly. Shortly after completion, Glendon was asked to add two additional names:

> A chap came in one day and he was very flustered. He said, 'I don't see my brother's name on this.' And I said, 'Well, I've the list, these men would have gone through this'; and he said, 'No, my brother is buried out here, I know that.' And what happened a couple of years later, I got a phone call from Brother Leonard and it was that there were two boys who were away on family

Case Study: Artane Oratory

holidays, and had died whilst on holidays, but there was nowhere to bury them so they were buried here. But they weren't in the school records as having died in the school, so it's just at the bottom of the inscription; there's two additional names, and they're the two boys. So that's how careful the brothers were, in recording everybody, but the summation insofar as I say, they were all a family group. (Glendon, 2019)

A Liam McCormick Church
The Artane chapel design refers to some idioms seen in a number of Liam McCormick's earlier churches. The continuous strip window running the circumference of the walls – at clerestory level – separating walls from roof, is a much simplified version of the stained glass at St Aengus Church at Burt (Co. Donegal, 1967, Imogen Stuart; also a motif used at St Nicholas, Carrickfergus, 1981). Artane's deep-set window openings with asymmetrical reveals are similar to those in the side chapel at St Michael's Church at Creeslough (Co. Donegal, 1971, with stained glass there by Helen Moloney), as is the curved corner of the high blank walls. The square plan with curved corners is also seen in St Mary's in Maghera (Co. Derry, 1974). The strip skylight above the ambulatory is similar to those at Laytown (Church of the Sacred Heart, Co. Meath, 1979) and Clogher (St Patricks, Co.Tyrone, 1979), while the plan of the Artane Chapel, with its ambulatory and entrance spiralling out from the church body, is redolent of the latter.

The skylight over the altar was a regular motif of McCormick's churches, with the cylindrical collar particularly reminiscent of Creeslough and Maghera. A number of the motifs – the narrow continuous clerestory window, the punched windows, the side wall flicking away from the entrance door, and obviously, the upturned eave – owe a debt to the famous pilgrimage chapel of Notre Dame du Haut (1955, Ronchamp in eastern France) by Le Corbusier.

An avid sailor and enthusiastic traveller, McCormick was familiar with the work of leading modernist architects on the continent. He visited the World Fair in Paris in 1937 while a student in Liverpool, and later cited Le Corbusier's Pavilion Suisse, Alvar Aalto's Finnish Pavilion, and the UAM Pavilion as formative in his design education. An admirer of Alvar Aalto, he sailed to the Baltic in 1956, and again in 1959. He regularly went to Switzerland to visit churches and (also in 1959) visited France, Switzerland and Germany with Frank Corr and Fr Anthony McFeely, the client for the church at Murlog. Fr McFeely accompanied him to Ronchamp around 1962.

Cover of brochure to celebrate opening of Liam McCormick's church at Maghera, Co. Derry in 1974 (Private collection)

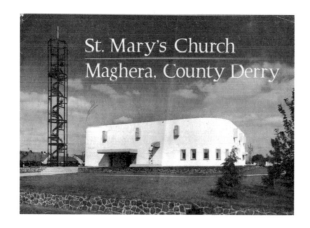

From some angles to the south our chapel in Dublin's Artane is mildly reminiscent of the Creeslough Church, although the curved corners in this instance are the graveyard walls, rather than the church proper. McCormick typically played a significant role in selecting sites for churches, especially in county Donegal and regularly rejected the originally proposed site – in Milford, spotting a hitherto unconsidered 'small hillock' on the way back from the initially proposed site; for Desertegney, selecting a site within view of Lough Swilly; at Burt, contacting the owner of the site he wanted (a Protestant businessman, who agreed to donate a site of McCormick's choosing), rather than build on the existing Catholic Church lands; at Creeslough, selecting a site to the north of that proposed, to use Muckish mountain as a dramatic backdrop. But McCormick had no such indulgence here in the suburbs of North Dublin.

Designed to protect the graveyard, which had become a 'haunt of vandals' (McCormick, undated document in Christian Brothers' Archive), the location of the oratory was immovable. So, unlike many of his Donegal churches, and that at Fossa, Killarney, which benefit from dramatic landscapes, the setting here is entirely flat and unremarkable topographically. Instead, the landscape is marked by low-lying suburban construction whereby the opposite site is occupied by a drive-thru McDonalds.

This is a largely concrete building, with concrete block walls, cavity fill, beams, and foundations. The curved soffit of the roof – although it has the appearance of plasticity associated with concrete – is made of expanded metal on battens and plywood forms. Similarly, the depth of the window reveals and the irregular form of the piers is formed by plastered stud walls. The clerestory strip window that runs the whole circumference of the main body of the church gives the impression that the roof floats. This seamless

Case Study: Artane Oratory

effect, inside and outside, is created by steel rods set into the ring beam, which support the roof. A run of glazing to the exterior, and the stained glass to the interior, hide these.

Artane Oratory could be said to be made up of four parts: the oval making up the body of the church; the ambulatory with its 35-foot memorial wall; the attendant spaces, including the prayer room and sacristy, arranged in a square plan behind closed doors at the west end of the ambulatory; and the graveyard itself, surrounded by high walls, and forming the greater part of a square with curved corners, wrapping around the south-east of the church.

A lesson was learnt from Creeslough, where the fan-shaped plan located the majority of the congregation far from the sanctuary. At this later chapel in Artane, we are truly in the post-Vatican II design phase of Irish Catholic churches (see Donaghmede case study). Here the sanctuary is at the wider end of the oval, addressing the congregation at an angle. The

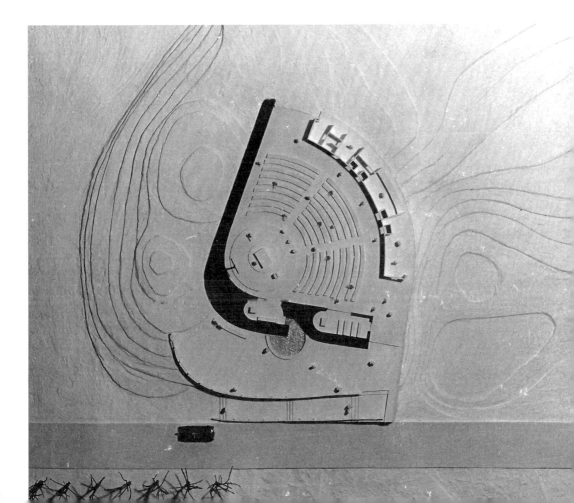

Model of plan for McCormick's church at Creeslough, Co. Donegal, 1971 (Courtesy of Flemming Rasmussen collection)

altar table and lectern (both of Portland stone) are not set behind altar rails – rather, the kneeler to the front pews creates the effect of an altar rail. The two piers which separate the ambulatory from the nave (technically forming a colonnade), are nearly as broad as the spaces between, and each an irregular rhombus shape in plan. These line up with the pews and the tiles, to create a strong visual connection between the ambulatory and the four stained-glass windows. These windows give out onto the graveyard, although due to their opacity and rich colouring, there are no views. The deep irregular reveals give the impression of forming radii converging on a distant point.

The ambulatory contains the 35-foot memorial wall, which is lit from above along its length by the strip roof light. This wall, made from Portland stone, contains the names of the brothers and boys buried in the adjoining graveyard, set out in chronological order. The adjacent sacristy does give views onto the graveyard. The graveyard was landscaped, with paths and trees, and enclosed by high concrete walls. Externally, the distinction between the graveyard walls and the church walls is not great, due to blank elevations. The roof is visible in long views, with its distinctive upturned coving.

Facts and Figures

The oratory is located at 18–21 Kilmore Road, Beaumont, Dublin 5. It was commissioned in 1979, construction began in 1982, and the building opened in August 1983, with work on the memorial stone carving continuing into 1984.

The architect was Liam McCormick (1916–96). Born in Derry, the son of a dental surgeon, he grew up in Donegal. Educated as a boarder at St Columb's College, Derry, he trained as an architect in Liverpool, graduating in 1943. Following local government work (Derry Corporation and Ballymena Council) and a bout of tuberculosis, he teamed up with Frank Corr, a classmate of both St Columb's and Liverpool, to win a competition for the design of a new Roman Catholic (RC) Church in Ennistymon, Co. Clare in 1947. They subsequently set up office in Derry (with Joe Tracey as assistant) as the partnership, Corr and McCormick, (formalised in 1949). Several commissions from the RC Church followed including numerous school buildings in Northern Ireland, and a large number of churches in Donegal, Derry, and elsewhere in Ireland.

McCormick's partnership with Frank Corr was dissolved in 1968, after which he formed Liam McCormick and Partners, which was renamed McCormick Tracey Mullarkey in 1979 when Tom Mullarkey (another former assistant) became partner. McCormick retired from practice in 1982 but continued as a consultant to the practice for some years. His other works in Dublin are the Met Éireann building in Glasnevin (1979) and the Church of the Ascension of the Lord in the south Dublin suburb of Sandyford (1982, Balally). He was the recipient of the 1968 Triennial Gold Medal from the Royal Institute of Architects of Ireland (RIAI) for St Aengus Church at Burt in Co. Donegal, and the Royal Institute of British Architect's commendation for Our Lady of Lourdes Church at Steelstown, Derry.

Builders: Spanstruct of Iona Villas
Stations of the Cross: Caroline Bond
Stained glass windows: Ruth Brandt
Memorial lettering: Thomas Glendon
Tabernacle and surrounds: Leo Higgins (later altered)

Sources

Unpublished
Bro Aodh Caomhánach (probable author), untitled unpublished undated account of the Artane Oratory, c.1993, including press clippings from opening ceremonies. Architectural drawings of earlier design, uncatalogued. Christian Brothers' Archive, Dublin
Dublin City Council planning registry, including planning application plan ref. 2121/81 (application for church) and plan ref. 4049/80 (application for shopping centre, community centre and public open space, which served as outline permission for chapel), both available from Dublin City Library and Archives

Published
Anon., 'Concern at Orphans' Graves Plan', *Irish Independent*, 17 July 1975
Anon., 'Ryan Opens Oratory', *Sunday Tribune*, 28 Aug. 1983
Anon., 'Oratory memorial in Artane', *Irish Independent*, 29 Aug.1983
Anon., 'Why compete with the Eiffel Tower', *Sunday Independent*, 29 July 1984, p. 13
Cantwell, Wilfrid, 'Ecclesiastical Architecture', *Irish Architect* (Vol. 82, Jan./Feb. 1991), pp 61–3
Cantwell, Wilfrid, 'The Churches of Liam McCormick', *Irish Architect* (Vol. 83, Mar./Apr. 1991), pp 60–4
Daly, Cyril, 'Orphans' graves at Artane' (letter to the editor), *Irish Times*, 15 July 1975
Hurley, Richard, 'Cities for God', *Irish Arts Review* (Summer 2008), pp. 125–9
Kennedy, Maev, 'Some of McCormick's later churches reflect influence of Vatican II in character', *Irish Times*, 25 July 1978
Larmour, Paul, and O'Toole, Shane, *North by Northwest: The Life and Work of Liam McCormick* (Gandon Editions, 2008)
Mullane, Dermot, 'Artane residents dissatisfied with plans for housing estate development', *Irish Times*, 13 Sept. 1972
O'Driscoll, R. Q., 'Orphans' graves at Artane' (letter to the editor), *Irish Times*, 17 July 1975
Pollard, Carole, *Liam McCormick: Seven Donegal Churches* (Gandon Editions, 2011)
Viney, Michael, 'The architect's dilemma', *Irish Times*, 4 Dec. 1963
Viney, Michael, 'Property company and local people agree on new centre site', *Irish Times*, 14 Oct. 1975

Case Study
Willow Field, Park Avenue, Sandymount, Dublin 4, 1984

Merlo Kelly

Willow Field is a private housing development in Dublin's coastal Sandymount. Elegant and urbane, the scheme was envisaged as a series of planted courtyards which could potentially be constructed in phases. It is composed of 78 single and two-storey houses organised around a series of five shared courts which serve as car parks. The Willow Field site is long and narrow with a tree-lined road, forming a central spine off which the landscaped courts and dwellings are accessed. The houses were composed in clusters of 12, with each house enjoying access to the shared courtyard in front, and a landscaped garden to the rear. To minimise overshadowing of neighbouring lands, a series of single-storey dwellings were constructed around the perimeter of the scheme, adjacent to the boundary. In a clever move, these perimeter dwellings project forward slightly, creating the desired sense of enclosure for each cluster of houses.

Plans for Willow Field evolved during a period in which there was considerable pressure to construct high-density affordable housing developments on greenfield suburban sites. Density policy in Ireland was traditionally mired in the issue of inner city overcrowding and the mitigation of poor urban living conditions. However, in the 1980s and 1990s it became a tool with which to regulate housing standards. Minimum areas and room sizes were introduced, as were guidelines regarding external space, amenities, and general quality of life. As an inner-suburban scheme, Willow Field displays a successful attempt to provide well-designed, low-budget housing in a calm, landscaped setting, while achieving the desired density. Architect Tony Horan observed that on completion in 1984, the houses in Willow Field were largely acquired by young single women. He attributes this to the fact that mortgages for single women had just been made available for the first time, creating a new demographic. This signified an interesting social change at the time and is reflected in the fact that 36 houses (nearly half of the houses built in the scheme) were one-bedroom dwellings.

The main phase of construction was completed in 1984 and a second and final phase was completed in 1985. Though several houses have undergone alterations, in the form of extensions and conservatories to the rear, and minor additions to the side, the shared areas remain relatively unchanged since their conception. The development is run by a group of residents under the name Wilf Limited, who in 2012 were collecting an annual charge per household of €300 per annum for general maintenance, gardening, communal lighting, public liability insurance, and audited accounts. The façades presented to the street remain uniform, and this is perhaps due to a level of control imposed on homeowners by the residents themselves. The landscaped grounds remain very well maintained, and the houses generally appear to be in excellent condition.

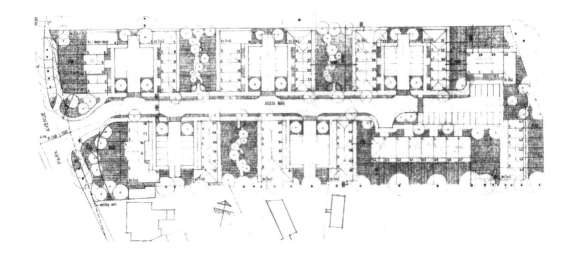

Site plan (Courtesy of Tony Horan image collection)

A Balance of Shared Space and Privacy

Willow Field is situated in Sandymount, a southern suburb of Dublin, four kilometres from the city centre. The development is accessed from the main suburban (leafy) thoroughfare of Park Avenue and is generally located within a larger residential area, 600 metres from Sandymount Green. Park Avenue is predominantly made up of large two-storey red-brick houses, fronted with generous front gardens. The entrance to Willow Field is signalled by planted green areas to either side, with mature trees set back from the public footpath, and by a large willow tree. A granite garden wall breaks to allow access to one of the gardens, and red-brick walls define the development from this point on. Despite the low level of communal public space, landscaping is pivotal to the scheme. The paths along the main spine are lined with grass and mature trees and are maintained by the council – a seamless continuation of the planting strategy along Park Avenue and adjacent streets.

The houses are generally grouped in terraces of six, with five two-storey dwellings concluding with a single-storey house. The terraces of six are paired to form an arrangement of 12 houses around each court. Within each grouping, the single-storey structures project forward, framing the space and creating a sense of enclosure. The pattern of the site is broken to the rear boundary where three groups of houses wrap around the southeast corner and car parks line the street edge. A small area of communal garden space is located in this corner.

The two-storey houses are entered via a small lobby with access to a living room and kitchen/dining room with a hearth. Bedrooms and bathrooms were located on the first floor. The living, dining and kitchen areas are

Case Study: Willow Field, Sandymount

combined in the single-storey houses, with the bedroom and bathrooms located to the rear. The architectural language is consistent throughout the scheme. The form of the houses is traditional, with masonry walls and hipped roofs (pitched roofs that slope upwards from all sides). A modest single-storey projection with a pitched roof announces the entrance to each house and contains an entrance hall within. Similar small-scale projections are found to the rear, roofing a fuel store, and providing a small covered outdoor area. The houses are rendered cavity wall construction – 'a Renovo coloured finish' (*Irish Times*, 21 Mar. 1986), with tiled roofs and red-brick boundary walls. The walls, floor and attic space were fully insulated (*Irish Times*, 12 Oct. 1984), reflecting newly emerging values regarding the thermal performance of private dwellings.

The use of traditional materials and building techniques was driven by the limited budget for the project. However, the efficient manipulation of form, space, and landscaping reflects innovative planning and design. The tightly planned scheme groups the dwellings in such a way as to maximise the sense of open space while maintaining a sense of privacy for each. The plain palette of materials is enhanced by a creative approach to landscaping design, with low redbrick walls delineating the shared open areas, screening the waste bins, and accommodating common seating areas. Planted timber trellises and flower beds further subdivide the dwelling

Floor plans, two of the three house types, as published in Portfolio Presentation to Laing O'Rourke (Courtesy of Tony Horan image collection)

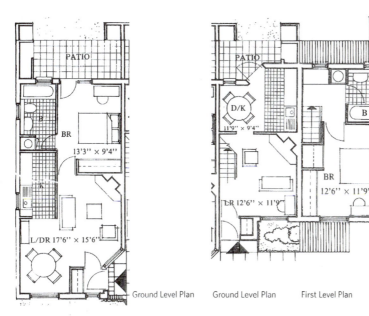

Ground Level Plan   Ground Level Plan   First Level Plan

HOUSE TYPE 01
1-Storey 1-Bedroom Dwelling

HOUSE TYPE 02
2-Storey 1-Bedroom Terrace

(above)
Willow Field, aerial view (Courtesy of Tony Horan image collection)

(below)
Signage, Willow Field (Courtesy of Tony Horan image collection)

zones externally, while providing a visual screen between properties. A layer of planting separates each house from the common footpath and softens the impact of the car parking within the courts. This planting allows a level of personalisation of space within an otherwise homogeneous landscape.

The communal garden spaces to the rear of the houses are enclosed by high redbrick walls which finish in a curve, forming a border along the shared street. This green space can be shared by all 12 houses or subdivided into individual private gardens. A central path and planted pergolas allow for smaller private spaces. Access to this garden is directly from the dwellings, and by a secondary entrance from the footpath. Despite the restricted budget, bespoke decorative tiles were commissioned from a company in Lewes, Sussex for use in signage and house numbering. This small additional expense added, according to the architect Tony Horan, a 'touch of quality' to the appearance of the scheme.

A Natural Extension of the Village Street

Willow Field was one of a number of private housing developments emerging around the outskirts of Dublin in the early 1980s. The development integrates comfortably into the grain of the residential neighbourhood surrounding it. Rather than assuming the architectural armoury of a gated community, the development feels like a natural extension of the streetscape. The presence of Sandymount Green, in the heart of Sandymount village, just half a kilometre from the site for Willow Field, was fundamental to the design of the scheme. Horan is quoted as saying that 'the need to respond to, and indeed, create an extension of this 'village' formed the basis of the layout and detailed design' (*Irish Times*, 27 July 1984). The proximity of Willow Field to Sandymount village, Sandymount Strand and the DART line (the suburban coastal train line) became a major selling point for the scheme, as documented in newspapers at the time.

The selected plot off Park Avenue in Sandymount, an affluent suburb of Dublin, seemed an unlikely site for relatively low-budget housing. Horan Cotter were requested by the client, Killeavy Properties Limited, to design a scheme comprising two-storey dwellings, for under £45,000, in Dublin 4. When purchased, the proposed site for Willow Field had planning permission for 87 apartments, ranging from two to four storeys in height. The architects advised revising the scheme to provide houses instead of apartments, in an effort to avoid the higher development costs associated with apartment schemes. Horan Cotter devised a new design strategy for the site and planning permission was subsequently granted for 78 houses. This resulted in a residential density of 25 dwellings per acre – a relatively high figure for a suburban housing scheme – and greatly reduced the site cost per house.

Thus, Horan Cotter succeeded in the challenge presented by their client to provide dwellings for under £45,000 in Dublin 4. The range of house prices proved competitive, with one-bedroom units advertised on the market for £34,450 (*Irish Times*, 12 Oct. 1984), and three-bedroom units advertised at £57,990 (*Irish Times*, 27 July 1984). An added bonus was that the houses qualified for the £1,000 government grant available at the time, and for the £3,000 mortgage subsidy offered to purchasers (*Irish Times*, 12 Oct. 1984). This made it attractive to younger buyers and, as Horan notes, to young women who had the opportunity to avail of mortgages for the first time. One of the successes of the Willow Field scheme was that it addressed this shifting demographic, to accommodate a cohort that had largely been excluded from the housing market previously.

Willow Field, artist's sketch, 1984 (Courtesy of Tony Horan image collection)

Facts and Figures

The first and main phase of housing at Willow Field was completed in 1984, with a second phase completed in 1985. The client was developer Pat Conlon of Killeavy Properties Limited who also developed the nearby Windermere Apartment scheme in Sandymount.

Architect: Anthony (Tony) Horan of Horan Cotter Associates. Horan Cotter was established in 1978 by Horan and fellow architect, Tony Cotter. Previously, following graduation from Manchester University, Horan had worked with Ernő Goldfinger in London, and in 1967, returned to Dublin as an associate with Stephenson Gibney & Associates (SGA). His projects at SGA included Gaeltarra Éireann Head Offices, a hotel at Ballyferriter, and the DIAS School of Theoretical Physics, Dublin (1972, see MTCB Vol. 2). Horan founded his own practice in 1973, which evolved to become Horan Cotter Associates. The firm developed a particular expertise in housing and was awarded the RIAI Medal for Housing for Richmond Hill, Monkstown, in 1975. Other housing projects included Monkstown Valley, Co. Dublin (1980), Balnagowan housing scheme, Dublin 6 (1982), and Smock Alley Court, Dublin 8 (1997). In 1992 the company Horan Keogan Ryan Chartered Architects (HKR) was formed between Tony Horan, John Keogan and Jerry Ryan, and in 2008, Tony Horan and Brian Rainsford established Horan Rainsford Architects.

Willow Field featured as a case study in a 1999 Government Publication *Planning Issues Relating to Residential Density in Urban and Suburban Locations* (McCabe, O'Rourke, and Fleming, 1999). The report focused on a series of housing developments across Ireland. Willow Field was chosen as an interesting example of smaller dwelling sizes forming a low-rise, high-density scheme. Analysis tabled in the report gave an overview of the planning strategy for Willow Field, categorised as 'inner suburban'. The density is recorded as 62 dwellings per hectare (25 per acre) and the floor area per acre is 1,708 sq. metres giving a plot ratio of 1:0.42. The scheme was acknowledged for addressing changing demographic demand for housing in the later years of the 20th-century.

Sources

Unpublished
Tony Horan Archive, private

Published
Anon., 'The village of Willow Field', *Irish Times*, 27 July 1984
Anon., 'Use of private open spaces dominates development', *Irish Times*, 12 Oct. 1984
Anon., 'Final phase is now on market at Willow Field' *Irish Times*, 15 Nov. 1985
Anon., 'Southernside comforts', *Irish Times*, 21 Mar. 1986
Anon., 'Willow Field special prices', *Irish Times*, 18 Apr. 1986
Anon., 'Willow Field courtyards', *Irish Times*, 13 June 1986
Anon., 'Willowfield's last offer', *Irish Times*, 2 Oct. 1986
McCabe, Fergal, Bryan O'Rourke, Margaret Fleming, *Planning Issues Relating to Residential Density in Urban and Suburban Locations* (Department of the Environment and Local Government, 1999).

Case Study
The Irish Life Centre, Lower Abbey Street, Dublin 1, 1978 and 1985

Carole Pollard

Described by its developers in the 1970s as a city within a city, the Irish Life Centre occupies a large footprint within the north city centre area, stretching from Abbey Street Lower to Talbot Street and from Marlborough Street to Beresford Lane. The Centre comprises a mix of office, residential, leisure and shopping facilities, built predominantly in brown brick, with chunky white concrete arcades and shimmering reflective bronze glass. A nine-storey tower dominates the development, overlooking the main entrance plaza where Oisín Kelly's powerful sculpture 'Chariot of Life' gallops through shooting spouts of water. The various blocks are linked externally by a series of plazas and covered walkways where predominantly hard landscaping imposes a harshness that has come to personify the Centre. However, hidden deep within the development are two raised and lushly planted gardens that provide a wonderful, unexpected counterpoint to the otherwise bleak urban environment. These gardens, with dappled shade of trees, secluded seating areas and background hush of gurgling water, remain a closely-guarded secret known only to a few Dubliners. Their existence peels away the presumption that the Irish Life Centre is a dusty remnant of Dublin's 1970s office block 'boom period', providing a glimpse of the ideological aspirations of the architects and their clients.

The Irish Life Centre is made up of 15 separate blocks: eight completed in 1977 and seven in 1985. They range in height from three to nine storeys, and despite being built over a period of more than ten years, form a unified assembly of buildings. The Centre has a strong architectural identity which is most distinctive around the entrance plaza. But the sporadic appearance of its trademark white concrete colonnade and brown brick façades along Abbey Street, Talbot Street, and Marlborough Street reveal the full scale and ambition of the project. Most of the buildings are in office use and all workers have access to an integrated leisure centre which includes a swimming pool, gym, and squash courts. There are 69 residential apartments in total, 50 in the Talbot Street block and 19 overlooking the Abbey Court Garden. A ground-floor shopping mall, known as Talbot Mall, acted as a north-south pedestrian route through the scheme, while a secondary east-west pedestrian route traversed the entrance plaza, linking Gardiner Street (via Beresford Lane) to Northumberland Square, just off Lower Abbey Street. Parking for 320 cars was provided at basement level.

The Irish Life Centre was commissioned by Irish Life Assurance Company and has been its headquarters since 1977. The office blocks remain in office use, though not all are occupied by Irish Life. Most of the apartments are in private ownership, although a small number were retained by Irish Life. The least successful element of the complex is the shopping mall, which since it opened in the early 1980s, has had a chequered history. Despite several makeovers it failed to attract long-term retail tenants, and in 2021 was converted to a supermarket. Refurbishment works elsewhere in the

Block plan for Phase 1 development showing office blocks arranged around central garden courtyard, 1973 (Courtesy of Robinson Keefe & Devane image collection)

complex threaten to whittle away the integrity of the original design. In 2018 re-paving works were carried out to the external circulation areas including the main plaza and Northumberland Square (Bernard Seymour Landscape Architects). The 'Chariot of Fire' and pool were relocated forward in the main plaza and now have an arguably better relationship with the public street. However, alteration works to the conference centre in the Abbey Court Garden have resulted in the loss of its Frank Lloyd Wrightian ambience. Ongoing replacement of reflective bronze glazing with a blue-hued alternative similarly alters the original architectural character of the complex.

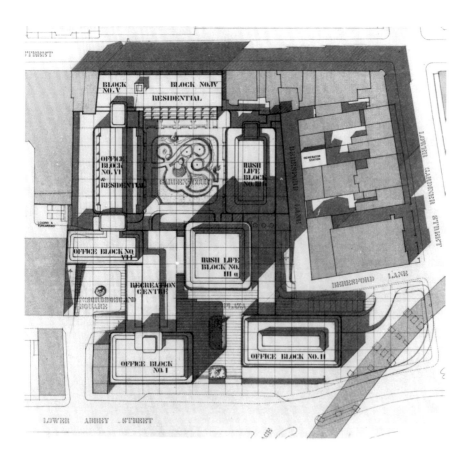

Gardiner Revisited: A Big Development North of the Liffey

The Irish Life Centre was conceived in the early 1970s as a new city quarter, combining office, retail, residential, recreational, civic, and landscape amenity and car parking. It was the first attempt to build a modern mixed-use development in the centre of Dublin city, and the first large scale redevelopment north of the river Liffey since the Georgian period in the 18th century when Luke Gardiner, and his descendants, built Henrietta Street, Parnell Square, O'Connell Street, Mountjoy Square, Gardiner Street, and their environs. Its conception as an integrated mixed-use development is important for its rarity. Devane's argument in his 1975 essay 'Space about buildings' (from the RIAI's *Dublin: A City in Crisis*) was predicated upon his belief that urban living in the heart of the city could be appealing to professionals too.

The catalyst for the redevelopment of this part of the city centre was a fire in July 1970 which caused extensive damage to the Brooks Thomas builder's provider's premises on Abbey Street. The property manager at Irish Life Assurance Company, Michael Lucey, who had worked previously with Dublin Corporation, had unique insight into the development potential for the north side of the city. As Dublin Corporation's Chief Valuer, he had worked on projects relating to the Abrams Report into planning in Ireland (1960) and the Lichfield Plan for Dublin's northside (1969). Recognising the possibilities of a large site so close the city centre, Lucey advised Irish Life to buy the fire-damaged premises. He then set about purchasing adjoining properties, including those belonging to Varian Brushes and the Educational Company of Ireland who both moved in the 1960s to the new industrial estates in Walkinstown on the city's south-west fringes. The secondary acquisitions provided Irish Life with valuable street frontage on busy Talbot Street and included considerable back land sites adjoining the former Brooks Thomas premises. Later acquisitions on Marlborough Street enabled the expansion of the Centre in the 1980s.

Since 1964 Irish Life was based at their headquarters on Mespil Road, in Dublin 4, one of the first office blocks to be constructed on the south bank of the Grand Canal. By the early 1970s, the company had outgrown that accommodation with staff spread across several buildings in the city. The Abbey Street development allowed them to consolidate in one location with better proximity to bus and rail services. It also enabled the provision of on-site parking, a facility that was much encouraged by Dublin Corporation's

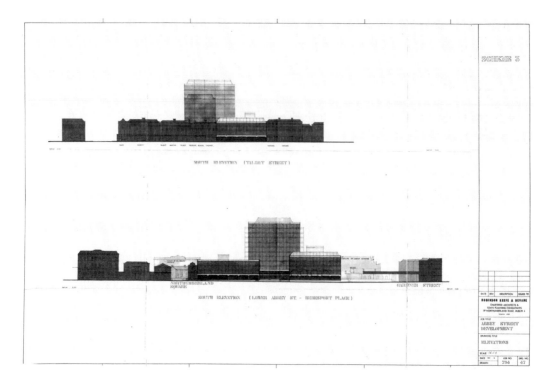

Sections through proposals for Phase 1 development, 1973 (Courtesy of Robinson Keefe & Devane image collection)

planning department at the time. Importantly, the Abbey Street development meant that Irish Life could future-proof their expansion while at the same time produce an investment income by leasing surplus office space to other tenants.

According to Bill Nowlan, who was a member of Irish Life property team that assembled the site, good design and landmark architecture were key elements of the success formula for transformative projects like that at Lower Abbey Street. The brief given to the architects was to make a handsome scheme on a tight budget which would stimulate urban renewal in this part of the city, while always celebrating Irish Life's corporate identity; not forgetting to provide a block of accommodation for Irish Life's chief office.

The first planning application was lodged with Dublin Corporation in 1973. In defence of the scale of the development, the applicants argued that the scheme would greatly enhance the economy and amenity of the neighbourhood. In addition, the applicants argued that the decision of Irish Life to relocate their headquarters to the north inner city would act as a catalyst for the revitalisation of the area and attract other high-quality developments to the north side of the city. The planning process was not without controversy however, and two serious disputes forced appeals to An Bord Pleanála, one by third parties and the other by the developers and their architects.

Case Study: Irish Life Centre

Aerial view of completed Phase 1 and Phase 2 development, 1987 (Courtesy of Robinson Keefe & Devane image collection)

The first dispute involved the demolition of 15 houses in Northumberland Square – a compact enclosed street with only one entry/exit point onto Lower Abbey Street. Despite Dublin Corporation Housing Department's assessment that Northumberland Square was not derelict, permission was granted to demolish the houses to facilitate the development. This sparked a campaign by the Living City Group to save the houses and the community based there. An Taisce and the Dublin Civic Group also made representations on the issue. The developers argued that they would provide residential accommodation in the new development, however The Living City Group and their allies did not consider the provision of luxury apartments adequate compensation for the loss of an established community. The subsequent grant planning permission was appealed to An Bord Pleanála but failed to overturn Dublin Corporation's decision.

The second dispute was spearheaded by the development's architect, Andrew Devane. Dublin Corporation refused permission for the proposed 12-storey central block, stipulating that it must be reduced to nine storeys. Devane was adamant that such loss of height on the scheme's architectural centrepiece would seriously compromise its composition and be detrimental

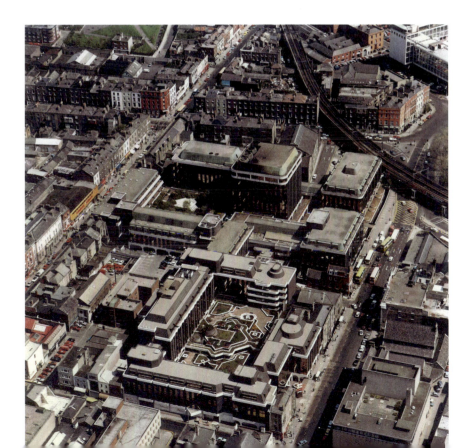

Conference Centre in Abbey Court prior to alteration works in 2019. Photography by Paul Tierney, 2018. (Courtesy of RKD image collection)

to the architectural harmony of the development. For Irish Life, the loss represented a significant reduction in revenue. The appeal to An Bord Pleanála was unsuccessful; not surprising given that building heights were very much the subject of public debate at the time. The dispute over height at the Irish Life Centre ran concurrently with the controversy over the Central Bank which had been built higher than planning permission allowed (see Central Bank case study). Devane very reluctantly changed his design of the central tower by reducing the floor-to-ceiling heights and squeezing ten floors into the nine-storey height stipulated by Dublin Corporation.

In the early 1980s Irish Life acquired adjoining lands which allowed the extension of the Centre to Marlborough Street. Devane took a lesser role in this second phase of development, but the design is primarily his. His colleagues at Robinson Keefe & Devane implemented the same design principles and used the same palette of materials.

Despite the pioneering attitude of the developers and their architects in imagining and implementing a large, complex development in one of the most dilapidated parts of the city, the Irish Life Centre garnered little attention in the press when it was officially opened. Coverage in architectural and construction journals was limited to short articles in *Plan* and *Build* magazines which were essentially regurgitations of press statements.

Case Study: Irish Life Centre

Space About Buildings

Devane was appointed by Irish Life as the architect for the Irish Life Centre just as work was being completed on his first Irish Life collaboration, Stephen Court (1972) (see *MTCB* Vol. 2). Devane had been in architectural practice since the early 1940s, but Stephen Court was his first office block commission. The leap from designing an infill office block at Stephen Court to designing an entirely new city quarter at Abbey Street was great, but Devane was unperturbed. The appointment allowed him to put into practice contemporary town-planning theories and urban design policies that he had first tentatively explored at Stephen Court.

Since 1970, Devane was chairman of a specially convened group under the RIAI Planning Committee, known as the *Dublin Urban Study*. In 1975, the group's research work was published as *Dublin: A City in Crisis* (RIAI), a series of essays written by some of Dublin's best-known architects. Devane's essay, 'Space about Buildings', was a discourse on the relationship between buildings and their surrounding space(s), in the context of Dublin's townscape. Devane suggested how the transition from a legacy of decay and dereliction to a modern city might be handled. He envisioned a revitalised city built around new transport infrastructure, a clean-flowing River Liffey and tree-lined boulevards flanked by gleaming modern buildings. Landscape was an essential element of his proposal, used to soften edges,

control, and maintain human scale, and provide a pleasant backdrop for buildings built with modern materials and new technologies.

Devane's concepts aligned closely with those of Frank Lloyd Wright, with whom Devane had apprenticed in the United States during the 1940s: promoting harmony between human habitation and the natural world. Devane used drawings of the Irish Life Centre to illustrate his *City in Crisis* essay, describing how integration of built form and nature would counteract the disadvantages of 'the surrounding environment [which was] dreary and noisy with traffic and trains.' He proposed

> a large landscaped garden with mature trees surrounded by residential, recreation and office buildings of varying heights is set at the heart of the complex... to provide what is hoped will be a homely and peaceful haven for the use of occupants and their friends. (*Dublin: A City in Crisis*, 1975, p. 78)

The palette of materials for the new Irish Life HQ was like that selected by Devane at Stephen Court. The external finishes included exposed white concrete columns, beams, arcades, parapets and fascias constructed in-situ with a textured bush-hammered finish. The combination of dark brown clay brick and bronze-tinted reflective solar glass set in bronze-anodised aluminium framing has become the instant defining feature of the scheme. However, when viewed in its totality – as Devane intended – the shifting heights of the various blocks, with their rounded corners and shapely copper roof profiles created a soft, non-adversarial hierarchy that responded well to the adjacent buildings on the surrounding streets, and to each other. The two landscaped garden courts, situated deep within the development as amenity spaces for both office workers and residents, provide relief from the unrelenting urban conditions that surround the Centre.

Devane created different conditions depending on where each edge of his scheme met the city. At Talbot Street, a typical Dublin retail street lined with brick-faced houses with shopfronts at ground-floor level, Devane simultaneously integrated into, and disrupted, the existing streetscape. He retained the street edge and existing parapet line but recessed the new shopfronts deep within the ground-floor concrete arcade. The main entrance to Talbot Mall was therefore weakened and the bronze tinted shopfronts did not entice shoppers inside. Many subsequent alterations and upgrades – including the appointment of a Swedish shopping centre specialist in the

Mosaic mural in Abbey Court Garden by Desmond Kinney, now demolished (Courtesy of RKD image collection)

1980s – failed to resolve the shopping mall's inherent flaws, and it has now been subsumed into one large supermarket premises. Similarly, the later phase frontage onto Marlborough Street has failed to engage fully with the street, but Irish Life have plans to upgrade here.

Northumberland Square – the residential enclave demolished to facilitate the development – was the name given to the smaller of the two main external plazas and held the second entrance to the Talbot Mall. It is the intersection between the first phase of the development completed in 1978 and the later phase completed in 1986. Despite recent upgrading, it remains a dull space because it is overshadowed by the surrounding buildings for most of the day.

The Irish Life Centre's most successful engagement with the city is on its southern edge where the raised main plaza spills out onto Lower Abbey Street with a clear vista to the River Liffey. Three large, round-edged office blocks (ten storeys, six storeys and five storeys) define the edges of the plaza which has been recently re-paved (2018/19). Known throughout his career for his collaboration with Irish artists, Devane was instrumental in appointing Irish sculptor, Oisin Kelly (1915–81) to create the plaza's centrepiece – 'Chariot of Life' – a depiction in bronze of a warrior and horses in a raised pool and fountain. Unfortunately, Kelly died before the piece was installed. In 2019 the public sculpture was relocated closer to the plaza's street edge and given a new two-tiered fountain setting.

More Than Concrete Blocks Volume 3

Conference Centre
set in Abbey Court
Garden. 1985
(Courtesy of RKD image
collection)

The muted brindle palette – of varying shades of brown, and of rough concrete juxtaposed with smooth bronze surfaces – made the Irish Life Centre a building very much of the late 1970s. Since its completion, there has been little nostalgia for this aesthetic. For most Dubliners the Irish Life Centre was a remnant of a brief and tumultuous 1970s heyday and the complex was most closely associated with the grim recession of the 1980s. Recent upgrading works by Irish Life, who still own and manage the complex, indicate their intention to invest in the future of the Centre, however it remains to be seen how changes will impact the integrity of Devane's original scheme.

Facts and Figures

Andrew Devane of Robinson Keefe & Devane was appointed architect in 1971. Phase I and Phase II of the scheme were completed in 1978 and included eight blocks. Blocks 1 and 2 faced onto the main plaza and were let to other tenants. Blocks 3A, the ten-storey tower, and 3B behind it, were occupied by Irish Life as their headquarters. The scheme included another office block facing onto Northumberland Square, a recreational centre and two blocks of apartments. A shopping centre filled the ground floor of the Talbot Street apartment block and fed under a raised garden court, exiting onto Northumberland Square. The basement carpark could accommodate 320 cars.

Phase III was completed in 1985 and comprised seven office blocks (A–G) arranged around the Abbey Garden courtyard. Blocks A and B faced onto Lower Abbey Street, while Block C faced onto Marlborough Street. Blocks D, E, F and G formed the north and east edges of Abbey Court and had no public street façades. Block G contained 19 apartments.

The buildings were set out on a square grid of 7.5 metres. The total area is approximately 41,000 sq. metres including 31,000 sq. metres of offices, 7,500 sq. metres of retail space, and 2,500 sq. metres of residential accommodation.

Architects: Robinson Keefe & Devane Architects
Lead Designer and Project Architect – Andrew Devane assisted by Roddy McCaffrey and Philip O'Reilly. Because of the scale of the development and the duration of its construction, many other Robinson Keefe & Devane employees were involved in the project also.

Andrew Devane was born in Limerick and studied architecture at University College Dublin (UCD) where he graduated in 1941. In 1943 he sat examinations to become a town planning consultant. In 1946 he travelled to Frank Lloyd Wright's Taliesin Fellowship where he spent 14 months. On his return to Ireland, he re-joined Paddy Robinson and Cyril Keefe in the architectural practice of Robinson Keefe. In 1948 he became a partner in the practice, renamed Robinson Keefe & Devane (later RKD Architects). He was a prolific and versatile designer. His early works include the Mortuary Chapel at Naas (1948) and the GI Unit at the Meath Hospital (1954, see MTCB, Vol. 2). His portfolio of buildings includes churches, hospitals, primary schools, and technical schools. He is probably best known for his house at Howth, Journey's End Lodge (1961), St Fintan's Church at Sutton (1973), and his major campus developments including St Patrick's College, Drumcondra (1964), AIB Bankcentre (1979), the Irish Life Centre on Abbey Street (1978 & 1982).

Roddy McCaffrey, a nephew of RKD founding partner, Cyril Keefe, studied architecture at UCD. On graduation in 1953 he spent a short time at RKD before travelling to work in the United States. He returned to the practice in 1962 and worked there until his retirement. McCaffrey was Devane's right-hand man, working closely with him on all his projects.

Philip O'Reilly graduated from Bolton Street in 1971 and, having worked in Robinson Keefe & Devane as a student, joined the firm on graduation. Initially, he mostly worked for partner Fred Browne but in 1973 he was transferred to Andy Devane's team to work on the Irish Life Centre, eventually becoming the project architect. He remained on the Irish Life project until he left RKD in 1982.

Quantity Surveyors: Boyd & Creed
Structural Engineers: O'Connell & Harley / Horgan & Lynch
Mechanical & Electrical Engineers: Delap & Waller
Air-Conditioning and Mechanical Services installed by Climate Engineering Ltd
Landscape Architects: Brady Shipman Martin
Main Contractors: John Sisk & Son (Dublin) Ltd
Letting Agents: Jones Lang Wootton

Artists: Oisin Kelly: *Chariot of Life* in main plaza (See *MTCB*, Vol. 2, Garden of Remembrance); Alexandra Wejchert: triptych sculpture in entrance lobby; Desmond Kenny: mosaic murals in Abbey Court Garden and in restaurant; John Behan: sculpture of rising birds in central pond in Secret Garden

Sources

Unpublished
Vincent Delaney, interview by Carole Pollard, Apr. 2018
Philip O'Reilly, Philip, interviewed by Carole Pollard, Apr. 2018
Roddy McCaffrey, interviewed by Carole Pollard, June 2018
Bill Nowlan, interviewed by Carole Pollard, May 2020
Colman Billings, interviewed by Carole Pollard, Mar. 2021
Bowtell, Philip, interviewed by Carole Pollard, Apr. 2021
Anon., *General Brief for Chief Office New Building for Irish Life Assurance Co. Ltd* (Nov. 1972)
Irish Life archive file of promotional brochures
Greenfield, J., *Report for Planning Appeal Hearing* (14 Oct. 1973)
Pollard, Carole, 'Andy Devane and the Architecture of the Modern Irish Office Block, 1963–1979' (unpublished PhD thesis, UCD School of Architecture, July 2022)
RKD archive No. 794 – job files and drawings

Published
Anon., 'Group Aims to Save Square's Community Life', *Irish Independent*, 29 Mar. 1973
Anon., 'State to Probe Irish Life Furniture Deal', *Irish Press*, 14 Jan. 1976
Anon., 'Irish Life Centre', *Plan* (Vol. 8, Oct. 1977)
Anon., 'Irish Life, Bronze Bastion', in *Build* (June 1978)
Anon., 'New Look for the 90s', in *Plan* (Issue 7, 1993)

Crume, Agnes, 'Design Seen. Roof Garden, Irish Life Centre', in *Landscape Architecture* (Mar./Apr. 1983)

Devane, Andrew, 'Space About Buildings', *Dublin: A City in Crisis* (RIAI, 1975)

Ferriter, Diarmaid, *Ambiguous Republic: Ireland in the 1970s*, (Profile Books, 2013)

Grogan, Dick, 'Irish Life Development to Transform City Centre', *Irish Times*, 25 Nov. 1976

McDonald, Frank, *The Destruction of Dublin* (Gill & MacMillan, 1985)

Harwood, Elain and Alan Powers (eds), *The Seventies: Rediscovering a Lost Decade of British Architecture* (c20th Society, 2012)

O Beirne, Tomás (ed.), *A Guide to Modern Architecture in Dublin* (Architecture in Ireland, 1978)

Stephenson, Sam, 'Importance of Layout in Office Design', special supplement in *Irish Times*, 19 Nov. 1968

Tansey, Paul, 'Irish Life in the Hot Seat', *Irish Times*, 15 Jan. 1976

Case Study
Juvenile Court, Smithfield, Dublin 7, 1987

Merlo Kelly

The Juvenile Court (formerly the Children's Courthouse, known today as Children's Court) occupies a long narrow plot at the junction of Smithfield and New Church Street. The three-storey building neatly reinstates the corner of the former Jameson Distillery site and introduces a modest formality to the square. Embedded within the historic context of Smithfield Market (which dates from 1660), the scale, rhythm, and materiality of the redbrick and limestone façades reference the adjoining redbrick houses and neighbouring warehouse structures. The building presents a solid defensive edge to the industrial urban block. Its deep-set splayed openings and punctured square vents to the ground floor are reminiscent of the defensive architecture associated with the medieval tower house.

The Jameson Distillery complex was under threat of demolition in the 1980s, and this informed the selection of a site for the new courthouse in the early stages of the project. The introduction of a contemporary architectural language, while respecting and referencing the historic setting, was fundamental to the design approach. The smooth limestone base of the courthouse was carefully stitched into the rough distillery warehouse walls in an effort to deter demolition and preserve the industrial heritage. The curved copper roof of the motor room, which has turned green over time, was intended to reference the copper domes of the Dublin skyline. Another underpinning principle was the creation of an 'internal street' within the building. In the classical tradition, the primary spaces of the courthouse are arranged in a symmetrical composition along a central axis – a top-lit atrium. The central doorway, marked by a keystone motif and flanked by columns, allows access to this internal street. The visitor is drawn in through the entrance hall to the waiting gallery via a top-lit staircase. The remaining workings of the building are rendered subordinate to the public areas, the relatively modest office spaces and ancillary rooms contrasting with the generosity of the stair hall and surrounds.

Patterns of use have altered somewhat since the original building conception. A significant change is the exclusion of the public from the first floor waiting area. This measure was apparently taken to limit noise levels on the upper floors which had become a hindrance to court proceedings. With the exception of the recently assigned Victim Support Office, the upper floor is used primarily for file storage. The external walkway connecting the judges' block to the upper floor is no longer in use, which stems the circulation flow. The detention rooms, shown as two large rooms on the original plans, have been subdivided to create four holding cells with WC facilities. Stone benches with bull-nosed edges were formed as part of the entrance elevation with the intention of providing a place to sit and experience the life of the square. These benches have since been removed to discourage lingering, and later developments have greatly altered the character of Smithfield market and of the urban block within which the courthouse sits.

More Than Concrete Blocks Volume 3

Section drawing by John Tuomey, Project Architect at OPW (Courtesy of Irish Architectural Archive and OPW)

Layered Façades and a Public Core

The commissioning of a new Juvenile Court arose at a time when sub-standard court conditions had come under scrutiny, and court reform was on the government agenda. The Children's Court in the basement of Dublin Castle was no longer viable and it was proposed to move the courts temporarily to the Four Courts until new accommodation was acquired. This was deemed unsatisfactory as it was not policy to allow children into (adult) courts until they were at least 15 years old, and many of the defendants were younger. At the same time, judges' quarters were in need of reform. All of these issues were to be addressed in the creation of a new courthouse.

In 1980, the New Works V department in the Office of Public Works (OPW) was given the brief to provide a new Juvenile Court in Dublin. The complex brief called for two courtrooms with public circulation and waiting areas, offices for staff, judges, and Gardaí, holding cells for defendants and separate circulation routes for defendants, judges, staff, and visiting members of the public. The previous court, which was housed in the basement of Dublin Castle in grim conditions, was temporarily moved to the Four Courts. As an architect in the OPW, John Tuomey was asked to survey the site of the Linders car showroom, on the corner of Smithfield and Haymarket, which was under consideration for adaptation as a Juvenile Court. Furthermore, Tuomey was given the task of examining the Jameson

Case Study: Juvenile Court, Smithfield

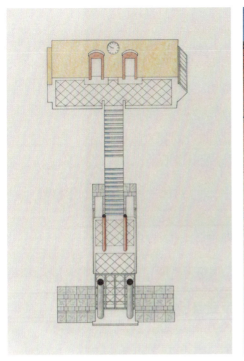

Floor plan study by John Tuomey, Project Architect at OPW (Courtesy of Irish Architectural Archive and OPW)

Front of building shortly after completion (Courtesy of Irish Architectural Archive and OPW)

distillery buildings, also in Smithfield. On inspection, the Linders building proved unsuitable for adaptation as a court and instead the corner site of the Jameson Distillery block across the square was proposed for the project. Following a survey, the site was pronounced suitable and the project for a new courthouse formally commenced in 1983.

The prospect of building within the historic context of Smithfield presented certain design challenges. Though accepted in the European context, the notion of a 'conversation with history' was one which had not been fully embraced in the Irish context. The writings and works of Swedish architect (and modernist), Erik Gunnar Asplund, document his efforts to work within a regional context while bringing contemporary ideas from the world of architecture. Young architect John Tuomey aspired to this ideal of Asplund's, drawing from the fabric of the historic urban setting – in this case, historic Smithfield – while introducing a contemporary 1980s language.

Studies of classical models, and the work of architects like Andrea Palladio and Thomas Ivory led to the exploration of a stripped-down classical form, expressed in the Post-Modern idiom. The plan of the courthouse owes much to the Irish courthouse tradition, and Tuomey cites the central courthouse in his native Dundalk as inspiration. The Dundalk Courthouse, which sits prominently on the town square, is a classical revival building

Elevation to New Church Street (Courtesy of Irish Architectural Archive and OPW)

based on the Temple of Theseus in Athens, dating from 1819 and designed by Edward Parke. A sequence of external spaces within the Dundalk building, in the Greek tradition, was key to the later Smithfield building's design concept.

Though rationally composed in plan, closer study reveals a complex system of circulation at Smithfield. The brief called for the separation of defendants, the public, judges, and staff which resulted in three entrance points and four vertical circulation routes. All the workings of the court operate around a light-filled atrium space, the public realm. In an article on the courthouse for *The Architects' Journal* architectural historian John Olley likens this illuminated core to 'a theatre of the law, a public forum before the seat of justice which sits behind the inner façade' (Olley, 1988, p. 36). A progression along the primary axis is punctuated by a series of layered façades, terminating at this inner façade which allows access to the courtrooms. The secondary spaces serve the axially placed public realm and introduce a labyrinthine quality to the organisation which is heightened at ground level. The holding cells are connected to a concealed staircase which allows separate access for the defendants to the courtrooms and borrows natural light from the courtrooms by means of glazed clerestory panels.

Case Study: Juvenile Court, Smithfield

The layered spatial composition of the interior echoes the work of the Swedish architect, Asplund. The columns to the main entrance are mirrored by a second set of columns in the entrance hall. A third façade is presented on the first floor addressing the waiting area, where the doors to the courtrooms feature a Post-Modern abstraction of the historic segmental pedimented doorcase. A large clock with Roman numerals terminated the axis completing the composition of the inner façade (a replacement clock now hangs in its place). Olley notes similarities with Asplund's public buildings in the placement of the clock and the axial stair rising through an enclosed space (Olley, 1988, p. 36).

The long narrow plot lent itself to this sequential progression through the principal spaces, devised as a means by which to extend the public realm of the street into the building. The sense of the exterior within is compounded by the stripped-down aesthetic – the ruled and lined plaster of the concourse echoing that of the classical courthouse, and the steel handrails and bare strip lighting creating this interior 'public realm'. A sectional isometric drawing by the architects perfectly illustrates this concept of a dominant public core.

The timing of the Smithfield courthouse commission coincided with the UCD Dublin City Quays symposium (see 1980s essay) and vertical-structure college project – a project in which all years of the School of Architecture were engaged. John Tuomey and Sheila O'Donnell led a group investigating the future of Smithfield and its connections to the Liffey quayside. This academic endeavour was prompted by a perceived planning crisis, specifically ignited by Dublin Corporation's radical road-widening proposals and plans for a central transport hub on the quays. Olley notes O'Donnell & Tuomey's aspirations to 'remake the city by fusing its fragments to make a sequence of spaces rather than a collection of objects' (Olley, 1988, p. 36). Tuomey's work on the courthouse undoubtedly reflects this ambition.

A 'House-Sized' Building

Despite classical influences and a defensive presence on the square, the new Children's Court was conceived as a 'house-sized building', signifying a move away from the formality of the conventional courthouse. A deep recess in the side elevation allows the massing of the structure to be broken down, and the form of the courtrooms to be expressed. It is also a device that allows the judges' quarters to assume the scale and separate identity of a house. The small, naturally lit, naturally ventilated courtrooms further reject the formality

(left) Interior of
courtroom, 1987
(Courtesy of Irish
Architectural Archive and
OPW)

and intimidation of a traditional courtroom. Solicitors' offices were provided in the building so that meetings could be held outside of the courtroom, and welfare officers were given accommodation with the idea that the courthouse could become an accessible place for consultations and advice.

The structure of the courthouse is reinforced concrete, clad in smooth redbrick and textured limestone blocks, a reference to the materials of the adjacent houses on the square and the limestone warehouses of the Jameson distillery complex. The weighty limestone base comprises alternate bands of bush-hammered plain limestone, fossilised wet sand rubbed limestone, and plain wet sand rubbed limestone over a bevelled plinth. At the front and side entrances, the plinth terminates in an elegant, splayed detail as it reaches the door jamb. This accomplished use of assorted limestone finishes, along the banded layers of the stone base, adds a textural richness to the façade and establishes a rhythm, delineating the dimensions of the window openings and deep-set square vents overhead. The solidity of the stone base is offset by the lightweight qualities of the projecting canopy to the front façade, the bay window to the waiting area, and the pitched glazed roofs of the courtrooms. The two upper storeys are expressed in redbrick and borrow their proportions from the adjoining redbrick buildings fronting the square. Existing parapet lines are respected on both elevations.

The interior workings are revealed externally through the expression of the various elements in the composition of the façade. A rather mannered steel and glass canopy crowns the recess and balcony to the entrance elevation, announcing the roof-lit public space within. The banded limestone columns flanking the main entrance and curved step introduce this central interior space which spans the depth of the building to the courtrooms. The flat roofs are asphalt and gravel, with steel frame rooflights over the central atrium space and perched on the front façade. An angular steel frame bay window projects through the south elevation signalling the waiting gallery.

The tiled surfaces, ruled and lined plastered walls, mild steel handrails, and timber benches of the public areas reinforce the sense of the exterior, and contrast with the softer materiality of the modest courtrooms. The courtrooms, diffused in natural light, bring about a shift in scale and exude a sense of privacy and intimacy essential to the Juvenile Court process. This is reinforced by the timber parquet floors, panelled walls, and carefully crafted oak furniture. Painted steel radiator covers display cut square perforations echoing the square motif of the external vents and the courtroom door surround.

Case Study: Juvenile Court, Smithfield

The double-skin roof structures over the courtrooms aspired to introduce natural light and ventilation to spaces that had not enjoyed such conditions in their previous incarnation. This design approach reflects the drive for reform, driven by the 'Dickensian' conditions of the former Children's Courts embedded in the basement of Dublin Castle (Tuomey, July 2014). The innovative roof system was devised to establish a system of cross ventilation through the void and to minimise solar gain within the spaces, allowing the passage of fresh air though a series of outlet louvres at eaves level. A continuous gap along the ceiling edge was designed to allow this cross flow. For various reasons, attributed to excessive noise levels and over-heating, the louvres were blocked, and extract vents were installed.

Facts and Figures

The project architect (New Works V, OPW) was John Tuomey (working under John Cumming)

John Tuomey, partner in O'Donnell + Tuomey Architects, was born in Tralee in 1954 and graduated from the School of Architecture in UCD in 1976. On graduation he moved to London and worked for the office of Stirling Wilford Associates where he worked on the Staatsgalerie in Stuttgart, among other projects, until his return to Dublin in 1980. He was engaged as an architect at the Office of Public Works from 1981–7, and was responsible for various public projects such as the Abbotstown Laboratory and the Juvenile Courthouse in Smithfield. He received a Masters of Architecture in 2004, publishing a book on his research entitled *Architecture, Craft and Culture* (Gandon Editions, 2004). For more on Tuomey, in practice with Sheila O'Donnell, see IFI Case Study.

The Juvenile Court was given an AAI Award in 1987, and Tuomey was the recipient of a Millennium Award for Architecture from the Lord Mayor in November 1988.

Architectural technicians: Brendan Walsh and Leonard Whyte
Assistant Principal Architect (New Works V, OPW): John Cumming
Senior Architect, OPW: David Slattery
Principal Architect, OPW: Noel de Chenu
Services Engineer: Tom Glynn, OPW
Quantity Surveyor: Aiden Quinn, OPW
Structural Consultant: Donald Keogan Associates

Sources

Unpublished
John Tuomey, interviewed by Merlo Kelly, July 2014
Children's Court Smithfield, collection of drawings – OPW Library & Archives (Trim, no photography permitted)
O'Donnell + Tuomey website: http://www.odonnell-tuomey.ie (accessed 2014–23)

Published
Anon., '*Irish Times*' journalist receives Millennium award', *Irish Times*, 1 Dec. 1988
Becker, Annette, John Olley and Wilfred Wang (eds), *Ireland. 20th-Century Architecture* (Prestel, 1997)
Casey, Christine, *Dublin: The City within the Grand and Royal Canals and the Circular Road with the Phoenix Park* (Yale University Press (Buildings of Ireland series), 2005)
Graby, John (ed.), *Building on the Edge of Europe* (Gandon Editions, 1996)
McDonald, Frank, 'Juvenile Courthouse, Smithfield', *Irish Times*, 18 Aug. 1988
Murray, Hugh, 'Smithfield Courthouse', *Irish Architect* (Issue 65, Feb./Mar. 1988), pp. 33–7
O'Connor, Ciaran and John O'Regan, *The Architecture of the Office of Public Works, 1831–1987* (AAI, 1987)
O'Donnell + Tuomey, *Buildings and Projects* (Gandon Editions, 1988)
O'Donnell + Tuomey, *Profile* (Gandon Editions, 1997)
O'Donnell + Tuomey, *Space for Architecture* (Artifice Books, 2014)
Olley, John, 'Dublin Courts', *The Architects' Journal* (Vol. 187, No. 28, 13 July 1988), pp. 32–43
Tuomey, John and O'Donnell, Sheila, *Architecture, Craft and Culture: Reflections on the Work of O'Donnell and Tuomey* (Gandon Editions, 2004)

Case Study

Atrium/Loos Bar, Trinity Dining Hall Restoration, TCD, Dublin 2, 1987

Aoife O'Halloran

Trinity College Dublin's Dining Hall building has fed the university for over 250 years. Sitting to the north of the university campus' Front Square and opposing the later Reading Room (1928–37) and Campanile or bell tower (1853), the Dining Hall is one in a collection of classical stone buildings which forms the social quarter of the university. Providing cheap lunches to the city and commons (the daily evening meal) to Trinity's fellows and scholars, the Dining Hall is familiar to many. A fire in 1984 precipitated an extensive restoration and adaption project. It is these works, carried out by architects de Blacam & Meagher, which find this 18th-century building in this volume. de Blacam & Meagher restored, replanned, and regularised the building which had been left roofless and open to the elements. In all, the works involved over 68 different subcontracts, lasted three years, and was duly recognised with the Europa Nostra Award for conservation.

The rigour with which the firm restored the building was carried through to subsequent interventions made within it. Of these, most notable is their insertion of a lofty, four-storey galleried timber atrium; not forgetting their playful insertion of a handed replica of Austrian modernist architect, Adolf Loos's 'American Bar'. Here, the famous Viennese bar, built in the image of America, is recreated in Dublin nearly 80 years on. Built originally in 1908 in 290 square feet, the American Bar in Vienna, or 'Kärtner Bar' as it is now known, is an architectural fascination. Materials such as silk, marble, onyx, brass, and mahogany compose a rich interior. Mirrors above eye level on three sides, reflect the columnar room to infinity; at once intimate and expansive. This intense orchestration is fastidiously recreated in Trinity in using Kilkenny marble, painted MDF and plywood. Though Dublin's model departs from Vienna's where economy and circumstance dictate, the replication is impressive. Manned daily at lunch and ahead of commons, the bar is a quirk still enjoyed by Trinity's fellows and senior staff.

de Blacam & Meagher's other intervention, the Atrium, was worked a little harder. It played a significant role in the successful reconfiguration of the building, connecting the Dining Hall's generally disparate elements and serving as ante-room to the building's eating and drinking. Despite its masterful integration within its existing context, students and staff remain somewhat ambivalent to the structure. With an un-programmed space at its centre, the atrium does not fulfil a daily role in the College's life. Rather, hosting conferring photo shoots, graduation drinks and the occasional theatrical performance, amongst other miscellany, the Atrium sits largely underused. This has perhaps aided the preservation of its fine timber stairs and shutters, which after 35 years of wear might otherwise be in poor order. In any case, the Atrium's significance is perhaps best viewed in the context of the Irish architectural community. de Blacam & Meagher's work here is a statement around the reuse of existing buildings which has been read and reread, drawn and redrawn, in the many fine architectural interventions they and other's made in existing buildings since the 1980s, across Dublin and Ireland.

Lower ground floor plan (Courtesy of de Blacam & Meagher collection at Irish Architectural Archive)

Ever-Shifting Structures: Histories of Trinity's Dining Hall

Designed by Hugh Darley, the Dining Hall Building was substantially complete by 1765. It was preceded, however, by an earlier ill-fated Eating Hall which was built in 1743 and designed by Richard Castle. This earlier Eating Hall was razed 18 years after its construction following the collapse of its vaults. Sheds were built specifically to house elements salvaged for reuse in the new (1760s) Dining Hall. The old Scotch flags were re-laid on the floors of the new hall for example, Ionic capitals – that is, scrolled volutes – were reused in its façade, and it is thought that the timber panelling which lines the walls of Darley's Hall is that which once lined Castle's.

Five bays wide, three storeys tall, Darley's Dining Hall sits over vaulted stone cellars known as The Buttery. Entrance steps lead from Front Square, through a portico, into a vestibule and on to a great Dining Hall known to public, scholar, and fellow alike. The original plan was simple – entrance vestibule with Common Room above and Dining Hall beyond, both of which were served from the west by a tall ceilinged kitchen and from vaulted cellars below. Insufficient for a university which has grown multi-fold since then, the building has been subject to significant alteration. By the 1970s, the circulation of people and plates had become arduous and complicated; up,

Case Study: Atrium/Loos Bar, Trinity Dining Hall Restoration

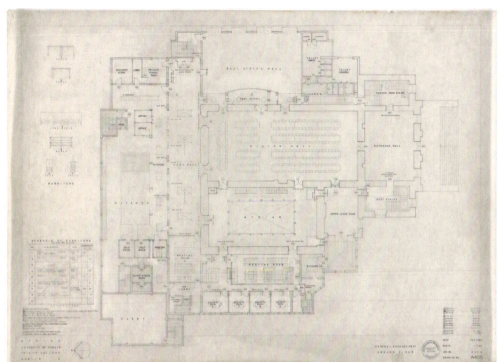

Ground floor plan (Courtesy of de Blacam & Meagher collection at Irish Architectural Archive)

down and across floors. A building that was already complex in terms of both function and ritual had become overwrought.

In 1984, a second major salvaging operation happened; this time, as a result of fire. On Friday 13th of July an electrical fire spread rapidly through the 200-year-old roof timbers of the Dining Hall. Yellow, black acrid smoke was reported to have risen over Trinity College. The Dining Hall's bell fused and melted, while the building's roof timbers collapsed, crushing and burning furniture below. Damage caused from fireman's hoses outweighed that caused by the fire itself: thick masonry walls and vaults were soaked through; the oak panelling lining the Dining Hall was left sodden; and some minor rooms flooded. In the immediate aftermath, College Architect Ian Roberts of McDonnell and Dixon made a posthumous record of the building from memory, from photographs and from salvaged debris. This record would form the basis of initial stabilisation works carried out by well-known contractor G&T Crampton.

While unfortunate, the fire was well timed as it coincided with changes already afoot for the Dining Hall. In the preceding years, the College had embarked on a process of expansion and appraisal of its building stock ahead of its 1992 quatercentenary (that is, 400-year-old) celebrations.

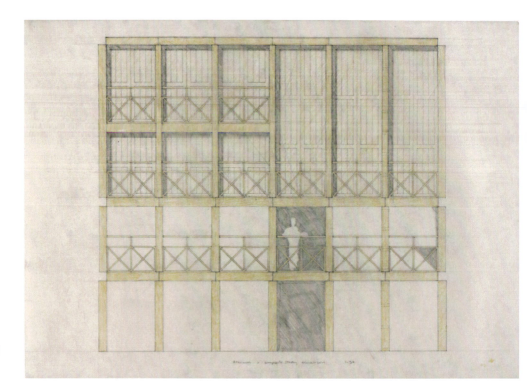

Study of internal elevations (Courtesy of de Blacam & Meagher collection at Irish Architectural Archive)

Dublin-based architects de Blacam & Meagher, supported by Paul Koralek of Ahrends Burton Koralek (ABK) Architects (see *MTCB* Vol. 2, Berkeley Library case study), had won a competition by interview to engage with the College in this regard. Preceding the fire, a study of the re-use of existing buildings of Front Square had concluded with the decision to replan the Dining Hall building. Where the expansion of the College had previously demanded increased catering facilities, the growth in cafes and casual dining in Dublin city centre, outside the College, now necessitated its reduction. As such, a brief was drawn up to reduce the catering capacity of the building and introduce student society rooms in its place. de Blacam & Meagher, already appointed to design and build the upcoming Samuel Beckett Theatre for the University, were thus engaged for works to the Dining Hall.

A New Life for the Dining Hall: Restoring and Replanning

de Blacam & Meagher's proposal at this stage was compromised by a limited brief which drew a line through the plan, segregating eating to the east and society facilities to the west. This limited the architects in their resolution of the building's inherent planning issues, born of the piecemeal development of the preceding years. In many ways, the devastation caused by the fire, facilitated a deep re-thinking process. The building now required

Portfolio presentation panel of images (Courtesy of de Blacam & Meagher collection at Irish Architectural Archive)

comprehensive weathering, structural and decorative works, substantial replacement of internal fittings and furniture and regularisation to comply with of-the-day fire safety standards (as required by the college's insurers). Conflating the building's existing issues, the fire thus expedited and expanded works, allowing the architects and Trinity's Building Committee a substantially freer reign.

de Blacam & Meagher presented revised plans within four weeks of the fire and were appointed under two separate contracts. The first was for restoration work to the Dining Hall and was administered by the College Architect, Ian Roberts. Roberts was engaged in structural repairs of the walls and roof while de Blacam & Meagher were charged with the restoration of internal fabric. Works were carried out in intimate collaboration between the two firms. The second appointment related principally to the replanning and refitting of the building. This was a straight de Blacam & Meagher appointment, the resolution of which was undoubtedly informed by that of the former.

The revised replanning of the building was based on sensible architectural ideas around circulating and lighting a deep plan. It eliminated two small rooms from the entrance vestibule, revealing its original scale and readmitting southern light from Front Square. The Common Room above and

(left) Detail of timber balustrade (Courtesy of G. & T. Crampton Photograph Archive, UCD Digital Library and Prof Joseph Brady)

Dining Hall beyond were to be unchanged beyond their restoration. Two new stairs to the east and west of this vestibule were introduced, both leading to corresponding new lower ground floor entrances to/from Front Square and are the predominant entrances used today. These were paid for by insurers to comply with fire safety requirements but in fact served as a planning devise to simplify the circulation of students and staff at either end of the building. The architects proposed to excavate the volume of the original kitchen, rediscovering its height. They placed within it a four storey, galleried timber atrium. While admitting light into a deep plan, the structure also served as an organisational tool to circulate through the building, connecting common room with kitchen, Buttery Bar with Dining Hall etc.

Restoration work in Irish architecture was still a novel process in the 1980s. For instance, the first Irish educational programme (the Masters in Urban and Building Conservation, University College Dublin) was not established until 1986; that is, two years after the Dining Hall fire. The state and a handful of other practitioners were the only people carrying out

Case Study: Atrium/Loos Bar, Trinity Dining Hall Restoration

this scale of restoration in Ireland at the time. Prior to its disbandment by Margaret Thatcher, the Greater London Council along with English Heritage proved very useful to the architects. They advised on guiding conservation principles and fire proofing of existing fabric. Conservation works proceeded on their advice.

A detailed measured survey of existing fabric was made and drawn by Martin Donnelly, project architect. Remarkably thorough, the drawings provided a measured record of each element of the building which could then be tagged to facilitate accurate reinstatement following their restoration or replication. Each panel was separated, cleaned by immersion, dried out, reglued, and restrained before being refitted. Battens were fixed to the reverse side to prevent warping of timbers. Elements which were beyond repair were pieced in with the rigour of a cabinet maker or sculptor. The panelling was adjusted in places, secret jib doors to the atrium and food hall were incorporated, the dado cornice used to conceal uplighters. In fact de Blacam & Meagher's fire proofing of original 18th-century doors was a first for Ireland; the Dining Hall doors being the first instance in which Dublin Corporation waived the requirement for certificates of standard construction.

Atrium and Loos Bar

A handed replica of Adolf Loos's Kärtner Bar on the first floor of the building is perhaps a side story to that of the atrium. Placed within what was formerly a staff lunchroom, the bar is de Blacam & Meagher's solution to a request by senior members for a drink's cabinet to the restored senior Common Room. Made exclusively from books, drawings and photographs, the replication is impressive.

The bar is simple, a black and white checkerboard of mosaic tiles frames a central isle with bar to one side and booths to the other. In Vienna the bar is to the left, in Dublin it is to the right. Where Vienna's model is marked by its subtle opulence, Dublin's is marked by its economy. Marble in Vienna is painted MDF in Dublin for example, leather is upholstery, and so on. Loos's marble coffered ceilings, trimmed with brass is replaced with layers of MDF in Dublin, marbleised in paint. Where Loos's original materials are employed, they are gainfully executed; unpolished black Kilkenny marble forms the bar top for example, leather and brass provide arm and foot rests, etc. Perhaps the greatest deviation from the original is this: in Vienna there is no fourth wall, glass blocks to the street-facing elevation emit northern light, whereas in Dublin, this opportunity is not taken. Instead, the mirrored effect is developed on all sides. creating a particularly insular environment.

Naturally, there are unanticipated idiosyncrasies in any replication. Loos's bar, for example, contained a portrait of Viennese poet Peter Altenberg, who in Vienna, faces the bar on the left. A near perfect replication of this, made by Irish artist Alice Hanratty, also looks to the left however, as she was not told the bar would be handed. Be it a quirk, an amusement, a folly, the bar is light-hearted and playful: a delight enjoyed regularly, if only by the few.

Linked to the Loos Bar by its sense of a stripped classical geometry and absence of decoration, the atrium is de Blacam & Meagher's principal intervention in Trinity. Having taken apart the panelling of the 18th-century Dining Hall, they were well placed to put a version of it back together in the making of the Atrium. Elegant and practical, the four-storey, galleried structure is composed of steel columns and beams clad in beech and infilled with large tilting panels of same, battened and strengthened as in the Dining Hall. The four façades are braced by timber galleries at their perimeter, linking the otherwise independent structure back to the existing walls. Its façades are graduated, recessing at successive levels.

Case Study: Atrium/Loos Bar, Trinity Dining Hall Restoration

The trabeated elevations present a simple and restrained geometry back onto itself, a subtle abstraction of the classicism it is set within.

The Atrium has been compared widely to American architect Louis Kahn's Yale Centre for British Art, a project on which Shane de Blacam worked during his time in the renowned architect's office. At Yale, exhibition galleries and shops circle two lay-lit courts whose internal façades are made up by a trabeated concrete structure infilled with timber. Laylights in the TCD atrium's earlier design align it more closely with that of Kahn's. Their omission here, however, allows the structure to interface delicately with the existing roof trusses. While its debt to Kahn is clear, successive sketch iterations speak of other influences at play; from the pivoting walls of John Soane's art gallery in London to that of a central stage set, overlooked from all angles. The final elevations sit somewhere between those of a Venetian Palace's courtyard and an Italian Rationalist's façade.

An issue often tabled at the Atrium is that it lacks a natural entrance. Positioned within the warren of existing building, the atrium relies on the familiarity of Trinity's students and staff, with many newcomers unaware of its existence. With an unprogrammed space at its centre and irregular footfall through, the Atrium sits largely underused, fulfilling more termly requirements than daily. This aside, the Atrium is an important project for de Blacam & Meagher. The open-minded patronage of Trinity College and particularly their Building Committee, presented the architects with an opportunity to test and retest architectural preoccupations. Preceded by their 1979 entry to an architectural competition for a Taoiseach's Residence and State Guesthouse in The Phoenix Park, the Atrium in Trinity is a further reworking of an architectural concept which would be tested again in the redevelopment of Cluain Mhuire – Galway-Mayo Institute of Technology's (now, Atlantic TU) library and School of Art and most famously, in Cork Institute of Technology's (now Munster TU) library. While these are perhaps better-known examples, the atrium in Trinity was the first large-scale, institutional employment of an architectural language which would come to represent de Blacam & Meagher. Having taught much of the current generation of Irish architects, the significance of opportunities given to architects, such as that given to de Blacam & Meagher by Trinity College's Building Committee, cannot be underestimated.

The dining hall restoration and attendant works were carried out from 1984–7. The architects were de Blacam & Meagher. Shane de Blacam and John Meagher formed de Blacam & Meagher Architects in 1976. In 2021 the firm was awarded the RIAI James Gandon Medal in recognition of their sustained contribution to the advancement of Irish architecture. Their portfolio is extensive, ranging from private homes to large residential, educational, and commercial schemes. The quality of their work has been recognised both nationally and internationally through publication, exhibition, and award. de Blacam & Meagher represented Ireland at the 2010 and 2018 Venice Biennale, an international showcase of architectural solutions to contemporary societal, humanistic, and technological issues.

Shane de Blacam, born in 1945, was educated at University College Dublin and University of Pennsylvania, US, where he graduated with a Masters in Architecture. He worked in London with Chamberlain, Powell and Bon and Louis I. Kahn in Philadelphia, and in 1972 he returned to Ireland as first year master at the School of Architecture, University College Dublin. de Blacam's portfolio is extensive with projects such as the Wooden Building in Dublin (2000), Abbeyleix Library in Laois (2010), Dining Hall, Atrium (1987) and the Beckett Theatre (1993) in Trinity College, Dublin, and the firm's own principal headquarters (2007) that are located in 4 St. Catherine's Lane West, Dublin 8.

John Meagher, born in 1947, died 2021, was educated at the School of Architecture, College of Technology in Dublin and at Helsinki University of Technology, School of Architecture, Finland. See Meagher biography with Castle Street essay.

Structural Engineers: Ove Arup and Partners, Dublin
Quantity Surveyor: Patterson Kempster and Shortall
Mechanical and Electrical Engineers: Robert, Jacob and Partners
Main Contractor: G&T Crampton (appointed under both contracts)
Mechanical Services: T. Bourke & Co.
Electrical Services: F. Worthington
Plasterwork: N. Creedon
Joinery: G&T Crampton, Ballingly Joinery, Joe Byrne (Loos Bar)
Stonework: Stone Developments
Structural Steel: Reads Engineering
Services: Kennen & Sons
Tiling: Verso Tiling
Furniture: Michaell Carroll, Eric Pierce, Christopher O'Neill & Sons, J. P. D. Design, P. Spain & Sons, Keith Moss

Sources
Unpublished
Drawings, Archive of de Blacam & Meagher, Irish Architectural Archive
Martin Donnelly interview with Aoibheann Ní Mhearáin, July 2021
Edward McParland interview with Aoibheann Ní Mhearáin, July 2021 and with Aoife O'Halloran, Feb. 2022

Published
dePaor, Tom, Maybury, Peter, Deegan, Cian, Casey, Alice, *Irlanda: of de Blacam & Meagher: Archive: Drawings Construction Photography–Essay: Photography Writings* (Gall Editions, 2010)
de Blacam, Shane, Lecture, FD Lecture Series (7 Jan. 2016, CEPT University) (Video)
de Blacam, Shane, 'The Practice of de Blacam & Meagher', Lecture at Architectural Association, London, School of Architecture (30 Jan. 2001, AA School of Architecture) (Video)
Gillespie, Elgy, '… from blaze', *Irish Times*, 14 July 1984
Olley, John, 'Rebuilding in a Classical Tradition', in *The Architects' Journal* (17 June 1987), pp. 37–51
Prown, Jules David, *The Architecture of the Yale Centre for British Art* (Yale University Press, 2009)
Reihill, Ann, 'The Restoration of the Dining Hall, Trinity College, Dublin', in *Irish Arts Review* (Vol. 3, No. 1/Spring 1986), pp. 26–37
Sarnitz, August, *Adolf Loos, 1870–1933: Architect, Cultural Critic, Dandy* (Taschen, 2003), pp. 33–47

Case Study

Treasury Building, Grand Canal Street, Dublin 2, 1990

Carole Pollard

The Treasury Building is an adaptation of the former Boland's Bakery on Grand Canal Street which, for the second half of the 20th century, was the tallest building in the Grand Canal dock area. Its conversion from an industrial facility to a high-specification office building in the late 1980s was unique in the city at the time. Indeed, the Treasury Building was a herald of the Celtic Tiger transformation of the Grand Canal Docks that took place in the succeeding decades. With its distinctive blue industrial-style glazing and soaring glass and marble-clad atrium at its eastern end, it was designed specifically for the expanding financial services sector that came to dominate Dublin's commercial landscape.

Boland's Bakery was part of a complex of buildings owned by Dublin's largest and best-known milling and baking company. It was built to accommodate the expansion of the business from the 18th-century stone Boland's Mills warehouses that stand on the edge of the water at nearby Grand Canal Dock. For almost 100 years, Boland's was one of the largest employers in this part of the city, but during the 1970s the company experienced severe financial difficulties and closed in 1984. Three years later it was purchased by Dublin's most ambitious upcoming developer Johnny Ronan who would go on to build a substantial commercial property portfolio in the city. Ronan identified the Bakery building, with its vast floor to ceiling heights, large expanses of glazing and distinctive Modernist industrial aesthetic, as a unique opportunity for an office conversion. He specifically wanted to target the demand for financial services sector offices in Dublin, which was being driven by the newly constructed International Financial Services Centre (IFSC) at Custom House Docks (1987).

The Treasury Building was fitted out to the highest office specifications of the time, with Belgian glazing systems, marble from Italy and Norway, and luxury executive suites aimed to attract high-calibre financial companies. Tenants included blue-chip institutions who took advantage of Ireland's favourable tax legislation in the 1990s, designed to incentivise investment in the city. One of the building's most high-profile tenants was the National Treasury Management Agency (established in 1990) which was tasked with managing the national debt. The agency gave its name to both the building and to Ronan's property company, Treasury Holdings. When the severe financial downturn of 2008 occurred, more than €2 billion of Treasury Holding's loans came under the control of the National Asset Management Agency (NAMA), but Ronan managed to retain ownership of the Treasury Building. Ironically, in 2011 NAMA took a lease in the Treasury Building and established the headquarters there. Ronan eventually sold the building to Google in 2020 for €120 million.

Boland's Mills, Grand Canal Street Lower, 1950s (Courtesy of G. & T. Crampton Photograph Archive, UCD Digital Library and Prof Joseph Brady)

The Last to Surrender

Patrick Boland first established a bakery business at 133–136 Capel Street, Dublin in 1870, and in 1873 relocated his thriving business to the south side of the city on the quayside of the Grand Canal dock. Boland's Mills occupied two six-storey stone warehouse buildings dating from the 1830s and, over the years that followed, expanded production facilities on the site. Boland's became the largest milling facility in the country, and in 1874 the company built the City of Dublin Bakery across the dock from the mill. That complex of buildings included bakery buildings, a residence for the manager, and a retail shop. It was here also that the company's rolling stock of distribution vans were manufactured and stored. Up until the 1980s, Boland's Bakery vans were a familiar sight all over the city.

Boland's Mills major claim to fame in Dublin folklore was its role in the 1916 Rising. On Easter Monday, Commandant Eamon de Valera marched

Case Study: Treasury Building, Grand Canal Street

with a column of less than 100 men from Liberty Hall to the limestone mill buildings and hoisted a tricolour. The men fortified the building with flour sacks to protect themselves against shell fire both from the land and from the Helga Gunboat in the river Liffey. Despite the heavy shelling, the walls of the mill buildings remained intact. The following Sunday, de Valera and his men – all of whom survived – were the last garrison of Irish Volunteers to surrender to the British.

Boland's continued to thrive in the early years of the Free State and in the 1940s a new Bakery building was constructed on Grand Canal Street, completed in 1951. This is the building that subsequently became the Treasury Building. Designed by Belfast-based architects, Samuel Stevenson & Sons, the Bakery was a state-of-the-art industrial bakery with a vertical production line. Flour and other ingredients were brought into the building at one end and shipped in elevators up to the top floor. The ingredients were poured into large hoppers and dropped through holes in the floors where they were mixed in vats and dropped again to the first floor where the ovens were housed. Baked goods were transferred down to the ground floor where the vans were lined up to receive them. The floor to ceiling heights on each floor were intentionally high, the highest being the first floor, where the ovens were located, which measured 7 metres. The air quality was controlled by

Aerial view of Boland's Mills, Grand Canal Street Lower, undated (Courtesy of G. & T. Crampton Photograph Archive, UCD Digital Library and Prof Joseph Brady)

Boland's Mills under construction, c.1950 (Courtesy of G. & T. Crampton Photograph Archive, UCD Digital Library and Prof Joseph Brady)

means of an air-conditioning system that used long cotton funnels shaped like large socks. These filtered the air, keeping the building cool while at the same time capturing the flour particles in the air.

Throughout the 1960s and 1970s Boland's, like other Irish bakers and millers, faced intense competition from imported flour, bread, and biscuits. In the mid-1970s the company was taken over by Barrow Milling, although the products retained the Boland's name. Throughout the 1970s the company was plagued by rising competition from smaller Irish bakeries and imported products, and by the intransigence of the trade unions. Despite several efforts to rationalise the business including attempts to introduce new more efficient shift hours and the implementation of a series of redundancies, Boland's went into receivership and finally closed its doors in 1984. Later that year, its owners sold the Boland's Bakery premises on its 3-acre site to Duke House Properties (DHP) for £500,000.

DHP obtained planning permission to develop the entire site with a new type of inner-city development – low-rise own-door office units. The scheme was designed by Arthur Gibney & Partners. The first phase, known as Clanwilliam Square, was completed in 1987 at the east end of the site. DHP did not proceed with the next phase of the development, which included the demolition of the former Bakery building, and in 1986 sold the building to Johnny Ronan for a sum in the region of £500,000, although some reports say he paid as low as £400,000.

Case Study: Treasury Building, Grand Canal Street

Ronan's timing in the purchase of Boland's Bakery was excellent. In 1987, the Irish economy was beginning to slowly improve, largely as a result of government policy that favoured development. Devaluation of the Irish pound in 1986 was followed by tax reforms and development-oriented policies such as the control of public utility prices and employment-based grants. One of the most significant factors for increase in activity in commercial development in Dublin was the establishment in 1987 of the International Financial Services Centre (IFSC) in the north city docklands. The Irish Government secured EU approval to apply a 10 per cent corporate tax rate for designated financial services activities, and this attracted large numbers of international companies to the city. The designation of the IFSC lands as a Special Economic Zone (SEZ) drove the urban regeneration of the north docks area, but the south docks – which included Grand Canal Dock – remained underdeveloped for many years. Nonetheless, although most companies had registered offices at the IFSC, a significant number chose to locate in the south-east city central business district, meaning that the IFSC had a beneficial ripple effect across the city.

Ronan's recognition of the potential of Boland's Bakery was revolutionary in Dublin at the time, particularly because of its location slightly off the beaten track on a street with no established commercial pedigree. The neo-classical Sir Patrick Dunn's Hospital (1818) was located directly across the road but had closed in 1986 and lay empty. The area was predominantly residential to the east and west with tracts of industrial land (mostly unused) to the north. However, Ronan's risk exposure was lessened by the fact that the site lay only one block north of Lower Mount Street, the main artery to Merrion Square North from the desirable environs of Ballsbridge. Ultimately, his decision to redevelop Boland's Bakery as a financial services hub was prescient: such is the level of development in the area since the late 1990s, that the Treasury Building now occupies a prime location between the vibrant South Docks and the traditional Georgian business district.

Aspiration

The original building designed by Samuel Stevenson & Sons comprised a monolithic five-storey structure clad in brick with stone trimmings and unbroken horizontal bands of glazing along its front façade. Stair towers stood at either end, acting as bookends to the building, with narrow vertical windows running the entire height and topped off with a raised, stepped

(above)
Schematic layout for second floor offices (Courtesy of Henry J. Lyons image collection)

(below)
Perspective drawing of proposed office building (Courtesy of Henry J. Lyons image collection)

parapet and slender flagpole. At the west end, a curved brickwork wall, c.12 metres high, turned the corner into Macken Street and carried the Boland's name in tall, slender raised lettering. The original form of the building is still very much evident, with the only major addition being the atrium block attached to the east end. An additional floor was added on top, but it is recessed behind the parapet and is not visible from the street below.

Ronan purchased the site with planning permission to demolish the existing structure and build a low-rise office complex, however, he had an entirely different vision. The low-rise option was not financially lucrative when considered alongside the refurbishment potential of the existing five-storey building. With its robust steel frame, extensive floor plates and very generous floor to ceiling heights, the building offered huge opportunity to create an atmospheric post-industrial office complex of the type that was very much in fashion in other international cities at that time. Regarding the conversion, Ronan was advised by his property agents to increase sub-letting possibilities by sub-dividing the floors with a central atrium. He rejected that advice on the grounds that potential tenants would prefer large open floors in which to lay out their trading desks. This was the model he had seen in operation in London and the one he wanted to introduce in Dublin.

Ronan appointed Henry J. Lyons as the architects for the refurbishment of the building, instructing them to retain the full floor areas on each floor. The problem remained regarding how vertical circulation would work, and how to introduce the 'wow' factor that would attract high-calibre tenants away from the IFSC to Grand Canal Street. Ronan's brief demanded the creation of an impressive entrance space, open and accessible circulation spaces, lavish offices for senior management, and the use of high-quality finishes in the shared areas.

The team at Henry J. Lyons was led by partner Martin Henihan, who had worked with Ronan's father in the past. The Grand Canal Street project was Ronan's first major venture into office speculation. While it was underway, Ronan also commissioned Henry J. Lyons to design a mixed-use scheme (offices and apartments) at Percy Place which was completed in 1992. The same team of architects at Henry J. Lyons were involved in both projects as is evident in the similarity of the stylistic rendering of the elevations in both buildings. Each has a distinctly Post-Modern aesthetic that was popular at the time, but which is relatively rare in Dublin because of the dearth of development during the 1980s and early 1990s.

Case Study: Treasury Building, Grand Canal Street

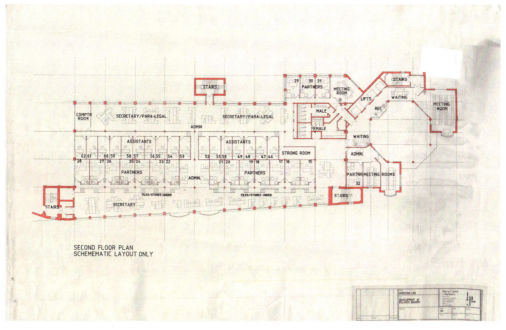

More Than Concrete Blocks Volume 3

At Grand Canal Street, the prolific use of pink granite is also symptomatic of the aesthetic trends of the time. The six-storey glazed octagonal atrium built on the eastern gable is flanked by walls of Norwegian pink granite trimmed with bands of cream Carrera marble. In the interior, the colour scheme is reversed so that the walls are lined with cream marble trimmed with pink granite banding and with black granite skirtings and architraves. The glazing system used on the atrium and in all the windows was a specialist cladding system manufactured by a Belgian company called Chamabel. Chamabel was first employed in Ireland at the IFSC where green window frames and green tinted glass were used extensively. Ronan was intent on making his building at Grand Canal Street equally as attractive to tenants as the IFSC, and instructed his architects to use the Chamabel system at Grand Canal Street too. Architect Derek Byrne was sent to Belgium to visit the plant and oversee the manufacture of the windows: each opening had to be measured by hand because each was slightly different in size. Byrne also travelled to stone quarries in Italy with Ronan where he chose *lapis lazuli*, a semi-precious stone to be used in keystones above the lift doors. The high standard of finish was extended to the toilet facilities too where the architects specified American sanitaryware with infra-red controls – an innovation in Ireland at that time.

The new atrium was a dramatic, soaring, light-filled space with the entrance lobby at ground level sitting on a podium slightly above street level. A bank of four lifts and concealed stairwell rose through it with individual reception areas on each floor and balconies from which to view activity above and below. Large boardrooms and conference rooms were accessed directly from the atrium balconies. The use of Art Deco flourishes, for example the keystones over openings and the elaborate brass railings to the balconies, were inspired by both the modern industrial character of the original Bakery and by the Post-Modernist trend of applied decoration. Post-Modern architecture, which was internationally very popular in the 1980s, rejected of the austerity of Modernism which had dominated previous decades. At Grand Canal Street, the keystone motif is dominant. As well as adorning the interiors it features on every window bay on the elevations.

The main body of the building provided office accommodation, toilet facilities, and staff canteens fitted out by individual tenants. A new recreation centre was proposed at the west end of the building, contained inside the curved wall at the Macken Street corner but was not built. Parking was at basement level accessed via a curved ramp to the rear of Macken Street flats where ground level parking was also provided.

The refurbishment works greatly enhanced the thermal performance of the building. The existing steel structure was encased in concrete, providing reinforcement, fire protection, and thermal upgrade. The new double-glazed windows were set into a new brickwork façade built outside the existing brick structure. This was a complex process because the existing brickwork was not plumb, and every section had to be measured by hand and individually drawn. New stone mouldings were made to match the existing to retain the existing character of the building. The addition of a new floor at roof level allowed for the installation of a major plant room enabling sophisticated new building services, including large water tanks.

Despite Ronan's optimism that tenants would rush to occupy his new building, a slowdown in Ireland's economy in the early 1990s meant that the building remained unoccupied after completion. However, Ronan's fortunes turned when the newly formed State body, the National Treasury Management Agency (NTMA), signed the lease for the top floor. The building was named the Treasury Building in honour of its new tenants, and Ronan and his business partner Richard Barrett named their property development company Treasury Holdings in similar acknowledgement. They located their own offices in the building also.

In 1995, Ronan commissioned Irish artist, Rowan Gillespie, to design a sculpture to adorn the building. The sculpture was to be called *Aspiration* as a commemoration of Ireland's struggle for freedom. Gillespie proposed a naked male figure climbing the atrium wall as a symbolic metaphor. However, when Ronan saw a miniature version of Gillespie's proposal, he insisted that the male figure be changed to a female. The bronze sculpture became one of Dublin's best known public artworks until it was removed in 2020 when the building was sold. In 2022, Dublin City Council granted planning permission to the building's new owners, Google, to increase the height of the building from six storeys to eight storeys.

Facts and Figures

Boland's Mills commissioned the construction of their new Bakery in 1948 and the building was completed in 1951. It remained their primary bakery facility until the company closed in 1984. The building and its site were bought by Duke House Properties who obtained planning permission to demolish the existing structure and build a low-rise own-door office complex designed by Arthur Gibney. The first phase of this development was Clanwilliam Square which was completed in 1989.

Duke House Properties sold the Bakery building to Johnny Ronan in 1987 and Dublin Corporation granted planning permission to refurbish and extend the building in 1988. Works began in 1989 and were substantially complete in 1990. The first major tenant was the National Treasury Management Company whose offices were fitted out by Henry J. Lyons. The building was named the Treasury Building as a result. Ronan and his business partner Richard Barrett named their development company Treasury Holdings. The architects carried out fit-out designs for a number of tenants including the ASK Group, an asset and wealth management company who took a lease in the early 1990s.

Developer Paddy McKillen was one of the investors who helped finance the project. When Treasury Holdings went into liquidation in 2012 with debts of €2.7 billion, Ronan and his group of investors managed to retain ownership of the Treasury Building. The National Asset Management Agency that took over Treasury Holding's debt became a tenant in the building. Ronan and his investors subsequently sold the building to Google in 2020 for €120 million.

The architectural team at Henry J. Lyons included Martin Henihan, Derek Byrne, Paul O'Brien, Susan McDonnell (who was primarily responsible for designing the elevations), Stephen Rafter, David Owens and Triona Milner.

The main contractor for the works was John Sisk & Sons, led by contracts manager Michael Barnwell. The site engineer, Mary Daly, was the first woman engineer employed by Sisk. Matt Murphy was the foreman, and the Sisk quality surveyor was John Dignam. The Design Team included structural engineer, Brian Hendrick and the Stonework was carried out by Chris Gaffney of Longford-based company Cullen Stone (later Monuclad). The glazing systems were manufactured and supplied by Chamabel, Belgium. The pink granite was sourced in Norway, and this was the first time it was used in Ireland. The interior marble came from Carrera in Italy. The sculpture *Aspiration* was designed by Irish artist Rowan Gillespie.

Sources

Unpublished
Derek Byrne, interviewed by Carole Pollard, July 2020
Mary Daly, interviewed by Carole Pollard, Aug. 2020
CBRE Sales Brochure, undated, c.2017
Treasury Building job files, Henry J. Lyons Archive, Dublin

Published
Anon., 'Boland's Bakery building sold for c.£500,000', *Irish Times*, 4 June 1986
Anon., 'Bolands Mills, since 1873', www.bolandsmills.com, accessed Aug. 2020
Fagan, Jack, 'Government agency to open HQ at Bolands', *Irish Times*, 15 May 1991
Fagan, Jack, 'US computer firm to open HQ at Treasury Building', *Irish Times*, 4 Mar. 1992
Murray, Cormac, 'Aspiration' in *Irish Independent* online edn, 27 Nov. 2012

Case Study

Stanhope Green, Focus Ireland housing, Stanhope Street, Dublin 7, 1991

Ellen Rowley

Tucked away in a corner of Dublin 7, is the almost mythical world of Stanhope Green, Focus Ireland's campus or mini city of various housing types. It is a place apart: a retreat and a refuge which provides over 70 individual homes in 2020s Dublin. Incorporated into a handsome brick and stone convent building (c.1907, designed by George C. Ashlin of Ashlin Coleman), Stanhope Green was the late-1980s vision of Sr Stanislaus Kennedy (Sr Stan), Focus Ireland's founder together with architect, Gerry Cahill. Having managed to persuade her order of nuns, the Sisters of Charity, to 'give' her the empty convent building – thereby saving it from inevitable demolition – Sr Stan entrusted the task of conversion to the young architect, Cahill. The nun and the architect had first met in the late-1970s through the Combat Poverty Agency. Their shared values and pursuit of social justice was to sustain them through this first commission and later housing projects.

At Stanhope Green, Gerry Cahill kept the hardy brick convent at the centre of his design strategy: firstly, by rehabilitating the surviving elements of it; secondly, by placing terraces of new low-rise housing at key junctures in relation to it; and thirdly, by creating open spaces around and within it. We encounter the first new housing terrace upon entering the site, under the original arch where ten small two-storey homes form a street facing Ashlin's large convent façade. Next, we move through the original convent entrance and into the building where the warren of nuns' parlors and rooms were converted into a range of studios and bedsits. Enlarged and refreshed corridors wrap around a courtyard, feeding communal areas and leading out to a cloister of new housing beyond. This new housing, contained in a pair of two-storey blocks facing each other, again invokes the city terrace. It is enclosed visually by a single-storey unit – originally a workshop but today, adapted into another home.

Cahill's materials and geometries, all chosen to respect the convent and to extend its housing accommodation, speak to their late-1980s design origins. Their pitched roofs, mixture of porthole and regular windows and colourful paint schemes express something of a local Post-Modern architecture. Where the new housing out front is yellow brick, responding to the convent's polychromatic brick front, the cloister housing at the back of the site is hewn from grey textured Forticrete blocks, in response to the rough masonry of the convent's rear. Forticrete was a relatively new reinforced concrete block technology at the time and the cloister was awarded the 10th Irish Concrete Society award in 1991.

Robust, realistic, modest and well-mannered, Cahill's adaptation of Stanhope Green convent for Focus Ireland has endured. Originally, he and Sr Stan provided 96 units along with a host of communal functions such as a library, a renowned restaurant for residents and the public alike, and a homework club. In c.2011, many of these communal rooms swapped function, becoming staff offices or restful sitting rooms. Meanwhile, the original 96 homes were reduced to 72 due to changing prescriptions around minimum housing standards. This meant knocking two or three units into one larger apartment, and so on. Material upgrades to Cahill's original architecture include uPVC windows replacing timber ones and the insertion of a new lift. Today, Stanhope Green is the setting for a quietly thriving residential community of families, couples, new Irish, elderly people, single people, long-term residents and those in transition from homelessness: a microcosm of Dublin and a lesson of what can be done on a tight budget.

FELLOWSHIP: Without Homes in 1980s Dublin

As with any meaningful and enduring project, architectural or otherwise, Stanhope Green as a new community of homes was in gestation for years before its realization. But in the end it happened quickly. While physically it came out of the donation of the convent, its social origins were rooted in the work and life experience of one nun, Sr Stan. Through the 1960s, Sr Stan was based in Kilkenny, working with the local bishop, Bishop Peter Birch of the diocese of Ossory. Sr Stan points to Birch and this Kilkenny period as key to the formulation of her social view. Being a forward-thinking humanitarian – what Sr Stan termed, a prophetic activist – Birch established the Kilkenny Social Services project in 1963 which was about improving and making new community social services. Through the 1970s, there were influential national conferences on poverty and social matters held in Kilkenny, out of which the Combat Poverty Agency was founded with Sr Stan appointed as its chair. Then in 1983, Sr Stan was moved by her order, the Sisters of Charity, to Dublin where she took the time to reflect on this pioneering social intervention through a senior research fellowship at UCD. Her fellowship focused on the nature and extent of homelessness amongst women in Dublin. And after two years looking closely at this problem, Sr Stan set up Focus Point (later, Focus Ireland) in 1985 as an organisation which would help people to move on from homelessness.

It began with the leasing of a building in Temple Bar which could act as an information hub, with a restaurant and drop-in advice service. By 1986 and in between researching, publishing and lobbying, Sr Stan persuaded her order of nuns to give her their convent building – they were moving to a smaller new premises on the site – to transform into homes. What had been evolving was Stan's philosophy and practicable theory that homelessness

Site Plan (Courtesy of Gerry Cahill Architects image collection)

was not a *state* of being but rather, a *stage* in one's life; that to be homeless should not define a person; that there is no one typical homeless person; and critically, for our story here, that hostels are not an appropriate housing solution for homelessness.

The architectural origins of Stanhope Green's adaptation unfolded over a similar formative period: through education in the 1960s and activation in the 1970s. Gerry Cahill's introduction to architecture at UCD in 1969 coincided with the arrival of the 'Flying Circus', visiting architect-teachers from London's Architectural Association (AA) under Ivor Smith. And on to London, where he ultimately encountered the confident end-stages of London's post-war house-building project. Through his work at Camden borough and then, with Levitt Bernstein architects, Cahill engaged in meaningful urban renewal, through often massive housing schemes. It was in London too, following two bountiful years at the AA, that Cahill learned more about building fabric and the rigours of the building site, as he and a small group of fellow students set up as a construction company, converting a Victorian house into two flats.

Like Sr Stan, Gerry Cahill was called back to Dublin at the dawn of the 1980s – by love and marriage in his case – where he took on a housing research fellowship, sponsored by Cement Roadstone, at UCD's School of Architecture. It was 1979 and Dublin city centre was an abuse of derelict sites and decimated streets. Cahill's research and subsequent publication, *Back to the Streets* (UCD, 1980), examined the neighbourhood of the

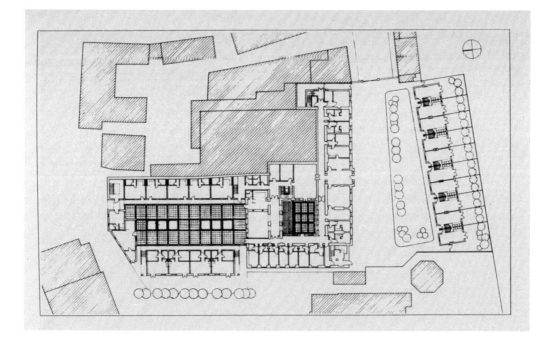

Design Strategy, axonometric (Courtesy of Gerry Cahill Architects image collection)

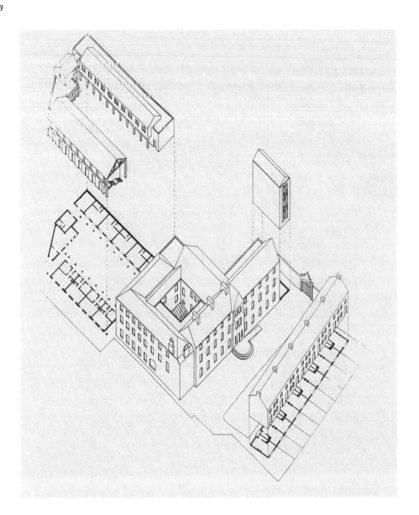

Liberties. Close to Dublin's medieval core, the Liberties was then and continues to be characterised by low-rise high-density housing; streets of artisan dwelling cottages are interrupted by churches, the occasional market building, small warehouses and commercial arteries. In short, its morphology represented an image of traditional Dublin to the young architect and yet, in front of his eyes, that morphology was being bulldozed while its community was being hollowed out.

Back to the Streets was something of a call-to-arms. In the vein of Jane Jacobs' activist urban writing, Cahill's study lamented the loss of residential populations from the city; the loss of mixed activity from the streets. But

Case Study: Stanhope Green

beyond those initial and legitimate laments, Cahill called for community, housing co-op and bureaucratic mobilization. He called for a new 'Inner City Renewal Agency' to be set up, inciting alternative economic models of land distribution and collaboration to overcome dereliction:

> Multi-disciplinary area teams appointed by the Agency consisting of a Community Worker, Social worker, Lawyer, Economist and Architect could liaise with community groups and representatives to determine the optimum use for derelict or decaying sites and buildings. (Cahill, 1980)

On his journey through the Liberties, Cahill had been introduced to such a multidisciplinary group, SCARP or the South City Area Research Partnership, which was connected to the Combat Poverty Agency. For Cahill, the architect's tools of surveying the site and proposing design solutions could be made more meaningful in the context of the social and community worker. This would be the way to remediate urban dereliction: incrementally, with integrity, and taking the lead not from the planner or the commercial developer, but from the social activist.

So it was that Gerry Cahill met Sr Stan.

Following deep research through their respective UCD fellowships, both Sr Stan and Gerry Cahill were at the coalface of social and urban dereliction in 1980s Dublin. Sr Stan established Focus Point in 1985: Cahill established Gerry Cahill Architects in 1984. Where Stan was watching and doing, gathering like-minded professionals to bring pioneering social services to impoverished Dubliners, Cahill was searching for solutions for a physically beleaguered Dublin. His interest in city was an interest in housing: her interest in people experiencing homelessness was also an interest in housing. When Sr Stan managed to procure the convent building in 1986, she knew the very architect who could help. Her purpose was to make alternative 'emergency' and long-term housing. And Cahill's knowledge of building fabric and his design pursuit of or aspiration for alternative housing forms and types, placed him well. 'Alternative' being the key issue. Furthermore, and from the outset, this convent-conversion project was about more than accommodation — it was about hope, ambition, rehabilitation, fellowship and dreams. Cahill not only understood this, but he and his design team, and the builders, embraced it.

Practically speaking, as Cathal Crimmins pointed out in his critique of

Elevation of 10 houses, 1991, photograph by Bill Hastings in Irish Architect (No. 83, Mar./Apr. 1991)

Stanhope Green, the architect(s) 'fulfilled a role of not only designers for this project, but fundraisers as well' (Crimmins, 1991, p.30). Of course, economics were to the fore of this endeavour. As it was a new innovative objective, the bureaucratic and funding infrastructure had to follow. Focus Point established an Approved Housing Body (AHB) wing, Focus Housing Association, on to which Cahill was co-opted. In this way, the typical separation of client, builder, designer, developer was overcome at Stanhope Green. Another critical element towards the utopian project's realization was the new housing legislation – the 1988 Housing Act – which tackled homelessness at its heart and allowed £20,000 per unit created as against £2,000 previously. Combined with Sr Stan's persistence and doggedness which brought her to then Minister for the Environment, Padraig Flynn, who subsequently awarded the project over £1 million – as a special provision in the 1989 budget – the making of a community of homes, with priority to single people, was on.

A Piece of City: A Promenade of Homes

Little remained of the original institutional architecture by the time Gerry Cahill and his team, including architect and fellow-teacher at UCD, Jim Murphy, came to the site. The 1810s Manor House predating the Sisters of Charity's arrival on the site, was demolished in 1987. At the same time, the nuns' 1860s chapel (designed by George Ashlin) was also demolished. What was there, on this site up the hill on Stanhope Street, was a bulky three-storey polychromatic brick building which was developed, again by Ashlin, in the early 1900s. Externally, this symmetrical block with its medley of brick hues – brown, blues and yellows – was resplendent with Neo-Gothic features, typical of nineteenth-century British and Irish religious buildings: the steeply pitched roof, marked with decorative crosses; the large statue of Mary presiding over the entrance from her roofline pediment; the

 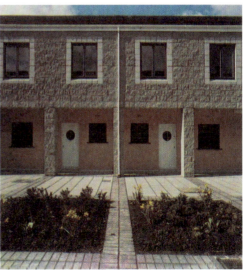

(left)
Original Cloister, 1991, photograph by Bill Hastings in Irish Architect (No. 83, Mar./Apr. 1991)

(right)
Elevation detail of cloister housing, 1991, photograph by Bill Hastings in Irish Architect (No. 83, Mar./Apr. 1991)

projecting central bays; the granite dressings delineating the large windows, were all in good condition and demanded dominance. Adding a new stair block to the east end, as well as a ramp to the side of the entrance, Cahill's moves were quiet, enabling the original façade's continued dominance with some repointing, repairing of windows and cleaning of dressings.

Internally, the former convent was another story where, according to Cahill's extensive survey, not much of note survived except for a difficult floor plan, and dry and wet rot. Homes were to be made, wherever and however possible. As the architects sketched out possibilities, they worked to upgrade the building's fabric and especially, the circulation routes for fire safety. The close attention paid to the original provided the architects with the logic of the emerging floor plan: nuns' rooms were to become the basis of single person homes; services were to be housed in enlarged corridors; into the principal stairway was inserted a diminutive lift shaft while another (east end) staircase was added overall; windows and details like skirting or ceiling decoration mostly remained the same.

Upon figuring out how a body enters the main building, then moves through, up and around the spaces, the architects could position communal areas. Pacing the public and the private, Cahill pushed the old convent building to contain small dwellings, feeding them from the bright and hard-working corridors. Then, stop: interrupt both circulation route and private home with larger sitting room, homework club, library and public restaurant. The floor plan was wrought, even overwrought and was experienced in this way; like a rhythm of compression or tightness, interspersed with

Sr Una, Vicar General of Sisters of Charity, with Gerry Cahill, Architect, at laying of foundation stone, October 1989 (Photograph by James Maguire, Courtesy of Gerry Cahill Archive)

openness. After all, the architecture was quasi-Victorian Catholic institutional architecture at its heart. The public rooms at both ground and first floors provided just those open breathing spaces, attempting to bring reprieve from the institution.

The next move was to assess where new structures could be placed. From the outset, Cahill was drawn to the convent's siting. At a height and bearing south, it looked over the city. After that, it was a hemmed-in affair with a large commercial laundry to the east and the newly built 'downsized' convent (Cantrell Crowley, c.1987) to the west. The site conditions became the next determinant. And constraints, as ever with Cahill and this generation of Irish architects, were to be celebrated. The convent's oblique positioning off the sloping Lower Grangegorman, together with the arched gateway entrance, already brought a sense of drama to the place, as a journey. The architects carried this self-conscious journeying through the whole project. Movement and sequence underpinned the unfolding masterplan. For that is what it was: a masterplan.

Sr Stan and the architects wanted to make homes. They wanted to make as many homes as they could, without resorting to crowding or ghettoising. As such, the architects interpreted the convent and its curtilage as a campus, to be reshaped. Cahill describes his adaptation with a pen in his hand, more or less drawing one precise albeit sweeping gesture from gateway to green; through and in to the convent; around and out the back to a new cloister. He is clear that this journey or promenade is a single one, however many encounters happen along the way. And through it, the

Case Study: Stanhope Green

building starts to reveal itself from entrance, to courtyard, to cloister.

From that premise, the new housing was made in three forms. Firstly, at the new green, and facing the convent, Cahill designed the terrace of ten two-storey houses. At only 60 square meters each, they are so diminutive as to be barely noticeable upon arrival to Stanhope Green, especially in the shadow of the convent. Despite criticisms that this area is the least resolved of the new housing, much of the terrace's meaning comes from its small scale. In this, it invokes the ubiquitous Dublin artisan dwelling terrace. Front doors puncturing the yellow-brick walls with their navy machine-brick friezes, are invariably open: children and adults come and go, sit at thresholds supervising one another. These are long-term homes for families.

As we know, the architects were somehow unafraid to tackle the institutional accommodation of the former convent. Perhaps interpreting this main block as the scheme's own city centre, at higher density than the rest of the campus, Cahill grappled with the task. This was the first time that a convent had been converted into any form of social housing in Ireland. How to go about that? How could it be kept, yet changed so that it would work socially and financially? Such issues of bottom-line economics and social crisis, coupled with the unprecedented architectural challenge, drove the project on. With Sr Stan crunching numbers and pushing a pioneering social agenda around homeless housing, Cahill and his team soon provided 61 single-person dwellings across the three floors of the old building. Technologically, each unit held waste and water infrastructure, ventilation and independent electricity. Domestically, this translated as a self-contained

Original Courtyard, 1993 (Courtesy of Gerry Cahill Architects image collection)

kitchen, bathroom and bedroom/sitting room. Existentially, it amounted to a room-as-home of own's own: to privacy, to retreat.

Cahill speaks of the structural and design decisions, in response to the economic and social imperatives to provide as much as possible. The old building had a structural logic, running through its three floors, that he worked with and then asked, 'what is the smallest unit that won't make you go mad?' Seemingly *well-being*, in its late-1980s iteration, was the common denominator in this remarkable residential project.

The third housing structure, the cloister, was undoubtedly the architectural surprise and climax of Stanhope Green. Here a pair of two-storey pitched-roof ranges, with colonnade elevations at ground level, enclosed a rectangular courtyard. A lot has transformed since the architects completed the original hard-edged scenography in 1991: today, this place bristles with biodiversity and human activity. It is a verdant oasis, a secret garden, in Dublin's north city. Not only has plant life invaded the concrete spaces but Cahill's colonnades have been filled in, thereby changing how the two blocks touch the ground. While this change from columnar rhythm to wall/window articulation is significant, making a more substantial and

Case Study: Stanhope Green

blocky block than the architect intended, the overall design ethos is not compromised. If anything, such easy transformations speak to the clear yet absorbent geometries, to the strong yet elastic form and functions informing Cahill's architecture for Focus Ireland here.

This cloister is not a universal place where 'one size fits all'. But as a residential setting, it must work harder than most in bringing a mix of long-term homes and shorter-term stepdown dwellings together, into a tight space. In this way, the architecture is a backdrop: not neutral or passive but never willful or overbearing. Architectural historian, John Olley commented on how the scheme created cohesion. Contrasting it to the contemporaneous group project 'Making a Modern Street' for the Liberties, which Olley claimed to be a 'jamboree of tricks and contortions', Stanhope Green provided for 'a generosity of space and outlook and a comfortable relation between privacy and community' (Olley, 1993, p.76).

Perhaps the generosity to which Olley refers comes from the pragmatics of this project. Material pragmatics are also at play in the cloister architecture where Cahill introduced a fairly radical but affordable concrete block, Forticrete. Choosing a rough textured Forticrete block to compliment the back of the convent building with its rough stone walls, the material brings sensory richness to the space. As a reinforced concrete block system, it provides its own structure. It looks different. It feels particular to the cloister, reminding us that we are in another part of the scheme; showing us that each part of Stanhope Green, while unified, could have its own character. Indeed, in this diversity and particularity, Stanhope Green is a piece of city. Enabled by, what Olley calls a 'quiet and unpretentious architecture', the scheme is a 'miniature city with a hierarchy and diversity of accommodation linked by its own public amenities' (Olley, 1993, p.76).

Years later, Cahill reflected on his practice, and what he concluded resonates for the Focus Ireland community at Stanhope: 'As architects, the challenge of our engagement with communities is to deliver not what they thought they wanted but what they never thought they could have' (Cahill, 2005, p.32). From the level of need within the homeless community to the prescription of the pre-existing building, Gerry Cahill and the design team with their quantity survey, the engineers and the builders wrestled with the pragmatic and in the end, they created poetry.

Facts and Figures

Focus Point was established in 1985 by Sr Stan and Focus Housing Association was established in 1988, with the Stanhope Green conversion following soon from this. The first terrace of houses was complete in 1989 and the overall scheme was complete in 1991.

Stanhope Green's cloister architecture in Forticrete won the 1991 Irish Concrete Society Award for excellence in design and construction in concrete.

The architects were Gerry Cahill Architects (GCA), including Gerry Cahill, Jim Murphy, Enda MacMahon and Hilary Vandenberghe.

Gerry Cahill studied Architecture at UCD and the Architectural Association (AA), London. Graduating in 1975, he worked on large housing renewal projects across London. From 1978, Cahill worked between London and Dublin, publishing his study into urban regeneration and the Liberties neighbourhood, *Back to the Street* in 1980; teaching at the UCD School of Architecture; and establishing GCA in 1982. From the outset GCA was a practice interested in housing, urban renewal, social justice and the environment. Other convent housing adaptations after Stanhope Green include George's Hill (Focus, 2000) and Mercy Convent, Cork Street (Sophia Housing, c.2005). While Cahill's most notable and award-winning housing schemes are New Street (NABCo, 1998), Allingham Street (Sophia Housing, 2000) and Clarion Quay (DDDA, 2001). With Derek Tynan and McGarry Ní Éanaigh, Gerry Cahill co-founded Urban Projects in 2000 and designed this large apartment scheme at Clarion Quay (186 units) for Dublin Dockland Development Authority, winning the RIAI Silver Medal for Housing (2002-3). Cahill was a regular contributor to architectural journals, writing and researching. He was an important force and popular studio tutor at UCD Architecture, influencing two generations of Irish architects between the late 1970s and 2010s. Both locally and internationally, Gerry Cahill's work is of great ethical and environmental significance and often overlooked, though in 2001 he was awarded the Lord Mayor's Award for his service to Dublin and in 2008, his Cork Street Sofia housing project was exhibited as part of the 11th Architectural Venice Biennale. He was pioneering in his prioritisation of sustainable and affordable building materials, in his insistence on variety of housing types and in his working for Approved Housing Bodies. In 2013, GCA ceased to trade. Cahill is consultant with McQuillan Architects (MQA).

Born in Kerry, Sr Stanislaus Kennedy joined the Religious Sisters of Charity in 1958, at the age of 18. Beginning her social work with the Kilkenny Social Services in the 1960s, she later worked with homeless women in Dublin and established Focus Ireland (formerly known as Focus Point) in 1985. Sr Stan has written several books and edited collections of scholarly essays on poverty, homelessness and related issues such as *Who Should Care?* (1981); *One Million Poor* (1981, Turoe Press); *But Where Can I Go?* (1985, Arlen Press); *Focus on Homelessness* (1988, Columba Press); *Focus on Residential Care in Ireland* (1996, Focus Ireland). Having served as the Chair of the Combat Poverty Agency, she went on to coordinate the EU's rural anti-poverty programme and in 2001 she set up the Immigrant Council of Ireland. For the past 20 years or more, Sr Stan has concentrated on meditation and spirituality through mindfulness. She has published many books on these practices (with Transworld and Columba Press), and established the Sanctuary – a home and place for retreats – next door to Stanhope Green.

Consulting Engineers: Johnny Rooney of Fearon O'Neill Rooney
Services Consultant: Frank Quigley
Quantity Surveyors: Charlie O'Connor of Burton & O'Connor
Main Contractor: Cleary & Doyle

Sources

Unpublished
Sr Stanislaus Kennedy and Gerry Cahill, in conversation with Ellen Rowley, May 2023
Nieve White, Jan Mingle, Therese Towey, Emma Moore, tour of Stanhope Green, April, July 2023
Gerry Cahill Architects Archive

Published
Anon., 'Sr Stanislaus Kennedy', *Irish Times*, 26 May 2010
Cahill, Gerry, *Back to the Street* (Housing Research Unit, UCD, 1980)
Cahill, Gerry, 'SubURBIA' in *Building Material* (No. 6, Spring 2001)
Cahill, Gerry, 'Between Ethos and Expediency' in *Building Material* (No. 14, Winter 2005)
Cahill, Gerry, 'Sanctuary and Congregation' in *Building Material* (No. 18, Spring 2009)
Crimmins, Cathal, 'Stanhope Street Refuge' building review in *Irish Architect* (No. 83, Mar./Apr. 1991)
Focus Ireland. 'Focus Ireland – History, Mission, Vision and Values', www.focusireland.ie/ (accessed May – July 2023)
Housing Act, 1988: www.homelessdublin.ie/info/policy (accessed July 2023)
Kennedy, Stanislaus RSC (ed.), *One Million Poor? The Challenge of Irish Inequality* (Turoe Press, 1981)
Kennedy, Stanislaus RSC and John Blackwell (eds.), *Focus on Homelessness. A New Look at Housing Policy* (The Columba Press, 1988)
O'Keefe, Maurice, 'Sr. Stanislaus Kennedy Interview' in *1922-2022, A Century of Change. Irish Life and Lore* (29 Sept. 2021, Audio, 47:53) https://www.irishlifeandlore.com/product/sr-stanislaus-kennedy/ (accessed May 2023)
O'Keefe, Maurice, 'Gerry Cahill Interview' in *1922-2022, A Century of Change. Irish Life and Lore* (2 Dec. 2021, Audio, 1:02:53) https://www.irishlifeandlore.com/coc-229-gerry-cahill/ (accessed May 2023)
Olley, John, 'The Theatre of the City: Dublin 1991' in *Irish Arts Review* (Vol. 9, 1993)

Temple Bar Case Studies, 1991–96:
Editors' Note to Readers

Highlighting the Temple Bar Framework Plan and the key urban space of this masterplan, Meeting House Square (finished 1996), the first Temple Bar essay introduces a series of case studies which describe the urban and architectural reimagining of Temple Bar as Dublin's cultural quarter from 1991, through the 1990s. We tell this exemplary and internationally-renowned architectural history through the examples of two cultural institutions – both predate the Temple Bar competition but were subsequently folded in to the Temple Bar Framework Plan: the Irish Film Centre, later the Irish Film Institute (1992) and Temple Bar Gallery and Studios (1994) – one housing scheme, the Printworks (1996) and the supposed nucleus of the masterplan, the urban space of Meeting House Square (1996). In this way, each Temple Bar case study essay focuses on a particular site and related aspect of the architectural, cultural or urban intentions. Chronologies, like the commission mechanisms and the design influences, overlap and interweave.

Architecture is complicated and its recent history is particularly slippery when dealing with an extra-ordinary procurement process. The story of Temple Bar's 1990s reinvention is a story of David versus Goliath in terms of small critical architectural practices engaging in the wholesale redesign of a chunk of city; also in terms of cultural development winning out over commercial infrastructure. Afterall, this area which later became known as Temple Bar comprised 40 acres of densely-woven buildings and narrow streets – an image of Dublin as it was before the late 18th-century rationalisation by the Wide Streets Commission. This was a substantial bank of land running between the River Liffey (to the north) and Dame Street (to the south), and book-ended by College Green to the east and Christ Church to the west. Firstly, how the government decided to save the area from Modernist infrastructural development and to create an architectural competition through an alternative development body (Temple Bar Properties) is remarkable. Secondly, how a group of young architects coming from eight practices, gathered themselves into a consortium called Group 91 so as to win that architectural competition is also remarkable – unprecedented and not since repeated.

Our telling of this story comes from key witness accounts as well as from international contemporary commentary and from lesser-known specialist reports. We recall the oft-told facts of CIÉ becoming a benignly negligent landlord, buying most of the buildings in this neighbourhood from 1975 so as to demolish them all for their American-designed transportation hub (Skidmore Owings and Merill, 1975–81). By the late-1980s CIÉ's plans were stalled. Having rented to artists and musicians, students and small business owners – a 'meanwhile use' for CIÉ's property portfolio – the neighbourhood had become culturally-rich and interesting. Nobody, not least the Taoiseach of the day, Charles Haughey, would sanction the area's demolition then. The 'meanwhile use' was coupled with An Taisce's 1985 archaeological and architectural study of the area which defined the 'Temple Bar Area', named physical attributes from setts to buildings and pointed to the place's Bohemian nature. This report spawned the Temple Bar Study Group which in turn recommended Ireland's first area action plan for Temple Bar. Published in 1990, the Temple Bar Action Plan proposed tax incentives to develop the area and identified desirable elements such as greater pedestrian permeability which became key goals and eventual features of the Temple Bar Framework Plan, 1991.

The following four case study essays should be read almost like a tiffin box: layers of independent goodies but ultimately interrelated, with each essay to be enjoyed as its own layer, contributing to the overall story and experience of the place, 30-plus years later.

Temple Bar Framework Plan, 1991 and Meeting House Square, Dublin 2, 1996

Merlo Kelly

Temple Bar street, Inner City Survey, 1985 (Courtesy of Irish Architectural Archive)

Meeting House Square is named after the Presbyterian Meeting House on Eustace Street (now the Ark) which dates from 1728, and the former 19th-century Quaker Meeting House which housed the Irish Film Centre (now the IFI). The proposal for a new public space and 'cultural hub' formed part of the collaborative Group 91 entry in the 1991 Temple Bar competition. Group 91 was made up of 13 architects from a number of small practices and their 'Temple Bar Framework Plan' identified three new 'hearts' which would animate the east-west pedestrian route through Temple Bar – Temple Bar Square, Meeting House Square and Market Square.

Meeting House Square, designed by Paul Keogh Architects, was intended to serve as an 'outdoor room' – an open-air performance space formed by cultural buildings around its perimeter. A series of secondary pedestrian routes converge on the space, creating a gathering point within the 'cultural cluster'. These meandering pedestrian routes were fundamental to the design strategy and echo the spirit of the Group 91 framework plan. Forming explorative connections, they were designed to open up new streets and spaces within what were predominantly derelict urban blocks.

The creation of a square was envisioned as part of a new urban sequence from Temple Bar Square and Curved Street through the square and on to Essex Street East. A north-south route cut through the Irish Film Centre via an historic laneway, connecting Dame Street to the Liffey. McGarry Ní Éanaigh's 'Wibbly Wobbly Bridge', a pedestrian footbridge at the mouth of the Poddle River, was designed to continue this route across to the north quays, bringing footfall through the square, but this never materialised. The omission of this bridge and the construction of the Millennium Bridge on axis with Eustace Street, means that the flow of pedestrian traffic from Dame Street bypasses Meeting House Square. Without this footfall, the square lacks passive surveillance. Since 1996, the square has been locked at night, allegedly for security reasons following reports of anti-social behaviour. Many would argue that this is contrary to the spirit of the Temple Bar Framework Plan and that it has fundamentally changed the nature of the square as a shared civic space. The proliferation of bars within the area has also played a role. As Frank McDonald commented in 1997, 'Given that one of the primary goals of the Temple Bar project was to create

'Dublin's Left Bank as Cultural Flagship', Frank McDonald, Irish Times, 30 May 1990 (Courtesy of Irish Times)

new "public spaces", the need to erect gates around Meeting House Square and to close them – even for eight hours every night – is an admission of failure. However, it is an inevitable consequence of the way the licensed trade has overwhelmed Temple Bar." (McDonald, 1997, p. 16)

The square underwent significant changes in 2011 when Sean Harrington Architects designed four giant retractable umbrella canopies to provide shelter in inclement weather. At this time the paving was altered to include a checkerboard panel to the centre in limestone and granite. These works were completed for the 20th anniversary of the Temple Bar Framework Plan.

A Series of Small-Scale Urban Interventions

Interest in the area between Dame Street and the River Liffey was triggered by a controversial development proposal along the quays in the late 1980s. The scheme for a colossal transportation hub spanning across the river was designed by American firm Skidmore, Owings & Merrill, and CIÉ had acquired numerous properties in the vicinity to ensure its completion. Short

leases were issued locally as many properties were earmarked for demolition in preparation for this. However, as Catherine Slessor observed, 'This nurtured an eclectic and vibrant mixture of small-scale users – cafes, art galleries, shops, clothing factories and recording studios – attracted by the cheap rents and bound together by a spirit of optimistic bohemianism.' (Slessor, 1993, p. 42)

A state agency Temple Bar Properties was established following the Temple Bar Renewal and Development Act 1991. Funding was obtained from the European Regional Development Fund, and a competition was announced to develop an Architectural Framework Plan for Temple Bar. The assessors were Paddy Teahon, Piaras Beaumont, Michael Collins, Owen Hickey, David Mackay, Laura Magahy and Gay McCarron. Twelve practices were invited to enter the competition, and Group 91, an architectural consortium formed in 1991 to celebrate Dublin's designation as the European City of Culture, submitted the winning entry. Group 91 was made up of 13 architects, from eight small architectural practices. Paul Keogh Architects was one of those practices. The assessors' report outlines the particular merits of the Group 91 scheme, and makes specific reference to the treatment of open space:

Proposed Transport Hub for Temple Bar and Dublin 7, 1975-81, Skidmore Owings and Merrill (Courtesy of CIÉ archive)

> The spacing and treatment of the various public open areas is extremely successful in this plan. This was the only scheme which proposed that Meeting House Square open directly to East Essex Street and the assessors were particularly impressed with this scheme's treatment of the Square. (Assessors' report, 1991)

Contemporary developments in Barcelona were undoubtedly a source of inspiration for Group 91 in the design of their Framework Plan. Keogh recalls trips to Europe as a studio tutor in University College Dublin (UCD), School of Architecture, in particular a trip to Barcelona where the contemporary urban interventions and elegant public spaces made a distinct impression on

Group 91, winning team: back row, from left: Michael McGarry, Derek Tynan, Sheila O'Donnell, Shelly McNamara, Niall McCullough (d.2021), Shay Cleary and John Tuomey
Front row, from left: Paul Keogh, Rachel Chidlow, Siobhán Ní Éanaigh, Yvonne Farrell, Valerie Mulvin and Shane O'Toole (Courtesy of Group 91 collection at Irish Architectural Archive)

him (Keogh, Nov. 2019). He cites Bach & Mora's Plaças de Gràcia (1981–5) as a particular influence, most notably their Plaça del Sol (1985).

As it happened, David Mackay, one of the assessors of the 1991 Temple Bar competition, was based in Barcelona. He had been in partnership with Oriol Bohigas and Josep Martorell since 1962, and their practice MBM Arquitectes was responsible for several urban projects in Barcelona, most notably the design of the Olympic Village and Port for the 1992 Olympics. Mackay, Bohigas and Martorell were key figures in the Barcelona Renaissance, gaining recognition in the 1980s for their '100 projects' – a series of small-scale urban interventions designed to stimulate urban renewal. Bohigas, who was Head of Urban Planning Department (1980–4) and Councillor of Culture (1991–4) in Barcelona City Council, advocated this incremental approach to urban design.

> I believe that this understanding of the city as the sum of its neighbourhoods or identifiable fragments has also been one of the basic criteria in the reconstruction of Barcelona. Controlling the city on the basis of a series of projects rather than uniform general plans makes it possible to give continuity to the urban character, the continuity of relative centralities. (Bohigas, 1999, pp103–8)

Temple Bar Framework Plan and Meeting House Square

'Walking Through Temple Bar' proposed routes, Group 91, 1991 (Courtesy of Group 91 collection at Irish Architectural Archive)

In practice, Mackay and Bohigas sought to highlight the distinction between urban planning and urban design: 'We're against urban planning, as it's known. There's a space between urban planning and architecture, which is urban design.' (Eaude, 2014). In his introductory essay to the *Temple Bar Lives* publication, Mackay laments the absence of a role for the architect in urban design decisions.

> For too long in Europe there has been not only a neglect of responsibility towards understanding the historical significance of the public space, the on-going creation of new places, but cities have not even been aware that it is their responsibility. This is no doubt due to the fact that architects themselves have neglected to exercise their professional skills in this task of urban design. They have allowed the decisions about the form of the public space to be determined by sectoral interests. These, however valid they may be, have led in many instances to the destruction of the multiple identities of our cities and neighbourhoods. (Mackay, 1991, p.11)

Group 91 had exhibited their 'Making a Modern Street' proposals for the Liberties in May 1991 and won the Temple Bar competition in the autumn of that same year. Derek Tynan recounts how they were the 'new kids on the

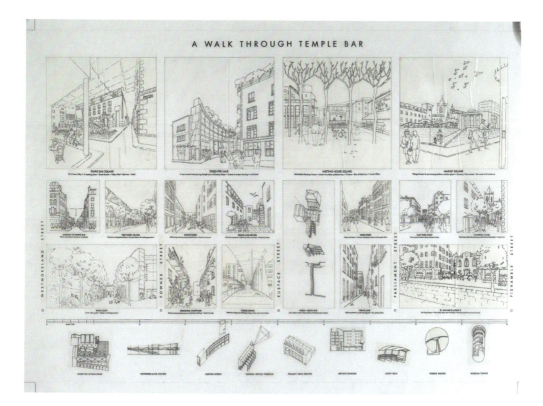

block', hungry for work. The prize for the Temple Bar competition was to be 'a significant commission' involving the design of a series of public spaces. Paddy Teahon was appointed by Haughey to oversee the commissioning process (Tynan, Nov. 2019), and negotiations to determine the exact scope of works were held with representative members of Group 91. Laura Magahy and Owen Hickey were also involved in negotiations, with Derek Tynan acting as managing director for Group 91 (Keogh, Nov. 2019). The first phase was to include three 'cultural clusters' within the Framework Plan, one of which was Meeting House Square. Once this was determined, Temple Bar Properties set about acquiring the relevant properties (Tynan, Nov. 2019).

A Magnet for Activity

Meeting House Square was to be located at the centre of the proposed cultural district, envisaged as a 'magnet' for activity in Temple Bar. Formerly a surface car park owned by the Linders Group, it was strategically located on various axes of pedestrian routes through Temple Bar. The site was adjacent to the Irish Film Centre (now the IFI) and open to Sycamore Street. There were aspirations within the Group 91 Framework Plan for a continuing route west to Crampton Court, linking the square with the Olympia Theatre and the Project Arts Centre, but this was never realised. In their Framework Plan, Group 91 outlined their intentions for the new square:

> A tourist information centre on a square lined with cafés. Both Meeting Houses refurbished. A place for meetings, for indoor and outdoor cinema and theatrical performances, a civic-scaled foyer to the surrounding cinemas and theatres. Projecting glass canopies, a passage to Crampton Court. A dramatic new bridge at the mouth of the Poddle. (Group 91 Framework Plan, 1991)

The cross routes resulted in three openings to the perimeter of the square. There were level changes to be navigated, given that the ground along Eustace Street was considerably higher than that within the square and adjacent Sycamore Street and Essex Street East. The approach from Curved Street is through an elegant stone-clad stepped archway alongside Shane O'Toole and Michael Kelly's Ark, a Children's Cultural Centre which forms the east edge of the Square. Opposite is Paul Keogh Architects' Mixed Use Building with a restaurant to the ground floor, entered from Sycamore Street. A slim red-brick block closes the south edge of the passageway to Sycamore Street. Despite initial plans for demolition, the 'kitchen shop', a two-storey red-brick building to the corner of Sycamore Street and Essex Street East was retained. O'Donnell + Tuomey's Photographic Archive and Photographic Gallery form the north and south walls of the 'outdoor room'. The square can also be accessed from the IFI (1992), another O'Donnell + Tuomey project, which predates the Framework Plan and was itself conceived as a 'room in the city'.

Meeting House Square, measuring 750 square metres, is laid out in Wicklow granite, with sections of limestone inlaid to trace the intended east-west route through it. Four trees punctuate the west edge of the square, and provide screening for the seating area outside the café. The presentation of the square as a room was dependent on a conversation between the various buildings, each of which had a particular aesthetic and character. The palette of materials presented to the square in the façades is various – red brick, Portland stone, granite, limestone, render, steel, copper, zinc and glass. The design of the space was developed by Paul Keogh Architects in consultation with the various architects (Keogh, Nov. 2019). Thresholds and junctions were considered, with continuous paving extending out from the interior in the case of the Photographic Archive. AAI assessor Michael Hussey observes – 'In Temple Bar Square, it is the built form which borrows from the exterior, while in Meeting House Square, it is the external room which borrows from the building interiors.' (AAI, 1997, p. 60).

The square was intended for outdoor performances, film screenings, and music recitals with the enclosing buildings specifically designed to serve this function. Encased in a copper-clad proscenium arch, Santiago Calatrava's elaborate theatre curtain forms a centrepiece within the red brick façade of the Ark. This folding metal screen opens up to reveal a stage while forming a sheltering curved canopy. The projecting plinth below the stage is clad in Portland stone. Portland stone also forms the façade of the Photographic Gallery, a pale and reflective screen-like surface befitting its function. The principal opening to the façade incorporates a zinc-clad recessed screen, allowing films to be projected onto it from the Photographic Archive across the square. Zinc panels also feature on the red-brick façade of the Photographic Archive.

Roving oak and steel wheelbarrow benches were designed by Paul Keogh Architects for public use within the space. These were constructed from oak slats fixed to a curved steel frame. Comprising seating on two levels, the benches were fitted with cast-iron wheels to allow them to be moved around the square as required. Stage lighting was fixed to the building façades, around the perimeter of the square, and a circle of uplighters was placed within the paving to the centre of the square.

All the building uses lining Meeting House Square reflected the aspiration to create a cultural hub. In addition to the Children's Cultural Centre, the Photographic Archive and Gallery, and the Irish Film Centre, the Gaiety School of Acting occupied the upper floors of the Mixed Use Building. Eden Restaurant was located on the ground floor, with a fit-out designed by architect Tom de Paor. During the design process Paul Keogh Architects proposed a demountable weather covering for the square, as used at the outdoor opera festival in Garsington, Oxfordshire (Group 91 meeting minutes, 19/01/93, IAA), but this was not included in the final scope of works.

Rooms of the City

In tracing formative influences, it is important to note that many of the Group 91 architects had studied together in UCD, some under architect Ivor Smith who was Professor of Architecture in UCD from 1969–72. Smith and his so-called 'Flying Circus' cohort, which included Ed Jones, Kenneth Frampton, John Miller, Chris Cross and Neave Brown among others (Keogh, Nov. 2019) would fly in from London to teach each week. After years abroad following graduation, in London and further afield, Paul Keogh, Rachael Chidlow and many of their Group 91 colleagues returned to Dublin, with aspirations to transform attitudes to urban inhabitation. Several were appointed as studio tutors in UCD by Professor Cathal O'Neill, who was head of the School of Architecture from 1972–96 (Keogh, Nov. 2019). Indeed, the UCD Dublin City Quays project (1985–6), which was led by Gerry Cahill, Loughlin Kealy and Cathal O'Neill, was in many senses a precursor to the 'Making a Modern Street' project and then, the Temple Bar Framework Plan.

Professionally, many of the Group 91 collective were already collaborating in the early 1980s, in their City Architecture Studio practice. In addition to a series of projects examining the quays and the docklands, they staged a number of architectural exhibitions in the Blue Studio Architecture Gallery at 42 Dawson Street (formerly the offices of de Blacam & Meagher Architects). The practice of Keogh and his colleagues was undoubtedly influenced by Aldo Rossi's writings and work, as is evident in their output from that period. Rossi's work was first exhibited in Ireland in the Blue Studio in May 1983. This event was staged in collaboration with Andreas Papadakis, who had written several texts on Rossi, and translated his essays into English (Keogh, Nov. 2019).

Leon Krier was another significant influence and in 1985 Keogh delivered a paper at the UCD Dublin City Quays Symposium entitled 'Leon Krier and the Reconstruction of the Traditional City.' Keogh writes how Krier was influenced by Rossi's seminal 1965 publication *Architecture of the City*, and outlines a number of principles which became precepts of Krier's work. What is evident in the writings of Rossi and Krier is the changing role of the architect in urban design. Rather than assuming a *tabula rasa* approach, the architect was reliant on existing fabric and historic precedent.

Central to Krier's Postmodernist design theory was the requirement for an in-depth analysis of the historic city. As Keogh elucidated:

> He [Krier] rejects the idea that the form of the city and of its public spaces could be a matter for personal experiment. These public spaces, he argues, should be built in the traditional form of streets and squares, whose dimensions and proportions can be obtained and verified from the culture of urban civilisation [...] He cites the example of a well-proportioned room which is symmetrical and bright and has elegant architectural detail. So it is with rooms of the city, their forms can be measured from past examples and reconstructed along these lines. (Keogh in Cahill and Kealy, 1986, p. 56)

This methodology was particularly applicable to the Temple Bar Framework Plan, and the appropriation of public spaces as 'rooms of the city', following scale and proportion of historical urban space, became a pivotal strategy within the Group 91 approach. As John Olley summarised in 1997:

> In Temple Bar the fabric of the city is being recycled, whether in its standing form or by the reuse of its materials. The interventions of Group 91 are stitching new uses and activities into the spaces and buildings of the existing fabric. The urban tapestry is enriched while its material worth is conserved and an ecological alternative is formulated to suburban expansion and the process of destruction and rebuilding. (Olley, 1997, p. 161)

Facts and Figures

Meeting House Square was commissioned in 1991 and was completed in 1996.

Architects: Paul Keogh Architects (part of Group 91) – Paul Keogh, Rachael Chidlow, Cormac Allen, Cathie Curran, Kevin Nolan.

Group 91 was a consortium made up of eight architectural practices and 13 architects, formed in 1991 to celebrate Dublin's designation as the European City of Culture: Shay Cleary Architects – Shay Cleary; Grafton Architects – Yvonne Farrell, Shelley McNamara with Mark Price; Paul Keogh Architects – Rachael Chidlow, Paul Keogh; McCullough Mulvin Architects – Niall McCullough, Valerie Mulvin; McGarry Ní Éanaigh Architects – Michael McGarry, Siobhán Ní Éanaigh; O'Donnell + Tuomey Architects – Sheila O'Donnell, John Tuomey; Shane O'Toole Architects – Shane O'Toole, Michael Kelly with Susan Cogan; Derek Tynan Architects – Derek Tynan.

Group 91 submitted the winning competition entry to design an 'Architectural Framework Plan for Temple Bar' in 1991. In the period leading up to the Temple Bar competition, Group 91 staged an architectural exhibition, 'Making a Modern Street', which tested new ideas for urban living on a street in the Liberties area of Dublin.

PKA or Paul Keogh Architects was established in 1984. Paul Keogh and Rachael Chidlow are both practice directors. Paul Keogh studied architecture in UCD and the Royal College of Art in London, where he received a Masters in Environmental Design. He worked for James Stirling in London, and de Blacam & Meagher and the Office of Public Works in Dublin before establishing Paul Keogh Architects. He has taught and lectured in Ireland, UK, Europe, USA and Asia. He was president of the Royal Institute of Architects of Ireland from 2010–12 and is a Fellow of the RIBA. Rachael Chidlow received a BA from Manchester University and a Masters in Environmental Design from the Royal College of Art in London. She worked with de Blacam & Meagher before joining Paul Keogh Architects. She is a member of the Society of Designers in Ireland and was awarded the Goldsmiths Company Prize and the Glen Dimplex Award for her work in interior design.

Client: Temple Bar Properties
Contractor: P. Rogers & Sons Ltd
Quantity Surveyor: Bruce Shaw
Archaeology: Margaret Gowen

Sources

Unpublished
Paul Keogh, interviewed by Merlo Kelly, Nov. 2019
Derek Tynan, interviewed by Merlo Kelly, Nov. 2019
'Making a Modern Street' (exhibition models), Irish Architectural Archive
Group 91 Archives (drawings, models and documentation), Irish Architectural Archive:
Group 91 Archive ref. 2009/152; Paul Keogh Collection ref. 2007/106; Shane O'Toole Collection ref. 2004/166; O'Donnell Tuomey Archive ref. 2012/008

Published
AAI, *New Irish Architecture 12. AAI Awards* (Gandon Editions, AAI, 1997)
Anon,. 'Aiming to create an ambience of Montmartre', *Irish Times*, 28 Nov. 1991
Anon., 'Meeting House Square, Dublin', in *Architektur + Wettbewerbe Journal* (No. 154, Jun. 1993)
Bohigas, Oriole, 'Ten Points for an Urban Methodology', in Tim Marshall (ed.), *Transforming Barcelona* (Routledge, 2004)
Campbell, Hugh, 'Urbanism: Saving the City: Dublin's Temple Bar Renewal', in *Architecture Today* (No. 81, Sept. 1997)
Cole, Richard, John K. Billingham, and Urban Design Group, *The Good Place Guide: Urban Design in Britain and Ireland* (Batsford, 2002)
Eaude, Michael, 'David Mackay Obituary', *The Guardian*, 23 Nov. 2014
Graby, John and Royal Institute of the Architects of Ireland, *Building on the Edge of Europe: A Survey of Contemporary Architecture in Ireland Embracing History, Town and Country* (RIAI, 1996)
Graeve, Jobst and Temple Bar Properties, *Temple Bar Lives!* (Temple Bar Properties, 1991)
Keogh, Paul, 'Leon Krier and the Reconstruction of the Traditional City', in Gerry Cahill and Loughlin Kealy (eds), *Dublin City Quays: Projects* (The School of Architecture, University College Dublin, 1986)
McDonald, Frank, 'The Future Wins at Temple Bar', *Irish Times*, 13 Aug. 1992
McDonald, Frank, 'Temple Bar fails to meet objectives but its visitors drink the atmosphere', *Irish Times*, 21 April 1997
McDonald, Frank, 'Building Sight', *Irish Times*, 2 Sept. 2006
Olley, John, 'Temple Bar. Dublin 1991 – 6', in Becker, Annette, John A. Olley, Wilfried Wang (eds), *Ireland: 20th-Century Architecture* (Prestel, 1997)
Slessor, Catherine, 'Dublin Renaissance', in *Architectural Review* (No. 1151, Jan. 1993, republished online Feb. 2012, https://www.architectural-review.com/buildings/dublin-renaissance)

Case Study
Irish Film Centre, 6 Eustace Street, Temple Bar, Dublin 2, 1992

Merlo Kelly

The Irish Film Institute (IFI), formerly the Irish Film Centre (IFC), is located in the former Quaker Meeting House and school, in the heart of Temple Bar. The site for the IFI comprised a collection of nine buildings, ranging in quality and scale and dating from as early as 1692, loosely assembled around a covered yard. Through the adaptation of this collection of historic buildings, the architects (O'Donnell + Tuomey) succeeded in creating a 'secret urban room' and a lively centre for film culture. The story of the buildings, and their evolution over a period of 300 years, is revealed through the layered architecture. The decision to locate the principal cinema in the former men's meeting room and the second cinema in the former women's meeting room underpinned the design of the complex. A central atrium space, around which the workings of the IFI hinge, was formed on the footprint of the historic courtyard.

The IFI is embedded within an urban block, bound in by Eustace Street and Sycamore Street. The centre has no conspicuous street presence and is accessed by a series of narrow laneways which cut through the block and lead the visitor to the central atrium. O'Donnell + Tuomey have created a social hub that is criss-crossed by this series of urban paths, an opening-up of concealed city fabric to the public. The building is unannounced, the interior spaces become an extension of the surrounding streetscape, and the inner court assumes the qualities of a lively public square. This permeability of the urban block is key to the project, and ties into the ethos of Group 91. Though the IFI, which was commissioned in 1986, predates the Group 91 Temple Bar Framework Plan, it encompasses many of the ideals and principles that were integral to the collaborative scheme, and indeed O'Donnell + Tuomey were pivotal players in Group 91. The film centre was, in many senses, the pilot project for the regeneration of Temple Bar as a cultural quarter. The aspiration to create a 'cultural cluster' was compounded by the later addition of the Irish Film Archive, the Photographic Gallery, the Photographic Archive, the Ark Children's Centre and the Gaiety School of Acting, all of which connect to Meeting House Square which was completed between 1995 and 1996.

Several alterations have been made to the IFI since its completion in 1992. The original steel stairs in the bar area were removed and replaced in the mid-1990s. Modifications were made to the seating in the main cinema in c.2003, and again in 2020. The acoustic maple proscenium arch which framed the screen in the main cinema was removed during these works to accommodate a larger screen. In 2009, O'Donnell + Tuomey were involved in further alterations to the building. The works included the addition of a third studio cinema within an existing meeting room on the first floor, and the refurbishment of the bar including provision of a new staircase. Historic toilet fittings had been re-used in the original toilet facilities along the entrance corridor, but these facilities were relocated, and remodelled. The bookshop, originally housed off the central atrium space, was moved to its current position along the entrance corridor from Eustace Street.

Ground floor plan, 1994 (Courtesy of O'Donnell + Tuomey collection at Irish Architectural Archive)

Public Realm Within an Urban Block

The National Film Institute (NFI), now the Irish Film Institute (IFI), was founded in 1943. In 1986, a film centre was proposed in Dublin's Temple Bar to house the IFI. The brief, which evolved in the early stages of the project, was to provide a building that would accommodate various aspects of film culture. It was to include two cinemas, a film archive, a bookshop, a restaurant, a bar, education rooms and film production offices. It was intended as part of a cluster of cultural buildings and became a pilot project for the subsequent Temple Bar developments. Referring to the brief and design concept for the project, O'Donnell + Tuomey describe their intention 'to extend the public realm of the city into the centre of the urban block' (O'Donnell, Oct. 2011).

The proposed site, a former Quaker Meeting House complex, was accessed through the discreet pedimented doorway of no. 6 Eustace Street, a seven bay four-storey commercial palazzo designed by Millar & Symes in the 19th century. The nine buildings on the site were acquired by the Irish Film Institute in 1986. Prior to the design process, the architects carried out a meticulous site survey, recording the existing structures and spaces in detail. The design intention was to regenerate the layers within the complex block, retaining as much original fabric as possible whilst introducing new elements to make sense of the disparate pieces. The careful judgement executed in the decision to manipulate the existing forms and

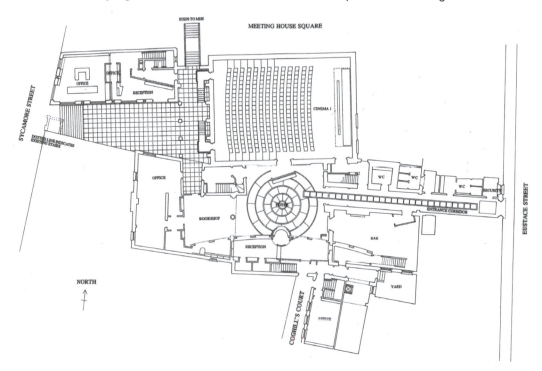

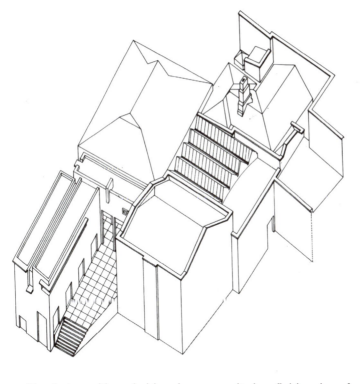

Axonometric drawing (Courtesy of O'Donnell + Tuomey collection at Irish Architectural Archive)

the sensitive juxtaposition of old and new, results in a fluid series of spaces stitched into the historic block. As the architects explained, 'Our site-specific strategy for the new film centre — comprising new interventions, surgical demolitions, simple conversion, and invisible mending — was intended to continue the process of gradual change and incremental adaptation that had characterised the historical development of this complex site'. (O'Donnell + Tuomey, 2007, p. 32).

The block is effectively turned inside out, the primary public gathering space becomes internal instead of serving the street. The skilful manipulation of existing historic fabric and sensitive insertion of new material results in a rich and complex spatial experience. The original scheme consisted of two screening rooms, a café/bar and restaurant, a ticket kiosk, bookshop, offices and toilets all accessed from the central triple height atrium. The existing structures accommodated the cinemas, their brick and granite-lined openings retained and incorporated into the linings of the structure where possible.

Primary access to the film centre is through no. 6 Eustace Street via a long vaulted corridor, with varying ceiling height. An illuminated film-strip of etched glass set into the floor lines the dimly-lit passageway and projects into the bright atrium space. The centre is also accessed from Meeting House Square and Sycamore Street via a raised courtyard concealing an

Sketch of proposed internal courtyard space (Courtesy of O'Donnell + Tuomey collection at Irish Architectural Archive)

archive store and workshop below, and from Dame Street through Coghill's Court. A strip of neon light along the underside of the limestone-clad projection suite signals the entrance from Meeting House Square.

A limestone colonnade delineates the paved courtyard, which is overlooked by the Irish Film Archive and serves as an external café area. Catherine Slessor describes how the 'matrix of tentacle-like entrance routes draw visitors in from the surrounding streets to converge in an airy, skylit courtyard. Within the courtyard, an expressive dialogue between the old and new is immediately established'. (Slessor, 1993, p. 49).

The external qualities of the atrium space are accentuated by the industrial glazed roof, the limestone and steel floor, the weathered brick façades of the surrounding buildings and the robust steel furniture. An inserted wall, 'gently curved like a lens' (Ó Laoire, 1993, p. 30), creates the southern edge of the space, extending into the former schoolroom to form the bar and contain the restaurant gallery at first floor level. This smooth ochre wall, punctured by a series of mild steel-lined openings, is clearly articulated and presented as a contemporary element. A careful selection of materials such as steel, glass, neon, pigmented plaster and limestone, further articulates the juxtaposition of old and new and yet the scheme reads as a seamless whole.

The adjacent position of the screening rooms, within existing structures at right angles to each other, meant that the projection suite could be strategically located between the two cinemas. This decision anchored the design process and the auxiliary spaces were organised accordingly within the remaining structures and voids. Thus construction began with a process of selective demolition.

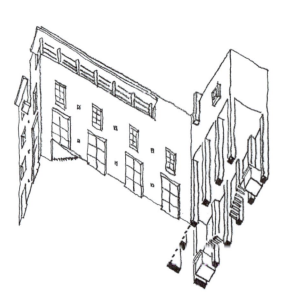

Materials were carefully selected to highlight new insertions while presenting a coherent aesthetic. Exposed I-beams support the industrial glazed roof which covers the atrium, formerly the courtyard. The Ballinasloe limestone floor is arranged in concentric circles neatly articulated within mild steel bands. Three historic granite Doric columns, two of which are engaged, support the upper wall

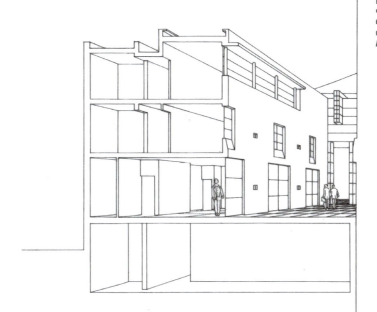

Sectional perspective drawing (Courtesy of O'Donnell + Tuomey collection at Irish Architectural Archive)

of the second screening room and subdivide the common space. The insertion of the curved plastered wall, coloured with natural ochre, highlights this contrast yet manages to unite disparate elements – the bar, the ticket booths, the restaurant and the offices overhead. The openings within this wall are lined with oiled and waxed mild steel, and display inset lighting in their soffits. Fine profile steel windows occupy the upper level openings in the curved wall, which have chamfered integrated sills. The ticket kiosk and gallery balustrades are also mild steel with walnut handrails and countertops. The curved steel panels in the kiosk are fixed with exposed rivets, creating an industrial feel. The existing brick façades remain relatively unaltered and display a patina of age, their textured surfaces contrasting with the clean lines of the insertions. A display wall made up of layers of polished plaster brightly pigmented with cobalt, is splayed to announce and screen the entrance to the main cinema.

The cast-iron gallery overlooking the men's meeting room was sacrificed in the design process but the upper level doors were retained in their entirety (frame and leaf). The resultant floating Classical doorcases present a surreal composition within the main cinema space. Similarly, the windows on the west façade of the main cinema were retained, the central opening framing the projector. A maple proscenium arch, layered with acoustic insulation and housing all the technical requirements for the screen, was the only built insertion in the main cinema. The roof structure of the second screening room (housed within the former women's meeting room) was retained, complete with cornicing and acanthus scroll supports, as was the semi-circular seating.

Archaeology and Architecture

O'Donnell + Tuomey's film centre is a crafted intervention into a complex layering of urban fabric. The former Meeting House Headquarters had evolved and accumulated over centuries. The unveiling of material within the assemblage of structures and interstitial spaces displays technical ingenuity and an innate understanding of the site. The balance between existing and new is finely judged, enabling modern insertions to reanimate existing fabric, leading conservation architect, Loughlin Kealy, to laud the project: 'Projects such as... the Irish Film Centre within the Quaker complex in Eustace Street, point to a changed perception of the role of historic buildings. There is nothing romantic about these projects. They meet new needs with the technology of the present and an acute awareness of the context.' (Kealy in Graby, 1996, pp 77-8).

The process began with an understanding that their contribution to this collection of historic buildings was merely another phase in its evolution. They carried out a meticulous survey of the existing fabric, in an effort to understand the layered history of the site. The design intention, underpinned by the values of continuity and renewal, was 'to continue the process of gradual change and incremental adaptation that had characterised the

View of internal courtyard (Courtesy of O'Donnell + Tuomey and Irish Architectural Archive)

historical development of this complex site.' (O'Donnell + Tuomey, 2007, p. 32). They adopted an archaeological methodology in the initial stages of brief development and design.

> The architects see an analogy between archaeology and architecture. They regarded the process of discovering, understanding and recording the site as one that provides the basis for the architectural intervention. Buildings are always changing and the architects' contribution is but another layer in the evolution. (Brooker and Stone, 2004, pp 237–42)

The design approach, opening-up the inner workings of an urban block, invites a new reading of hidden city fabric and creates 'a sequence of atmospheric spaces rich in spatial and textural effect' (Casey, 2005, p. 432). The palette of materials –stone, steel, brick, plaster, reflects the modest character of the surrounding Temple Bar streets and warehouse buildings. John Tuomey recounts his delight on seeing a 'No bicycles' sign posted on the wall of the foyer, an implication that the space was perceived as an extension of the streetscape. The cinemas, by contrast, have the intimacy of a private room – comfortable lined spaces within a robust shell. The historic artefacts within the existing structure – window openings, cornices, door surrounds and roof trusses – add a rich layer to the cinematic experience.

The spatial progression through the embedded spaces and the galleried courtyard has echoes of an Italian piazza, and brings to mind Florian Beigel's Half Moon Theatre in London. The space is clearly theatrical, invoking a sense of performance which indulges the public desire to see and be seen. In his critique Seán Ó Laoire makes reference to this notion. He likens the scenario to that of a Fellini film, and notes the *Cinecittà* parallels – *cine* (cinema) and *città* (city), the rare and magical blend of film and cityscape that is found within the walls of the

centre. As Ó Laoire noted, 'This project magically balances substance with veneer and provides Dublin with a place where citizens' repressed desire for promenading can be relieved to a limited extent.' (Ó Laoire, 1992, p. 31).

This close assembly of buildings relating to film – screening rooms, education rooms, lecture rooms, a bookshop, a film archive, film production rooms, together with the Photographic Gallery and Archive and open-air screening space – results in a lively cultural quarter, a unique urban atmosphere. It has become a cultural hub, 'an appropriately lively environment for the viewing and discussion of films' (Ryan, 2002, p. 17) – the intention of the architects fulfilled. In addition, the establishment of this 'cultural cluster' prompted the emergence of several film related companies in the area at the time, among them Filmbase (Curved Street) and Access Cinema (Meeting House Square). As Colm Ó Briain writes in 1996, 'The commitment to this cultural infrastructure marks the first coherent, planned provision of buildings for cultural purposes since the founding of the state.' (Quinn, 1996, p. 58)

In many ways, the methodology for the IFI project informed the trajectory for subsequent work by O'Donnell + Tuomey, and established values which they still uphold today. 'Working slowly on this project, through the processes of research, survey, design, demolition, repair, reuse, building, and rebuilding, set us on a course by which we still steer today — the belief that the task of architecture is continuity and renewal.' (O'Donnell + Tuomey, 2007, p. 32).

In 1988, O'Donnell + Tuomey won the AAI Downes Medal for the unbuilt design of the Irish Film Centre, an unusual feat. Assessor, Mike Gold stated: 'You get the feeling from this – even though it is still only drawings – that it will shine as a building.' (AAI, 1988, p. 5). And in the words of Seán Ó Laoire, 'Shine it did' (Ó Laoire, 1993, p. 30).

More Than Concrete Blocks Volume 3

Facts and Figures

The Irish Film Centre/Irish Film Institute was commissioned in 1986; it went to site in 1991 and was complete in 1992. The architects were Sheila O'Donnell, John Tuomey and Sean Mahon.

Sheila O'Donnell and John Tuomey, both graduates of UCD School of Architecture, formed the practice O'Donnell + Tuomey in 1988. Their first project as an office, the Irish Film Centre, commissioned in 1986 and completed in 1992, heralded the start of a significant new phase in urban regeneration. They were co-founders of the award-winning collaboration Group 91 and went on to design the Gallery of Photography, the Irish Film Archive and the Photographic Archive in Temple Bar. As a practice, their subsequent works include Ranelagh School, the Furniture College Letterfrack, Centre for Research into Infectious Diseases (CRID) UCD, the Glucksman Gallery University College Cork, An Gaeláras Derry, the Timberyard Housing Dublin, the Lyric Theatre Belfast, the Photographers' Gallery London, the London School of Economics Saw Swee Hock Student Centre and phase one of the Central European University Budapest.

Current projects in their practice include the development of competition-winning designs for the V&A East Museum and Sadler's Wells dance theatre in London's East Bank, an Academic Hub and Library for TU Dublin, a new School of Architecture for Liverpool University, new Cultural Quarter in Swords and a range of housing projects for Dublin City Council. O'Donnell + Tuomey have won the AAI Downes Medal for Excellence in Architectural Design seven times, been shortlisted for the RIBA Stirling Prize five times and in 2005 were awarded the RIAI Gold Medal. In March 2010, Sheila O'Donnell and John Tuomey were elected as Honorary Fellows of American Institute of Architects, and in 2015 they were awarded the RIBA Royal Gold Medal, in recognition of a lifetime's work. In that same year they were awarded the American Academy of Arts and Letters Brunner Prize.

O'Donnell + Tuomey have also published several significant architectural monographs and have exhibited six times in the Venice Biennale. Both are members of Aosdána.

The Irish Film Centre won the AAI Downes Medal in 1988, an RIAI award in 1993 and joint first prize for the *Sunday Times* Building of the Year Award in 1995. The building was a finalist in the Andrea Palladio International Award in 1993.

Contractor: Cleary & Doyle
Structural Engineer: Fearon O'Neill Rooney
M&E Engineer: EDA
Quantity Surveyor: Boyd & Creed

Sources

Unpublished
Sheila O'Donnell, interview with Merlo Kelly, Oct. 2011
O'Donnell + Tuomey Archives – Selected drawings and sketches, various dates
O'Donnell + Tuomey Architects, Planning permission application – Ref: 1309/08 (Dublin City Council)
Irish Film Institute – Members' Newsletters (1992–5)

Published
AAI, *New Irish Architecture III. AAI Awards* (Gandon Editions, 1988)
Brooker, Graeme & Sally Stone, *Rereadings: Interior Architecture and the Design Principles of Remodelling Existing Buildings* (RIBA Enterprises, 2004)
Comiskey, Ray, 'Film Institute on the Move', *Irish Times*, 24 Apr. 1986
Hegarty, Trish, 'Central Focus for Irish Films', *Irish Times*, 18 Sept. 1992
Kealy, Loughlin 'Buildings from the Past', in John Graby (ed.) *Building on the Edge of Europe* (Gandon Editions, 1996)
McDonald, Frank, 'What the Young Architects Are Doing', *Irish Times*, 30 Jan. 1986
O'Donnell, Sheila and John Tuomey, *O'Donnell + Tuomey: Selected Works* (Princeton Architectural Press, 2007)
O'Laoire, Seán, 'Irish Film Centre', in *Irish Architect* (No. 93, Nov./Dec. 1992), pp 29–33
Olley, John, 'Irish Film Centre, Temple Bar Dublin 1987–92', in Annette Becker, John Olley and Wilfred Wang (eds), *Ireland: 20th-Century Architecture* (Prestel, 1997)
O'Toole, Shane, 'Renovation of the Temple Bar Urban District in Dublin', in *Domus* (Vol. 809, Nov. 1998)
O'Toole, Shane, 'Coming of Age', in Architektur Zentrum Wien, *New Building Today: European Architecture of the 1990s* (Birkhauser Verlag, 1995), pp 280–3
Quinn, Patricia (ed.), *Temple Bar: The Power of an Idea* (Gandon Editions for Temple Bar Properties Limited, Dublin 1996)
Ryan, Ray 'Making Room for the Movies at Temple Bar', in *The Architects' Journal* (Vol. 196, No. 21, Nov. 1992), pp 17–19
Ryan, Raymund 'Six Medals: The Unprecedented Success of O'Donnell & Tuomey', in *Irish Architect* (No. 174, Feb. 2002), pp 53–4
Slessor, Catherine 'Irish Reels', in *Architectural Review* (No. 1151, Jan. 1993), pp 46–9
Royal Institute of the Architects of Ireland, *Irish Architecture 1993: RIAI Regional Awards* (RIAI, 1993) p. 5
Wigham, Maurice J., *The Irish Quakers: A Short History of the Religious Society of Friends in Ireland* (Historical Committee of the Religious Society of Friends in Ireland, 1992)

Case Study

Temple Bar Gallery + Studios, 5–9 Temple Bar, Dublin 2, 1994

Ellen Rowley

In the heart of Temple Bar, in the heart of the city, facing the river on one side and Temple Bar Square on the other, stands a citadel of contemporary art: Temple Bar Gallery + Studios (TBGS). Though founded in 1983 and coming to occupy part of the present site in the 1980s, this TBGS building was converted from a former shirt factory and updated by McCullough Mulvin Architects from 1992 and finished by 1994. While TBGS predates the Framework Plan, it was one of the catalysts that brought about Temple Bar's reimagining. And as the building was reconfigured by some of the Group 91 architects, it sits happily within the Temple Bar cultural building portfolio. We count it as our third Temple Bar case study.

The building stands as a gridded block of white, black metal and glass – almost like an exploded Piet Mondrian painting. In this, it seems to be all about its walls and its surfaces. Indeed it is hard for the passer-by to imagine the world of art that bustles within. Hints of that activity can be found at ground level, where expanses of glass meet the busy Temple Bar pavement. Peering in, the passer-by will find a White Cube gallery space. There are more hints if the passer-by leans back and looks up to see a painted steel circular sign and artwork, 'Our Union Only in Truth' (Garrett Phelan, 2013). Here, at roof level where the building wall is pushed back and clad in metal, different things are happening. This is what the architects call the 'metal 'town' above the city' (*Generation*, p. 103); where we sense a community or population of people, set apart from the rest of us.

Indeed, the stars of this show are the artists' studios: a quasi-hidden ecosystem of creativity made up of differently shaped and oriented artists' rooms, barely visible externally from the first-floor windows upwards. As TBGS Director, Cliodhna Shaffrey observed, 'one room lies alongside another quiet room. 30 in all. In each, artists are testing, experimenting, wrestling, struggling, winning, failing, making. At times it feels like a version of paradise, so much spark and magic.' (O'Malley, 2022, p. 171) This is a private world, access to which is given to professional artists who, after a rigorous application process, become short and longer-term tenants of their own creative domain. They enter and exit on Fownes Street, through industrial-style painted metal panel doors, recalling the building's industrial heritage. Signage along this façade also describes the building's idiosyncratic function but most people fail to notice as they negotiate the narrow street's uneven cobbled ground.

More than any single building or public area in this volume, TBGS speaks to the aspiration, transformation and challenge of the Temple Bar project. It arose from artist-led activism and collaboration when urban space was undervalued and cheap. While a beautiful success story – it programmes independent cutting-edge art exhibitions, tours and talks while hosting a community of variously-focused artists – TBGS seems under siege in 2020s Dublin. On the one hand, demand for artists' studios rises as the national housing crisis worsens and on the other hand, Temple Bar's cultural quarter identity shrinks under the weight of tourist-based consumerism. In 2022, and to international critical acclaim, TBGS curated the Irish pavilion for the Venice Biennale with artist Niamh O'Malley. In 2023, TBGS celebrates 40 years in existence; and to date, more than 500 artists (Irish and international) have worked or exhibited at TBGS. The building's interior of exposed surfaces is fundamentally in good condition, due to conscientious maintenance by the TBGS administration, while its public-facing gallery space enjoys a constant process of reinvention. Other than revealing more of the gallery's concrete structure, there have been no significant architectural alterations to the building since 1994.

A Potted History: From Shirt Factory to Makeshift Studios to Utopia?

Jenny Haughton, an independent arts administrator and curator who was influenced by artist-led movements internationally, might be hailed the originator of Temple Bar Gallery + Studios, referred to at its start in 1983 as the 'Temple Bar Centre'. Indeed, as Haughton saw it and as it developed during the first decade of its life – before it got the refurbished and extended building designed by McCullough Mulvin – this organisation was a nucleus, a hub, a centre: a centre for artists of most media; a centre for making art; a centre for watching art-house films; a centre to gather and discuss art. As well as a dance studio, there was a crêperie for a short time. And at different intervals, this Temple Bar Centre hosted a weekend food market.

For the first four years, with Haughton at the helm as secretary and administrator, the centre evolved into Temple Bar Gallery + Studios. Participating artists became members and decisions were taken collectively, through the structure of two committees – a gallery and a house committee. Communality, sociability and the collective underpinned the place's workings. As issued in a memo of February 1987: 'Temple Bar is for working artists [...] If you have a problem with your neighbour, deal with it immediately [...] There are approximately 30 people coming in each day to work. Please introduce yourselves!' (*Generation*, 2013, p. 44).

Haughton and the founding artists whipped up a storm of cultural activity while somehow establishing the painting studios as the pillar or mainstay of this vibrant centre. During these formative years, Haughton also managed to persuade the Arts Council of Ireland of the centre's legitimacy: funding rose from a paltry £300 starting grant to a sizeable £30,000 by the time she left in late 1987. From the outset and unsurprisingly, the issue of building leases was a hot topic. Leases were taken on a two-year basis from CIÉ, the state corporation that owned most of the properties in this four-acre area of Dublin centre. And as such, these first years of occupation at the Maureen Buildings were marked by the insecurity of the short-term lease. This insecurity was exacerbated by the lack of building insurance. Resulting from the original building's fabric and then the makeshift timber partitions brought in by the artists, no insurance company would touch the place. Precarity, it would seem, reigned supreme during these first years.

Having launched the 'ship', Haughton moved on. Her successors – Clair Stanbridge for two years; then John Hunt from 1988 to 1990; and Ruairí Ó Cuív from 1991 to 1996 – gradually formalised the organisation

(left)
Maureen Buildings (pre-1992 view), Shirt Factory, T. J. Cullen (Courtesy of McCullough Mulvin image collection)

(right)
Ground Floor Plan, Temple Bar Gallery and Studios (Courtesy of McCullough Mulvin image collection)

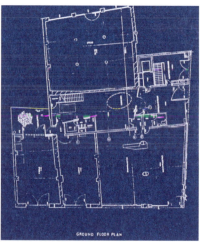

and ultimately, by 1994, Ó Cuív oversaw the redevelopment of the Maureen Buildings from improvised studios and art centre to the Temple Bar Gallery + Studios building that we know today.

While there had been rumblings of a better lease from CIÉ – certainly, Haughton was pushing for this from day one and reputedly offered CIÉ £150,000 for the building in 1987 – the prospect of less precarity and instability only came with the Temple Bar Area Renewal and Development Act of 1991 and, in turn, with the establishment of Temple Bar Properties and Temple Bar Renewal Limited. The new director of TBGS, Ó Cuív, worked closely with this new landlord body which was also the developer (on behalf of the government), Temple Bar Properties, to broker a deal for the art centre and studios. With the backing of TBGS's voluntary board, comprising three artist members and other professionals such as a solicitor and accountant, Ó Cuív and Temple Bar Properties reached a 'Cultural Use Agreement' which centred on a 40-year licence (as against, lease) for TBGS in the Maureen Buildings site. At this point though, the decay of the original building's fabric was stark and seemingly, irreversible. Leases were soon eclipsed by the necessity of a new building or at least, a deep redevelopment of the existing one.

Post-Industrial Architectural Space for Dublin's Artists
What excited most of the artists who took over the four floors or 12,500 square feet of the Maureen Buildings in 1983 were the spaces with their openness and particular quality of daylight. As one artist, Mairead Byrne exclaimed, 'Space and light are a material which you can't buy in the shops. But they're as important as the materials you can buy and they influence

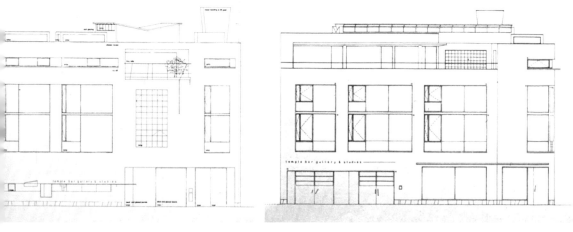

(left)
Fownes Street Elevation (Courtesy of McCullough Mulvin image collection)

(right)
Temple Bar Elevation (Courtesy of McCullough Mulvin image collection)

the form of one's work' (*Generation*, 2013, p. 48). At least three of the pioneering artists – Brian Maguire, Patrick Graham and Sean Fingleton – made bigger work in response to their new circumstances. Reputedly, Fingleton's oil paint overflowed from canvas to corridor (Dunne in Coyne, 1994, p. 7).

Such was the physical freedom inherent in this large non-precious factory building, bounded by glass walls and mostly unobstructed internal spaces. The large floor plates lent themselves well to architectural improvisation. And the improvised natures of the interiors lent themselves well to creative expression. The flipside of such informal architecture was the neglect, typically, of those more prosaic issues like mechanical services and fire safety; or the perfunctory conditions of poor thermal behaviour and ever-present water ingress. In these ways, TBGS's shirt factory was failing. While the initial maelstrom of creativity and multidisciplinary activity sustained the community, by 1988 these building failures were increasingly intrusive and problematic. And by the time Ruairí Ó Cuív took the reins in 1991, there were complaints about the upper floor studios being either too cold or too warm. The steep mansard glazed roof – a later 1950s addition to the original Cullen building – was leaking badly. Initially lauded for its daylighting properties, the glazed roof felt hazardous and by 1990, the Arts Council conceded to fund its repair. Ó Cuív also pointed to the wet and dry rot that was appearing through the building, stating that the former shirt factory was 'nearing its end as a habitable building' (Ó Cuív in Coyne, 1994, p. 15).

Another aspect of the building which was lauded initially but within a decade of occupation by the artists had become challenging, was its open floor plan coming from the deep floor plates. As the Maureen Buildings' structure was of concrete post and beam, or frame construction, interior

Model, Temple Bar Gallery and Studios (Courtesy of McCullough Mulvin image collection)

spaces were eminently adaptable and indeed, such ease of subdivision was evident in the artists' subdivision of floors by means of timber partitions; leading to what Ó Cuív called, 'a warren of passageways and a potential firetrap.' (Ó Cuív in Coyne, p. 15). Clearly, extreme action was needed and TBGS (with a steady sub-committee under the direction of architect, Neill Monahan) appointed the young architect, Valerie Mulvin to survey the building. Apparently, Mulvin was already known for her sympathetic leanings to older but not necessarily canonical buildings, which the sub-committee recognised as her sensitivity towards and ability with complex projects. Good fortune, luck and sure-footedness managed to turn this initial survey engagement into a wholesale building commission. In early 1992, the architects McCullough Mulvin were appointed to develop Maureen Buildings and the factory's adjacent derelict site.

So much of the original T. J. Cullen building that had inspired the artists also inspired the young architects. Mulvin and her partner Niall McCullough were stimulated by the existing structure and by the essence of the place. They were motivated by the potential to extend the life, the use and the physicality of the original factory. One of the earliest and according to Mulvin, most 'obvious' moves was her stretching of the old building along to the corner edge of Fownes Street. This was done in something of a land-swap whereby the single-storey sculpture gallery beside Maureen Buildings was exchanged for the derelict corner site on Fownes Street. As the new building would now turn the corner, folding and moving from Temple Bar to the river quay, the new elevation along this narrow old street could accommodate novel function, namely a semi-private entrance for the artists and the many hefty pieces of work coming in and out of studios. Breaking with any sense of what it should be, this elevation hosts a veritable smorgasbord of opening types: from aluminium-framed curtain wall glazing to square-headed windows, and from the part-glazed metal double-leaf doors to the metal-panelled doors crowned by the painted exposed steel lintels. All of these doors and windows serve to enliven and articulate the building's envelope of smooth white rendered walls. The white walls seem to spring from limestone plinths running along the juncture of the building with its footpath – an outdoor skirting board. And above, high up towards the top of the building, the wall surface is enlivened further by a projecting concrete sill and then, a projecting metal balcony.

The architects were having fun. But it wasn't glib. The industrial origin of the building was more than inspiration. The architects understood this as the anchor, the character, the steer of the place and without following this steer, their new building could never endure or have integrity. Having studied in Rome – in the sites and through Nolli's historic maps (1740s) – both McCullough and Mulvin were fascinated by the city (any city) as a layered place. During this post-graduate experience, they also encountered the Italian architect and theorist, Aldo Rossi (writer of such books as *The Architecture of the City,* MIT Press, 1966). They returned to Ireland, full of faith in the potential of historic buildings and the nature of a local architecture; and they set about exploring Ireland's architectural tradition, publishing a deep gazetteer of building types from across time entitled, *A Lost Tradition. The Nature of Architecture in Ireland* (Gandon Editions, 1987).

Mulvin's design work for TBGS was the first large public commission for the practice. As such, much of McCullough Mulvin's theoretical and research interests could be played out through this project, in earnest, for the first time. Indeed, many design tendencies later identified with the practice took root here. Their emphasis on preserving the character of Maureen Buildings while ensuring that any additions and adaptations were of the highest quality – were 'contemporary' in terms of technology and materials – became the practice's approach. This has become known as architectural grafting: bringing or grafting new fabric and materials onto pre-existing, so as to strengthen and embolden the pre-existing. In a 2004 monograph of McCullough Mulvin, the

introduction remarked that the practice appreciated and re-used 'existing architectural fabric together with the simultaneous emergence of idealistic spatial form' (Ryan in Arets + Ryan, 2004, p. 7). At TBGS, that idealistic form emerged most visibly at its exterior with the new prominent geometrically-strong corner. Arguably the new building's stepped-back habitable roof, seemingly hewn out of trash-bag metal, becomes another instance of idealistic form.

What's appearing through this critical description of the extended and new studio and gallery building is a play of forms, surfaces, superficial geometries. Unsurprisingly, all of these forms emanated from industrially-inspired references like the black and primary coloured grid paintings of Piet Mondrian, or the chaotic and complex jumble aesthetic of architect Rem Koolhaas and others. According to the architects, the playful metal profile patterning on the building's roof refers to a favourite Cubist still-life painting (with guitar) by Juan Gris. Mulvin holds this Gris reference higher, or closer even, when we move into the building and understand the place's new internal organisation. Pointing to the guitar strings, emphatic black lines which run across the canvas like a horizon, Mulvin reveals the dominant axis through the building, running from east (Fownes Street) to west (a shared courtyard with the Black Church Studio). The axis is first announced with the massive steel industrial pivoting door, through which artists, bicycles and big objects come; and then into a sequence of ante-rooms becoming an atrium and stair hall. The atrium could claim to be the interior's climax. An oval hole cut through three floor plates reaching from ground to roof, this atrium was a request of Ó Cuív's in an effort to help artists to lift big pieces through the air.

However useful or used this oval hole has been in practice, it quickly became the leitmotif for the new building, generating a TBGS logo. The dizzying repeat of ovals as one looks up or down the atrium is certainly memorable and dramatic. But more than any of that, the atrium is a spatial punctuation mark for the building. This building is overwrought in terms of its many functions. It must work hard at all times. In the first instance then, the idiosyncratic atrium becomes sensually significant, bringing a change in volume – the body looks up/looks down/glimpses light/senses height. Secondly, we know of the atrium's basis as a hoist route. Thirdly, and most impactfully, this is the stair hall around which all the circulation marches and flows, and from which the reconfigured studios are reached. Fourthly, as a rectangular space, marked by the oval void, it is the point in the plan where old and new are connected.

Case Study: Temple Bar Gallery and Studios

McCullough Mulvin knew Temple Bar Gallery + Studios before they were commissioned to help repair the old building and develop the site. Visiting exhibitions there during the 1980s was an exhilarating experience. Mulvin remembers the raw energy and creativity captured in the Maureen Buildings. She recalls the white painted floorboards and through the close survey later, she felt the power of the industrial flooring and the generosity of the factory glazing. The commission was as much about preserving these energies and robust features, as it was about improving the studio experience and making the public gallery accessible. The key was to bring the thick floors with their undulating floorboards into an insulated, secure and accessible new structure. Improved functionality and upgraded building technology meant that the architects removed the glazed roof, creating a four-storey building containing studios from first to third floors. In all, 30 studios were made, ranging from 20 square metres to 70 square metres: each one lit by floor-to-ceiling windows and sporting its own large Belfast sink. After those essential considerations of daylighting and decent plumbing, the studios are all different – as individual, as inconsistent, as hardworking as each artist. Ó Cuív, as client, wanted to make a series of universal studios. No specificity. Meanwhile, as Mulvin commented. '..basic needs were all the same. The artists wanted the building to be warm, dry and to have running water' (*Generation*, 2013, p. 102). The material palette of poured concrete and mild steel ensured an interior robustness; what Mulvin referred to as simple finishes, minimising maintenance and 'meant to feel like a rough, industrial workspace, something that isn't too precious' (*Generation*, 2013, p. 102).

There are smart design moves underpinning TBGS. From the top, the replacement of the glazed roof with an interesting 'cap' of indoor offices, outdoor roof terrace/room, studios and gathering space is carefully considered. And echoes of the glazed mansard roof resound in the glazed butterfly roof now. More than a landing, the gathering space houses the odd seat and many indoor plants. This is a shared space. But it is also circulation. In fact, on each floor the studios (privately) are fed off these shared circulation landings. On each floor, more publicly, we find a kitchen, toilets and a shower. Understanding that making art is not a 'nine-to-five' occupation, the reworked TBGS provides elements of the domestic in this workplace. And understanding the need to segregate and congregate, the building's circulation routes are more generous than corridors. If we want to stop and commune, we can.

Case Study: Temple Bar Gallery and Studios

After the studios, the atrium, the playful roof and the entrance sequence, the last remarkable element is the ground-floor gallery. Enlarged to twice its previous size, the gallery is at once White Cube and shopfront. Ruairí Ó Cuív, as curator, sought a public space for this gallery, almost as an extension to the footpath. He boldly pushed for the wall to be glass and hey presto, Temple Bar Gallery, as part of TBGS, was made. Such a public-facing gallery is not for the faint-hearted but likely the muscle of the artists' presence on the site – though only in part relating to the activities of the gallery – brings confidence to such a space. The gallery engages in an ongoing process of reinvention when it is moulded afresh with each exhibition. We are reminded of the architects' mission: 'From our perspective, the project is about the potential relationship between art and architecture – and the appropriate representation of the power of art through architecture.' (*Generation*, 2013, p. 103). In the instance of the gallery then, the architects made a neutral or mute interior. In keeping with the clean-lined White Cube aesthetic, the gallery's internal structure was originally boxed off and ceilings covered, however these elements have been exposed today, revealing a more muscular and raw space. Notwithstanding subsequent alterations, the point is that once again with the TBGS project, the architects interpreted the artistic programme. And the architecture came out of that.

TBGS is a citadel for the studio artists. Their art-making seeps and oozes out of McCullough Mulvin's building, barely contained. The place is remarkable for Irish culture, in its hardiness and in its generosity. It comes out of an exceptional confluence of factors – site, client, landlord, funding, architect. As founding studio artist Robert Armstrong reminisced, the artists came, made the place interesting and for once, were not removed by the force of urban development and property value: 'It was a genuine cultural quarter and it couldn't be countenanced that the people who started it would be kicked out' (*Generation*, p. 100). The exhibitions, happenings, gatherings, talks that have come out of TBGS are too many to mention. In terms of the impact of Temple Bar Gallery + Studios, in cultural-urban terms, Aidan Dunne best summed it up in 1994: 'many of the potentialities identified by Jenny Haughton in her original conception of the Temple Bar Centre are now being enacted on the wider canvas of the area as a whole, in the shape of the various cultural centres overseen by Temple Bar Properties. In this sense, the original Temple Bar Centre was a microcosm of what the area was to become.' (Dunne in Coyne, 1994, p. 12).

Facts and Figures

Temple Bar Gallery + Studios, 5–9 Temple Bar is situated on the north side of Temple Bar Square, on the west side of Fownes Street Lower and on the river, occupying Crampton/Wellington Quay. The original shirt factory was designed by T. J. Cullen and was known as the Maureen Buildings. The extension and refurbishment was mooted in 1990, following an Arts Council grant to repair the roof of the older building. Valerie Mulvin was hired to survey the building in 1991 and following the establishment of Temple Bar Properties, McCullough Mulvin Architects were commissioned to refurbish and develop the site in 1992. The 'new' building opened in 1994.

Part of the project, for the Black Church Print Studio, won the Downes Bronze Medal in the AAI New Irish Architecture Awards in 1996. The project lead for TBGS and the former Black Church Studio was Valerie Mulvin. Born in 1956 in Dublin, Mulvin and her partner, Niall McCullough (1958–2021) graduated from UCD in 1981 and in 1986, they established their architectural practice, soon joining forces with other small critical practices to form Group 91. Architects working on TBGS with McCullough and Mulvin were Grainne Hassett, Dermot Boyd, Eva Byrne, Charlotte Sheridan and Paul McClean.

TBGS was McCullough Mulvin's first major public building commission and as part of Group 91, they contributed to the Temple Bar Framework Plan, out of which the practice designed the Music Factory and Curved Street (with Shay Cleary). McCullough Mulvin Architects are known for their research and publications, and for their interest in renewing older buildings. This aspect is evident in their many celebrated cultural and educational buildings in Ireland and beyond such as the Model Arts and Niland Gallery, Sligo (2000, shortlist RIAI Gold Medal, Europa Nostra Award), Trinity College Dublin's Ussher Library (2002, shortlist RIAI Gold Medal), Source Arts Centre, Thurles (2006, shortlist RIAI Gold Medal) and Blackrock Public Library (2014, International Architecture Award). Strengthened by Ruth O'Herlihy and Corán O'Connor as co-directors, the practice's work continues apace; despite Niall McCullough's untimely death in 2021 which was deeply felt by the local architectural community. Notable recent projects for Trinity College Dublin (Printing House Square, RIAI Education Award 2023) and Poetry Ireland (ongoing, Parnell Square) certainly speak to McCullough's interest in the potential of roofscapes. In 2020 McCullough Mulvin finished their biggest project to date, for the University in Patiala, India which has firmly established their international reputation. In 2021 Valerie Mulvin published her book on the origins and potentials of Irish towns, *Approximate Formality* which harks back to her M.Litt of 1991. She is a member of Aosdána.

TBGS Director, 1999–96: Ruairí Ó Cuív (*b.*1957) is a curator who educated in Art History and Archaeology at UCD. He has worked as a curator and art handler in many contexts including TBGS and the Douglas Hyde Gallery. Since 2008 he has been Public Art Officer with Dublin City Council.

TBGS Board Chairperson: Neil Monaghan, architect and art advisor to the Bank of Ireland chose Valerie Mulvin
Contractors: G&T Crampton
Civil and Structural Engineer: Jim Mansfield of Kavanagh Mansfield and Partners
Services Engineers: Abbott and Partners
Quantity Surveyors: Bruce Shaw Partnership

Sources

Unpublished
Anon. *Temple Bar Lives! Winning Architectural Framework Plan; Catalogue of exhibition of entries to the Temple Bar Architectural Competition* (Dublin: Temple Bar Properties, 1991) Irish Architectural Archive Ref. No. RP.D.312.7
Valerie Mulvin, interview with MArch students Brian O'Shaughnessy and Lilu Savage, Apr. 2021
Ruairí Ó Cuív, interview with MArch students Brian O'Shaughnessy and Lilu Savage, Apr. 2021
Cliodhna Shaffrey (TBGS director) and Orla Goodwin (TBGS education and engagement), walks through the building with Ellen Rowley, Nov. 2018, Aug. 2020, Apr. 2022
TBGS studio artists – Tanad Williams, Andreas Kindler Von Knobloch, interview with MArch students Brian O'Shaughnessy and Lilu Savage, Apr. 2021
TBGS studio artist – Brian Fay, informal conversation with Ellen Rowley, Apr. 2022

Published
Anon., 'New Temple Bar Gallery and Studios', in *Build* (Dec. 1994), p. 3
Coyne, Alexa (ed.), *Temple Bar Gallery and Studios. Aris* (Gandon Editions, 1994) (essays by Aidan Dunne 'A Big Idea' and Ruairí Ó Cuív 'Temple Bar Gallery and Studios – The Building')
Temple Bar Gallery + Studios (multiple contributors), *Generation: 30 Years of Creativity at Temple Bar Gallery + Studios* (TBGS, Language, 2013)
O'Malley, Niamh (ed. and artist), *Gather* (Temple Bar Gallery + Studios, The First 47 design, 2022)
Arets, Wiel and Raymund Ryan (eds), *Work: McCullough Mulvin Architects* (Anne Street Press, 2004)
Battersby, Eileen, 'McCullough and Mulvin, Space Explorers', *Irish Times*, 20 May 1999
Hutchinson, John, 'The Temple Bar Centre', *Irish Times*, 8 Nov. 1983
McCullough, Niall and Valerie Mulvin, *A Lost Tradition: The Nature of Architecture in Ireland* (Gandon Editions, 1987)
McDonald, Frank, 'Architecture Couple Inspired by Old and New', *Irish Times*, 15 Apr. 2004
McKenna, Mary, 'Temple Bar Gallery and Studios', building review, in *Irish Architect* (No. 105, Jan./Feb. 1995), pp 7–11
Pollard, Carole, 'RIAI Women in Architecture

2021 with Valerie Mulvin and Ruth O'Herlihy', 24 June 2021, https://www.youtube.com/watch?v=9JywKRyjM_I&t=17s

Pollard, Carole, 'Valerie Mulvin biography', in Brown, Lori A. and Karen Burns (eds), *The Bloomsbury Global Encyclopedia of Women in Architecture, 1960–2015* (Bloomsbury, 2024)

Quinn, Patricia, *Temple Bar: The Power of an Idea* (Temple Bar Properties, 1996)

Scanlon, Emmett, 'Valerie Mulvin – Group 91', *What Do Buildings Do All Day?* (No. 39, 31 Aug. 2022), https://podcasters.spotify.com/pod/show/whatbuildingsdo/episodes/39--Valerie-Mulvin--Group-91-e1n73aj

Case Study

Temple Bar: The Printworks, East Essex Street, Dublin 2, 1994

Merlo Kelly

The Printworks development by Derek Tynan Architects is a collection of ten apartments embedded within a historic block in the heart of Temple Bar. The site was that of the former two-storey Curtis Printworks on Temple Lane, which dates from c.1935 and was reclaimed as part of the scheme. The scheme had its genesis in the 'Architectural Framework Plan for Temple Bar' in 1991 and Derek Tynan was one of the Group 91 architectural consortium. Central to the Group 91 vision was the establishment of 'a community of 3,000 citizens living in the city' and proposals within their strategy reflected this desire to reinhabit the city centre, placing an emphasis on conservation and renewal. Many of the ideals set out in their manifesto were enshrined in the Printworks project.

Robert Maxwell makes reference to 'an agile lightness of touch in the work of Derek Tynan' (Quinn, 1996, p. 84). A dense urban block is carved out to create a complex inner world, while presenting an understated exterior. The use of existing structures to Temple Lane and Essex Street East allows the Printworks to disappear within its context. Retail units line the street along the north boundary to Essex Street East, and studios and offices address Temple Lane. Thus, the commercial units form a podium, creating a presence at street level, while the residential accommodation occupies a private world above. The layering or stacking of units is resolved in a complex manner which is revealed in section, with clever interventions allowing light to the rear of the commercial spaces. This sectional device is key to Tynan's design strategy, allowing the upper levels of the block to benefit from light and privacy while creating a shared intimacy internally which is far removed from the streets of Temple Bar below. What emerges is an architecture that is responsive to context and orientation in form and materiality – the muted red-brick façade and shopfronts to Essex Street East, the industrial frontage and stepped façade to Temple Lane, and the unfettered volumes to the inner court.

The Printworks was awarded the AAI Downes Medal in 1995, and the RIAI Silver Medal for Housing 1994–96. The project was also shortlisted for the Mies van der Rohe European Architectural Award. This development is a thoroughly considered ensemble of uses and volumes, consistently and thoughtfully detailed with a scale and orientation that make it an oasis in the midst of street-level urban activity. It stands as a singular example of how highly crafted design can contribute to the quality of renewal and regeneration for the future of urban living.

A lamentable change to the Essex Street East elevation is the loss of the original façade and interiors to nos. 26–27. The limestone surround and steel-framed glazing were replaced with pastiche timber shopfronts, and the retail units are occupied by fast-food restaurants. These changes were implemented within years of completion. Despite the vicissitudes of commercial ground-floor uses – in particular, the abuse of the unit 25/26

View of Temple Lane c.1992 (Courtesy of Derek Tynan Architects image collection)

beside the stairs and entrance – the apartments retain their quality helped in no small part by the active inhabitation and occupation of the raised court. Sadly this 'active inhabitation and occupation of the raised court' (so-named in Derek Tynan Architects' Citation, *Irish Architectural Review*, 2001), has been greatly undermined by the transient nature of the current rental market in Temple Bar. With the exception of the occasional pot plant, the shared spaces are now devoid of landscaping, and the sense of ownership that was so evident in the decade following completion of the scheme has been undermined.

Case Study; Temple Bar, The Printworks

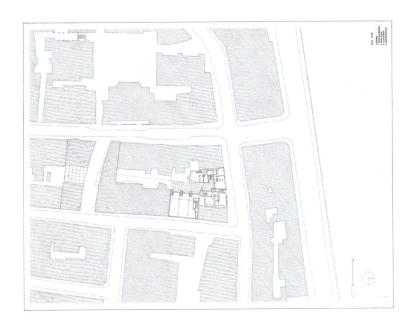

Plan of Printworks set within the context of the urban block (Courtesy of Derek Tynan Architects image collection)

Re-Inhabitation of the City

The mid-1980s signified a new phase in Dublin's urban history, culminating in a rejection of modernist ideals and the embrace of a more contextual approach to urban development. This shift in attitude was evident in the theoretical work of emerging architectural practices at this time, particularly notable in the work of collectives such as City Architecture Studio, of which Derek Tynan was a key player. Tynan, like many of his contemporaries in practice, was teaching during this period. The 1986 UCD School of Architecture publication *Dublin City Quays – Projects* includes a paper delivered by Tynan at the UCD Dublin City Quays symposium in 1985. This essay is entitled 'The Value of the Proposition – Urban Design Projects for Dublin 1980–84' and presents a number of works which offer a reinterpretation of the city. He highlights the phased development of the city through time and is critical of work which undermines the historic narrative.

> The city may be compared to a narrative: it describes, through the development of its physical fabric, an historical process, with each successive 'chapter' or period of time contributing to the elaboration and transformation of various themes in a continuous process, building layer upon layer of reference and meaning. But if we consider the most recent 'chapter' in the history of Dublin in this light we are presented with a disturbing spectacle; for not only over the past twenty-five years has there been no significant addition to the continuity of the narrative, but rather it is being destroyed. (Tynan in Cahill and Kealy, 1986, p. 57)

More Than Concrete Blocks Volume 3

(above)
Printworks model
(Courtesy of Derek Tynan Architects image collection)

(below)
Printworks model
(Courtesy of Derek Tynan Architects image collection)

He laments the prevalence of pastiche developments and instead proposes an approach which respects historic precedent but accommodates a contemporary interpretation of urban patterns and expression.

Fundamental to the principles of Tynan and his colleagues at the City Architecture Studio was an aspiration to embrace 'what might be possible rather than what is probable', leading to a re-interpretation, re-imagination and re-inhabitation of the city. This re-inhabitation of the city was a key focus, while development plans for the city at the time promoted an exodus to the suburbs. In describing one of the proposals by the City Architecture Studio, a mixed-use project on Bachelors Walk which accommodated 'shops, offices and apartments with roof gardens overlooking the quays', Tynan muses on the visionary nature of such proposals: 'These projects might be considered as visionary ideals without hope of realisation. In one sense, one cannot argue with that description; in another, one must restate the necessity, within one's own discipline, to make a proposition as a contribution to the debate upon the city'. (Tynan in Cahill and Kealy, 1986, p. 59)

This altruistic approach to urban design implied an inherent sense of civic duty, and desire to improve the cityscape for city dwellers. The focus shifted from the insertion of self-referential built works, or 'severe bouts of object fixation' as referred to by Tynan, to the placing of an element which forms part of a greater urban context, physically, culturally, and socially. In promoting this debate, Tynan and his colleagues created a platform for discussion which would eventually lead to a testing of these principles in built format.

In the period leading up to the Temple Bar competition, Group 91 staged an architectural exhibition, 'Making a Modern Street', which tested new ideas for urban living on a street in the Liberties area of Dublin. The proposals were intended to be provocative, to ignite debate and bring focus to the plight of Dublin's neglected inner city streets. Prior to this, many of the architects involved had participated in the UCD Dublin City Quays project and symposium in 1985, where they examined sections of the city along the river Liffey with students in the School of Architecture and made proposals for urban interventions (see 1980s essay).

In 1991, Temple Bar Properties, under the Temple Bar Renewal and Development Act 1991, announced a competition for an Architectural Framework Plan for Temple Bar. Group 91 submitted their Framework Plan which encapsulated many of the ideologies and theories that had been

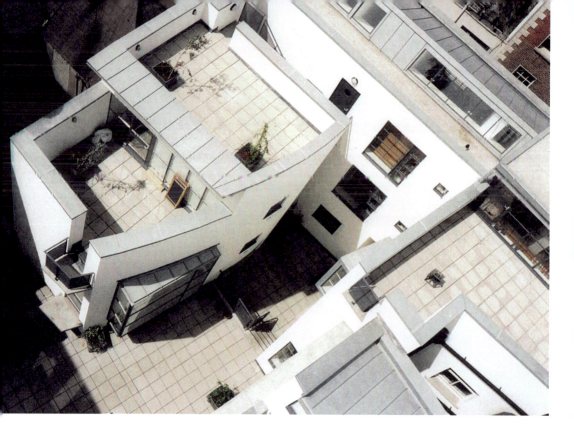

Aerial view of completed development (Courtesy of Derek Tynan Architects image collection)

explored in their collective design projects and exhibitions during the 1980s. In this regard, they were poised to tackle the challenging brief, and won the competition. A negotiation process with Temple Bar Properties began to establish which projects could be commissioned immediately, one of which was Tynan's Printworks. Group 91 submitted an 'Advanced Feasibility' document in May 1992, 'intended as a primer for the advancement of both spaces and buildings with a view to completion of projects by Summer 1994' (Group 91, 1992). There were significant differences between the early Printworks schemes and the final iteration of the project, most notably a dramatic curved wall to the inner court which carried down to the lower level. On 31 July 1992, a planning application for the Printworks development was lodged to Dublin Corporation along with 20 other schemes within the Temple Bar Framework Plan, on behalf of Temple Bar Properties.

The influence of earlier studies by the group became evident, with aspects of the Derek Tynan and McGarry Ní *Éanaigh* corner building in 'Making a Modern Street' emerging in the built Printworks project. The scheme arguably had its genesis in that study, with several elements reappearing, most notably the commercial podium and narrow stair access to a raised internal courtyard. Tynan's studies under Colin Rowe in Cornell

Case Study: Temple Bar, The Printworks

View of internal courtyard (Courtesy of Derek Tynan Architects image collection)

University undoubtedly had a profound effect on his subsequent practice. Rowe's seminal text *Collage City* (MIT Press, 1978) presented a critical re-examination of urban planning theory and re-defined the role of the architect in the context of contemporary urban design. Architectural theorist and teacher, Colin Rowe was preoccupied with urban form and was highly critical of the Modernist approach to urban design. Like Aldo Rossi, Rowe presented a study of the traditional city, and explored the layered evolution of contemporary cities against the backdrop of classical theory. Tynan and his contemporaries were very much part of this new phase of thinking.

In practical terms, this contextualism promoted by Rowe was embraced by Group 91, who sought to introduce contemporary elements into the historic urban setting of Temple Bar while retaining the existing fabric. This respect for historic context is manifest in the adaptation of existing structures in the case of the Printworks. Though the historic structures are only partially retained, the re-inhabitation of these elements established a scale and rhythm that sits comfortably within its context. The urban grain is respected, and new elements respond.

More Than Concrete Blocks Volume 3

A Wonderful Reference to the Mechanics of Urban Life

Temple Lane South was formerly called Dirty Lane, and the historic block within which the Printworks is located originally stretched south to Dame Street. However, in 1995 a new street, Curved Street, was constructed through the block as part of the Group 91 Framework Plan. A ramped street designed to connect Curved Street to the Printworks through the block also formed part of the strategy but remained an enclosed route within McCullough Mulvin's Music Centre.

A narrow double-height slot alongside the historic façade to Essex Street signals the entrance to the complex, giving way to a narrow staircase leading to a raised internal court. All the apartments are accessed from this datum, which was designed as a shared, landscaped space, in such a way that recalls for Ryan, a Rubik's Cube: '… as an assemblage of cubic forms with specific programmes and interpenetrations which have been judiciously inserted into its urban setting.' (Ryan, 1999, p. 34) The 'cubic forms' referred to by Ryan are only revealed within the block, though glimpses of the overlapping volumes are afforded from Temple Lane, where stepped duplex units were added to the original Printworks building. There are three elements overlooking the shared court – duplex apartments over the Printworks to the east, the refurbished 18th-century house and the four-storey 'house and return' to Essex Street East. A single dwelling occupies the 'return'. These elements are expressed as white volumes, which are prised apart to accommodate staircases and terraces; what Christine Casey refers to as 'Simple lines, opaque glass and thin steel detailing creates an elegant luminous space, almost Japanese in character'. (Casey, 2005, p. 442)

The elevation of three duplex studio apartments over the former Printworks is punctured by three stairway alleys which ascend from the court, in what Shane O'Toole refers to as a homage to Le Corbusier's Maison Citrohan. The saw-tooth roof profiles and vertical stair voids lend a rhythm to the composition, reducing the apparent scale internally. The staggered façades to the east allow private balconies to overlook the street. In addition to the 'hollowing out' of the interior to form a central court, a series of private open spaces serve the apartments. This connection to external space is an essential feature of the development, eroding the density of the block. The stepping of volumes allows light to enter to the rear of the Temple Lane studio while the stepped façades, internally and externally, maximise light to the internal spaces. This exploitation of section also allows

Case Study: Temple Bar, The Printworks

a manipulation of views over the city while retaining a level of privacy.

> From the street, in the crowded design-conscious world of Temple Bar, it is almost an act of camouflage. It is simultaneously one building and many different buildings. Remarkable as an example of assemblage, it is a modest composition of easily identifiable, three-dimensional fragments which is also a believable proposal for urban living. In this, it is both didactic and practical, a methodological exercise for the public good. (Ryan, 1999, p. 29)

Praise for the hidden world within the raised courtyard was counterbalanced by a critique of the muted expression to Essex Street, or lack of contemporary expression externally. Limitations in this regard were dictated by the historic context, and this lack of presence on the principal street only serves to heighten the qualities of the private world sequestered behind the façade. This separation of public and private is described by assessor Felim Egan as 'a wonderful reference to the mechanics of urban life.' (AAI, 1995, p. 10).

The selection of materials reinforces this separation between the inner world and the street. Along the principal elevation to Essex Street East, a red-brick skin with regular rhythmic openings references the neighbouring buildings in scale, materials, and fenestration pattern. The shopfront (since altered) maintains the proportions of the adjacent properties but presents a contemporary interpretation with steel-framed glazing set within a smooth limestone façade. In the upper court the aesthetic shifts, borrowing an industrial language and material palette from the former Printworks. Here, lighter elements project from the solid white volumes – concrete balconies, steel balustrades and zinc-clad bay windows. Sills and parapets are dressed in zinc. Pitched zinc-clad roofs to the perimeter blocks incorporate large sections of glazing which channel light to the upper levels. The limited palette of materials allows the various elements to form a cohesive whole – rendered walls, steel-framed doors and windows, expansive glazing, glass block and concrete paving. Gates and railings are steel, with mesh detailing to the balustrades.

The industrial aesthetic carries to the interiors which are light-filled with generous fenestration, white reflective walls and sparse detailing. Steel and timber balustrades outline stairs and balconies. The remodelled Printworks Building, which originally served as a studio for fashion designer John Rocha, is spatially complex. A double-height pattern room is flooded with natural light from clerestory windows to the rear. Polished timber floors and clean white planes are offset by exposed concrete soffits, steel glazed balustrades and a spiralling staircase.

Urban renewal and re-inhabitation were central to the ethos of the Printworks scheme, in a part of the city where vacancy and dereliction was prevalent. The 'Living over the Shop' or LOTS scheme was introduced as part of the 1994 budget, offering tax incentives for building owners to include residential accommodation on floors over shops on certain designated streets. In his essay 'Living over the shop', Frank McDonald cites the Printworks as a model for contemporary urban development.

> Temple Bar has deservedly won awards for the quality of so many of its LOTS schemes – notably the Printworks (by Derek Tynan Architects) which won the Architectural Association of Ireland's Downes Medal in 1995, not least because it offered a new model for city-centre living, with apartments arranged around a courtyard at first-floor level. (McDonald in Quinn, 1996, p. 43)

In a critique, Alan Mee lauds the Printworks scheme as 'a built celebration of urbanity, with all of the complexity and ingenuity, excitement and beauty of any city environment.' (Mee, 1995, p. 22). He denounces the proliferation of 'boom' apartment types in previous years, suggesting that the Printworks may have served as a housing prototype had it materialised earlier.

> Many of the individual aspects of the Printworks which have been praised should, in fact, be the fundamentals of good building design in the city; mixed-use brief, suitably scaled development, adequate space allocation, natural light and ventilation as basic necessities for comfort, diversity of unit, size etc. This exceptional building in some ways seems to come from a time in the history of Dublin when an urban sensibility in design was regarded as quite ordinary. (Mee, 1995, p. 23)

Assessor Michael Cullinan echoes this sentiment in the 1995 AAI Awards, expressing a hope that the Printworks might influence housing developments to come: 'If this had been presented prior to the current inner-city apartment building, I would say that it must be given the highest award in the hope of influencing what is yet to come. I think it's a wonderful critique of what was missed.' (AAI, 1995, p. 10).

Case Study: Temple Bar, The Printworks

Facts and Figures

The Printworks is located at 25–27 Essex Street East and 12–13 Temple Lane South, Temple Bar and was completed in November 1994.

Architects: Group 91/Derek Tynan Architects
The architects who worked on Printworks were Derek Tynan, Esmonde O'Briain (Project Architect), Mel Reynolds, and Marcus Donaghy
For Group 91, see Meeting House Sq essay

Derek Tynan graduated from UCD School of Architecture in 1977 and, in 1981, received a Master's in Architecture from Cornell University where he studied as a Fulbright Scholar. He was Assistant Professor in the University of Virginia School of Architecture from 1981–82. In Dublin he was Head of Urban Design Unit in the National Building Agency from 1986–89. From 1989–90, he was Urban Design Consultant at Koetter Kim & Associates International. There he acted as consultant to the London office on Canary Wharf Phase 2, and the Masterplan for Isle of Dogs. He established Derek Tynan Architects in Dublin in 1990, which was incorporated as Derek Tynan Associates or DTA Architects from 2005. From 1998–2010, Tynan was Managing Director of Urban Projects Ltd, a collaborative urban design practice formed between Derek Tynan Architects, McGarry Ní Éanaigh Architects and Gerry Cahill Architects. Tynan was a visiting critic at various schools of architecture, including Tulane School of Architecture, University of Virginia, Harvard GSD, Kent State Florence Program, Syracuse University, the Architectural Association London, and the University of Jordan (Amman). He was a regular reviewer at University College Dublin, Dublin School of Architecture (now TU Dublin) and Queen's University Belfast.

Client: Temple Bar Properties
Structural Engineers: Thorburn Colquhoun & Partners
Mechanical/Electrical Engineers: RN Murphy Associates
Quantity Surveyor: Brendan Merry & Partners
Fire Consultant: John A. McCarthy
Archaeologist: Margaret Gowen
Main Contractor: Cleary & Doyle Contracting Ltd

Sources

Unpublished
Derek Tynan, interview with Merlo Kelly, Nov. 2019
Derek Tynan/DTA Archives, Dublin
Group 91, *Temple Bar: Advanced Feasibility* (1991)
Making a Modern Street (exhibition models), Irish Architectural Archive
Group 91 Archives, Irish Architectural Archive Ref: 2009/152
Derek Tynan Collection, Irish Architectural Archive Ref: 2010/053

Published
AAI, *New Irish Architecture 10: AAI Awards* (Architectural Association of Ireland, 1995), pp 6–11
Anon., 'Aiming to create an ambience of Montmartre', *Irish Times*, 28 Nov. 1991
Anon., 'The Printworks, Temple Bar, Dublin 2', in *Irish Architectural Review* (Vol. 3, 2001), pp 56–61
Becker, Annette, John Olley and Wilfried Wang (eds), *Ireland: 20th–Century Architecture* (Prestel, 1997)
McDonald, Frank, 'The Future Wins at Temple Bar', *Irish Times*, 13 Aug. 1992
McDonald, Frank, 'Building Sight', *Irish Times*, 2 Sept. 2006
Slessor, Catherine, 'Dublin Renaissance', in *Architectural Review* (Jan. 1993)
Mee, Alan, 'The Printworks, Temple Bar', *Irish Architect* (No. 105, Jan./Feb. 1995), pp 21–4
Murray, Peter, 'New Irish Architecture: The Architectural Year Reviewed', in *Irish Arts Review Yearbook* (Vol. 14, 1998)
O'Toole, Shane, 'A Prototype for Urban Living. The Printworks', Essay 29, in *One Hundred & One Hosannas for Architecture: A Chronicle of Architectural Culture in Millennial Ireland* (Gandon Editions, 2017)
Quinn, Patricia (ed.), *Temple Bar: The Power of an Idea* (Gandon Editions for Temple Bar Properties, 1996)
Ryan, Raymund, 'A Building as a Contextual Machine: the Printworks in Dublin', in *Architectural Research Quarterly* (Vol. 3, No. 1, Mar. 1999), pp 29–42
Graby, John, and Kathryn Meghen, (eds), *The New Housing* (Gandon Press in association with the RIAI and the Department of the Environment and Local Government, 2002), pp 88–91
Irish Architecture '95: RIAI Regional Awards (Royal Institute of the Architects of Ireland, 1995), p. 10
Tynan, Derek, 'The Value of the Proposition: Urban Design Projects for Dublin 1980–84', in Gerry Cahill and Loughlin Kealy (eds) *Dublin City Quays: Projects* (The School of Architecture, University College Dublin, 1986)

Case Study
British Embassy, Merrion Road, Dublin 4, 1995

Merlo Kelly

Dublin's British Embassy in Ballsbridge can be interpreted as a 1990s expression of the 'house of the middle size' that was found throughout the 18th-century countryside of Ireland and Britain. The arrangement involves a collection of buildings, varying in scale, grouped around a central courtyard. The landscaped grounds and productive garden (an orchard) complete the composition of the country house. In response to criticism that the building was not constructed from brick like its neighbouring buildings, British firm Allies and Morrison cited influences from further afield. They likened the composition to that of a 17th-century Parisian hotel or an Italian Renaissance *palazzo*, while also pointing to the Wicklow granite and Portland stone of notable 18th-century Dublin public buildings.

Security was a primary design consideration and consequently the outward appearance is not an honest expression of the construction. The granite cladding, aluminium frame and slate roof panels mask a concrete bunker beneath. There is an impenetrable quality to the main block, which is the frontispiece to a high security compound. The defensive language prevails in the landscaping of the forecourt with the presence of a moat. It was intended that public visitors traverse this moat (since drained and planted) to enter the building. Despite this language of security there is a spatial fluidity between the interior and exterior, with expanses of glazing and breaks in surface allowing a blurring of the perceived building envelope. This notion of layers, which is introduced in the main façade, carries through to the inner workings of the embassy building where spaces are defined by a series of screens and planar divisions.

Changes to the embassy building have been minor, with no extensions or significant alterations to date. Following the destruction of the earlier British Embassy in Merrion Square in 1972, and the decades of political unrest that followed, security became paramount in its running. For security reasons, any construction process or maintenance work has to be carefully monitored by a designated security team; a hugely time-consuming process which drives costs up. The functions of the two sections of the building have altered, with allocated uses redistributed. Currently the main building houses the public desk and the central access point for visitors. The visa/consular section has reduced access to the public as recently, passport and visa applications are primarily online, limiting the requirement for visitors to the building. Externally, the granite cladding has been intensively cleaned and the aluminium framework to the façade has been cleaned, sanded and repainted. A bullet-proof glass security screen has been installed in front of the main entrance to allow protected vehicular access for the ambassador.

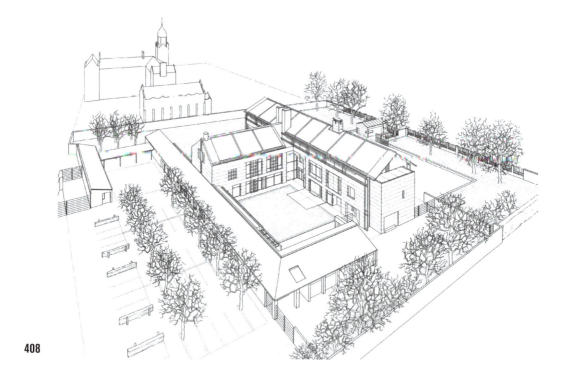

Perspective drawing (Courtesy of Allies & Morrison image collection)

A Politely Defensive Country House

Set within the context of Merrion Road on the former lands of Thomas Prior Hall (now a hotel), the British Embassy takes on the scale of the neighbouring red-brick villas and the composition of an Irish country house. The principal embassy building, a gabled block, presents a formal frontage to the street concealing the more private workings of the embassy to the rear. These functions are housed in the return and the single-storey stable block, in this case an office wing addressing the inner court. The material expression of the structure, with its granite cladding and aluminium frame, sets it apart from the surrounding streetscape. Only the office wing to the rear references the red-brick of the adjacent houses and Thomas Prior Hall. The Merrion Road elevation is restrained and formal, its solidity broken down by the gridded rhythm of the applied façade. The architectural language of the building and surrounds, with its thinly-clad concrete frame, layered screens, elegant moat and high railings is politely defensive.

The configuration of the embassy façade represents an abstraction of the typical classical arrangement, formally and proportionally. The main building, a two-storey structure with its *piano nobile* (or grander first floor) and attic storey, was conceived as two distinct elements and this division is expressed in the façade. The five-bay embassy wing is restrained in its expression and centres around a formal entrance. The three-bay wing,

Case Study: British Embassy, Merrion Road

Site plan (Courtesy of Allies & Morrison image collection)

home to the visa and consular section and open to the public, presents a peeling back of the façade and introduces a certain degree of openness and informality. The selection of materials introduces a hierarchy to the arrangement where the main block and return are clad in Wicklow granite with insets of Portland stone, and the secondary office accommodation to the rear is clad in brick, traditionally regarded as a more modest building material.

The crisp detailing of the building envelope – a term used by architects to define the outermost layer of a building – is particularly accomplished. The solidity of the base structure, effectively a defensive bunker, is somewhat alleviated by an applied skin, which serves to break down the mass and introduce a precise architectural language. An aluminium frame delineates floors and piers, establishing a rhythm and bringing a lightness to the composition. The structure is made up of an in situ concrete frame, clad in bush-hammered Wicklow granite. The door and window openings are placed within a grid-like framework. In the more formal frontage of the embassy section, a series of deep-set square window openings puncture the ground floor, articulated by a recessed surround. Tinted security glazing

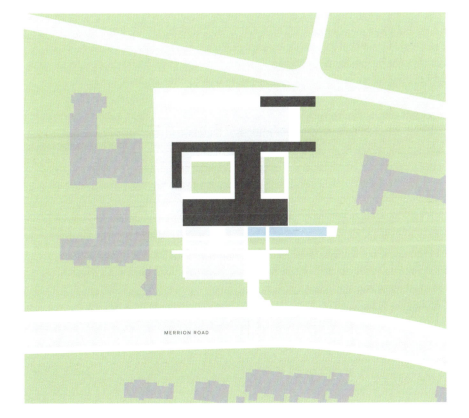

is used throughout. A decorative timber panel displaying the British coat of arms is placed centrally over the recessed entrance bay, with timber panels mirroring this composition on the courtyard façade. The aluminium frame of the façade is revealed within the three-bay visa/consular section, dispensing with the compositional formality. The inset bay is lined in Portland stone, with an integrated bench adding textural richness to the façade.

The single-storey L-shaped structure to the rear houses offices and incorporates a sheltered parking bay. A concrete structure, clad in brick with a pitched natural slate roof, the building mimics the traditional construction of a stable wing. Recessed vertical channels delineate the bays, and timber rafters protrude beneath the eaves, expressed as dentils. These carefully detailed 'rafters' sit on a concrete shell, and the brick wall panels form a vertical skin.

The embassy building is naturally ventilated by means of a series of narrow vertical ventilation grilles which are incorporated into the window design. These weatherproof panels allow cross ventilation through the eight-metre plan depth. The in situ concrete structure acts as a thermal mass, absorbing and storing heat, with night-time cooling facilitated by the ventilation grilles.

Case Study: British Embassy, Merrion Road

There is a flow to the interior spaces which pivot around a brightly lit central stair hall and gallery. A series of folding doors and screens allow physical and visual connections between the spaces. The plan organisation is layered, with the main block forming a barrier or filter through to the more private spaces behind. The rooms are pared down and reflective with white painted walls, Portuguese limestone floors, white American oak stairs, handrails and folding screens, glass and timber balustrades. Decorative wall hangings, coloured rugs and powder blue carpets introduce colour to the central spaces. The detailing is meticulous, with each element forming part of the larger composition. This considered and calm interior is perhaps designed to put occupants and visitors at their ease which might be deemed an essential consideration in the culture and architecture of diplomacy.

As in the case of the 18th-century country house, the building dominates and surveys the grounds, offering extended views from within. The outdoor landscaping is composed as an extension of the building echoing its materials and forms: from brick and granite screens, Portland stone paving, bridge to the powder-coated aluminium canopy and railings. A courtyard forms the inner kernel of the embassy around which all the key spaces connect. The landscape is compiled of planar surfaces and screens interrupted by planting and water and is cleverly manipulated to create more intimate zones within the court and garden. The Portland stone paving is conceived as a continuous fluid surface which is eroded to expose planting, water, gravel and grass. The orchard to the west, overlooking Thomas Prior Hall, contains pear, apple and fig trees. A number of sculptures by London-based artist, Susanna Heron were commissioned for placement in the landscape, intended as symbols of peace.

Diplomatic Architecture – Tension and Formality
Until 1972, the British Embassy was housed in a rented Georgian premises at nos. 30 and 39 Merrion Square. In February 1972, in the aftermath of Bloody Sunday, protests mounted around the British Embassy culminating in the burning down and complete destruction of no. 39. The need to rehouse the embassy prompted the acquisition of land in Ballsbridge, an inner suburb in south Dublin. In 1973, the present Ballsbridge site was acquired for £0.5 million, formerly the property of An Foras Talúntais, the Agricultural Institute. The embassy then occupied two existing houses on this site.

Moat and walkway photographed by Peter Cook, 1985 (Courtesy of Allies & Morrison image collection)

In 1988, it became evident that these houses were no longer appropriate for the embassy functions, and the British Overseas Estates Department purchased part of the grounds of Thomas Prior House from the Royal Dublin Society (RDS), comprising 2.4 acres of land, for the sum of £1.5 million. The generous grounds allowed the construction of an enclosed 'compound' facilitating the required security measures, and a new purpose-built embassy building.

An architectural competition for the design of a new embassy was announced, with a brief to create a single embassy complex accommodating 40 staff and nine diplomatic officers. A shortlist of four architectural firms were invited to submit sketch proposals, all of whom had experience in embassy design: Ahrends Burton Koralek (ABK), Percy Thomas Partnership, Forum Architects and Allies and Morrison. In the final stages of the competition, Arthur Gibney was appointed as a Dublin-based adviser and architectural consultant for the project. Allies and Morrison were successful, gaining the commission which had an estimated building cost of £6.5 million and a projected start date on site of June 1993. It was officially opened in early 1996, predictably generating considerable public interest.

In the light of the contentious history and particularly the violence shown the precedent embassy in Merrion Square, it is unsurprising that a conservative architectural language was chosen for the design of the new Dublin embassy. Jane Loeffler ponders the imprudence of an over-emphasis

Case Study: British Embassy, Merrion Road

on 'pomp and ceremony' in the design of embassy buildings: 'Buildings that had expressed openness, adventure, and hope for the future in the 1950s seemed arrogant and ostentatious to later critics, both outside and inside the profession' (Loeffler, 1990, p. 278).

As mentioned in the essay's introduction, the architects for this Dublin building chose to summon the architecture of an 18th-century country house, expressing the typology in a contemporary language. The scale and composition of the buildings, clustered around the inner courtyard, echo this precedent. Set back considerably from the main road, with a gate lodge and high railings, the building assumes a defensive air despite its restrained architectural expression. Andrew Saint refers to the Dublin embassy as 'a nervous building – the half-conscious outcome of a process of reflection on Anglo-Irish relations.' (LeCuyer, 1996, p. 12).

There is indeed a tension to the formality of the main elevation, accentuated by the crisp detailing and the carefully defined rhythm of the façade. This tension dissipates as you enter the tranquil space of the enclosed court, which has something of the atmosphere of a monastic cloister. This landscaped space becomes a focal point within the house, the

(left)
Detail of façade photographed by Peter Cook, 1985
(Courtesy of Allie & Morrison image collection)

(right)
Detail of interior with staircase photographed by Peter Cook, 1985
(Courtesy of Allies & Morrison image collection)

kernel of the embassy building, much like the courtyard of a country house. All the primary spaces within the building relate directly to this space. As the architects comment: 'The provision of such a space, noticeably lacking in the existing embassy, and implicit rather than explicit in the client's requirements for the new building, creates a focus for life within the building, like the traditional hall and staircase of a country house' (Allies and Morrison, 2002, unpaginated).

There is a repeated theme of layering throughout the design; in the textured skin of the façade and in the complex of screens internally and externally. These accentuate the division between the public realm and the private inner world of the embassy. The theme of layering carries through to the landscape; in the sculptural brick and stone screens set up controlled vistas. The pale stone screens of the courtyard contribute to the cloister-like qualities of this inner garden. Further layering is revealed in the rear façade of the main block overlooking this space, where pockets are carved out to reduce the bulk and scale of the block.

Facts and Figures

Planning permission for the construction of the building was granted in February 1992. The new embassy building began operating on 22 August 1995, and was officially opened by the Princess Royal on 19 January 1996. The British Embassy received an RIBA award in 1997.

Architects: Allies and Morrison established their practice in 1984 following success in a competition for the redesign of a public square in front of the National Gallery of Scotland in Edinburgh. They are a London-based practice with a significant body of work throughout the UK and on the international scene. Their practice work encompasses architecture, interior design and conservation, planning consultation and research. Bob Allies graduated from the University of Edinburgh in 1977 and went on to work in the practices of Peter Collymore, Martin Richardson, Michael Brawne and Michael Glickman. Graham Morrison graduated from the University of Cambridge and won the Brancusi Prize to travel to Finland and study the work of Alvar Aalto.

Allies and Morrison have received 39 RIBA awards and have been shortlisted for the RIBA Stirling Prize twice – for the Royal Festival Hall in 2008 and for the New Court Rothschild Bank with OMA in 2012. Their London studio building won the RIBA London Building of the Year in 2004.

Associated Architectural Consultants: Arthur Gibney & Partners (See Merrion Hall case study for Gibney biography)
Contractor: Pierse Contracting
Structural Engineers: Whitby & Bird (UK) and KML Consulting Engineers (Dublin)
Mechanical and Electrical Engineers: Max Fordham & Partners (UK) and VMRA Consulting Engineers (Dublin)
Quantity Surveyor: George Corderoy & Company (UK) and Desmond MacGreevey & Partners (Dublin)
Landscape Architects: Livingstone Eyre Associates (UK) and Mitchell & Associates (Dublin)
Art Commissioner: Public Art Commissions Agency

Sources

Published

Allies and Morrison, 'The British Embassy Dublin' brochure (Allies and Morrison, 2002)
Anon., British Embassy press release, *Irish Architect* (No. 84, May/June 1991)
Anon., 'August Opening for Embassy', *Building* (Jun. 1995)
Anon., 'A Diplomatic Solution', *Architects' Journal* (Nov. 1995)
Anon., 'An Irish Solution', *Architectural Review* (Apr. 1996)
Becker, Annette, John Olley and Wilfred Wang (eds), *Ireland: 20th–Century Architecture* (Prestel, 1997)
Johnston, Ewan, 'Sense and Sensitivity: The British Embassy, Dublin, Ireland', *World Architecture* (Feb. 1998)
LeCuyer, Annette (ed.), 'British Embassy, Dublin 1995', in *Allies and Morrison. Michigan Papers – Two* (University of Michigan, 1996)
Loeffler, Jane C., 'The Architecture of Diplomacy: Heyday of the United States Embassy-Building Program, 1954–1960', *Façade* (Sept. 1990)
O'Reilly, John E. 'New British Embassy, Dublin', in *Irish Architect* (Oct. 1995)

Case Study
Parsons Laboratory, Trinity College, Dublin 2, 1996

Merlo Kelly

Set within Trinity College campus, the Parsons Laboratory presents a boldly sculptural response to the 1895 Parsons Building. Commissioned by Trinity's Department of Mechanical and Manufacturing Engineering in 1994, designed by Grafton Architects and completed in 1996, the complex brief called for the provision of a workshop, laboratories, and staff offices. The various functions are presented as individual elements – a podium, a cube, and a bookend. These abstract forms collectively respond to their context and are playfully juxtaposed against the solemn 19th-century Parsons Building, while respecting its scale and composition.

The solidity of the podium was driven by the client's desire to conceal the interior 'gritty' workings of the engineering workshop and minimise views into the workspaces, though slots and gaps woven into the construction offer glimpses within. The floating black basalt-clad cube housing the Fluids and Acoustic Engineering Laboratory is poised above the weighty granite-clad base. The form of the extension is context-driven, taking its cues from the surrounding buildings and landscape. Though it appears skewed, the cube is perfectly aligned with the front façade of the Chemistry Building, and its geometry reflects that of the wider campus.

A second extension was also designed by Grafton Architects and completed in 2006. The addition comprised a three-storey block to the west end of the original Parsons block. This phase saw the provision of accommodation for the Engineering with Management programme and the Trinity Centre of Bioengineering. A second-degree programme was established, which enabled the department to address the increasing demand for training in Engineering Management. New integrative teaching methods evolved across the department, ensuring a more efficient use of space and staff resources. Former head of department Prof. John Monaghan notes that the Grafton extensions enabled them 'to kick-start the movement of engineering in Trinity into the twenty-first century' (Monaghan, Sep. 2014).

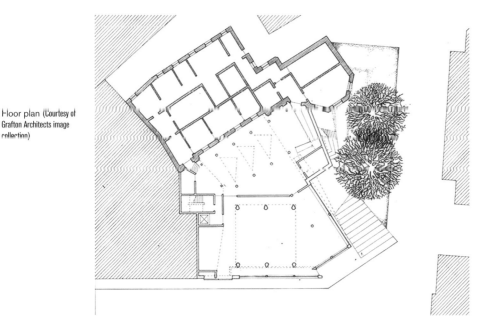

Floor plan (Courtesy of Grafton Architects image collection)

Creative Solution to a Complex Brief

The former College of Pathology building, designed by Robert Stirling, completed in 1895 and now known as the Parsons Building, was home to Mechanical and Manufacturing Engineering in Trinity College since its creation as a department in 1981. By the early 1990s, the building was overcrowded, and its structure deemed unsuitable for the heavy laboratory equipment that was required for teaching. Consequently, the department was dispersed, and large classes were accommodated in various parts of the campus and on Pearse Street.

In the context of departmental developments, the teaching and practice of mechanical engineering had changed radically in the decade preceding the construction of the Parsons Laboratory. New courses were emerging, and technology was rapidly evolving, bringing with it new requirements of the teaching laboratories and workshops. When John Fitzpatrick became head of the Department of Mechanical Engineering in 1984, he realised that the Parsons Building, the former Pathology Building, was no longer suitable for the required teaching functions. For instance, the heavy machinery in the workshops was causing the historic structure to vibrate. Furthermore, student numbers were rapidly rising, challenging the building's capacity. Resultantly, classes were dispersed throughout the college campus. Fitzpatrick set up a committee to raise funds for a new department building and presented the case to the university authorities and to the Higher Education Authority (HEA). By the early 1990s funds had been sourced and the decision was made to extend the Parsons Building at a pivotal time when the teaching technology required a purpose-built facility. Following the sale of the Lincoln Place buildings to the Dental Hospital, a budget was approved and in 1994 six architectural firms were called to interview for the project, among them Grafton Architects. The site for the proposed extension, which was to house laboratories, workshops, teaching spaces, staff offices and study areas was limited to the forecourt of the Parsons Building to the south-west of the campus.

By Grafton Architects' own account, they had understood the brief to comprise a refurbishment of the existing buildings on Lincoln Place. On discovering during the interview that the brief called for a complete extension to the Parsons Building, the architects Shelley McNamara and Yvonne Farrell quickly responded describing a design strategy centred around the retention of the two mature trees on the site. Trinity's Buildings Committee were so impressed by McNamara and Farrell's ability to think creatively and spontaneously that they appointed them as architects for the job. Trinity College

has a long-standing tradition of architectural patronage, with Grafton's Parsons Laboratory forming an exemplary addition to the succession of notable 20th-century contributions to the campus such as the Berkeley Library (ABK, 1967, see *MTCB* Vol. 2) and the Beckett Theatre (de Blacam & Meagher, 1992, see Outline Survey) among others.

The brief was a complex one incorporating specific technical requirements for each workspace and presenting the challenge to create a fluid connection to the accommodation within the existing Parsons Building. Extensive consultations were necessary between the architects, the mechanical/electrical (M&E) engineers and Alan Reid, the technician within the Trinity College department. The specific requirements for machinery and equipment meant that there was no room for error in terms of services, and this process was skilfully handled and facilitated by clear communication within the team. The architects' scheme ably met the requirements of the brief, allowing the integration of the new spaces into the workings of the existing building and successfully accommodating the expanding department. The Parsons Laboratory and the subsequent extension by Grafton Architects in 2006 meant that the previously fragmented department could adopt a more integrated teaching approach, a move that was pivotal to their consolidation and expansion within the university.

On completion the Parsons Laboratory was critically lauded and celebrated. The sculptural nature of the composition juxtaposed against the 19th-century Parsons Building was indeed a brave gesture. The large-scale splayed columns and expanses of raw concrete within the workshop are reminiscent of the uncompromising concrete structures by the Brazilian architect Paulo Mendes da Rocha. Grafton Architects later acknowledged the influence of Mendes da Rocha on their work in their exhibit for the 2012 Venice Biennale. Another cited influence was Dutch architect, Rem Koolhaas. The placement of columns within the engineering laboratories to the rear, perpendicular to the soffit, creates a distorted perspective which is reminiscent of Koolhaas' work on the 1992 Kunsthal in Rotterdam.

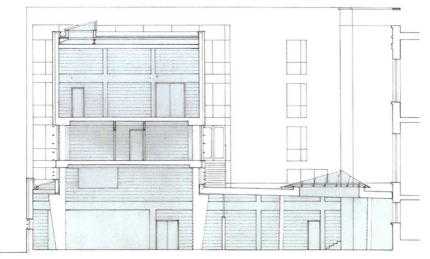

(above) Section (Courtesy of Grafton Architects image collection)

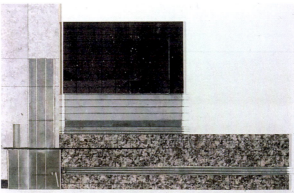

(below) Materials study (Courtesy of Grafton Architects image collection)

Counterbalancing a Floating Cube

The architects adopted a contextual approach in their extension to the Parsons Building, located in the southeast of the Trinity College campus to the rear of a terrace of houses on Lincoln Place. Given the historic context, a creative and sensitive response to the site was required. This was something to which the architects were attuned from early design concept stage. Indeed, evidence of the site's early origins became apparent when the foundations were being laid for the extension. As excavations proceeded the ground-scape flooded; testament to its location on a historic flood plain which was once a tidal zone in Dublin's early history.

The confined site posed several design challenges that were skilfully handled by the architects. There is a significant drop in level to the site from the Nassau Street entrance. Prior to the Grafton extensions (phase 1, 1996 and phase 2, 2006), the 19th-century building was accessed by means of a

Exterior view (Courtesy of Grafton Architects image collection)

formal stepped approach. Grafton Architects' extension introduces a podium level, establishing a raised forecourt and creating an arrival point. This central podium or plinth allows all parts of the building to be easily accessed through a series of layers, like stepped terraces, while the irregular footprint of the plinth mediates the conflicting geometries of the site.

The building comprises an in-situ concrete structure, which reads as two primary elements – the podium and the cube. A corner of the cube is cut away, lighting the laboratory, and providing a viewing point over College Park. The separation of the sculptural cube element is accentuated by the glazed connecting strip which encloses the staff offices and allows clerestory lighting to enter the workshop and engineering laboratories below. Minimal openings within the podium allow controlled light, views and ventilation. The massive profiled concrete columns which dominate the workshop space perforate the office floor to support the acoustic laboratory (cube) above. The columns within the engineering laboratories, adjacent to the workshop, are cast at right angles to the sloping podium thus appearing skewed at ground level.

The sculptural quality of the scheme is borne out in a collection of early conceptual sketches for the project. The dominance of the cube form is balanced by the weight of the podium which reconciles the varying site

Case Study: Parsons Laboratory

Interior of engineering workshop (Courtesy of Grafton Architects image collection)

lines. The podium, a hefty element clad in Wicklow granite, is accessed by a set of splayed concrete steps and flanked by stepped benches carved into the landscape. A decision to retain two existing mature lime trees on a landscaped incline to the west of the site underpinned the early design strategy. The stepped ramp allows the slow reveal of the Parsons Building on ascent, and a further set of steps leads to the upper podium level. Here, three angular rooflights assume the rhythm of the existing façade, penetrating the podium and bringing natural light to the teaching laboratories below. These aluminium rooflights were designed by the architects in collaboration with façade consultant Seán Billings to give the effect of patent glazing, with sharp profiled edges and gutters on a mild steel frame. A linear rooflight at podium level along the north façade allows additional light to this space. The cube is clad in honed black basalt lava panels with mitred edges and open joints. Deep-set window openings are formed within the cube envelope allowing light to the acoustic laboratory. Aluminium windows with a naturally anodised finish form a glazed storey enclosing the offices. The finishes within the workshop are raw and industrial – exposed concrete floors, walls and soffits with surface-mounted services throughout the space. The bookend element is finished in Marmorino pigmented polished plaster. It houses seminar rooms and forms a distinct edge, transitioning in scale to the four-storey Dental Hospital. A full-height sliding metal door to the

base of the bookend facilitates large-scale deliveries to the workshop and laboratories.

The selected materials complement the palette of the adjacent campus buildings – the Wicklow granite and the basalt panels echoing the stone façades and the blue-grey slate of the rooftops within the college. A debate arose at planning stage, regarding the use of black basalt for the cube. The planners wanted Portland stone cladding, and the architects presented basalt, perceived as a radical proposal for this traditional setting. The final decision was in the hands of the planners. To avert any delays in programme, the façade had to be re-designed by the architects to allow the windows to be inserted and deemed weather-proof prior to the installation of the cladding panels. Because of this, a level of ingenuity was required in the detailed design of the cladding. As McNamara recounts, Trinity suggested finding a paler shade of black:

> It never would have occurred to me, as a way around a planner to find a paler shade of black! So, we got samples of a paler shade of black, and we laid them out for the planner, walking him through the forecourt, pointing at the roofs saying that the palette was Portland stone but was also the blue-grey slate colour of the roofs. I remember standing down there with all the samples up against the wall in the sunshine and he said yes. (McNamara, Oct. 2014)

The selection of the basalt lava cladding was inspired by the work of Dutch architect, Ben van Berkel (b.1957), specifically his REMU Transformer Substation (Amersfoot, 1994). Having read about the project while visiting Amsterdam, Yvonne Farrell and Shelley McNamara went to visit the substation in Amersfoort and decided to use the material for the acoustic laboratory cube. Ben van Berkel came to Dublin to present an Architectural Association of Ireland lecture, and Shelley McNamara recalls his visit to the Parsons Laboratory construction site: 'The cladding was up; he came to look at the building and he said, 'Is it the one that doesn't go white after ten years?' … I remember for a month going down and counting the white spots on that building, counting the fossils! I was terrified'. (McNamara, Oct. 2014)

Having worked predominantly on residential projects and schools, where every millimetre is accounted for and finishes are controlled, the architects describe the experience of working on a gritty large-scale workshop as a liberating one. The placement of a 'floating' cube called for a certain amount of structural creativity. Grafton Architects had experience of working with large-scale concrete structures having previously collaborated with Roughan O'Donovan Engineers on the design of a motorway bridge. The introduction of massive, profiled columns into the workshop introduces an industrial scale to the space, a counterbalance to the suspended cube. The columns taper to meet the ground, and terminate above to support the sloped podium, while allowing slender columns to rise above plinth level and carry the concrete frame of the cuboid structure above. The concrete structure is exposed throughout, giving clarity in the structural expression, with the slim columns visible through the glazed office storey. The cube form ingeniously overhangs the glazing and structure below, assuming the geometry of the adjacent buildings and not the existing Parsons Building, thus setting itself apart from the composition.

Facts and Figures

The Parsons Laboratory was constructed as a phase 1 extension to the Parsons Building which formed part of the Department of Mechanical and Manufacturing Engineering at Trinity College, Dublin 2. The project was commissioned by the Department of Mechanical and Manufacturing Engineering in 1994 and was completed in 1996. Staff members across the department were consulted in the development of a detailed brief, with Professor John Fitzpatrick as head. Other staff members involved included Professor John Monaghan, Jennifer Gill, Alan Reid, Darina Murray. Tim Cooper was Director of Buildings in Trinity and led client discussions with the architects.

Architects: Grafton Architects, including Shelley McNamara, Yvonne Farrell, Eilis O'Donnell, Ger Carty, Philippe O'Sullivan, Alistair Hall, and Lisa O'Regan.

Yvonne Farrell (b.1951) and Shelley McNamara (b.1952) co-founded Grafton Architects in 1978 (with Shay Cleary, Frank Hall and Tony Murphy), having graduated from University College Dublin in 1974. They are Fellows of the RIAI, International Honorary Fellows of the RIBA and elected members of Aosdána, the eminent Irish Art organisation. Today the practice is run by founding directors Farrell and McNamara, and directors Philippe O'Sullivan and Gerard Carty. Both McNamara and Farrell taught at the School of Architecture at University College Dublin from 1976 to 2002 and were appointed Adjunct Professors at UCD in 2015. They have been visiting professors at EPFL, Lausanne, held the Louis Kahn chair at Yale University and the Kenzo Tange chair at GSD Harvard. They have been visiting critics at the London Metropolitan School of Architecture and Cambridge University, and have lectured extensively in Irish, European and American Schools of Architecture. They are currently Professors at the Accademia di Archittettura, Mendrisio, Switzerland. Grafton Architects were co-founders of the award-winning collaboration Group 91 (see Temple Bar essays). They were awarded the World Building of the Year Award 2008 for the Università Luigi Bocconi in Milan and were awarded the Silver Lion at the 12th International Venice Biennale for their exhibit, Architecture as New Geography. In 2018, Yvonne Farrell and Shelley McNamara were the curators of the Venice Architecture Biennale. In 2020 they were awarded the RIBA Royal Gold Medal and the same year, were selected as the 2020 Pritzker Prize Laureates. The Parsons Laboratory was the recipient of an RIAI Regional Award in 1996, followed by an AAI Award in 1997. In December 1996 it was designated 'Building of the Year' by Frank McDonald in the *Irish Times*, who celebrated the building's gutsy nature.

Structural Engineers: Arups & Partners

Glazing/Façade Consultant: Sean Billings, Billings Design Associates

Quantity Surveyors: Patterson Kempster & Shortall

Contractors: John Paul Construction

Sources

Unpublished
Grafton Architects Archive, Dublin
Shelley McNamara & Eilis O'Donnell, interviewed by Merlo Kelly, Oct. 2014
Yvonne Farrell, interviewed by Merlo Kelly, Aug. 2014
Professor John Monaghan, interviewed by Merlo Kelly, Sept. 2014

Published
AAI, *New Irish Architecture 12: AAI Awards* (AAI 1997)
Anon., 'Finely Tuned: Trinity College Dublin's New Department of Mechanical and Manufacturing Engineering', *RIBA Journal* (Vol. 103, No. 3, Mar. 1996), pp 38–45
Anon., 'Department of Mechanical Engineering, TCD', *Irish Architect* (No. 119, July/Aug. 1996) pp 9–14
Hatz, Elizabeth, 'Mind-Matter of Cool Passion', in John O'Regan (ed.), *Grafton Architects: Profile* (Gandon Editions, 1999)
McDonald, Frank, 'Triumph for Diversity as RIAI Picks a Bumper Architectural Crop', *Irish Times*, 13 Jun. 1996
McDonald, Frank, 'Building of the Year: A Cube to Cherish', *Irish Times*, 31 Dec. 1996
Montague, John and Ellen Rowley, 'Trinity College Dublin: A Case Study', in Rolf Loeber, Hugh Campbell, Livia Hurley, John Montague and Ellen Rowley (eds), *Architecture 1600 – 2000, Volume IV, Art and Architecture of Ireland* (Royal Irish Academy, Yale University Press, 2014)

Case Study
Ranelagh Multi-Denominational School, Ranelagh, Dublin 6, 1995–8

Aoibheann Ní Mhearáin

The Ranelagh Multi-Denominational School (RMDS), an eight-classroom primary school, occupies a prominent site on a curve in the main Ranelagh Road. It sits in the historic Georgian context of Mountpleasant Square, and announces itself with four house-like brick structures tight to the street edge. The school site is small and rectangular, sloped and semi-urban, all unlikely characteristics for a school site, but a Church of Ireland school had been operating there since the 1960s, taking residence in an assortment of existing buildings. When, in 1988, the school patronage was transferred from the Church of Ireland to the newly established Ranelagh Multi-Denominational School Association (RMDSA), the active school community fought for a new building in the same location, to replace the unsuitable existing structures, and to serve the now growing student population. The architects, O'Donnell + Tuomey, who were first activists in the multi-denominational movement and later parents in the school, were formally appointed in 1995 after the Department of Education's failed attempts to secure planning permission with its designs, largely due to local opposition to their plans. In contrast, O'Donnell + Tuomey's design grew out of dialogue, with the neighbours, the school community and most crucially, with the site.

The conversation that developed during the design process questioned how to build in this constrained and historic context, and how to create school spaces that supported an educational ethos that was founded on tolerance, openness and sharing. The architects' design response produces a building keenly attuned to both its surroundings and its users' needs and rich with subtle invention as a result. Folded into its form, fabric and organisation is the intelligence of its Georgian context. We can see this most evidently in the four, two-storey classroom blocks on the street edge, that look like local Georgian houses, with their vertical proportions, reclaimed brickwork and large timber windows, but it is also there in the use of stepped levels, across the site and in the building, much like the split levels found in the Georgian house, but now to serve this new school model. To the south side, facing the yard and away from the road, the façade is open and constructed mostly of timber and glass, with a distinct verandah overhanging the long, glazed entrance screen. Echoing a much loved verandah from the original tin church on the site, and visible on the earliest sketches by Sheila O'Donnell, the verandah creates a space for lingering, for people to gather and to share, as they come and go from the school. It is an architectural gesture of generosity, aimed at creating connection and community, and that sensibility is repeated in the interior of the school, with its wide corridors, interconnected classrooms, shared garden space and carefully disposed windows that connect the students to each other and the wider world.

The building has continued in use as a school since its opening in 1998 and remains substantially as constructed, with the original interior colours retained and the timber to the exterior remaining unstained. The most

Sketch site plan set within map of neighbourhood (Courtesy of O'Donnell + Tuomey collection at Irish Architectural Archive)

significant change is a two-storey extension, built like a fifth 'house' similar to the classroom blocks, to the east of the school yard, with an elevation in brickwork matching the original. The extension provides a new staff room, a large art room, a single larger classroom space, support rooms, including resource teaching rooms that accommodate students' diverse needs and reflect changing educational requirements and methods.

Contextual School

The building's deep connection to its site and place, is evident in the resonance with the Georgian context, but also in the site planning and in the detailed materiality chosen. The primary move in organising the site, was to locate the school building along the northern edge, along the road, with the school yard to the south. The location of the school yard operates at a number of registers on the site; it is respectful to the existing terrace of houses at Old Mountpleasant, eliminating overshadowing and reducing the scale of impact of the school building, while also, at an urban scale, continuing the adjacent open space of Mountpleasant, and recalling the history of gardens on the site.

The four, two-storey classroom blocks, tight to the northern edge, facing the Ranelagh Road, are faced in reclaimed brick, salvaged from prison officer's houses that were demolished at Mountjoy prison, and these bring a patina to the façade that couldn't be achieved with new bricks. The existing railings on site were kept and re-used for the new perimeter to the school, including the new school gate, the stone on site was re-used, a laburnum tree is retained and the ground excavated for the construction was dispersed across the site, to create the new levels for the school. Detailing these design decisions, the architect John Tuomey described a sort of 'invisibility'

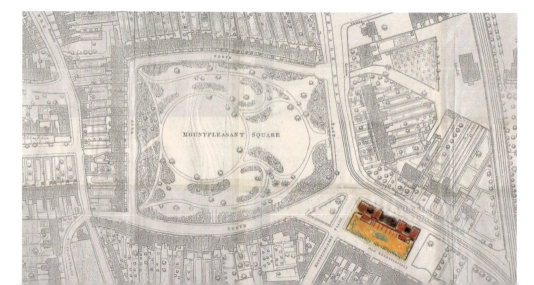

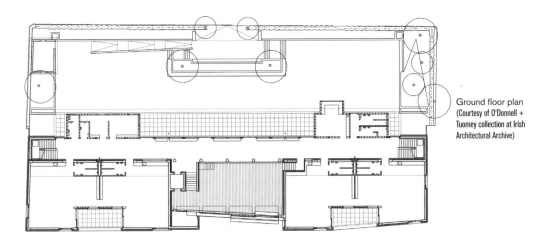

Ground floor plan (Courtesy of O'Donnell + Tuomey collection at Irish Architectural Archive)

to the building derived from its use of 'local materials, local scale, local brick, it does everything it can to embed itself into the continuity of Mountpleasant Square and Old Mountpleasant and position itself in relation to existing buildings.' (Tuomey + O'Donnell, Jul. 2021).

As noted in this study's outset, this connection with context is also evident in the use of levels across the site. Here we see them at the service of a school, however, rather than a house, which results in a carefully orchestrated sequence of spaces, starting from the arrival at the school gate and continues to the interior of the school. Arriving at the uppermost level of Old Mountpleasant, to the south side of the site, the students enter first through a repositioned original iron gateway, and from there immediately drop down a level to the school yard. The lower level of the yard operates like the 'area' of a Georgian house, the sunken space that separates the main house from the street, in this case separating the school building from the public street. From the yard the students enter the school underneath the timber verandah and arrive onto a wide corridor space that overlooks the general purpose hall (GP hall), sunken a half level below; the arrival space acts as a balcony to the theatre of children's activities in the school hall. The drop in level of the GP hall also achieves the greater ceiling height required for the hall, and brings its floor level down to match that of the main road outside, allowing a formal entrance to be located to the street, which also facilitates out of hours opening for the school and wider community. This stepping across the site is revealed in the building's short section, but though the changes in level can seem subtle and discrete on a drawing, they are in fact spatially impactful when experienced, and they work together to create a sequence of spaces that orchestrate the daily ritual of arrival at school, and through this foster a sense of place and belonging for the child and school community.

More Than Concrete Blocks Volume 3

A spatial ordering is evident in the more intimate spaces of the classroom too. There are eight classrooms in total, four located on the ground floor and four at first floor, with the classrooms on both levels arranged in pairs. The lower level classrooms, originally for the junior years, are larger than the upper ones, and are carefully zoned internally to provide a range of teaching spaces, as well as being linked to the adjoining classroom and a shared external area. The windows in the classroom offer different perspectives, including a window to the corridor, a glazed connection to the adjoining classroom, and a timber screen onto the shared external space, as well as the singular large window in the main brick façade that faces back to the city.

Linking all the interior spaces, both classroom and shared spaces, is the deployment of a distinctive colour palette. The interiors are remarkable for their dramatic use of the restricted colour scheme, composed of four selected hues of yellow, blue, brown and green, drawn from Renaissance paintings and frescos of Fra Angelico's, as distinct from the primary colours typically used in schools. The architects have used the colours deliberately to code the spaces, with yellow used for sunlit walls; blue for walls that are thought of as invisible (like the partition wall between the classrooms), brown for the stairs, wet area and floors, and green where there are cuts in the plan.

Case Study: Ranelagh Multi-Denominational School

Though the colour palette began with this school project, O'Donnell + Tuomey continued using these same colours throughout their future buildings. Indeed it was not just the colour palette that was influential on the architects' practice development, but they identify this school project, along with the Irish Film Centre (later the IFI), as seminal to the development of their practice. Though O'Donnell + Tuomey's formal appointment as architects on the school was made in 1995, their original sketches are made concurrent with the commissioning of the Irish Film Centre, in the mid-1980s.

These projects embody many of the key principles that O'Donnell + Tuomey have developed in their work in succeeding years; both projects are drawn from their surroundings, responsive to the existing condition, though still resolutely modern in their spatial ordering. In this approach, we can see the development of a new strand in Irish architecture that was to inform the coming generation. Emerging in Ireland in the 1990s, this architecture encompassed both the modern and the traditional with projects that embody many of the principles of modern architecture, in their plans and their expression, but that simultaneously countered the universality of modern architecture with designs that responded to the specifics of their climate, used local materials and embraced craft and traditional construction. Hugh Campbell identified this engagement of modernity and tradition in O'Donnell + Tuomey's work, work that was characterised by an ongoing conversation between 'continuity and renewal'. This dialogue between new and old, change and consistency, John Tuomey described as 'the task of architecture'. As with the Irish Film Centre, in the school in Ranelagh, this discourse is very much alive. The Ranelagh school is a building in a historic context, respectful of its neighbours in terms of scale, materiality and form, but concurrently informed by principles of modern architecture, housing a radical new type of school whose founders sought to transform one of the core institutions of Irish society.

(above)
Elevations
(Courtesy of O'Donnell + Tuomey collection at Irish Architectural Archive)

(below)
Elevations
(Courtesy of O'Donnell + Tuomey collection at Irish Architectural Archive)

Innovative School

Though RMDS was among the first multi-denominational schools established in the state when it was founded in 1988, its establishment speaks to one of the defining characteristics of education in Ireland in the 20th century, the near total dominance of the religious orders as school patrons. The highly influential Investment in Education Report of 1962 funded by the OECD, outlined this fact, noting that 95 per cent of schools were under the patronage of the Roman Catholic Church. The report highlighted many of the shortcomings of the educational system in Ireland and spurred a radical re-structuring of the Irish education system in the following decades, including the creation of the community and comprehensive schools, the introduction of free secondary education, the establishment of the Regional Technical Colleges, and the introduction of a more child-centred primary curriculum in 1971. Despite all these changes, primary and secondary schools remained, almost exclusively, under the patronage of the religious.

It was against this backdrop that a group of parents founded the first multi-denominational school, the Dalkey School Project (DSP) in 1978, surmounting considerable opposition and challenges, as they forged a new type of school. These parents wanted a choice in the type of education their children received, and were motivated by a desire to have a mixture of beliefs in the school. The emerging Troubles in Northern Ireland was an added impetus, and fuelled a desire to reduce division in society along sectarian lines. Central to their ethos was a child centred approach to education and respect for all in a co-educational environment that welcomed those of all denominations and none. In terms of administration, the multi-denominational school was run by a management committee with significant democratic involvement of the parents, and no representation from the parish or diocese.

In 1985 the DSP opened in a purpose built, eight-classroom school in Glenageary, Co. Dublin, designed by A. & D. Wejchert Architects. This design reflected the radical nature of the school structure and innovated by making paired, interlinked, octagonal-shaped classrooms, which the principal described as reflecting the school's policy of sharing and tolerance, and facilitated co-operation between all members of the school community. Like the later school in Ranelagh it was also a two-storey building, with terrace spaces at upper level for use of the first-floor classrooms.

Case Study: Ranelagh Multi-Denominational School

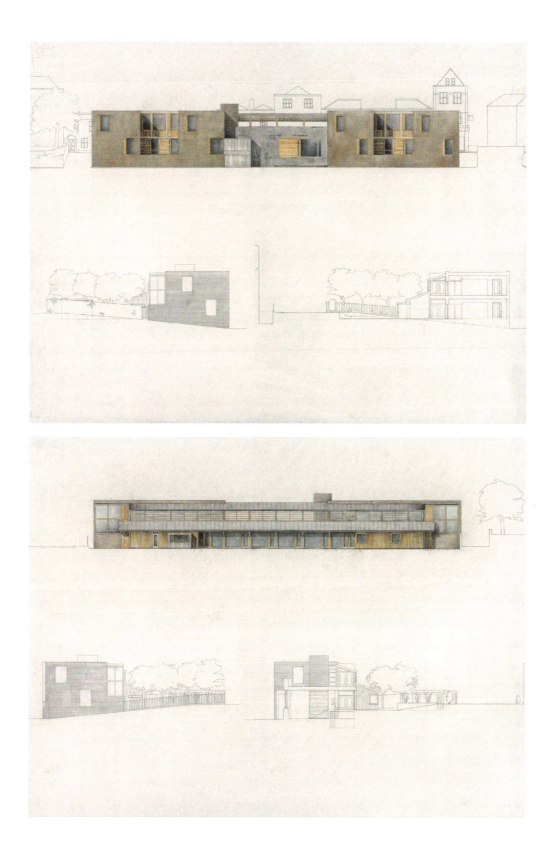

Model (Courtesy of O'Donnell + Tuomey image collection)

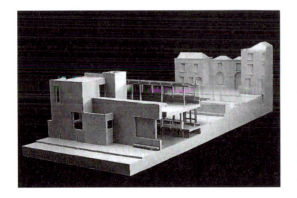

In the Ranelagh and Crumlin areas of Dublin in the 1980s parents similarly were advocating for a new type of school, now within the context of a society riven by referenda on abortion and divorce, issues that brought to the fore the role of the Catholic Church in people's everyday lives. Much like the founding of the DSP there was opposition to the establishment of this school, but equally the parents and multi-denominational community's commitment to the provision of the school, surmounted the opposition, securing the site on the Ranelagh Road, and in 1988 these parents successfully oversaw the first transition of a denominational school, St Columba's, from the patronage of the Church of Ireland, to the parent led patronage of the RMDSA. The school was officially founded in September 1988, with three teachers and an enrolment of 64 students, housed in the existing prefabs, 'Tin church' and caretaker's house on site.

The movement for an alternative school system coalesced in 1984 to become Educate Together, an umbrella organisation that acts as patron to multi-denominational schools. Its charter reflects the original ethos by which the DSP and following this, RMDS, was founded and there are now 95 primary-level, and 19 second-level multi-denominational schools in Ireland. This represents a huge growth in the sector in the space of 40 years, against considerable initial opposition, though this success must be viewed in the wider context, as multi-denominational schools represent less than 5 per cent of the schools in the country.

Case Study: Ranelagh Multi-Denominational School

School interior, photographed by Alice Casey (Courtesy of O'Donnell + Tuomey image collection)

More Than Concrete Blocks Volume 3

Case Study: Ranelagh Multi-Denominational School

Facts and Figures

Architects: O'Donnell + Tuomey. For a biography of Sheila O'Donnell and John Tuomey see IFI essay.
The project architect on RMDS was Will Dimond – who later set up Donaghy Dimond Architects with Marcus Donaghy – assisted by Peter Carroll, who also set up his own practice, A2 Architects, after working with O'Donnell + Tuomey.
The school has been recognised by many awards for its design including: the RIAI Triennial Gold Medal (1998–2000); The European Union Prize for Contemporary Architecture – Mies van der Rohe Award shortlist, 1991; AAI Downes Medal,1999; RIBA Award, Best building in Educational Category in Europe and RIBA Stirling Prize finalist, 1999

Contractor: Pierce Healy Developments
Structural Engineers: Fearon O'Neil Rooney
Quantity Surveyors: Boyd and Creed
Services Engineers: JV Tierney
Windows and timber screens: Gem Joinery

Sources
Unpublished
Irish Architectural Archive: O'Donnell + Tuomey Collection
Joan Whelan, former principal RMDS, interview with Aoibheann Ní Mhearáin, June 2021
John Tuomey and Sheila O'Donnell, interview with Aoibheann Ní Mhearáin, July 2021
Will Dimond, interview with Aoibheann Ní Mhearáin, June 2021

Published
Hyland, Áine, *A Brave New Vision for Education in Ireland: The Dalkey School Project 1974–1984* (Hyland, 2020)
Multiple Authors, *RMDS 21: The Story of Ranelagh Multi-Denominational School 1988–2009* (Ranelagh Multi-Denominational School, 2009)
O'Donnell, Sheila and John Tuomey, *O'Donnell + Tuomey: Selected Works* (Princeton Architectural Press, 2006)
O'Regan, John and O'Donnell + Tuomey, *O'Donnell & Tuomey*. Vol. 1 (Gandon Editions, 1997)
Tuomey, John, *Architecture, Craft and Culture: Reflections on the Work of O'Donnell + Tuomey* (Gandon Editions, 2008)
Tuomey, John and Sheila O'Donnell, *Space for Architecture: The Work of O'Donnell + Tuomey* (Artifice Books on Architecture, 2014)

Case Study
Castle Street Mixed-Use Building, Dublin 8, 1998
Carole Pollard

This mixed-use building, which turns the corner from Castle Street into Werburgh Street, both physically and aesthetically straddles the divide between Dublin's modern commercial core and its historic origins. Sited diagonally across from Christ Church Cathedral, which dates from 1028, its south gable nestles up against St Werburgh's Church built in 1719. Its adjoining neighbour at 4 Castle Street is designated as a Recorded Monument on account of its pre-1700 origins. When the site at 1–3 Castle Street was under construction in 1997, the discovery of medieval timbers embedded in the party wall between the two properties were thought likely to be the remnants of Elizabethan era timber-caged houses which had been demolished in 1812. 1–3 Castle Street is a remarkable achievement in terms of urban repair: it is a reinstatement of a broken street corner and a contemporaneous evocation of what may have stood there before.

The architects say that inspiration for their design, particularly the double height timber corner window, came from the discovery of drawings of Dublin's late medieval timber-framed houses. As such, it is at its corner that the building makes its boldest statement: starting from the recessed shopfront at street level, the building steps upwards and outwards, culminating in a massive six-metre-high projecting timber and glass box at the third and fourth floor. Soaring timber windows open out from a double height living space in the building's penthouse apartment, commanding magnificent views over Christ Church Cathedral. The building's materials are sympathetic to its environment with black framed granite cladding at ground floor and a dark brick consisting of many overburns employed to diffuse the volume of the building and carry the Castle Street elevation around the corner into Werburgh Street. The rendered panels at first- and second-floor on the Werburgh Street elevation were originally painted to match the stonework of St Werburgh's church (1170s, current building, 1790s).

No longer in residential use on the upper floors as originally intended, the building has lost much of the vibrancy that once made it a memorable landmark in the city. Passers-by can no longer catch evening-time glimpses into the spectacular penthouse living room from the street below, and the laughter of partygoers is no longer heard from the roof terraces. From the time of its occupation in 1999, an invitation to Castle Street on New Year's Eve became the hottest ticket in town where guests enjoyed a bird's eye view of revellers ringing in the New Year to the accompaniment of Christ Church Cathedral bells. Alas, the roof terraces are empty, as are the once lushly planted copper boxes that line the edges of the roof, undermining the hip neighbourhood vibe that 1–3 Castle Street once offered to this part of the city. For a short number of years, Castle Street presented a glimpse of what city living could be.

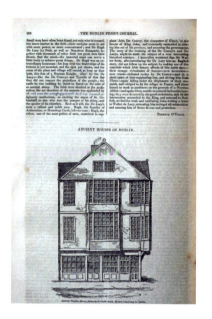

Historical Elizabethan house on Castle Street as featured in The Dublin Penny Journal, (Courtesy of Dublin City Library & Archive)

Making a Home in the Historic City

In medieval Dublin (c.1200–c.1500), Castle Street was part of the run of streets which comprised the medieval city's main thoroughfare: Castle Street, Skinner's Row and High Street were all situated within the city's medieval walls. Castle Street, as we know it now, wends its way from City Hall, past the gates of Dublin Castle to the junction with Werburgh Street. Despite the development of 20th- and 21st-century apartment block developments, the street retains its historic character and form. In 1997 when businessman Gordon Campbell bought the site on the corner of Castle Street and Werburgh Street, it was occupied by a three-storey concrete framed building dating from the 1960s with apartments on the two upper floors. The café on the ground floor enjoyed brief infamy as an anarchist hang-out called 'The Garden of Delight'. Set back from the Castle Street edge with a 'cut-out' chunk at its corner, its position, and unusual form was dictated by Dublin Corporation road-widening proposals which afflicted many parts of the city in the 1960s and 1970s.

Thankfully, road-widening plans for Castle Street were abandoned but it was not until the mid-1990s that the true heritage value of the street, particularly the remnants at its western end, were fully acknowledged and steps were taken to secure their survival. In 1996 Dublin Civic Trust began a campaign to save the adjoining building at 4 Castle Street from demolition on foot of the discovery of important 17th century building fabric on the site. This led to the Trust purchasing the building and restoring it to its former glory. That work was completed in 1999. When Campbell lodged

Case Study: Castle Street

planning permission for the redevelopment of his site in 1997, Dublin Civic Trust and An Taisce, raised concerns with the Planning Authority about the safeguarding of heritage. As a result, the grant of planning permission obliged the developer to undertake archaeological investigations prior to construction, and to ensure that the design of the foundations and layout of the building services would be dictated by any findings. In the end, the archaeological report had little impact on the design, however a section of Elizabethan era timber cage-work discovered in a party wall was required to be preserved and is exposed as a feature within the building.

    Gordon Campbell (d.2013) was a businessman with interests in the fashion retail business and he saw the potential to create a *pied-a-terre* for himself in the city centre. The site was adjacent to Temple Bar which was undergoing significant urban renewal at the time (see Temple Bar essays, p. x). From the mid-1990s, construction sector activity was increasing in tandem with the expansion of the Irish economy: empty city sites were being developed at a rapid rate. In addition to the substantial re-development of the Temple Bar area, a trawl through the architectural awards catalogues of the period reveals a proliferation of infill developments, mews houses, and period house restorations throughout the city. At the other end of the spectrum, speculative developers were building apartments which achieved only the minimum design standards of the time. For anyone wishing to buy or rent a spacious, attractive home in the city, there were few, if any options.

Campbell's original intention was to build an apartment building with residential use on each of the upper floors and a retail unit at ground floor but after planning permission was granted he decided that he did not want to share the building with other residents. A second planning permission was granted during the construction stage for change of use from residential to offices on the middle floors. The finished scheme comprised a retail unit on the ground floor, offices at first and second floor, and a grand penthouse apartment occupying the third and fourth floors. Private wrap-around roof terraces for the apartment provided an amenity that was unique in the city at the time. In addition to views of Christ Church Cathedral, the terraces enjoy views of Dublin Castle to the east and the Dublin Mountains to the south. One of the most important architectural feats of the scheme is the complete and masterful harmony that Meagher achieved in the design of Campbell's apartment interiors: light-filled and impeccably detailed spaces which flow from room to room and from inside to outside; not forgetting the book-lined mezzanine level befitting of any erudite urban dweller.

In 2002, Campbell sold the entire building to Harry Crosbie, one of Dublin's most famous property developers and the man behind the music venues at Vicar Street and The Point (later the O2 and then the 3 Arena). Crosbie used the apartment to provide accommodation for celebrities from the worlds of music, fashion, theatre, and film, including many of the headline acts performing in his music venues and their coterie of friends who came to Dublin to party. Since 2012, when Crosbie's property assets were taken over by the National Asset Management Agency (NAMA), the entire building has been in office use.

Case Study: Castle Street

Elevation study by John Meagher (Courtesy of de Blacam & Meagher collection at Irish Architectural Archive)

Rhythm and Grain

The architecture of de Blacam & Meagher is in many ways the foundation stone for the wave of architects who have brought Irish architecture to international attention in the 21st century. Shane de Blacam and John Meagher acquired international experience in both Europe and the United States at the beginning of their careers, absorbing design and cultural influences that they nimbly assimilated into their innate understanding of Ireland's built heritage. Both were born and raised in Dublin and gained their architectural education in the city, de Blacam in UCD and Meagher in DIT (now TU Dublin). From the beginning of their practice together in 1976, their early projects displayed an empathy with context. They also showed an ability to manipulate scale and materiality despite the limitations of tight budgets. By the late-1990s the practice, particularly the work of Meagher, had established a reputation in 'the mastery of residential form and space' (Keogh, Obituary, 2021). Meagher's versatility and skill is evident across the full spectrum of his housing work ranging from modest projects like Herbert Mews, to the more elitist and high budget houses which he designed for Ireland's wealthy. Castle Street was one of his first forays into that latter realm.

In his brief to the architects, Campbell expressed a wish for views of Christ Church Cathedral from his apartment: this mission provided much of the building's design meaning and intention. Constructed in untreated Iroko wood, the Elizabethan-inspired six metre-high projecting box contains accentuated window openings and ventilation shutters set in rhythmic basket-weave panelling. de Blacam & Meagher's masterful use of timber is seen in many of their projects including the oak panelled atrium at the Dining Hall in Trinity College (1987), the Samuel Beckett Theatre at Trinity College (1993) (Outline Survey) and the Wooden Building in Temple Bar (2001).

The rhythm of the timber panelling is accompanied by the quiet tempo of the unusual brick bond of two stretchers and one header which Meagher borrowed from renowned Finnish architect, Alvar Aalto's Helsinki University at Otaniemi where Meagher studied as a postgraduate. Another rhythm is set up in the nuanced stepping of the building's corner from recessed ground floor, to semi-recessed first floor, to the solidity of the second floor which anchors the projecting timber box above. Vertical incisions in the brickwork at the upper level reduce the brickwork mass and mediate the step back down to a two-storey building on the Werburgh Street edge. On

(above)
Floor plans (Courtesy of de Blacam & Meagher collection at Irish Architectural Archive)

(below)
Elevations (Courtesy of de Blacam & Meagher collection at Irish Architectural Archive)

this elevation, the existing concrete building is reinforced with steel beams expressed as frames around existing openings which are refitted with Iroko windows and shutter panels. Rainwater management is concealed internally so that there is no unintentional clutter on the building's façades. The same management of tempo and style is repeated in the building's interiors, most particularly in Campbell's two-storey apartment where the *tour-de-force* is the double-height living room, inside this Elizabethan-inspired timber window box. Timber is the predominant material, used on floors and doors, and in the bespoke built-in furniture. A steel and timber mezzanine level is lined with bookshelves and has access to the upper-level roof terrace. Light pours in on every level, and in turn almost every room has access to an outdoor terrace, so that Campbell's wish for views of Christ Church Cathedral is magnanimously interpreted to provide views in every direction over the city and its hinterland.

Structurally, the building contains the remains of the original 1960s concrete structure, alongside a new structural steel frame. Opening up works revealed that the original concrete frame was inadequate – old mattress springs were used as reinforcement bars – hence the use of steel reinforcement visible on the Werburgh Street elevation. At street level, the building is clad in black granite which wraps around the corner and the 'shopfront' is fitted with plate glass whose aluminium frames are recessed behind the granite so that it appears frameless. All windows on the upper floors are Iroko and those on the Castle Street elevation are deeply recessed, accentuating the shadows on the building's surface. Other external materials included copper flashings and coping details, complimented by copper planter boxes on the roof terraces. Zinc is used to clad the recessed penthouse roof level. Timber is used extensively in the building's interiors, tempered by smooth plasterboard walls and ceilings and tiled floor finishes in the public and common areas. The building has undergone some adaptation over the years, most notably in the ground-floor former retail unit which is now in use as offices, as are the floors of the former penthouse apartment.

One of Meagher's greatest gifts was his ability to communicate through drawing – 'drawing was his way of thinking' (de Blacam cited in Keogh, Obituary, 2021). As a teacher in the School of Architecture in UCD Meagher instilled that love of drawing in his students and it is one of the traits for which he is best remembered. Through drawing, Meagher developed his

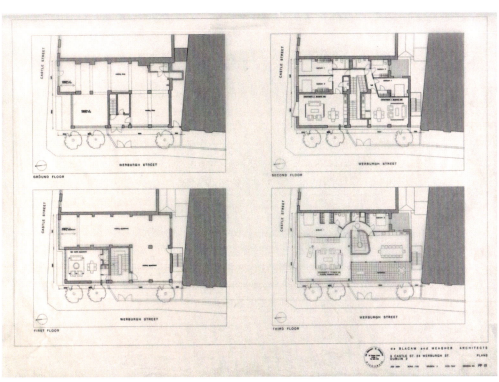
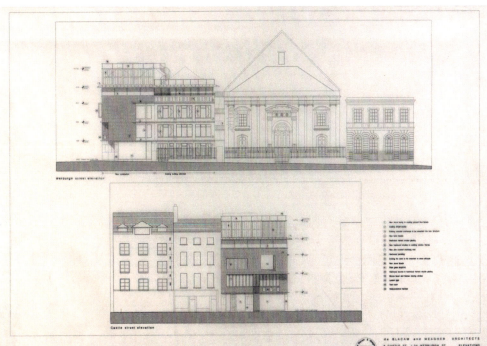

ideas and the touch and texture of his pencils, both graphite and coloured, evoked the texture and materiality that would eventually define the built outcome. Through drawing, Meagher connected his deep knowledge of the possibilities of building with his considerable understanding of context, which in this case was Dublin's late medieval urban grain. The result is a building which fits seamlessly into its context, not invisible but somehow an obvious solution. The building is an exemplar of how to build in an historic part of the city, how to repair a broken corner, and how to make a beautiful home deep in the heart Dublin. It is a small but valiant attempt to stop the erosion of Dublin's grain and structure. What Niall McCullough referred to as the 'gradual loss of the particular' (McCullough, 2007, p. 1) that spawned a generation of architects who rejected the phenomenon of universalisation, which by the closing decades of the 20th century permeated all aspects of life – from consumer goods, to popular culture, to architecture.

The architecture of de Blacam & Meagher heralds the emergence of 'Critical Regionalism' in Ireland as defined by architecture critic and writer, Kenneth Frampton. Frampton stated that, 'among the pre-conditions for the emergence of critical regional expression is not only sufficient prosperity but also a strong desire for realising an identity' (Frampton, 1983, p. 148). Increasing prosperity in Ireland from the 1990s, combined with increasing exposure to international ideas and greater confidence in Irish identity generally, laid the ground for a new type of architecture in Ireland.

Castle Street is the manifestation of that ethos: it draws on historical, cultural and urban reference points that are specific to its context. It is a small building with a lot to say, and perhaps if we had listened more closely, our city today would be more coherent, more inspiring and more vibrant. It is not very prescient to suggest – unsentimentally – that sustaining a singular urban and physical identity (or in fact any identity at all) might be a significant component of winning out in the 21st century.

View of roof terrace, c.2000 (Courtesy of de Blacam & Meagher Architects image collection)

More Than Concrete Blocks Volume 3

Facts and Figures

In 1997 Gordon Campbell purchased the Castle Street, appointing de Blacam & Meagher as architects. The project started on site in 1998 and was completed in June 1999.

John Meagher, partner at de Blacam & Meagher Architects, Dublin. Assistant architects: Trevor Dobbyn, Adrian Buckley and Caroline Lawlor. For full biography of de Blacam & Meagher, see Atrium case study.

John Meagher was born on 15th May 1947 and died on 30th March 2021. He was educated at the School of Architecture, College of Technology in Dublin and at Helsinki University of Technology, School of Architecture, Finland. He went on to work extensively throughout Ireland, Germany and the USA. Meagher commenced private practice with Shane de Blacam in 1976, forming de Blacam & Meagher, through which they have worked on the design of private and residential projects, both new build and restoration; residential complexes, and private homes in France, Ireland, Mexico, Portugal and Spain (Balearic Islands). John has been a consultant and adviser to PGA European Tour Courses for the past number of years. John's portfolio contains projects such as Lyons Demense, The Tony Ryan Academy for Entrepreneurship, DCU, Portobello Warf, Cap Martinet in Ibiza and PGA Catalunya, Spain and the firm's own Principle Headquarters, that are located in 4 St. Catherine's Lane West, Dublin 8.

Structural Engineers: Fearon O'Neill Rooney
Quantity Surveyors: John D Skelly & Associates
Services Engineers: R. N. Murphy
Joinery Subcontractor: McNally Joinery
Lighting: SKK Lighting, London
Landscaping to terraces: The Garden Supply Company
Main Contractor: Moston

Sources

Unpublished

Trevor Dobbyn, interview with Carole Pollard, Oct. 2014
John Meagher, interview with Carole Pollard, Oct. 2014
Drawing files at de Blacam & Meagher Architects archives, now in Irish Architectural Archive, Dublin

Published

Keogh, Paul, 'John Meagher Obituary: An Architect of Considerable Craft and Taste', in *Irish Times*, 10 Apr. 2021
O'Toole, Shane, 'No.1 Castle Street/No.24 Werburgh Street', in *Irish Architect* (No. 152, Nov./Dec. 1999), pp 21–5
Ryan, Raymund, 'Significant Facilities: Works of de Blacam & Meagher', in *A+U Architecture and Urbanism* (No. 346, July 1999)
Tóibín, Colm, 'New Irish Architecture, the Architectural Year Reviewed', in *Irish Arts Review* (Vol. 15, 1999)

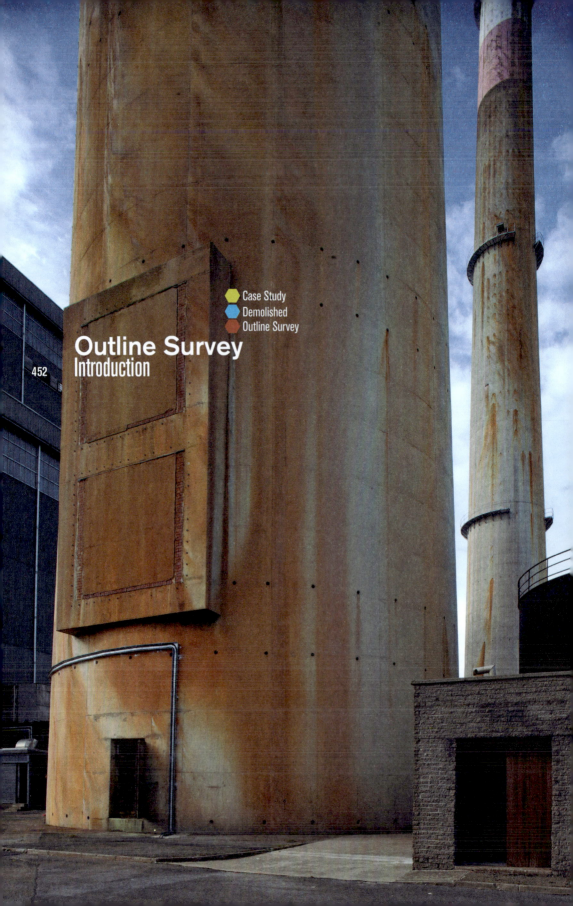

Outline Survey
Introduction

- Case Study
- Demolished
- Outline Survey

This overview in guidebook-style is *not* the 'best of' architecture from the period 1973 to 1999, but a representation of the types and forms of buildings which were designed, made and inhabited in Dublin City at the time. It is an Outline Survey which was originated by Shane O'Toole and developed since 2011 by the project team and the project commissioner, Dublin City Council Heritage Office.

In preparation for publication, in 2020, Shane O'Toole expanded the research of the survey of this period, and combined with recommendations from Paul Tierney and Charles Duggan, the survey grew to c140 sites. From 2020 to 2022, Lily O'Donnell and Cara Jordan (both MArch UCD students) undertook a significant fact-checking process. The sources which Cara, Lily and Shane consulted for dates, attribution and other information included materials from the Irish Architectural Archive's collections and library. Award schemes such as the AAI's New Irish Architecture from 1986, PLAN Magazine's Building of the Year and annual review scheme from 1982, the annual RIAI Gold Medal and Silver Medal for Housing schemes throughout the period 1973 to 1999 all served as markers of design excellence and relevance. Other sources from contemporary industry journals to witness accounts were followed closely. Practice collections, recently acquired by the Irish Architectural Archive (IAA) such as those for Group 91 or de Blacam & Meagher, were mined; as were more public materials such as Irish newspaper property pages and editorials.

All of the photographs for the Outline Survey sites were taken by Paul Tierney, in phases from 2011. Notably, some of these structures have since been demolished but we publish Paul's photographs where possible; in an act of recording the vagaries of recent architecture's legacy. In other instances, interiors or unbuilt projects or inaccessible sites are represented by an archive image. These have been sourced by Carole Pollard, through the IAA principally, and are credited as follows:

Palmerston House, elevation view (Courtesy of KMD Architects); Taoiseach House competition – site plan of De Blacam & Meagher, 2nd prize-winning entry (Courtesy of IAA); Life Association of Ireland as published in PLAN Magazine, Building of the Year 1982; Orwell Woods brochure, 1985 (Courtesy of Randal McDonnell); Women's Aid Refuge – Cloistered central courtyard (Courtesy of Peter & Mary Doyle Collection, IAA); Avonmore Zoo Pavilion, drawing by Paul Keogh (Courtesy of Paul Keogh Collection, IAA); Pillar Project competition entry, homage to Kazimir Malevich, 'Painterly Masses in Motion' 1915 by Shane O'Toole, Leo Higgins, James Scanlon (drawing by Niamh Butler) (Courtesy of Shane O'Toole); Café Klara – architects' presentation board (Courtesy of John Meagher Collection, IAA); Pavee Point/Free Church – McCullough Mulvin as published in *Irish Architect* No.81, Nov/Dec 1990 p. 27.

The Outline Survey rationales have been edited by Ellen Rowley and Carole Pollard, 2023.

More Than Concrete Blocks Volume 3

01 Texaco House
83 Pembroke Road,
Ballsbridge, Dublin 4

architect:
David Keane
company:
McCormack, Keane & Partners
start date:
1970
completion date:
1972

The corner site dictated the form of this exemplary 1970s Dublin central service-core office building. The result is one of the more stylish achievements of 1970s corporate architecture in Dublin. Technically significant too, it presents an early example of load-bearing precast concrete perimeter units and solar glass curtain walling. The original exposed white stone aggregate finish is no longer visible, following the application of a 'Sikagard' coating in 1986 to extend the durability of the concrete. A speculative development by David Lewis Group of London, the rent made headlines before construction was even completed. It was built by McLoughlin & Harvey and was called Catherine House before its first tenant, Texaco moved their head office from O'Connell Street, calling it Texaco House.

02 Alexandra College
Milltown Road,
Milltown, Dublin 6

company:
Ryan and Hogan
completion date:
1972

Originally located at Earlsfort Terrace, this was one of a number of educational establishments such as High School, Wesley College and University College Dublin that moved to greenfield sites in Dublin's south suburbs through the 1960s and 1970s. The new campus, comprising a series of two and three-storey brown concrete brick rectilinear blocks across a sloping green site was designed by Derek Ryan and Maurice Hogan. The school was officially opened on Friday 27 October 1972 by An Taoiseach Jack Lynch, at a ceremony attended by 1,500 guests.

03 Our Lady of Dolours
Botanic Avenue,
Glasnevin, Dublin 9

architect:
Vincent Gallagher
completion date:
1973

This is an enduringly novel Catholic church where the roof and walls are one, rising from the ground in a pyramid form to make a distinctive mark on the neighbouring skyline of Glasnevin. Its architect, Vincent Gallagher had just finished the 'temporary' Our Lady Seat of Wisdom at UCD Belfield and was evidently inspired by the architectural experiments encouraged by the liturgical reforms of Vatican II. Our Lady of Dolours was constructed in 1972, pre-empting the 1976 Dublin Diocesan church design competition in its adventurous roof, central floor plan and smaller size.

04 Fitzwilliam Lawn Tennis Club
Appian Way, Ranelagh, Dublin 6

architect: Sam Stephenson
company: Stephenson Gibney & Associates
commission date: 1969
start date: 1972
completion date: 1973

One of a series of buildings by Stephenson where the architecture is expressed as large-scale sculpture in brick; described by the architect as 'an essay in brickwork'. The indoor tennis arena has a steel structure to give large clear spans, while the clubhouse structure, with its banked spectator seating on the rooftop, is a combination of reinforced concrete and load-bearing brickwork. The building was commended in the RIAI Gold Medal for 1971-73. It was built following a land-swap arrangement with the developer, Marlborough Holdings, who took over the tennis club's original Wilton Place site. The complex was extended in 1992 by Horan Cotter & Associates, by Duff Tisdall in 2003 and by Douglas Wallace in 2020.

05 Molyneux House
67-69 Bride Street, Dublin 8

architect: Sam Stephenson
company: Stephenson Gibney & Associates
commission date: 1971
start date: 1972
completion date: 1973 (DEMOLISHED 2023)

The project involved the construction of a new façade and landscaped entrance courtyard to the remodelled interior of the former Molyneux chapel. The chapel was part of the Molyneux Blind Asylum but was deconsecrated and in use as a recreational hall for employees of Jacobs' factory. This was one of the most exciting architectural interiors of the time; it was an early example of an architect's studio moving away from the traditionally sober professional image conveyed by a suite of Georgian or Victorian consulting rooms. The design is expressed as brick sculptural architecture that reveals the monumental qualities inherent within the humble background building material of Dublin.

06 Merrion Hall
Strand Road, Sandymount, Dublin 4

architect: Arthur Gibney
company: Stephenson Gibney & Associates
commission date: 1965
start date: 1972
completion date: 1973

The first deep-plan office space and attempt at *Bürolandschaft* office planning in Ireland and an early example of an air-conditioned workplace, Merrion Hall is a serene perfect square of 7 bays, each measuring 7.2m square, with floor-to-floor heights of 3.6m. The office building was commended in the RIAI Gold Medal awards for 1971-1973, a rare accolade for a speculative office development. Its first tenants were Irish Shipping Ltd (who with the Insurance Corporation of Ireland, were its developers) and An Córas Tráchtála (The Irish Export Board). Construction costs rose to approximately £700,000. Generally, Merrion Hall and Sandyford Irish Management Institute, are regarded as Arthur Gibney's two great masterpieces.

RTÉ Campus
Montrose, Donnybrook, Dublin 4

architect:
Ronald (Ronnie) Tallon
company:
Michael Scott & Associates
commission date:
1960
start date:
1960
completion date:
1973

Combining the design ideals of German modernist architect Mies Van der Rohe (Miesian) with Irish culture, Tallon's masterplan for RTÉ follows the parkland campus ideal. Initially conceived as a singular structure housing diverse disciplines and services under one roof, the concept for the new broadcasting centre evolved in response to changing demands, to encompass a carefully composed landscape. The Television Building was completed in 1962, the Restaurant in 1967, the Administration Building (a Miesian three-storey glass and steel block supported on a ground floor colonnade) also in 1967, and Radio Building in 1973. Tallon worked on all the buildings ensuring continuity in design.

Castle House and Wicklow House
Nos 73–83 & 84–88 South Great George's Street, Dublin 2

architect:
Arthur Swift
company:
Arthur Swift & Partners
commission date:
1971
start date:
1972
completion date:
1973

An unusual intervention in Dublin, but typical of 1970s international urban block design, these two office buildings replaced an entire block – Pym's Department Store and some smaller buildings – to create a homogenous block with some dozen shop units at ground floor. Its street façade is uncompromising with its pre-cast concrete panels and non-opening windows, while its rear elevation is enlivened with balconies on to Dublin Castle. It was originally reported that the office building would be built with an adjoining multi-storey car park, so the motorist could park on the same level as the office in which they worked.

Lisney (infill office building)
24 St Stephen's Green, Dublin 2

architect:
Ronnie Tallon
company:
Michael Scott & Partners (later Scott Tallon Walker)
commission date:
1968
start date:
1970
completion date:
1973

Arguably the first good modern infill building in Dublin's Georgian core, the purpose-built headquarters for Lisney replaced a two-storey house with a mansard roof that marked a gap in the scale of the square. This was a hairdressers, 'Maison Prost', prior to the 1970 redevelopment. The offices are supported on four concrete columns, leaving the square floor plates column-free. On the ground floor this produces an elegant division of vehicular entrance, large display window and front door. The delicately proportioned steel curtain wall is painted white, with bronze-tinted glass. Built by G & T Crampton, for Lisney, it was awarded a High Commendation in the RIAI's European Architectural Heritage Year (1975) award.

Agriculture House
Department of Agriculture, Food & The Marine, Kildare Street, Dublin 2

architect:
Sam Stephenson
company:
Stephenson, Gibney & Associates
commission date:
1965
start date:
1970
completion date:
1973/4

An eight-storey 200,000 square feet office block in a sensitive context, this U-shaped building is unusual in that it incorporates a 20 feet high colonnade, and extensive use is made of large, structural, precast façade panels. It was the largest office building in Dublin at the time of its completion. The scale of the panels and the brown tones of the exposed Armagh limestone aggregate were chosen to harmonise with its monumental neighbour on Kildare Street, the National Museum. These panels underwent meticulous conservation and repair by Fleeton Watson, a specialist concrete repair company, in 2010. The meeting and conference facilities were designed by Shay Cleary in the 1990s.

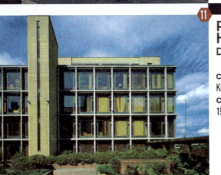

Palmerston House
Denzille Lane, Dublin 2

company:
Keane Murphy Duff
completion date:
1974

An unusual and lesser-known five-storey (plus plant room) office building, Palmerston House was designed by one of Dublin's most severely Modernist and reputedly Brutalist architecture practices, Keane Murphy Duff. Like their contemporaneous Texaco House project, this office block at the back of Merrion Square is articulated on its two long elevations with an external precast concrete frame. Another notable feature is the projecting slender concrete-brick stairwell on the south elevation, to Merrion Square.

River House
21–25 Chancery Street, Smithfield, Dublin 7

architect:
Thomas F. Sheahan
company:
Patrick J. Sheahan & Partners
start date:
1972
completion date:
1974 (DEMOLISHED)

Demolished to make way for a hotel in 2018, this much maligned five-storey block was oft cited as 'Brutalist'. Indeed in the style of Brutalism, River House made a strong visual image. The symmetry and order of the composition were best appreciated from a distance; at street level, the overhanging first floor lent a forbidding air. Some of its unpopularity may have emanated from its function as a motor tax office. Like many 1970s office blocks this was a speculative development (by I. & E. Investments), leased then by a government body. The architect, Patrick J. Sheahan died in 1965, and the Limerick firm was carried on by Timothy F. Clery, and Thomas F. Sheahan.

Bank of Ireland HQ, Miesian Plaza
50–55 Lower Baggot Street, Dublin 2

architect:
Ronnie Tallon (with Peter Doyle and Stephen Wolfe Flanagan)
company:
Michael Scott & Partners, later Scott Tallon Walker
start date:
1968
completion date:
1975

Built in two phases (1968-72 and 1973-75), this is the 'Rolls Royce' of Dublin offices which was inspired by the bronze-clad Seagram Building, New York (Mies van der Rohe, Philip Johnson, 1958) and Chicago's Federal Plaza (Mies, 1958-74). The Dublin bank HQ keeps the street line while also bringing in a corporate plaza, combining the best qualities of both. The three blocks enhance the streetscape and make a convincing whole of architecture, public space and monumental modern sculpture (with colourful works by John Burke and Michael Bulfin). The original curtain walls were made by Smith and Pearson (North Strand) in Delta manganese bronze. The complex underwent significant refurbishment (2015-8), becoming the first development in Ireland to achieve LEED Platinum V4 certification.

Chatham House
Chatham Street, Dublin 2

company:
Brian O'Halloran & Associates
completion date:
1975 (DEMOLISHED)

Demolished since 2022, Chatham House was notable for its three walls of glazing, combining frosted and reflective glass within an aluminium curtain wall grid. A corner building, it occupied its site fully, with shops at ground level and offices above. Notwithstanding its sleek design, in many ways, this is a typical speculative commercial building for early 1970s Dublin which succumbed to the property economics of the city's shopping district in the 2020s.

Darndale Housing Estate
Buttercup Park, Marigold Court, Primrose Grove, Snowdrop Walk and Tulip Court, Malahide Road/ Clonshaugh Road/ Greencastle Road, Coolock, Dublin 17

architect:
Arthur Lardner
company:
Lardner & Partners Architects, for Dublin Corporation
commission date:
1969
start date: 1973
completion date:
In phases from 1974 through 1976

Darndale estate was built following the Radburn principle (after Radburn, New Jersey), which separates vehicular and pedestrian traffic routes. The immediate example for the estate was Andover in England, and other high-density low-rise housing models built in greenfield sites by the Greater London Council from the late 1960s. The Darndale houses were built using an innovative dry concrete block system: quick to construct and eliminated the need for wet trades during construction. The estate layout and individual houses were significantly remodelled from the early 1990s.

Educational Building Society/EBS, Lafayette (Phase 1)
30 – 34 Westmoreland Street, Dublin 2

architect:
Sam Stephenson
company:
Stephenson Associates
completion date:
1975

The first phase of this EBS development, on the corner of Westmoreland and Fleet Streets, included a travertine-framed entrance which was removed during the second phase when the entrance was centrally relocated to the former Lafayette Building. This travertine entrance was reinstated in 2011 following a planning observation by DoCoMoMo Ireland. The dark reflective façade, with internal neon signage, was influenced by Norman Foster's Willis Faber and Dumas HQ and has been recently lost at ground level, impacting negatively upon Stephenson's original Post-Modern design intention.

Ulster Bank
33 College Green/ Trinity Lane, Dublin 2

company:
Boyle and Delaney
commission date:
1974
start date:
1975

Stretching from Suffolk Street to College Green, but most notable for its corner occupation along Trinity Lane, this mid-1970s bank building by Boyle and Delaney, was an addition to the 19th-century Ulster Bank (Thomas Drew, 1880s). Entailing the demolition and replacement of Drew's original Banking Hall, the 1975 structure is neat and hard-working, rising defiantly from its colonnaded street edge to the angular parapet roofline. Materials of prefabricated concrete and granite cladding compliment Drew's Ballinasloe limestone. With the closure of Ulster Bank in Ireland, the future of this building is unknown.

Grove House Apartments
Milltown Road, Ranelagh/Milltown, Dublin 6

company:
Henry J. Lyons
completion date:
1976

Grove House is a fairly massive and monolithic block of private apartments, representing the growing popularity of this typology in Dublin's housing market towards the middle of the 1970s. Its height – five-to-six storeys – is ameliorated by its horizontal massing and bulk, which in turn is articulated in light red-brick and concrete at its north, and stepped in balconied terraces at its south. This south elevation is at once the block's private and public front, enlivened with individual units' planters and bronze glazing and punctuated with public entrances and stairwells.

19 Wesley House/ Litton Hall
Leeson Park, Dublin 6

architect:
Robin Walker
company:
Scott Tallon Walker
start date:
1975
completion date:
1977

Wesley House is a housing complex, commissioned and managed by the Methodist Centenary Church and Christ Church. As a two-storey scheme, built of stack-bonded Forticrete blockwork, it was quick to construct, taking the builders, McLaughlin and Harvey Ltd., only 18 months. Forticrete would have interested the architect, Walker, as it was innovative and cheap. The zigzag layout of the scheme, emphasised by the aluminium corner windows, enabled individual shelter within a communal setting: something which intrigued Walker throughout his career. Wesley House is a fine modest scheme which retains its original use as sheltered and student housing.

20 Fitzgibbon Court
Fitzgibbon Street, Mountjoy, Dublin 1

company:
Dublin Corporation Housing/City Architects
start date:
1975
completion date:
1977

Fitzgibbon Court is probably the last example of the typical 1958-1970s Dublin flat type: the 5-storey, walk-up, deck-access maisonette block, which stacks a pair of duplexes above a ground-floor flat. By the mid-1970s, the type was running out of steam with the overt stylistic flourishes of the earlier 'butterfly-roof' maisonettes being stripped away. Traditionally these maisonette blocks paid little heed to their surrounding street grain but at Fitzgibbon Street, through the adoption of three blocks placed relationally, the architects have attempted to address the slope and to create a privacy threshold for the flats' residents. With 53 units, this scheme is medium sized.

21 Poolbeg Chimneys
Poolbeg Generating Station, Ringsend, Dublin 4

architect:
Maurice O'Keefe (engineer, ESB), Fred Browne (architect, RKD)
company:
Robinson Keefe & Devane for ESB Engineering Dept.
completion date:
Chimney A, Dec. 1971; Chimney B, Nov. 1978

The red and white striped chimney stacks are brick-lined concrete structures which are by now a representation of Dublin's skyline. Beginning their lives as crucial pieces of oil-burning energy infrastructure, later converted to gas (1984), they were decommissioned from 2010 and finally capped in 2015. Chimney A measures 207.48 metres in height and was completed in December 1971; Chimney B rises 207.8 metres and was completed in November 1978. They were both constructed using a radical slipform method of pouring and constructing concrete. And they are both tapered with a painted concrete outer shell, varying in thickness from 800mm at the base to no more 190mm at the top.

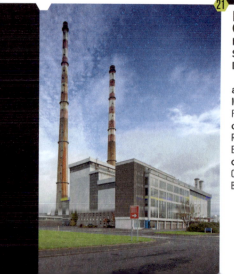

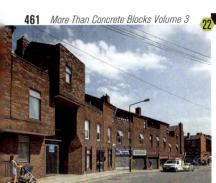

22 Ash Grove
The Coombe/Meath Street, The Liberties, Dublin 8

architect:
James Pike and Jim Barrett
company:
Delany McVeigh & Pike for the National Building Agency
commission date: 1968
start date:
1976
completion date:
1978

Possibly the finest example of a high-density low-rise, inner-city housing scheme, Ash Grove's innovative layout and plan forms stimulated the important City Quay housing competition of 1975-6. The scheme was realised through local residents' agitation; the Liberties Residents Association (LRA) commissioned the architects in 1968 to rethink collective housing for their area. At Ash Grove, street line and scale are respected, while internal pedestrian routes and corner shops are incorporated within the heavily modelled brick complex. The scheme eschews the use of modernist fenestration patterns in favour of more traditional 'portrait' windows punched through apparently solid brick walls. Ash Grove was Highly Commended in the RIAI Medal for Housing, 1977–78 and continues to be influential today.

23 PMPA HQ (now AXA Insurance)
46-52 Wolfe Tone Street, Wolfe Tone Square, Dublin 1

architect:
Robin Walker
company:
Scott Tallon Walker
commission date:
1972-3
start date:
1973
completion:
1978

Originally the PMPA headquarters (later, AXA Insurance), this office building by Robin Walker is a fine example of infill commercial architecture. PMPA displays all of Walker's urban and architectural preoccupations. Here we find an infill building which does not resort to pastiche; a design which is Walker's reading of a Miesian module (after Ludwig Mies van der Rohe); a gridded planar façade from steel and glass creating a tight skin, wrapping the volume; and 1970s contextualism for Dublin. Much of the original fabric and character of the elevation has been lost in the recent reglazing and refurbishment which enclosed the idiosyncratic, red giant order columns.

24 Talbot Memorial Bridge
Memorial Road (Dublin 1) to Moss Street (Dublin 2)

company:
Tyndall Hogan Hurley
completion date:
1978

This prefabricated concrete road bridge from Custom House Quay to City Quay was designed by modernist architects, Tyndall Hogan Hurley with De Leuw, Chadwick and O'hEocha Consulting Engineers. Constructed with three spans – two by 23 metres and one by 35 metres – the bridge won several engineering prizes. It was the first bridge over the River Liffey to be completed in the 20th century and was estimated to cost £750,000. It was named after the popular temperance figure of the mid-20th century Dublin Catholic Church, Matt Talbot.

25 Church of the Holy Trinity
Grange Road, Donaghmede, Dublin 13

architect:
Danuta Kornaus-Wejchert
company:
A. & D. Wejchert
commission date:
1976
start date:
1977
completion date:
1978

This church in a parkland setting, arising from the Dublin Diocesan Church Competition of 1976, is based on a design that was highly commended by the competition judges; they praised its 'unique structural system used to roof a cruciform plan' (Assessment, 1976). As the competition was for a notional suburban site, without reference to any particular context, the architect Danuta Kornaus-Wejchert gave emphasis in her design to the purity of the geometric form of the triangle. This was also a spiritual reference to the Holy Trinity. The form is simple and memorable, bringing abundant light to the interior. The church artist was Alexandra Wejchert, sister of architect, Andrzej Wejchert.

26 Taylor Galleries
16 Kildare Street, Dublin 2

architect:
Ross Cahill O'Brien
completion date:
1978

This adaptation of a medium-sized Dublin terraced townhouse into a private commercial gallery presented an interesting example of 'assemblage architecture', on a low budget. The gallery was established in 1978 by John Taylor and continued the tradition of small galleries in the city. The architect's interpretation of the house, for the purposes of a gallery, is in keeping with the shift towards contextualism in Irish architecture.

27 City Quay Housing
City Quay/Lombard Street East, Dublin 2

architect:
Paul Burke-Kennedy
company:
Kidney, Burke-Kennedy and Doyle for Dublin Corporation
commission date:
1975
start date:
1976
completion date:
1978

The City Quay housing scheme comprises a mixture of three types including two-storey over single-person units but mostly, two and three-storey family dwellings. Designed as one of the four winning schemes from the Dublin Corporation housing competition of June 1975, the first official housing competition in the history of the state, the results were announced in March 1976 and there were 85 submissions. As this terraced red-brick (mono) pitched-roof housing suggests, the competition sought an alternative to flat-block housing for central Dublin. The repetitive nature of the terraces, the strong street presence and the thresholds of small front gardens have endured and brought a new housing type to 1980s central Dublin. City Quay was awarded the RIAI Silver Housing Medal, 1979–81.

28. Trinity Arts and Social Sciences Building
Nassau Street and Fellows' Square, Trinity College, Dublin 2

company:
Ahrends Burton Koralek
start date:
1968
completion:
1978

Trinity College's Arts Building is a massive and typically overwrought late-1970s university building. Concrete with granite-cladding, sculptural and monolithic to Nassau Street, the block steps and slopes, with terraces and glazing to Fellows' Square. Following the successful New Library commission (1961-7), the architects (ABK) were retained for the Arts and Social Sciences Building, where they provided another library and lecture theatres at ground and basement levels, as well as a concourse and a cut from the city into the campus. The upper floors house academic departments, interspersed with light-well courtyards. A lightweight glazed sixth floor was added to the block in 2002.

29. Herbert Mews
Herbert Road, Ballsbridge, Dublin 4

architect:
John Meagher
company:
de Blacam & Meagher
commission date:
1976
start date:
1978
completion date:
1979

This terrace of six flat-roofed townhouses is a restrained, almost austere, essay in grey concrete brickwork, set back from the road among mature trees. Like the best townhouse developments of the period, it espouses a sense of communality and shared life. The ground floor is colonnaded to the front, leading to a roof-lit atrium in the centre of each house. Small courtyard gardens to the rear lead to a large communal lawn. The houses benefit enormously from passive solar house design, a precursor to *Passivhaus* building standards.

30. Martello Mews
Sydney Parade Avenue, Sandymount, Dublin 4

architect:
Denis Anderson
company:
Diamond Redfern Anderson
completion date:
1979

Martello Mews is a compact housing development of 15 or 16 dwellings on an awkward and small infill site, bringing a sense of urbanity to its suburban setting. Anderson's design here and famously at Castlepark Village, Kinsale (Co. Cork, 1974-82), was pioneering in how it made the shared external areas into a rich spatial experience. At Martello, the shared courtyards are brick-paved; at Kinsale, they are gravel. Many of the houses' living rooms are at first-floor level, with garages below. The scheme won the RIAI Medal for Housing, 1977-78, as well as a Europa Nostra diploma of merit in 1979.

AIB Bankcentre (now AIB Headquarters)
Merrion Road, Ballsbridge, Dublin 4

architect:
Andy Devane
company:
Robinson Keefe & Devane
commission date:
1972
start date:
1975
completion date:
1979 (DEMOLISHED)

Taking its cue from American examples, this was one of Ireland's first campus-style business complexes. The 40,000 square metres development was broken down into a series of six horizontally-modelled parkland pavilions and a taller central block, seamlessly integrated within the suburban context through its well-judged landscaped setting. There were interesting scale contrasts between the massively expressed structural elements and the minute mosaics with which the deep spandrels were clad. Alexandra Wejchert's sculpture, 'Freedom', is considered among the most ambitious large-scale public sculptures attempted in Ireland. The main block at the rear was almost doubled in size from 2003-8 (by RKD). The pavilions at the front were redeveloped from 2019 and nothing remains of Devane's Bankcentre.

Papal Cross
Acres Road, Phoenix Park, Dublin 8

architect:
Ronnie Tallon
company:
Scott Tallon Walker
commission:
1979
start:
1979
completion:
1979

The Papal Cross is an elegant monument marking the occasion when more than one million people attended an open-air mass celebrated by Pope John Paul II in the Phoenix Park: it was 29 September 1979. The cross, weighing 30 tonnes, is made up of six rolled-steel joists and required 5km of welding. It was fabricated in Clondalkin. Designed and built in just weeks, it was sized to the maximum height possible within the load and reach capacity of the largest mobile crane in Ireland. The base of the cross, a grass-covered concrete chamber, is an important part of the design, echoes of which are seen in Tallon's later 1798 memorial (Oulart, Co. Wexford), made in collaboration with sculptor Michael Warren.

Meteorological Office
65/67 Glasnevin Hill, Glasnevin, Dublin 9

architect:
Liam McCormick
company:
McCormick Tracey Mullarkey
start date:
1976
completion date:
1979

The Meteorological Office was designed by renowned architect, Liam McCormick, as a truncated pyramid. This unusual form allowed maximum sky-view for the meteorologists, while reducing the bulk of the building in its suburban setting of residential Glasnevin. The inspiration for the pyramidal form came from Justus Dahinden's 1971 Ferrohaus in Zurich but at Glasnevin, the walls incline at an angle of precisely 23 degrees, the same tilt as the earth's axis, and which gives us the seasons. With obvious geological references, the building is clad externally in Ballinasloe limestone (later replaced), with a limestone sculpture by long-time collaborator of McCormick's, Ruth Brandt.

Central Bank of Ireland
Central Plaza, Dame Street, Temple Bar, Dublin 2

architect:
Sam Stephenson
company:
Stephenson Gibney & Associates, Stephenson Associates from 1975
commission date:
1965
start date:
1972
completion date:
1979

The Central Bank is one of very few suspended buildings worldwide and the only example in Ireland. It was the first Irish office building to use the technique of continuous slip-forming concrete cores. Designed by one of Ireland's most famous 20th-century architects, Sam Stephenson for a major public institution, the landmark building has become one of the most recognisable symbols of the city. The 13-storey former bank building was significantly altered and refurbished between 2020 and 2023 (by Henry J. Lyons), to open up its basement, glaze in its roof-storey and incorporate retail and restaurant facilities as part of Central Plaza.

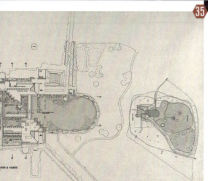

Competition for An Taoiseach's Residence and a State Guest House
Site of former Apostolic Nunciature, Phoenix Park, Dublin 8

architect:
Various
completion date:
1979

Closing on 30 March 1979, this international competition for a house for the Irish prime minister, An Taoiseach, attracted 300 enquiries and 97 entries. Among the assessors was Dutch post-war architect, Aldo Van Eyck. And among the submissions was one by Zaha Hadid – reputedly the first project in her office. A London duo, Eldred Evans and David Shalev won. Joint second place was awarded to young Dublin practice, de Blacam & Meagher, and a UCD School of Architecture team: Moore, Meagher, Farrell & Cleary with Peter Dudley. The assessors noted, 'the standard of the entries reflected the complexity of the brief, only a minority showing a sensitive appreciation of the requirements.' (Assessors' Report, 1979). With the replacement of Taoiseach in December 1979, the project was cancelled.

Investment Bank of Ireland/ Fitzwilliam Hall (Glandore)
Leeson Street Bridge, Lesson/Fitzwilliam Street, Dublin 2

company:
Frank Benson (consultant)
completion date:
c1980

This freestanding interpretation of a Georgian Dublin townhouse terrace is arguably the apotheosis of the 1970s (and into the 1980s) planning tendency for pastiche Georgian architecture across the South Georgian quarter. This speculative development is oversized and badly proportioned however its Neo-Georgian language of brick wall, symmetrical massing and large rectangular windows, proved popular with official Dublin, in part in reaction to the modernist concrete offices of the 1960s and 1970s.

Ilac Centre
Moore/Henry/Parnell Streets, Dublin 1

company:
David Keane & Partners, later Keane Murphy Duff
completion date:
1981

In development and construction through the late 1970s but not complete until 1981, this large shopping mall was of its time in both building type and urban attitude. Its cruciform low-rise bulk landed on top of the north inner city, erasing a warren of historic streets and traditional lanes in the process. Top-lit with moments of High-Tech aesthetics, it was a celebration of the suburban shopping centre, brought to town. Its interior emphasis did little to promote the market life of Moore Street and its surroundings. The Ilac Centre endures well in 2020s Dublin.

New Street Housing
New Street, Clanbrassil Street, Dublin 8

company:
Delany McVeigh Pike for Dublin Corporation
completion date:
1981

Coming off the success of the Ash Grove scheme for the Liberties, the architects were commissioned to design this nearby Dublin Corporation housing scheme on New Street. Here, the spirit is less experimental but echoes of Ash Grove are evident in the varied roof heights and strong street line. The red-brick houses, with deep-set arcuated front doors, are a mixture of two and three-storeys. The scheme occupies the site behind the main street line, with cuts made through to Cathedral Lane and axially lining up with the public park off Kevin Street.

Montrose House
1 Adelaide Road, Dublin 2

architect:
Robin Walker
company:
Scott Tallon Walker
completion date:
1981

Montrose House is a nine-storey commercial building which was a late project by Robin Walker, who retired in 1982. Was he responding to the increasing planning requirement in the city, that framed-buildings should be clad in brick which often resulted in 'pastiche' architecture? Or was this Walker's response to the rise of Post-Modernism, which offered certain freedoms from Modernist orthodoxy in relation to architectural detail and decoration? Here, the expressive, multi-coloured brick cladding is not superficially decorative, but adds subtle legibility to the unusual structural resolution of the building, which changes from front to back.

⬢40 Patrick Guilbaud Restaurant (former)
James' Place East, Dublin 2

company:
Arthur Gibney and Partners
completion date:
1981 (INTERIOR DEMOLISHED)

Patrick Guilbaud's restaurant is an institution for Dublin's elite as well as historically, for some in the architectural community. The AAI benevolent society annual lunch was held here, for instance. Before it moved to the Merrion Hotel, the restaurant was situated in this building off Baggot Street which was designed by Arthur Gibney and Partners. Though the interior with its reproduction Parthenon frieze is gone, the defensive brick exterior with its bulls-eye window still exists. The dining room rose into double height at the back while privacy was the design motivation with the roof-lights providing atmospheric daylighting.

⬢41 AnCO Training Centre (later Finglas Training Centre)
Poppintree Industrial Estate, Jamestown Road, Finglas, Dublin 11

architect:
Ronald Tallon
company:
Scott Tallon Walker
commission date:
1979
completion date:
1981

The Finglas AnCO Centre was one of only two purpose-built industrial training centres in the country. This building demonstrates superb integration of architecture and engineering, and stylistically the building is a fascinating and rare mix of quasi-British High-Tech structural aesthetics with aspects of Mies Van der Rohe or Miesian detailing. The 2 metre-high external lattice trusses support a clear-span roof structure over a single-space, column-free workshop measuring 115 metres long by 36 metres wide by 7.8 metres high. The first full year of courses were completed in 1982 and the building was officially opened in March 1983.

⬢42 Ringsend Housing Scheme
Pine/Bremen/ Kyle-Clare Roads, Sean Moore Road, Ringsend, Dublin 4

company:
Burke-Kennedy Doyle Architects for the NBA
completion date:
1981

Built by G & T Crampton for the National Building Authority (NBA) and designed by BKD, this colourful scheme of 115 units is a follow-on from the architects' City Quay scheme. Here, the terrace is set into more suburban idioms of culs-de-sacs, off the Sean Moore Road near the industrial edge of Dublin port. Indeed, all the estate's streets are named after charters and merchant ships. The scheme comprises mostly three-storey houses which are joined by the odd two or single-storey houses, all rendered and brightly painted. The young architect Ruairi Quinn, later Labour Party T.D and Minister for Education, worked on this scheme.

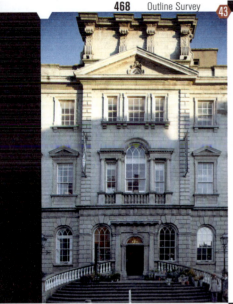

43

Powerscourt Townhouse Centre
59 South William Street, Dublin 2

architect:
James Toomey
company:
Toomey Architects for Power Securities (property investment)
start date:
1979
completion date:
1981

Mooted from 1977 for use as a higher education institute or a museum, the adaptation of Powerscourt Townhouse was a rescue mission for the Georgian building. A shopping centre won out, in response to the growth in suburban shopping centres, flourishing at the perceived expense of traditional urban street-front shops. The adaptation cost over £3.5 million. The townhouse's courtyard was roofed over, creating a sociable mall and an interestingly 'historic' shopping experience. The refurbished Powerscourt Townhouse was nominated as a national demonstration project to the Council of Europe for European Urban Renaissance year, 1981.

44

Port and Docks Board HQ (now Dublin Port Company)
East Wall Road, Alexandra Road, North Dock, Dublin 1

architect:
Niall Scott
company:
Scott Tallon Walker
commission date:
1976
start date:
1980
completion date:
1981

This refined precast concrete building is architecturally robust enough to sit comfortably within its large-scale industrial and city-edge context. Access to the headquarters is off a raised podium, with port-related lettable spaces below. Due to the unfavourable ground conditions, all plant and archive rooms are at roof level. Unusually, the form of the building is a perfect cube as the building's height, length and depth are identical.

45

Ballyfermot Public Library
Ballyfermot Road, Kylemore, Dublin 10

architect:
D. McMahon
company:
McMahon, Bloomer, O'Hara for Dublin Corporation (Dublin City Council)
completion date:
1981

When it opened in 1981, this public library for the suburb of Ballyfermot was, at 22,500 square feet, the largest public library in Ireland. Externally clad in brick, this is a low-lying single-storey building which is top-lit via bands of continuous rooflights. It is a modest industrial-type warehouse structure which has been cleverly divided and zoned internally. Considered colour schemes and partitions allow for the separation of activities and reading experiences. The library won the National Rehabilitation Board's Building Design Award Scheme in 1981, deemed a 'haven for recreation and education' (Assessment, 1981).

Northcliffe Apartment Complex
Martins Row, Chapelizod, Dublin 20

company:
Cleary and Hall
completion date:
1982

Northcliffe is an expressively unique residential development on a dramatic and challenging cliff-like site backing onto the Phoenix Park, to its north and overlooking the River Liffey, to its south. A large-scale object in the landscape, the monolithic brick scheme was conceived as an aqueduct-like structure with a repetition of piers on the front. There are deeply-incised balconies that ensure an appropriate sense of luxury in modestly-sized apartments by providing exemplary 'rooms with a view'. The scheme was jointly designed by Shay Cleary and Frank Hall. The sale of the apartments was pushed from November 1982 with the promotion of a free week in a Costa Del Sol timeshare, for five years.

Life Association Ireland Building
4–5 Dawson Street, Dublin 2

company:
Ryan O'Brien Handy
completion date:
1982

This office building was significant at the time, winning PLAN Magazine Building of the Year for 1982-3, among several accolades. It is a brown clay-brick building with projecting window bays at first floor and set-back windows across the second and third floors. Its structure is reinforced concrete holding a steel-framed roof; five-storeys over basement, with a terraced penthouse clad in natural slate. Set on to a podium of sorts, the shop-front ground floor is raised from the pavement and it is little changed since 1982.

Donnybrook Fire Station
19-23 Donnybrook Road, Donnybrook, Dublin 4

architect:
Dublin Corporation City Architects Dept
commission date:
1976
start date:
1981
completion date:
1982

The need for new Dublin fire stations was recognised in a government report on the Fire Service in 1975. In 1976, Dublin Corporation announced a plan to build six new fire stations, but this was shelved. Five years later, the Stardust Fire in February 1981 refocused the need to build fire stations across the city, and Donnybrook was the first of the new batch of stations to be completed. It is larger and more architecturally ambitious than its counterparts in Tallaght, Clondalkin, Blanchardstown and Swords, being a two-storey, four-bay structure with drill tower, built in reinforced in situ concrete with stone cladding externally. It was constructed by John du Moulin Ltd. at a cost of £784,000.

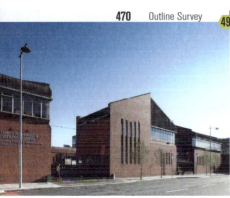

49 IDA Enterprise Centre (now Trinity Technology & Enterprise Campus)
Pearse Street, Dublin 2

architect:
Matthew Barry
company:
Barry and Associates
commission date:
1978
completion date:
1982/3

Built to house a cluster of small free-standing industrial and commercial units in the then-abandoned and decayed docks area, this enterprise development centre which was commissioned by the Industrial Development Authority (IDA) was heralded as an early success at urban regeneration. The original building was an iron-framed stone warehouse dating from 1862. It was significantly remodelled, to comply with fire regulations, into a craft centre and offices. This IDA Enterprise Centre won the RIAI Conservation award (1981-3) and was Commended in the RIAI Gold Medal award scheme (1980-82). Trinity College purchased the centre in 1999.

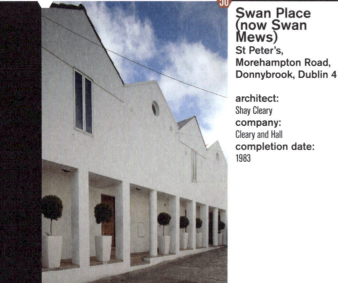

50 Swan Place (now Swan Mews)
St Peter's, Morehampton Road, Donnybrook, Dublin 4

architect:
Shay Cleary
company:
Cleary and Hall
completion date:
1983

This terrace of three mews houses is a refined essay in Post-Modernism, with 'historic' forms played off against the sleek white surfaces more typical of Modernist architecture. At the time, little value was placed on Dublin's secondary streets and lanes. Traffic set-backs for off-street parking, which were generally imposed as a condition of planning permission, were eroding the continuous walls that defined the city's lanes. The constricted site permitted no set-back here but instead, a new house type which evolved into a two-bay dwelling, each 3.3 metres wide, emerged, becoming a radical new model for mews lane redevelopment. Bedrooms were at ground level and living spaces were above.

51 Energy Centre, St James's Hospital
St James's Hospital Campus, James's Street, Dublin 8

architect:
Jim O'Beirne
company:
Moloney O'Beirne Guy & Hutchinson
commission date:
1975
start date:
1982
completion date:
1984

In 1975 the hospital launched a phased rebuilding programme and the Energy Centre was part of Phase 1B of this redevelopment. The Energy Centre is an industrially-detailed brick structure with a pair of slender metallic boiler-house stacks which are expressive of its function as a combined heat and power plant. The architect's decisive design move was the manipulation of site levels. The building remains the centre for energy distribution, as can be seen with the new taller stack of 16 flues which stand beside the original stack. Reassuringly present yet discreetly set behind trees, the silvery stacks are a local industrial landmark, axially visible along the approach to town from as far away as Emmett Road' to 'Newly visible beside the National Children's Hospital, the silvery stacks are a local industrial landmark.

52 Artane Oratory of the Resurrection
18-21 Kilmore Road, Beaumont, Dublin 5

architect:
Liam McCormick
Company:
McCormick Tracey Mullarkey
commission date:
1979
start date:
1982
completion date:
1983/4

The Artane Oratory is a rare Dublin church by renowned architect, Liam McCormick and is reminiscent of his rural Donegal churches: externally, in its battered or roughcast concrete curved walls; and internally, in its hidden top-lit or clerestory source of natural light. This is a memorial oratory, commissioned by the Christian Brothers' Northern Province following the closure of St Joseph's Industrial School in 1969, to celebrate the memory of those buried in the associated graveyard nearby. The building has recently been returned to its original colouring of deep Burgundy red with its new occupation by the Serbian Orthodox parish of St George.

53 Restoration of Casino, at Marino
Malahide Road, Marino, Dublin 3

architect:
Austin Dunphy and John Redmill
company:
O'Neill Flanagan and Partners for Office of Public Works
start date:
1975
completion date:
1984

The Casino building is Ireland's finest Neo-Classical folly and one of the finest small houses in 18th-century Britain and Irish architectural history. Designed by William Chambers for James Caulfield, Earl of Charlemont from the 1750s, it was in a state of decline by the 1970s when its restoration was initiated. Tunnels beneath the Casino had been used during the War of Independence (1916-22); while the Irish architects would annually make measured drawings of it for the AAI Downes Medal (up to 1917). Restoration took almost ten years, with Redmill becoming assistant to Dunphy in 1978. Much of the original interior fabric (16 rooms over three floors) had been damaged but in 1984, the Casino opened to the public.

54 Morehampton Mews
Morehampton Road, Donnybrook, Dublin 4

company:
Diamond Redfern Anderson
start date:
1982
Completion date:
1984

Morehampton Mews is a worthy example of the 1980s mews house typology, or private high-density low-rise housing which occupies secondary or infill urban sites. The architects, Diamond Redfern Anderson, were committed to pushing this architectural type in 1980s Ireland. Here, the pitched-roof brown-brick scheme snakes through the site, which is leftover space at the end of the Victorian villa terrace. Homes range from one-bedroom apartments in three-storey blocks, to two-storey small houses. Each has its own brick hearth, brick balcony or patio and neat kitchen, organised in a clever sequence of internal spaces.

55 Swan Centre
6 Rathmines Road, Dublin 6

company: John O'Reilly & Partners
completion date: 1984

The Swan Centre here represents 1980s suburban shopping architecture (such as the contemporary Frascati or Nutgrove Centres). It is a shopping arcade within a site which comprises 11 duplex apartments. Brick is the dominant material, used for internal and external elevations. The mall was floored with quarry tiles (since changed) and the structure is laminated timber. Notably, the roof is variously composed of a two-storey barrel vault with roof-lights and the hemispherical translucent dome (15 metres in diameter) which was brought inside in a single piece.

56 Cambridge Court (sheltered housing)
Cambridge Road, Dublin 4

architect: Cathal Crimmins
company: Crimmins Architecture for Dublin Corporation
completion date: 1984

Cambridge Court is a successful and beloved sheltered housing scheme for elderly people in the urban village of Ringsend. Originally, there were 22 one-person flats, eight two-person units, two enabled flats and then four one-person and three two-person cottages. The scheme is arranged as a perimeter block which holds the street line and brings elevations to the street which complement the neighbouring housing. The scheme is entered via a central entrance, marked out by a pediment housing a sundial, bringing the pedestrian through a tree-lined path to the scheme's communal centrepiece, the Common Room. Cambridge Court won Sunday Tribune Arts Award For Architecture, 1985.

57 Willow Field
Park Avenue, Sandymount, Dublin 4

architect: Tony Horan
company: Horan Cotter Associates
start date: 1972
completion date: 1984, main phase and 1985, phase 2

In the 1980s, as prices in Dublin's residential property market stagnated, townhouse developments offered the potential for increasing housing densities, particularly on infill sites in the inner suburbs. This involved the reinvention of traditional two- (and sometimes three-) bedroom terraced house concepts that would be attractive for sale to professional-class buyers. Willow Field is one of the best exemplars of this. It is an elegant, calm and urbane enclave in Sandymount, where as much design attention was paid to the landscaping of shared public spaces, including parking and communal gardens, as to the house plans and materials themselves. The houses were mostly sold between March 1985 and October 1986.

Orwell Woods
Orwell Park, Rathgar, Dublin 6

architect:
Randal McDonnell
completion date:
1985

This development of 61 houses nestles into the mature leafy suburb of Rathgar. Like its counterpart, Willow Field in Sandymount, it achieved a housing density much higher than the established local norm. The development consists of a mix of two-, three- and four-bedroom homes, arranged in detached, semi-detached and terraced groupings. Parking is thoughtfully managed. Red-brick is used judiciously on the projecting gables piers and boundary walls, offsetting the predominant presence of rendered blockwork. Wide expanses of timber-framed glazing allow light to penetrate the deep-plan houses, particularly in the narrow two-bed units.

Women's Aid Refuge
Rathmines, Dublin 6

company:
Peter & Mary Doyle Architects
start date:
1984
completion date:
1985

This was the first purpose-built refuge in the UK and Ireland for women who suffered domestic violence and abuse. The architecture is a response to the need for protection. The building is tucked behind a high wall, ensuring the building's external street presence is anonymous. Its scale is modest and non-assertive, while the materials used are typical of domestic architecture. The single-storey accommodation comprising bedrooms, living spaces, kitchens and classrooms grouped around a central courtyard where children can play safely. A verandah provides a sheltered place for women to gather and a place to keep toys out of the rain.

Irish Life Centre
Lower Abbey Street, Dublin 1

architect:
Andy Devane
company:
Robinson, Keefe & Devane
commission date:
1971
start date:
1975
completion date:
Phase I, 1977; Phase II, 1978; Phase III, 1986

One of the first examples of comprehensive redevelopment in Dublin's north inner city, the mixed-use development of shopping and offices also includes a sizeable residential content, overlooking a raised and luxuriantly planted, multi-level courtyard. The development is conceived as a citadel within the city complete with moat and retractable drawbridge, which was an idea made current by the Barbican complex (1965-76) in London. The architectural language is adopted from the same firm's Stephen Court on St Stephen's Green. Oisín Kelly's bronze sculpture, 'The Chariot of Life', commissioned in 1978 was posthumously unveiled in 1982.

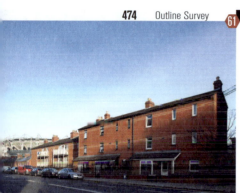

Brendan Behan Court
Russell Street,
Wellesley Place,
Dublin 1

architect:
Bernard Grimes
company:
Housing Architects Department,
Dublin Corporation
completion date:
1986

Russell Street is an exemplar of 1980s (post-City Quay competition) Dublin Corporation urban housing policy and subsequent form. Typical of this type of public housing for senior citizens, families and those with additional access needs, the scheme, comprising 65 units of varying size, makes the street edge and is of red-brick with pitched roofing. In all of this the Corporation references traditional Dublin housing such as the Dublin Artisan Dwellings and turns away from the five-storey maisonette flat block, a late example of which may be seen across the road at Fitzgibbon Street. Named in 1986 after beloved local writer, Brendan Behan, the scheme includes seven houses, eight maisonettes, 50 flats and a common room.

Avonmore Pavilion
Dublin Zoo, Phoenix Park, Dublin 8

architect:
Paul Keogh
company:
Office of Public Works
completion date:
1986 (DEMOLISHED)

This pavilion in Dublin Zoo (now demolished) was a witty exercise in Post-Modernism by Paul Keogh. It was a milking parlour for a single cow, set within a small amphitheatre built to demonstrate the milking process to urban children. Milk was served from an attached Belvedere tower. Ingeniously-scaled and evocative of vernacular farmyard structures, it perfectly captured key architectural ideas when, following the dissolution of architectural Modernism, young Irish architects were looking at historical sources: influential on Keogh were the drawings of Neo-Classical German architect, K F Schinkel and the writings of Italian architect Aldo Rossi, for instances. Later, Keogh was part of Group 91 who developed Temple Bar.

Blocks 1-2 Civic Offices
Wood Quay, Dublin 8

architect:
Sam Stephenson
company:
Stephenson Gibney and Associates, succeeded by Stephenson Associates, post-1975
commission date:
1968
start date:
1979
completion date:
1986

Possibly the most controversial buildings erected in Dublin during the 20th century, the Civic Offices blocks were the subject of mass protests during their planning because of their perceived threat both to the important Viking archaeological site and the setting of Christ Church Cathedral. The blocks' reputation was not enhanced by their monolithic militaristic appearance when they were eventually built: ten storeys, granite walls with strips of recessed glazing, prismatic and defensive, this form and aesthetic was absent from the architects' 1968 competition-winning design. Two of the proposed four towers were constructed in the first phase before the remainder of the project was abandoned, only to be completed according to a different concept and by other architects (Scott Tallon Walker) in the 1990s.

64 Mater Private Hospital
Eccles Street, Dublin 7

architect:
Tyndall Hogan Hurley
start date:
1984
completion date:
1986

The Mater Private Hospital was built on the site of No.7 Eccles Street, the home of the main character, Leopold Bloom, in James Joyce's *Ulysses*. This private hospital is co-located adjacent to one of the country's largest teaching hospitals, the Mater Hospital, founded by the Sisters of Mercy in 1852. Sr Gemma Byrne was the private hospital's first CEO when it opened in 1986. Strategically, the co-location of the two hospitals, one private and one public, was a primary factor in the decision to build on this tight urban site rather than on a greenfield site at the edge of the city. The hospital has expanded its services considerably since completion.

65 Usher's Quay Filling Station (now Circle K)
15-21 Usher's Quay, Dublin 8

architect:
Louis Burke Architects
commission date:
1985
start date:
1986
completion date:
1986

In 1985 the government introduced an Urban Renewal Scheme in Dublin, Cork and Limerick to address problems of inner-city decay. The petrol station at Usher's Quay was the first development to be completed in Dublin under that scheme. Its incongruity attests to a widespread lack of appreciation of the importance of traditional quay frontages to the integrity of the city's urban fabric. This is all the more pitiful for the fact that the UCD *Dublin City Quays Project* was published only months before planning permission for the filling station was granted. The petrol station forecourt is flanked by two slender office buildings with domed roofs and the scheme is dominated by the forecourt canopy with three large barrel-vaulted plastic roof drums and sweeping road access on either side.

66 The Dining Hall and Atrium and 'The Loos Bar'
Front Square, Trinity College Dublin, Dublin 2

architect:
Shane de Blacam
company:
de Blacam & Meagher with Trinity College Architect, Ian Roberts
commission:
1984
start:
1984
completion:
1987

This is a masterly restoration and reinvention of the Dining Hall and Senior Common Room complex following a catastrophic fire in July 1984. The four-storey, galleried-and-shuttered, American oak-clad Atrium or meeting place was slotted into the former kitchens of the Dining Hall, with the original roof trusses retained. The timber columns reduce in section as they ascend. A new interior, imitative of Adolf Loos's American Bar in Vienna, was also created for the use of the Senior Common Room members. The project won the RIAI Conservation Medal for the period 1984-86, an AAI Award in 1987 and a Europa Nostra award in 1988.

67 Merrion Village
Merrion Road,
Ballsbridge, Dublin 4

architect:
Brian O'Rourke
company:
Delany MacVeigh & Pike (later, O'Mahony Pike)
completion date:
1987

Merrion Village is a large private apartment complex formed in distinctive yellow brick and slate-clad mansard-like roofing. Comprising 150 apartments, a number of large terraced houses and a clubhouse with a swimming pool and gym for residents, Merrion Village was developed by Guy Kennedy. It represents an evolution from earlier private apartments, with increased amenity that would attract retired 'downsizers'. Fire regulations were a driving design force for the architects. The stepped balconies on the south-elevations provide private terraces and also a means of fire escape. In this unusual technological twist, the cascading balconies meant the architects were able to omit fire stairs from the scheme.

68 DIT Bolton Street Extension (now TU Dublin)
Kings Inns Street and
Loftus Place, Dublin 1

architect:
Gilroy McMahon Architects
completion date:
1987

The extension to the Dublin Institute of Technology college at Bolton Street provided a 60% increase in accommodation, including bespoke spaces for the Dublin School of Architecture. New facilities included a library, restaurant and Student Union spaces in an effort to elevate the building from feeling like a second-level educational building to presenting more like a third-level campus. The architects introduced new split-level spaces, and a triple-height atrium space overlooking an internal courtyard at the new Kings Inn Street entrance. The building's elevational treatment in red-brick and with distinctive blue aluminium windows is best along Loftus Lane where the unusual window alignment is a response to the configuration of internal spaces. The project won the RIAI Gold Medal, 1986-88.

69 Juvenile Court (now Dublin Children's Court)
Smithfield, Dublin 7

architect:
John Tuomey
company:
Office of Public Works
commissioning date:
1983
completion date:
1987

Dublin's first Juvenile Court is a mature and sophisticated essay in Post-Modernism that reinstates the street corner by extending the parapet and string course of the adjoining brick houses on Smithfield, and by taking the texture of the warehouse walls on New Church Street through in the form of a banded limestone base. The new court building expresses itself as a civic building, albeit of secondary importance, through its perfectly square and classically composed façade. It won an AAI Award in 1987 and resulted in John Tuomey being awarded The Lord Mayor's Millennium Medal for Architecture in 1988.

Dr Steevens' Hospital (now HSE HQ)
Steevens' Lane, Dublin 8

architect:
Arthur Gibney & Partners
completion date:
1987

Dr Steevens' Hospital, a 1730s building, closed in 1987 to become the administrative headquarters for the Eastern Region Health Authority (now Health Service Executive (HSE)). The adaptation involved conservation of the quadrangle and the east range of the complex, and conversion of the wards to office accommodation. The main entrance was relocated to the building's north façade which was remodelled to include new stone entrance steps, corner quoins, string course and pediment detail. The new landscaped forecourt facing Heuston Station is a positive addition to the area. The project won a Europa Nostra Award.

Clanwilliam Square
Grand Canal Quay, Dublin 2

architect:
Arthur Gibney & Partners
commissioning date:
1985
completion date:
1987

Built at the eastern end of a site formerly owned by Boland's Bakery, Clanwilliam Square is a low-rise own-door office scheme developed to meet the needs of a poorly functioning Irish (1980s) economy. Its scale reflects the fact that there was little demand for high-rise, high-specification office buildings. The buildings are arranged in short domestic-scale terraces with two octagonal pavilions at the main entrance. Originally the developers intended to build out this scheme across the entire Boland's site, but in 1986, even before the first phase was complete, they sold the remainder of the site to another developer. (See Treasury Building case study essay)

Friends Provident and Royal Hibernian Way
45-50 Dawson Street, Duke Lane, Dublin 2

architect:
Piaras Beaumont
company:
Costello Murray & Beaumont
commission date:
1982
start date:
1983
completion date:
1987/8

This sizeable office block, apartment building and shopping arcade came out of the lamented demolition and redevelopment of the Hibernian Hotel. Upon completion Frank Feely, then Dublin City Manager ran a naming competition for the scheme, resulting in 'Royal Hibernian Way'. The development rises to five storeys, with a penthouse and occupies a deep block between Dawson Street and Duke Lane, providing a new internal street and link to Grafton Street. The principal elevation addresses Dawson Street across twelve bays. This façade is strong and angular, enforced by the granite and black aluminium materials. Its muscular oriel windows were a condition of planning permission.

73. EBS Service Centre
155 Townsend Street, Dublin 2

architect:
Turlough O'Donnell and Paul Scully
company:
Turlough O'Donnell Associates
commissioning date:
1985
completion date:
1988 (DEMOLISHED)

Here we have an ingenious and assured use of a sharply triangular site, resulting in a building of real presence in a disadvantaged location. The form of the Service Centre is a right-angle triangle, with its long side facing the Dart (suburban coastal train) line and its street frontage on Spring Garden Lane. Only the apex of the building, a sharp arris of Post-Modern quoins, is on Townsend Street. Typical of the time, the architectural brickwork is offset with decorative bands of engineering brick marking each floor level. This project was shortlisted by Sean Rothery for The Sunday Tribune Arts Award for Architecture, 1988.

74. IDA Small Business Centre
Corner of Gardiner Street and Summerhill, Dublin 1

architect:
Ronnie Tallon
company:
Scott Tallon Walker Architects
start date:
1985
completion date:
1988 (DEMOLISHED)

This incubator unit for small start-up businesses was built (by the Industrial Development Authority (IDA)) to provide low-cost office space as part of a Dublin Corporation urban renewal programme. Like the nearby housing at Summerhill Court, the IDA units were set below the road level due to the sloping site. This, combined with the flat roofs and extensive planting to blend into the adjacent park, made them extremely low profile and self-effacing. The flat roof of the upper block was designed to be accessible from the street, in the manner of a park. The building was abandoned in 2005 and demolished in 2015.

75. The Pillar Project
O'Connell Street, Dublin 1

architect:
illustrated entry by Shane O'Toole, Leo Higgins, James Scanlon (drawing by Niamh Butler)
company:
various architects and artists submissions
commissioning date:
1988
start date:
1988
completion date:
1988 (UNBUILT)

The Pillar Project was a coming together to propose a potential replacement structure for Nelson's Pillar (bombed, 1966) on O'Connell Street. The project marked the loss of Nelson's Pillar as Dublin's only place of public resort at a height over the city. Shane O'Toole was the convenor. Reflecting the paper-project culture of 1980s Irish architecture, it encouraged collaboration between artists and architects. One interpretation saw Felim Egan with Sheila O'Donnell and John Tuomey, retaining the base of Nelson's Pillar as a viewing platform onto which a copy of the top, in white Portland stone, was stitched. O'Toole et al's entry was a homage to Russian artist, Kazimir Malevich. Nelson's Column was not 'replaced' until the Spire (Ian Ritchie) in 2003.

76 The Point Depot (now 3Arena)
North Wall Quay, Dublin 1

architect: Shay Cleary Architects
company: British Land
completion date: 1988

Shay Cleary Architects was commissioned to turn a large and abandoned cast-iron warehouse building (dating from 1878) into a multi-purposed concert, exhibition and conference centre. Although criticised for the quality of its acoustic installation, the building was significant for its adaptive re-use of Dublin docklands infrastructure. Its owner, Harry Crosbie, who is credited with transforming Dublin's music scene, operated the Point Depot between 1988 and 2007 as a venue for music concerts, boxing matches, operas and theatre productions. It hosted the Eurovision Song Contest on three separate occasions in the 1990s and the 1999 MTV European Music Awards. It was extensively redeveloped in 2007/8.

77 St Stephen's Green Shopping Centre
127-142 St Stephen's Green, Dublin 2

architect: James Toomey
commissioning date: 1983
start date: 1986
completion date: 1988

Standing on the site of the former Dandelion Market (closed 1981) known for its alternative vendors and site of U2's early music gigs, the five-storey St Stephen's Green shopping centre draws inspiration from historic European glass-roofed shopping arcades. In addition to having a glass roof, the building is clad almost entirely in glass with façades dressed in decorative white metal columns and grilles. Some have likened it to a wedding cake, others to a Louisiana steamboat. The building has undergone several upgrades since it first opened in 1988.

78 Royal Hibernian Academy (RHA) Gallery
Gallagher Gallery, 15 Ely Place, Dublin 2

architect: Raymond McGrath and Arthur Gibney
company: Arthur Gibney & Partners
start date: 1972
completion date: 1989

Designed and begun by Raymond McGrath, Australian Modernist architect and former principal of the OPW in 1972, this gallery project for the RHA was semi-abandoned, as an unfinished concrete shell, when McGrath died in 1977. Its realisation was taken up by Arthur Gibney from 1987 for two years (though work continued until 1991). Gibney commented on the challenges of finishing another's design, which was exacerbated by the difficult site on the plot of former Georgian houses. Oft reorganised internally and upgraded generally, most recently since 2007 by Henry J Lyons, the gallery is a rectangular box with limestone elevations replacing McGrath & Gibney's brick-clad frontage. Its asymmetric entrance sits on the long side of the building to the street.

79 Abbey Theatre Portico
Marlborough Street, Dublin 1

architect:
McCullough Mulvin Architects
start date:
1988
completion date:
1989

This addition to Dublin's famous Abbey Theatre (Ireland's National Theatre) is perhaps the most prominent work of Post-Modern architecture in the city. The two-storey Portland stone frame provides a theatrical Post-Modern 'tuning up' of the original box designed by Ronnie Tallon (of Scott Tallon Walker, see *MTCB* Vol.2). It serves to reconnect the National Theatre with the city on its doorstep, while opening a window that lets light into the first-floor bar. It makes a public event out of theatre-going. A long canopy leads the eye from Lower Abbey Street to the door and is finished by a balcony that looks towards the river.

80 Castle Hall and Conference Centre
Upper Yard, Dublin Castle, Dublin 2

architects:
Klaus Unger and Angela Rolfe
company:
Office of Public Works
commissioning date:
1984
start date:
1986
completion date:
1989

This phase of works undertaken at Dublin Castle comprised restoration of Castle Hall and the creation of a new Conference Centre. It involved the demolition of various dilapidated annexes in the Upper Yard and re-established the Georgian appearance of the buildings in their setting. The works cost £13.5 million and included the major restoration of four existing buildings, new works and the formation of new external spaces. The new two-storey structure is clad with alternative bands of Wicklow granite and Carlow limestone slabs. A lavish fit-out of the conference facilities was completed in time for the Irish Presidency of the EEC (now EU) in 1990.

81 Office Building (now Grattan Bridge House)
3 Ormond Quay, Dublin 7

architect:
Grafton Architects
commissioning date:
1986
start date:
1988
completion date:
1989

Here on Ormond Quay, the ornate Neo-Gothic limestone screen of the former Presbyterian church was retained at ground floor level, in an act of remembrance. It was collaged into a new Post-Modern façade composition for McNamara Construction, lending the infill office building a stature and presence that sets it apart from the houses lining the quayside. Rebuilt to accommodate offices, the decision to retain a portion of the existing façade – along with the proposal to construct residential mews houses on Little Strand Street to the rear – was regarded as a positive model for development by the planning authority. Nonetheless, the residential mews were later converted to office use.

Café Klara
35 Dawson Street, Dublin 2

architect:
John Meagher
company:
de Blacam & Meagher
completion date:
1989

Although it has had many iterations since it closed its doors as Cafe Klara, the conversion of the former Engineers Hall (1891) to an emporium of fine dining was selected for exhibition at the AAI Awards in 1990. Comprising a long internal space with curved ceilings, it is still considered one of the most beautiful dining rooms in Dublin. The architect, John Meagher conceived of the project as a total work of art, a *Gesamtkunstwerk* which embraced the interior forms and finishes, bespoke furniture, selection of table settings, menu design and even the contents of the wine list.

Treasury Building
Grand Canal Street Lower, Dublin 2

architect:
Henry J Lyons
commissioning date:
1987
start date:
1989
completion date:
1990

The Treasury Building is an adaptation of the former Boland's Bakery on Grand Canal Street which, for more than 50 years after it was completed in 1951, was the tallest building in the Grand Canal Dock area. Its conversion from an industrial facility to a high-specification office building in the late 1980s was unique in the city at the time, heralding the transformation in later decades of the Grand Canal Dock area. It is distinctive not only for its Post-Modern keystone motifs, blue industrial-style glazing and soaring glass and marble-clad atrium, but also for the naked figure 'Aspiration' which climbs the eastern gable. The building is undergoing major refurbishment in 2023.

Percy Lane Houses
Percy Lane, rear 13 & 15 Northumberland Road, Ballsbridge, Dublin 4

architect:
Edmondson Architects
start date:
1989
completion date:
1990

These three Percy Lane houses are notable for their generous display of Post-Modern motifs: an exuberant representation of the gimmickry that personified that short-lived architectural genre. Across four distinct volumes, there are four different roof treatments: a pedimented gable, a barrel vault, and tiled hipped roof and a mono-pitch. A salvaged Doric doorcase frames a set of first floor balcony doors, while an adjacent balustrade has hallmark Post-Modern diagonal bracing. The use of bright blue and red paint to highlight building details further solidifies the development's Post-Modern credentials.

482   Outline Survey

85 Pavee Point/ Free Church Traveller's Centre
46 Charles Street Great, Dublin 1

architect:
McCullough Mulvin Architects
completion date:
1990

This socially innovative project, a city-based community centre for Pavee Point – a NGO representing the Traveller and Roma communities – involves a revolutionary approach to adaptive re-use. Situated within the walls of an early 19th-century church (the Free Church), the architects' subtle but bold intention was to make a complete 'house', constructed in painted tin, within the confines of the existing church structure. The 'house' stands on legs on the ground rising between the existing church galleries. The new installation contains a library, workshops, offices, classrooms and a canteen.

86 International Financial Services Centre (IFSC)
North Wall Quay, Dublin 1

architect:
Benjamin Thompson (BTA+)
company:
Burke-Kennedy Doyle (BKD) Architects
commissioning date:
1986
start date:
1988
completion date:
1991

The big story of Dublin Docklands played out in the new millennium, but the transformation began in 1986 when special tax incentives were put in place to attract investment from international financial institutions. The development of the IFSC was the first attempt in more than 200 years to expand Dublin City eastwards. Originally intended to be a mini version of the City of London docklands covered by acres of trading floors, the collapse of the global markets on 'Black Monday' in 1987 limited the Dublin project's scope. American architect, Benjamin Thompson (1918-2002) of BTA+ prepared the scheme design in collaboration with the local architects, BKD. The residential, cultural and social elements of the masterplan were not realised until many years later, if at all.

87 Temple Bar Framework Plan
Temple Bar, Dublin 2

architect:
Group 91 Architects
commissioning date:
1991
completion date:
1991

Group 91 comprised a consortium of young Dublin architectural practices. Their winning competition scheme for the Temple Bar Framework Plan proposed interventions which involved stitching new uses into existing spaces and structures. The intention was to regenerate Dublin's Temple Bar area through the reuse of existing fabric, and to create a new cultural quarter. Their plan involved new streets and squares, new cultural institutional architecture and new housing. The scheme focused on the strength of Dublin's urban heritage and was pivotal in redefining government policy and implementing initiatives for the area. The Group 91 Temple Bar Architectural Framework Plan competition entry won the EU Mies Award 1996..

Irish Museum of Modern Art
Royal Hospital, Military Road, Kilmainham, Dublin 8

architect:
Shay Cleary Architects
start date:
1990
completion date:
1991

This adaptation of the Royal Hospital Kilmainham (1780s) to IMMA was accomplished and sensitive, enabling the 1780s building to house a museum of contemporary art. The form of the building allows for an enfilade of exhibition spaces overlooking the central court, with minimal intervention by the architect. A new entrance hall with a steel and glass staircase was located on the axis of the Great Hall, balancing the overall architectural composition. The courtyard is reanimated and has the qualities of a lively urban space.

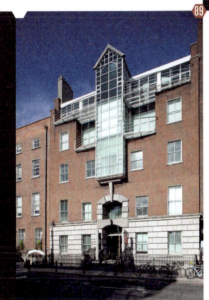

Office Building, Lower Mount Street
65-66 Lower Mount Street, Dublin 2

architect:
Paul Roche
company:
A & D Wejchert
start date:
1990
completion date:
1991

This office building presents an interesting combination of Georgian and Post-Modern architectures. Occupying a site that had lain empty for many years, the building repairs the gap with a blend of both architectural styles and a flamboyant treatment of the parapet and roof profiles. A collection of eclectic architectural motifs includes the brick façade with a stone base, capped by a recessed curtain wall. The central projecting bay window is clad and roofed in copper. White marble and polished Donegal pink granite mark out the entrance and reception walls, while black polished Kilkenny marble and stainless steel shine from the floors. The building won an RIAI Regional Award in 1992

Custom House – conservation and restoration project
Custom House Quay, Dublin 1

architect:
David Slattery
company:
Office of Public Works
commissioning date:
1984
start date:
1984
completion date:
1991

This major restoration of Gandon's Custom House led by David Slattery (conservation architect) arose from the critical need to repair hidden ferrous metal pin-pointing which was in various stages of failure. Many important lessons were learned about conservation and the future maintenance of the State's historic buildings, as a result of these extensive works which were carried out to the structural and decorative stonework. The restoration and reinstatement of the four allegorical figures above the south portico, which had lain in fragments in the grounds since the 1940s, was a fitting culmination of the painstaking process.

Larkin Theatre
Dublin City University (DCU) campus, Collins Avenue, Whitehall, Dublin 9

architect:
Deirdre O'Connor
company:
Arthur Gibney & Partners
completion date:
1991

The Larkin Theatre is the main lecture theatre in the DCU Business School. Taking the form of a brickwork drum, it mediates a sequence of pedestrian spaces on the Glasnevin/Whitehall campus. The façade of the two-storey structure is almost entirely blind, except for the main entrance doors which are located in an open ground-floor colonnade. The colonnade forms an outer concentric layer to the drum, where at first floor, the otherwise unadorned brickwork is subtly detailed into low-profile recessed panels. A concrete soffit is the only other decorative detail. The building contains a 400-seater lecture theatre used for both academic and entertainment events at the university. It is a heroic architectural moment in the DCU campus.

Earlsfort Centre
Earlsfort Terrace and Hatch Street, Dublin 2

architect:
Burke-Kennedy Doyle Architects
start date:
1989
completion date:
1991

Occupying the former Alexandra College (school) site and sitting directly across from the National Concert Hall (former University buildings of 1914), this is an extensive serpentine arrangement of office buildings. The elevational treatment is dominated by vertical redbrick bands and large expanses of mullioned glass at street level and on the upper floors. Projecting triangular glazing marks the main entrance on the corner with Hatch Street, also marking the entrance to the Alexandra House block which boasts a copper-clad mansard roof.

Stanhope Street Refuge
Stanhope Green, Stanhope Street, Dublin 1

architect:
Gerry Cahill Architects
commissioning date:
1989
start date:
1989
completion date:
1991

This much-needed sheltered housing scheme was an early collaboration between Sr Stanilaus Kennedy and architect Gerry Cahill on behalf of Focus Housing. Built in part to redevelop a range of the former convent building, Cahill brought new and old together: ten new houses were constructed to form a new courtyard that is empathetic with its surroundings. The architectural style is borrowed from Aldo Rossi, with two facing terraces of houses bookended by the rear wall of the historic convent and some single storey functional buildings. The result is reminiscent of a cloister, a place of sanctuary.

Mews Houses
10 and 11 Clyde Lane, Ballsbridge, Dublin 4

architect:
Yvonne Farrell and Shelley McNamara
company:
Grafton Architects
completion date:
1992

This pair of mews houses were conceived as two pavilions in the rear garden of a grand Victorian house on Clyde Road. While the two stone-clad façades on Clyde Lane are identical, the house volumes are distinctly different: one a cube with roof-garden, the other a long narrow volume with roof-lit first-floor studio for its artist owner. The stone 'mews' building accommodates a parking space for each house at ground level, accessed via large steel gates, with living accommodation at first floor. The gates open into the internal courtyard and shared garden overlooked by bedrooms and the studio. The scheme was nominated for an EU Mies Award 1992 and won a RIAI Regional Award in 1993.

Irish Film Centre (now Irish Film Institute [IFI])
6 Eustace Street, Temple Bar, Dublin 2

architect:
Sheila O'Donnell
company:
O'Donnell + Tuomey
commissioning date:
1986
start date:
1991
completion date:
1992

The Irish Film Centre, a crafted intervention embedded within an urban block in Dublin's Temple Bar, is seamlessly connected to its surrounding streetscape. In opening up an existing collection of buildings, the architects succeeded in creating a 'secret urban room' and a lively centre for film culture. The skilful manipulation of the buildings' existing historic fabric and the sensitive insertion of new material results in a rich and complex spatial experience, which is arguably the most successful and exciting interior sequence in Temple Bar if not, in Dublin centre. In many ways, the IFC served as a pilot project for the Group 91 Temple Bar regeneration scheme.

St Mary's Chapel of Ease/Black Church
St Mary's Place, Broadstone, Dublin 7

architect:
Healy Associates
completion date:
1992

This adaptation of a former church was one a number of such adaptations undertaken in Dublin during the 1980s and 1990s after the deconsecration of several Church of Ireland buildings. The Black Church, so-called because of the dark colour of its limestone exterior, was designed by John Semple and built in 1830. The building is remarkable for its parabolic roof which remains the key feature. The adaptation saw the insertion of galleried office spaces into the main volume, accessible by spiral staircases. The robust circular steel columns and tubular balustrades contrast with the slender and subtle detailing of the original structure.

Samuel Beckett Theatre
off New Square, Trinity College, Dublin 2

architect:
Shane de Blacam
company:
de Blacam & Meagher
commissioning date:
1990
start date:
1991
completion date:
1993

This theatre, associated spaces and teaching complex is an elegant oak-clad timber structure which is located at the north-eastern corner of New Square, Trinity College Dublin. Notable for being the only external timber-clad building on the Trinity campus, its grey weathered façades have allowed it to adapt to the context of the surrounding stone buildings. Named after the famous playwright and Trinity College alumnus, Samuel Beckett, the theatre is reminiscent of a timber Shakespearean Playhouse.

Ashford House/ DART Station
18–22 Tara Street, Dublin 2

architect:
Brian O'Halloran & Associates
start date:
1991
completion date:
1993

This was the first office building in Dublin to be constructed with direct access to a mainline and commuter train station. There are lingering touches of Post-Modernist aesthetics in its elevational treatment with heavy moulded parapets, bowed windows and a cross-braced projecting balcony high up on the corner. While the seven-storey building facing onto Tara Street is heavily stylised, the lower rear block adjoining the railway line is plain and utilitarian.

Waterways Visitor Centre
Grand Canal Quay, Dublin 2

architect:
Ciaran O'Connor
company:
Office of Public Works
start date:
1991
completion date:
1993

This visitor centre, which appears to float on the water of the Grand Canal Dock, quickly became a Dublin landmark and denoted the beginning of a new relationship between the city and its waterway amenities. The cubic form of the 'box in the docks' has nautical architectural detailing including white metal cladding, porthole windows and open guardrails on stairways and decking. A continuous band of glazing at the base of the box emphasises the floating effect both internally and externally.

100 Newman House
85–86 St Stephen's Green, Dublin 2

architect:
David Sheehan
company:
Sheehan & Barry Architects
commissioning date:
1989
completion date:
1993

Restoration works to No.85 were carried out over three phases, firstly to the Apollo Room on the ground floor and secondly, to the staircase and Saloon at first-floor level. Works included the removal of a number of nineteenth-century additions and the reinstatement of original decorative features including ornate stucco by the Swiss Lafranchini brothers. The third phase involved the cleaning, maintenance and repair of the façade and roof. This work received a Getty Foundation grant which stipulated that UCD architecture students be admitted for educational site visits. Later work to the upper floors of No.86 provided offices for the American University of Notre Dame.

101 Cusack Stand
28 Jones Road, Drumcondra, Dublin 3

architect:
Gilroy McMahon Architects
commissioning date:
1989
start date:
1992
completion date:
1994

The Cusack Stand was the first phase of the reconstruction of the GAA stadium at Croke Park, necessitated by safety concerns and growing demand for match tickets. Market research into the mix of spectators dictated the layering of the terraces and in turn dictated the architectural form. The overhang of the Cusack Stand roof was criticised for not providing adequate shelter from rain, and as a result the later stands had deeper cantilevered canopies. The completed development won the RIAI Gold Medal for 2001-2003.

102 Civic Offices
Wood Quay, Dublin 8

architect:
Scott Tallon Walker Architects
commissioning date:
1992
completion date:
1994

This second phase to the provision of Civic Offices for Dublin Corporation (now Dublin City Council) began with an architectural competition held in 1992. The winning scheme by Ronnie Tallon of Scott Tallon Walker has a totally different character to its predecessor of 1986, but shares some architectural features such as material cladding and building height. The Neo-Modernist structure, clad in grey Wicklow granite, addresses Dublin's south quay with an expanse of granite steps leading to the main entrance. The building houses an impressive civic space, finely detailed with a landscaped atrium which is traversed by elegant glazed bridges.

103

The Printworks
25–27 East Essex Street, Temple Bar, Dublin 2

architect:
Derek Tynan
company:
Group 91 Architects
start date:
1993
completion date:
1994

A mixed-use development comprising on-street commercial development, significant studio space, apartments and a shared raised courtyard space in Dublin's Temple Bar, the Printworks is part of the Group 91 Framework plan. The scheme is a well-crafted example of urban renewal, making something of a hidden landscape in the city which might be abstractly understood as an ensemble of sculpted voids and built forms. Most importantly, the Printworks brings healthy bright homes to Temple Bar. Unusually for Dublin, and signalling a new collective housing organisational form, these residential units are accessed via a raised internal courtyard.

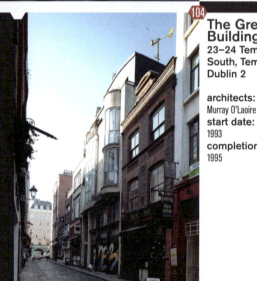

104

The Green Building
23–24 Temple Lane South, Temple Bar, Dublin 2

architects:
Murray O'Laoire Architects
start date:
1993
completion date:
1995

The Green Building was a showcase project for the regeneration of Temple Bar, designed as a flagship for energy technologies which would have minimal impact on the environment. According to the architects, it was a 'self-conscious exploration of the possibilities of greening the urban fabric.' As well as using several renewable energy sources – windmills, solar collectors and photovoltaic cells – the decorative elevation details are made from reused and recommissioned found objects such as balcony ironmongery shaped from bicycle frames.

105

Temple Bar Gallery and Studios (and Black Church Print Studio)
4 Temple Bar, Dublin 2

architect:
Valerie Mulvin
company:
McCullough Mulvin Architects
start date:
1993
completion date:
1995

Temple Bar Gallery and Studios (TBGS) was established in 1982 in the Maureen Buildings, a former shirt factory. Out of this commission, the architects moved the access to TBGS to the corner of Fownes Street while part of the site to the west was developed as the Black Church Print Studio. The latter was cited by the RIAI as 'a controlled essay in the use of classical modernist principles'. Though adjoined and designed by the same architects, the Print Studio and TBGS are separate entities folded into the Group 91 Temple Bar Framework Plan. As modern insertions into pre-existing structures, they architecturally epitomise the aspirations for Temple Bar.

The Ark
11 Eustace Street, Temple Bar, Dublin 2

architect:
Shane O'Toole and Michael Kelly
company:
Group 91 Architects
commissioning date:
1992
start date:
1994
completion date:
1995

This cultural centre for children – the first such purpose-built facility in Europe – is housed on the site of a former Presbyterian Meeting House (1728) and incorporates the carefully restored front façade of the church. The rear wall of the stage was designed with the assistance of Spanish engineer-architect Santiago Calatrava and allows the theatre space to address Meeting House Square. Here we find the first use in Ireland of ground-sourced, water-cooled, air-conditioning condensers, and of pre-patinated copper cladding.

Arthouse (later Filmbase)
Curved Street, Temple Bar, Dublin 2

architect:
Shay Cleary
company:
Group 91 Architects
commissioning date:
1992
start date:
1994
completion date:
1995

Curved Street was one of the major interventions in the Group 91 Temple Bar Framework Plan, opening up the east-west access by connecting Temple Lane South to Eustace Street and the newly created Meeting House Square. It was designed between Niall McCullough and Shay Cleary. The latter designed the largely glazed multi-media art centre, Arthouse, which forms the street's southern edge. Light is filtered through the building's three-storey atrium to alleviate dark shadows on the narrow street. The interior is a series of interlocking public spaces, supplemented with smaller offices and meeting rooms. Due in part to its overly-shallow site, it has been difficult to inhabit and is arguably the least successful of the Temple Bar cultural buildings.

Offices and housing at Ormond Quay
28-31 Ormond Quay Lower, Dublin 1

company:
Shaffrey Associates Architects
commission date:
1989
completion date:
1995

The site, formerly earmarked for a Bus Interchange, was bought by Patrick Shaffrey and his brothers in 1989. No.29, dating from 1680, was refurbished as offices for Shaffrey Associates with an apartment overhead. Subsequently, the derelict sites on either side were developed: No.28 contains seven apartments over a shop, while Nos.30-31 houses thirteen apartments. Materials include Flemish bond brickwork, natural slate and artist-commissioned mosaic decoration. The roofscape is particularly interesting with large decorative chimney stacks. The project represented a hopeful, well-considered and forward-thinking mixed-use interpretation of Dublin's quayside architecture.

109

Housing at Bride St / Golden Lane
Corner of Bride Street and Golden Lane, Dublin 8

architect:
Eugene Gribben
company:
Dublin Corporation City Architects
commission date:
1993
start date:
1994
completion date:
1995

Situated across the road from Iveagh Buildings (1904, MTCB Vol.1), the lively architecture of this social housing scheme mirrors its neighbour, using clay brick, reconstituted sandstone, copper and slate. The five-storey corner block is notable for its distinctive copper-clad barrel-vaulted roof with double-height glazing and triple-height panels of glass blocks on its corner edges. The barrel-vault detail is repeated on each street elevation. Influenced by contemporary housing schemes in other European cities, all but ten of the 59 dwellings have their own front door. To the rear, a small mews courtyard is lined by two-storey dwellings. Eight terracotta roundels on the façade commemorate Jonathan Swift's *Gulliver's Travels* (by Michael C Keane).

110

British Embassy
29 Merrion Road, Ballsbridge, Dublin 4

company:
Allies and Morrison
commissioning date:
1991
start date:
1993
completion date:
1995

With a formally composed granite façade to Merrion Road and a brick façade to the rear, the British Embassy reflects the character of the Ballsbridge Victorian villa context in which it is built. The embassy is arranged around a central courtyard, creating a private and protected external space. Security was a primary concern in the development of the design, yet the architects sought to create a grand villa appropriate to its affluent suburban location.

111

Millennium Tower
Charlotte Quay, Ringsend Road, Dublin 4

architect:
O'Mahony Pike Architects
completion date:
1995

One of the first brownfield developments in the Docklands area, this landmark building is home to 242 apartments, offices and a café/bar. Rising to 17 storeys, with adjacent blocks of five to seven storeys, the main volume is clad in white concrete with broad windows surveying the city. The tower responds to its significant location, placed firmly within the cityscape. It was the tallest residential building in Dublin at the time of its completion

112 Curvilinear Range
National Botanic Gardens, Glasnevin, Dublin 9

architect:
Ciaran O'Connor and Michael Carroll
company:
Office of Public Works
start date:
1991
completion date:
1995

When this project was commissioned, the glasshouse was in an advanced state of decay and was in fact, closed to the public. The restoration works undertaken are notable for their technical achievements in terms of how to re-forge and reform existing cast iron. In so doing, the restoration improved the material's structural strength. Much of the cast iron used was left over from a 1970s restoration works at the Kew Gardens Range in London. The Dublin project won a Europa Nostra Medal for the excellent quality of the restoration and for the innovation and development of cast-iron restoration techniques.

113 Temple Bar Square and Temple Bar Buildings
Crown Alley and Temple Bar, Dublin 2

architect:
Grafton Architects
company:
Group 91 Architects
commissioning date:
1991
start date:
1994
completion date:
1996

Temple Bar Square and Buildings form a pivotal social space in Dublin's Temple Bar; they were conceived as part of the Group 91 Temple Bar Framework Plan. The buildings comprise apartments over shops and restaurants. The façade composition of glass, steel and brick was inspired by the former Gas Retort House in Ringsend. Due to change in levels inhibiting universal access and commercial pressures pushing the change in uses of the public spaces, the success of Temple Bar Square has been compromised. It is being redeveloped by Dublin City Council at the time of writing (2023).

114 Dolan House
**Anglesea Road
40A Anglesea Road, Ballsbridge, Dublin 4**

architect:
Noel Dowley
completion date:
1996

This large house on a 'left-over' site in inner suburbia was one of Noel Dowley's (d.2023) last projects. He described it as a 'domestic expression of [the] Architecture of wall, light and garden'. A disciple (and former student) of Louis Kahn, Dowley's work is defined by modesty in nature, scale and expression. In this case, the expression is decidedly Modernist, with the use of reinforced concrete and glass block and slender flat canopies over the entrance doors.

115 Gallery of Photography (now Photo Museum Ireland)
Meeting House Square, Temple Bar, Dublin 2

architect: O'Donnell + Tuomey
company: Group 91 Architects
commissioning date: 1991
start date: 1994
completion date: 1996

Conceived as part of the Group 91 Temple Bar Framework Plan, the Gallery of Photography/Photo Museum of Ireland displays an elegant Portland stone façade and houses a shallow double-height gallery space overlooking Meeting House Square. The skilfully designed façade enables the screening of outdoor films from the National Photographic Archive (also by O'D + T, National Library of Ireland) opposite. In 2009, O'D+T added a new roof-level extension to the Gallery, called The LightRoom. This extension reads like a set-back glazed and canopied angular cap or cornice to the original Gallery.

116 Parsons Laboratory
Trinity College, Dublin 2

architect: Grafton Architects
commissioning date: 1994
start date: 1995
completion date: 1996

The Parsons Laboratory extension is an ably crafted and abstract addition to an existing 18th-century building. The form is context-driven: the solidity of the podium conceals the gritty interior of the engineering workshop while the apparently skewed basalt cube is perfectly aligned with the front façade of the adjacent Chemistry building. Continuing the university's notably excellent architectural patronage, this building makes a significant contribution to development of the Trinity College campus in the 1990s and a welcome element of good design to the campus' more hotchpotch east end.

117 Viking Centre/Smock Alley Theatre
6-7 Exchange Street Lower, Temple Bar, Dublin 2

architect: Gilroy McMahon Architects
commissioning date: 1991
start date: 1994
completion date: 1996

The former Church of SS Michael and John was purchased by Temple Bar Properties in 1991 with the intention of encouraging development at the western end of Temple Bar. Subsequent archaeological excavations revealed the original Smock Alley Theatre of 1662 and Gilroy McMahon's design responded accordingly. The building operated as a Viking Centre tourist attraction from 1996 until 2002. In 2012, it was converted (by O'Keeffe Architects) to once again become Smock Alley Theatre – a truly circular architectural history for this site.

118 Herbert Park Hotel and Apartments
Ballsbridge Terrace, Ballsbridge, Dublin 4

company:
O'Mahony Pike Architects
commissioning date:
1993
completion date:
1998

A technically accomplished large scheme on the banks of the Dodder, this primarily residential development consolidated O'Mahony Pike's reputation as one of Ireland's best housing architectural firms. Importantly, the scheme integrated the former backland site into Ballsbridge village and improved access to the public amenity of Herbert Park. The scheme includes a new bridge over the River Dodder connecting Anglesea Road with the park.

119 Heytesbury Lane
Mews House
78 Heytesbury Lane, Dublin 4

company:
de Blacam & Meagher Architects
start date:
1996
completion date:
1998

This mews house is an innovative design comprising a well-crafted timber atrium, which redefines the concept of an urban mews. The house, located on a narrow mews plot of a late Georgian terrace in Dublin, includes a living area on the ground floor which connects the entrance court in the east to the garden in the west. The internal atrium opens three sides of the house to natural light and creates a third façade.

120 Wolfe Tone Square
Jervis Street, Dublin 1

architect:
Peter Cody
company:
Boyd Cody Architects
completion date:
1998

This site was originally a graveyard for the Church of Ireland parish of Saint Mary's. The church sold it to Dublin Corporation in the 1960s, after which it was enclosed and used as a park. In 1998, as part of the 200-year anniversary of the 1798 rebellion, and in the name of the HARP urban renewal programme, Dublin City Council held an international competition for the space's landscape redesign. This was won by young architect, Peter Cody whence he designed the space in a more open albeit minimalist manner, with the buildings visually closing the space.

121 Ranelagh Multi-Denominational School
Ranelagh Road, Ranelagh, Dublin 6

architect: O'Donnell + Tuomey
start date: 1997
completion date: 1998

An elegant brick and timber building, this school's materials and scale successfully address its context on Ranelagh Road. The school comprises a complex and interwoven collection of interior and exterior spaces. The urban composition with Mountpleasant Square is considered, with a dialogue between the landscaped gardens to the rear and the adjacent Georgian terraces. The building has been nominated for many awards and received the RIAI Gold Medal for the period 1998-2000 and the AAI Downes Medal 1999.

122 O'Reilly Institute
Trinity College Campus (east end), Westland Row, Dublin 2

architect: Ronnie Tallon
company: Scott Tallon Walker Architects
completion date: 1998

The focal point of the O'Reilly Institute is a large glass atrium which acts as the interface between refurbished Georgian houses on Westland Row (city-side) and a new lab building towards the campus. This naturally ventilated space was the first atrium garden designed by Scott Tallon Walker Architects. In addition, the atrium reduced noise levels from the adjoining elevated railway line. The deep-plan laboratory building has a central garden to bring light into the scheme.

123 Trinity Dental Hospital
Trinity College, Lincoln Place, Dublin 2

architect: Ahrends Burton Koralek
completion date: 1998

The dental hospital presents another significant element of Trinity's extensive building programme of the 1990s. A sweeping curve of brickwork with Aldo Rossi's signature small square window openings connects the existing Victorian dental hospital (1896) with a new clinic building that sits on the curtilage of the university at Lincoln Place. A full-height glass atrium is enclosed between the old and the new buildings, acting as the circulation hub. A second stairwell at the hinge between the curved wall and the new clinic building rises above the parapet line as a slender glass block tower.

124 Smock Alley Court
Essex Street West, Temple Bar, Dublin 2

architect:
Horan Keogan Ryan Architects
completion date:
1998

Smock Alley Court is significant in being the only social housing scheme commissioned by Temple Bar Properties. Occupying most of the remaining city block to the west of Smock Alley Theatre, the red and yellow brick elevations are enlivened by a mint-green ceramic tiled finish to the ground floor shops on Essex Street and Fishamble Street. There is a landscaped courtyard at the centre of the scheme.

125 School of Design for Industry, NCAD
National College of Art and Design, 100 Thomas Street, Dublin 8

architect:
Mary Doyle
company:
Peter and Mary Doyle Architects /
Burke-Kennedy Doyle Architects
commissioning date:
1986
completion date:
1999

This building for the National College of Art and Design (NCAD) was originally commissioned in 1986 when Peter and Mary Doyle Architects were invited to devise a masterplan for the development of the campus. Works at that time included the creation of 'Red Square' which now acts as the building's forecourt. The project, which was to be the first new building on the campus, stalled and was eventually reactivated in 1994. Because of Peter Doyle's illness and death in 1995, Mary Doyle completed the project with the assistance of her daughter, Ann Doyle, also an architect.

126 Millennium Bridge
connecting Eustace Street, Dublin 1 to Ormond Quay Lower, Dublin 1

architect:
Sean Harrington
company:
Howley Harrington Architects
commissioning date:
1997
start date:
1998
completion date:
1999

The Millennium Bridge is the second pedestrian-only bridge to cross the Liffey after the Ha'penny Bridge (1815). A low-lying unobtrusive design, it was the winning entry to a competition in 1998 to select a design to celebrate the new millennium. The low profile creates a visual, as well as physical connection from one side of the river to the other. Its sophisticated detailing includes a gently arching timber walkway, brass leaning rails and custom-made manhole covers which commemorate its construction.

127

Entrance Pavilion Dublin Zoo
Dublin Zoo, Phoenix Park, Dublin 8

architect:
Michael Tallon
company:
Scott Tallon Walker Architects
commissioning date:
1997
completion date:
1999

The entrance pavilion to Dublin Zoo presents the visitor with a long, linear single-storey pavilion set between the lake and the public road. Its public or entrance façade, to the south is clad in Wicklow granite with a slender overhanging roof providing shelter from rain and acting as a *brise-soleil* (sun shade) to reduce solar heat gain in the interior.

128

Thirteen Denzille Preview Theatre (later Clarence Pictures)
13 Denzille Lane, Dublin 2

architect:
Shelley McNamara
company:
Grafton Architects
commissioning date:
1995
completion date:
1999

This preview theatre on Denzille Lane was Ireland's first and (at the time) only purpose-built movie preview theatre. Occupying a long and narrow mews plot, this well-crafted building makes a connection between the lane and main house, via the garden. Organised around an external staircase, the envelope and interior are skilfully detailed.

129

1 Castle Street
Corner of Castle and Werburgh Streets, Dublin 2

architect:
John Meagher
company:
de Blacam & Meagher
commissioning date:
1997
start date:
1998
completion date:
1999

No.1 Castle Street is a well-crafted corner building which addresses the scale and materiality of its surrounding context, in a historic part of Dublin city. Situated opposite Christ Church Cathedral and close to Dublin Castle, this prominent site on the corner of Castle and Werburgh Streets was redeveloped to provide a retail unit at ground level, offices at first and second-floor levels, and a penthouse apartment at third and fourth-floor levels.

Three Houses in Rathmines
Cambridge Lane, Rathmines, Dublin 6

architect:
Dermot Boyd, Paul Kelly, Deirdre Whelan
company:
Boyd Kelly Whelan Architects, later Boyd Cody Architects and FKL Architects
start date:
1997
completion date:
1999

This terrace of houses is an innovative interpretation of urban mews development, creating three adjacent homes along a Rathmines laneway. As an investigation into the changing needs of domestic housing, the scheme pushed the limits of mews development and achieved a new level of density for a back lane development in the inner suburbs. Designed for three individual clients (two of whom were the architect-owners), the terrace demonstrates the variation achievable within repeated forms.

The Bookend
18-22 Essex Quay, Dublin 8

architect:
Deirdre O'Connor
company:
Arthur Gibney & Partners
completion date:
1999

This unusual building turns its flank towards the River Liffey and addresses itself to the setting sun. Despite, or because of its quirky nature, it is regarded as a positive addition to the south-side quays. The west elevation, which contains recessed balconies, is framed by the floating ends of the front and rear walls and is capped by the slender roofline which hovers above the recessed upper floor. The tapering piece of ground on its west side forms a small urban park on the quays.

A&L Goodbody
North Wall Quay, Dublin 1

company:
Scott Tallon Walker Architects
commissioning date:
1997
completion date:
1999

Built as part of the IFSC development, this office scheme was one of the first of the docklands office buildings on North Wall Quay, and a herald of what was to come. The form evolved from a desire to maximise natural daylight to all working areas. The Dublin Docklands Development Authority, as the Master Plan commissioning body, stipulated that the river elevation had to be part of a continuous and connected street façade; meaning that the building is perhaps too squat for its width and within the context of the broad campshire in front.

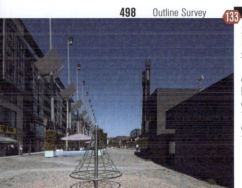

Smithfield Phase I
Smithfield, Dublin 7

company:
McGarry Ní Éanaigh
commissioning date:
1997
completion date:
1999

This scheme was the winning entry in the Dublin Corporation Smithfield International Design Competition of 1997. The design turned a windswept surface car park into a civic space with a capacity for approximately 12,000 people. The notable ground surface is made up of the original granite setts which were repaired and supplemented with granite slabs. The space is dominated by twelve 26.5m high gas brazier masts along the west side.

The Wooden Building
Exchange Street Upper, Dublin 2

company:
de Blacam & Meagher Architects
commissioning date:
1995
completion date:
2000

Here at the Wooden Building we find trademark de Blacam & Meagher architectural geometry and meticulous material detailing – including copper, brick and white render. These aspects ensure that the building sits comfortably within the tightly-packed site of west Temple Bar. The density of the development is relieved by an internal courtyard garden and generous terraces at third, fifth and eighth floors. Each apartment enjoys east-west orientation with views to the street and to the garden; and from the shared stairwell, to Dublin Castle. The building's distinctive roof profile includes a large copper canopy and a notched brick parapet. It has won several architectural awards.

Cow's Lane mixed use development
within the city block bounded by Essex Street, Fishamble Street and Lord Edward Street, Dublin 2

company:
Anthony Reddy Associates
commission date:
1995
start date:
1996
completion date:
2000

The clearance of a large industrial site between Lord Edward and Essex Streets allowed for the creation of a new street, Cow's Lane. Though wider due to contemporary fire safety requirements, Cow's Lane follows the alignment of an original medieval street. The bounding west-side structure is a five/six-storey apartment building, with shops at ground floor. Clad in brick and reconstituted stone with large timber windows and in-frame balustrades, the scheme is identified by a series of street lamps that run parallel to the façade. These interrupt the vista to the Church of Saints Michael and John, now Smock Alley Theatre, which has been cause for some criticism.

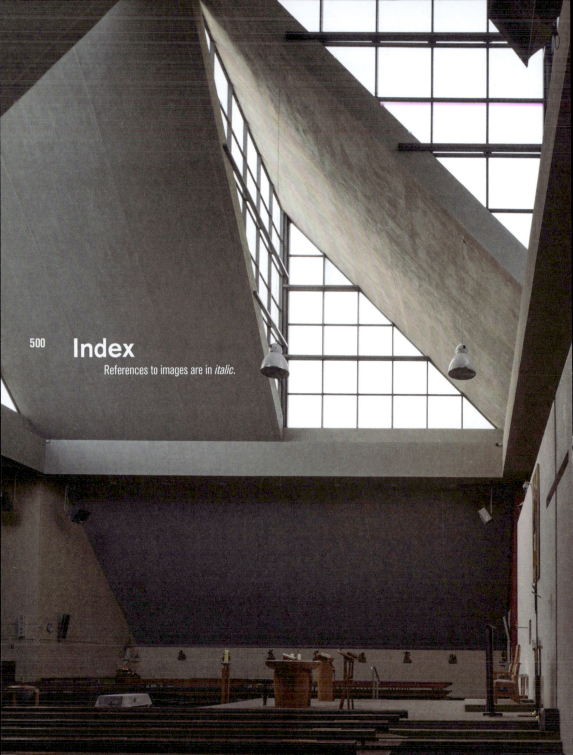

Index

References to images are in *italic*.

1 Castle Street, Dublin 2 496
3Arena (Point Depot) 479

Aalto, Alvar 269, 445
Abbey Homesteads 262, 264
Abbey Theatre Portico 480
abortion referendum 40, 436
Access Cinema 374
Act of Union (Ireland) (1800) 85
Agricultural Institute 411
Agriculture House, Dublin 2 457
Ahrends Burton Koralek (ABK) 29, 56, 312, 412, 463, 494
AIB Bankcentre, Ballsbridge 25, 29, 31, 45, 86, 174–87, 464
    artwork in 181
Air Pollution Act (1987) 253
A&L Goodbody, Dublin 1 497
Alexandra College, Milltown 29, 178, 454
Allies and Morrison 55, 407, 412, 415, 490
American Bar (Kärtner Bar), Vienna 309, 316
An Bord Pleanála 286–8
An Bord Tráchtála 77
An Foras Talúntais 411
An Taisce 44, 50–1, 287, 351, 443
An Taoiseach's Residence, Phoenix Park, competition for 465
AnCO 215–17
AnCO Training Centre, Finglas 214–23, 467
    roof structure 218
Anderson, Denis 463
Anna Livia sculpture 44
Archer's Garage, Fenian Street 55
Architectural Association, UK (AA) 337
Architectural Association of Ireland 36
architectural competitions 157, 226, 465 *see also* Dublin Diocesan Church Competition; housing competitions
Architectural Review 23, 30
Ardnacrusha hydroelectric station 108
Ark Cultural Centre for Children, Temple Bar 52, 35, 359–60, 367, 489
Armstrong, Robert 389
Art Deco 43, 328
Artane Boys' Band *265*
Artane Industrial School 262
    graveyard 262–5, 270, 272
Artane Oratory of the Resurrection, Beaumont 260–73, 471
Arthouse (Filmbase), Temple Bar 374, 489
Arts Council of Ireland 381, 383
Arup, Ove 191, 194, 198
Arup, Ove, & Partners 120, 198, 204
Ash Grove, The Coombe 28, 129, 134–8, 140–1, 144–5, 146, 461
Ashford House/DART Station, Dublin 2 486
Ashlin, George O. 005, 040
Ashlin Coleman 335
ASK Group 331
Asplund, Erik Gunnar 301, 303

Atkins, Annie 114
Atlantic Technological University (Galway–Mayo Institute of Technology) 317
AXA *see* PMPA headquarters

Bach & Mora 52, 356
Bachelors Walk 396
Ballyfermot Public Library 468
Ballymun 97, 101, 132, 138
Bank of Ireland 85–6
Bank of Ireland headquarters, Baggot Street 25, 29, 82–93, 177, 458
    artworks 88
    LEED rating 84
Bannon, Michael 121
Barcelona 52, 355–6
Barrett, Jim 461
Barrett, Richard 329
Barrett, Sylvester (Sylvie) 101
Barrow Milling 324
Barry, Matthew 237, 247, 470
Barry & Associates 237, 470
Beaumont, Piaras 477
Beckett Theatre *see* Trinity College Dublin
Beigel, Florian 373
Benson, Frank 465
Bernard Seymour Landscape Architects 284
Billings, Seán 423
Bird Market, Bride Street 64, 66
Birr Community School 38
64, 66
Black Church Print Studio 53, 488
Blackrock Shopping Centre 43
Bloody Sunday (1972) 27, 411
Blue Studio 35, 361
Blythe, Ernest 21
Bohigas, Oriol 356–7
Boland, Patrick 322
Boland's Bakery/Mills 321–5, 331
Bookend, Dublin 8 497
Boyd Cody Architects 493
Boyd Kelly Whelan Architects 497
Boyle + Delaney 29, 459
Bradley, John 42
Brendan Behan Court, Dublin 1 474
Bride Street/Golden Lane housing, Dublin 8 55, 64, 490
British Embassy, Ballsbridge 55, 406–15, 490
    former building 411–12
British Land 77
British Overseas Estates Department 412
Brown, Neave 361
Browne, Fred 110, 117, 460
Browne, Noel 101
BTA+ 482
Bulfin, Michael 93
    Reflections 88, 90
Burgh, Thomas 56
Burke, John 93
    Red Cardinal 90, 92

Burke, Louis, Architects 44, 475
Burke-Kennedy, Paul 462
Burke-Kennedy Doyle (BKD) Architects 53, 467, 482, 484, 495
Burolandschaft 79–80
Byrne, Derek 328
Byrne, Mairead 382–3
Byrne, Seamus 127

Café Klara, Dublin 2 481
Cahill, Gerry 35, 335, 337–45, *342*, 347, 361
Cahill, Gerry, Architects 55, 339, 484
Calatrava, Santiago 360
Cambridge Court sheltered housing, Dublin 4 472
Campbell, Gordon 442–6
Campbell, Hugh 433
Campbell Conroy Hickey 144
campuses 237, 249, 335, 342–3 *see also* RTÉ Campus; University College Dublin (UCD) Campus
    corporate 25, 175, 177–8
    hospital 253–5
    housing *see* Stanhope Green
    industrial 44
    school 29
    university 44, 309, 417–21
Caomhánach, Br 264
Carroll, Michael 491
Carroll's Factory, Dundalk 219
Casey, Christine 127, 400
Casino, Marino, restoration 471
Castle, Richard 310
Castle Hall and Conference Centre, Dublin Castle 480
Castle House, Dublin 2 456
Castle Street mixed-use building, Dublin 8 55, 440–51
Catholic Church 29, 149, 156, 434, 436
Celtic Tiger 53, 321
Central Bank, Dame Street 30, 39–41, 78, 177, 200–13, 288
Central Bank Currency Centre, Sandyford 30, 39–40, 203
Central Bank of Ireland, Temple Bar 203, 465
Chamabel 328
Chapel of Reconciliation, Knock, Co. Mayo 37
Chatham House, Dublin 2 458
Chidlow, Rachael 41, 361, 365
Children Court *see* Juvenile Court, Smithfield
Christian Brothers 261, 262–5
Church of the Holy Trinity, Donaghmede 29, 148–61, 462
Church of Our Lady, Blessington 156
CIÉ 351, 354, 381–2
Cinecittà 373
City Architecture Studio 361, 395–6
City of Dublin Electricity Works 108
City Hall 56
City Quay, Dublin 2 129–30, 136–7,
    140, *142*, 143–5, 146, 462
Clanwilliam Square, Dublin 2 477
Clarence Pictures (Thirteen Denzille Preview Theatre), Dublin 2 496
Cleary, Shay 56, 470, 489
Cleary, Shay, Architects 479, 483
Cleary and Hall 469, 470
Clyde Lane mews houses, Ballsbridge 485
Cody, Peter 493
Collins, Fr Joe 152–4, 160
Collins Barracks 56
Combat Poverty Agency 335–6, 339
Commercial Buildings, Central Bank Plaza 206–7, 210
Commitments, The 49, 93
community schools 38–9
Community Schools competition 36, 157
compulsory purchase orders (CPOs) 143
conservation 41, 52, 56, 139, 195, 309, 315, 372, 393, 483
Cooley, Thomas 56
Coombe North *see* Ash Grove, Dublin 8
Córas Tráchtála (CTT) 77, 80
Cork Institute of Technology 317
Corless, Catherine 263–4
Corr, Frank 269, 273
Costello, J.J. 165
Costello, Murray & Beaumont 42, 477
Cow's Lane development, Dublin 2 498
Craig, Maurice 50
Crampton, G&T 100, 311
Cranberries, the 49
Creeslough church, Co. Donegal 269–71, *271*
Cricketers' Way, Andover, Hampshire 97, 100
Crimmins, Cathal 339–40, 472
Critical Regionalism 448
Croke, Michael 194
Croke Park, Cusack Stand 487
Crosbie, Harry 444
Cross, Chris 361
Crown Hall, Illinois Institute of Technology 218
Cullen, T.J. 383–4
Cullinan, Michael 402
Curragh Carpets 193
Currency Commission 203
Curtis Printworks, Temple Lane 393
Custom House 56, 226
    conservation and restoration 483
Custom House Docks 44, 227–9, 321
Custom House Docks Development *54*
Custom House Docks Authority 53, 228
Custom House Docks Quarter 228

Dalkey School Project (DSP) 38, 434–6
Daly, Cyril 263–4
Dandelion Market 43
Darbourne, J.W. 144
Darbourne + Drake 141, 144
Darley, Hugh 310

Darndale Housing Estate, Coolock
  28, 94–105, 141, 458
  community centre 101
  refurbishment 95–6, 102–3
Dawson Street 42
de Blacam, Shane 317, 319, 445, 475,
  486
de Blacam & Meagher 42, 55, 56, 165,
  168–71, 309, 312–13, 316–17, 319,
  445, 448, 463, 475, 481, 486, 493,
  496, 498
de Burca, Máirín 28
de Paor, Tom 360
De Rossa, Prionsias 217
de Valera, Éamon 23–4, 322–3
de Vere White, Terence 165–6
Delaney, Miriam 141
Delany McVeigh Pike 140–1, 145,
  146, 148, 461, 466, 476
Denzille Lane Cinema and Apartments
  55
Department of Health 84
Devane, Andrew 31, 175, 179–84, 186,
  285, 287–93, 294, 464, 473
Diamond Redfern Anderson 30, 144,
  463, 471
Dinh, Raymond 98–9, 102–3
divorce referendum (1986) 40–1, 436
DMOD Architects 101
Dolan House, Ballsbridge 491
Donaghmede 149–50 *see also* Church
  of the Holy Trinity
  schools 150–1
Donaghmede Shopping Centre 149, 150
Donat, John 191, 195
Donnelly, Martin 315
Donnybrook Fire Station 469
Dowley, Noel 491
Doyle, Mary 38, 495
Doyle, Peter 29, 38
Doyle, Peter and Mary, Architects 473,
  495
Doyle, Roger 114
Dr Steevens' Hospital (HSE
  headquarters), Dublin 8 477
Drumalee Estate, Stoneybatter 145
Dublin
  European City of Culture (1991)
    49, 201, 355
  medieval areas 121, 139, 338,
    442, 448
  population 24, 54–5, 139, 240
  road planning 139–41
Dublin 4 area 72
Dublin Castle 56, 480
Dublin City Council 83, 208, 245, 329
  Heritage Office 453
Dublin City University (DCU), Larkin
  Theatre 484
Dublin City Quays Project *see* University
  College Dublin
Dublin Civic Group 287
Dublin Civic Offices, Wood Quay 56,
  474, 487

Dublin Civic Trust 50, 442–3
Dublin Corporation 20, 23, 25, 28, 73, 30,
  95, 129, 130, 138–9, 141, 143–5, 217,
  244, 285–8, 303, 315, 442
  Architects Department 102
  City Architects 145, 146, 196, 460,
    469, 474, 490
  Housing Committee 97, 138
  Housing Department 287, 460
  housing competition (1975) 129, 141–4
  Remedial Works Scheme 102
Dublin Diocese 149, 151–2
Dublin Diocesan Church Competition
  36, 149, 152, 155
Dublin docklands 53–4, 107, 114, 211, 225,
  228, 237, 245, 325, 361
Dublin Docklands Development
  Authority 54
Dublin Institute of Technology, Bolton
  Street extension 476
Dublin Open House 114
Dublin Port Authority 226
Dublin Port Centre Building, Dublin 1
  224–35
Dublin Port Company 225, 229, 468
Dublin Port and Docks Board 226, 228,
  229, 232
  Ballast Office 227
Dublin Urban Study 289
Dublin Zoo
  Avonmore Pavilion 474
  Entrance Pavilion 56, 496
Duggan, Charles 453
Duke House Properties (DHP) 324
Dundalk Courthouse 301–2
Dunne, Aidan 389
Dunphy, Austin 471
Dwyer, Conor 229–30, 235

Earlsfort Centre, Dublin 2 484
economic growth 23–4, 53, 226–7
Edmondson Architects 481
Educate Together 38, 436
education system 434–6
Educational Building Society (EBS)
  development, Dublin 2 459
  Service Centre 478
Education and Training Boards 215
Egan, Felim 401
Eighth Amendment to the Constitution
  40
Electricity Supply Board (ESB) 27–8,
  107–11, 113–15, 117
  headquarters 208
Emergency *see* Second World War
English Heritage 315
Enterprise Ireland 77
European Economic Community (EEC) 24
European Regional Development Fund 355
European Social Fund 216
Eustace Street, Temple Bar 53

Farrell, Yvonne 36, 41, 169, 419, 424, 427,
  485

Fay, Raymond 232
Fehily, Jim 181, 183, 186
Fehily, Monsignor Thomas 193
Fellini, Federico 373
Festival of Irish Arts and Culture, RCA (1980) 168–9
Fibonacci Square, Ballsbridge 176
Filmbase (Arthouse), Temple Bar 374, 489
Finance Act (1986) 44
Finglas 215, 217
Fingleton, Sean 383
Finnegan Menton 77
Firhouse 151
FitzGerald, Garret 102
Fitzgibbon Court, Dublin 129–34, 139–40, 146, 460
Fitzpatrick, John 418
Fitzwilliam Lawn Tennis Club, Ranelagh 455
FKL 55, 497
Fleischmann, George 109–11
Fleming, Lionel 107
Fletcher, Anne 41
'Flying Circus' 337, 361
Flynn, Pádraig 340
Focus Housing Association 340
Focus Ireland (Focus Point) 335, 339 *see also* Stanhope Green
Forbairt 77
Ford Foundation building, New York 78
Forticrete 335
Fouere, Olwen 114
Forum Architects 412
Frampton, Kenneth 361, 448
Franck, Martine 95
Frascati Centre 43
Friends of Medieval Dublin 28
Friends Provident Centre, Dublin 2 42, 477

Gaiety School of Acting, Temple Bar 360, 367
Gallagher, Vincent 454
Gallagher Group 151
Gallery of Photography (Photo Museum Ireland), Temple Bar 52, 359–60, 367, 492
Galway–Mayo Institute of Technology (Atlantic Technological University) 317
Gandon, James 56, 85
Gardiner, Luke 19, 285
Georgian architecture 19, 36, 41, 83, 86–7, 91, 121, 285, 429–31
    pastiche 54, 66, 166
Gibney, Arthur 61–9, 71, 73, 77–81, 204, 412, 455, 479
Gibney, Arthur, & Partners 29, 39, 53, 467, 477, 484, 497
Gibson, Sir Donald 210
Gillespie, Rowan, 'Aspiration' 329
Gilroy McMahon Architects 56, 476, 487, 492
Glenageary School 434
Glendon, Tom 193, 265–9
Gold, Mike 374
Good Friday Agreement (1998) 53
Google 321, 329

Government Buildings, Merrion Street 56
Grafton Architects 36, 55, 56, 417, 419, 420–2, 424, 480, 491, 492, 496
Graham, Patrick 383
Grange Abbey 149
Grangemore *see* Donaghmede
Grattan Bridge House, Dublin 7 480
graveyards 262–4
Greater London Council (GLC) 95, 97, 141, 315
Green Building, Temple Bar 53, 56, 488
Gribben, Eugene 490
Grimes, Bernard 474
Gris, Juan 386
Group 91 50–2, 351, 353, 355, 356, 357–9, 361, 367, 379, 398–9, 482, 488, 489, 491, 492 *see also* 'Making a Modern Street'
Grove House Apartments, Ranelagh/Milltown 459
Guinness 114
Guy Moloney & Partners 251

Half Moon Theatre, London 373
Hand, Matthew 155–6
Harrington, Sean 495
Harrington, Sean, Architects 354
Haughey, Charles 36, 51, 184, 201, 351, 358
Haughton, Jenny 381–2
Healy Associates 485
Helsinki University 445
Henihan, Martin 326
Henihan, Don 144
Herbert Mews, Ballsbridge 162–71, 445, 463
Herbert Park Hotel and Apartments, Ballsbridge 493
Heytesbury Lane Mews, Dublin 4 55, 170, 493
Hickey, Owen 358
Higher Education Authority (HEA) 418
Hines 211
Hirschfield Centre, Fownes Street Upper 27
homelessness 44, 336–7, 339–40, 343, 345
Hope, Cuffe & Associates 152–3
Horan, Tony 275, 278–9, 281, 472
Horan Cotter Associates 279, 472
Horan Keogan Ryan Architects 495
housing 54–5 *see also* public housing; social housing
    artisan 41, 129, 139–40, 143, 145, 338, 343
    high-rise 97, 138–9
Housing Act (1988) 44, 340
housing competitions 141–4
housing standards 55, 275, 336
Howley Harrington Architects 495
Hume Street, Battle of 28
hunger strikes 40
Hunt, John 381
Hussey, Michael 360
Hutchison, David 251, 259
Hutchison, Locke and Monk (HLM) Architects 251, 255, 259

Ilac Centre 30, 43, 466
'Image Changers' survey 102
Industrial Development Authority (IDA) 216–17, 239–40
   Enterprise Centre, Dublin 2 236–47, 470
   Enterprise Centres 238
   Small Business Centre 478
industrial growth 216, 240
Industrial Training Act (1967) 216
Industrial Training Authority see AnCO
infilll architecture 119–21,143, 289, 443
inflation 24, 80
Insurance Corporation of Ireland 73
interior design 62, 79–80
International Financial Services Centre (IFSC), Dublin 1 53, 228, 321, 325, 482
Investment Bank of Ireland/Fitzwilliam House, Dublin 2 465
Investment in Education Report (1962) 434
Irish Architectural Archive 453
Irish Continental Line 73
Irish Film Centre/Institute (IFI) 52, 352, 359, 366–77, 433, 485
   Irish Film Archive 367
Irish football team 49
Irish Goods Council 77
Irish Life Assurance Company 30, 177, 283, 285, 288
Irish Life Centre, Lower Abbey Street 25, 30–1, 86, 283–95, 473
   extension 288
   refurbishment 283–4, 293
Irish Mint see Currency Centre, Sandyford
Irish Museum of Modern Art (IMMA) 42, 51, 56, 483
Irish Parliament building, College Green 85
'Irish Renaissance' 35
Irish Shipping Ltd 25, 73, 75 see also Merrion Hall
Irish Women's Liberation Movement (IWLM) 26
Irishtown Nature Park 110
Italia 90 49

Jacob's Biscuit Factory 61–2, 64
Jameson Distillery 299–301
John Paul II, Pope, visit to Ireland 189–96
Johnston, Francis 85
Jones, Ed 361
Jordan, Cara 453
Judge, Chris 114
Juvenile Court, Smithfield 298–307, 476

Kahn, Louis 317
Kärtner Bar, Vienna 309, 316
Kaye Parry Ross Hendy 55
Kealy, Loughlin 35, 361, 370
Kean Murphy Duff 43, 457
Keane, David 454
Keane, David, & Partners 30, 43, 466
Kelly, Ambrose F. Partnership 43
Kelly, Deirdre 28

Kelly, Des 193
Kelly, Michael 52, 359, 489
Kelly, Oisín, 'Chariot of Life' 283, 284, 291, 296–7
Kelly, Paul 497
Kennedy, Sr Stanislaus (Sr Stan) 335–7, 339–40, 342–3, 347
Kenny, Tony 114
Keogh, Paul 355–6, 359, 361–2, 365, 474
Keogh, Paul, Architects 52, 355, 360–1
Kidney Burke-Kennedy Doyle 144, 146, 462
Kiely, Benedict 115
Kilkenny Design Workshops 77
Killeavy Properties 279
Kingston, Robert 155
Kinney, Desmond, mosaic mural 291
Koolhaas, Rem 386, 420
Koralek, Paul 312
Kornaus-Wejchert, Danuta see Wejchert, Danuta
Krier, Leon 361–2

Lacey, Dermot 115
Laheen, Mary 41
landscape 170, 289–90, 417, 423
landscaping 110, 137, 141, 163, 175, 178, 181–3, 189, 215, 225, 231, 256, 262, 272, 275–7, 283, 400, 407, 411, 413–14
Lardner, Arthur 105, 458
Lardner, Arthur, and Partners 95, 97, 105, 458
Lawlor, Aine 29
Le Corbusier 78, 269, 400
Leixlip Community School 39
Leonard, Br T.C. 264
LGBT+ rights 40–1
Liberties 36, 64, 134, 138–40, 238, 338, 345, 357, 396
Liberties Residents Association (LRA) 129, 140
Liberty Hall 204
Life Association Ireland Building, Dublin 2 469
Liffey Boardwalk 53
Lillington Gardens, London 141
Lincoln & Nolan 86
Lir Academy 237, 245
Lisney (infill office building), Dublin 2 456
Living City Group 28, 287
'Living over the Shop' (LOTS) scheme 402
local government 35
Local Government Act (1955) 26
Local Government (Planning & Development) Act (1999) 50
Loeffler, Jane 412–13
London City Council (LCC) 97
Loos, Adolf 309, 316
Louvre Pyramid, Paris 51
Lovett, Ann 41
Lower Mount Street office building 483
Lucey, Michael 285
Lydon, Frank 204
Lyons, Henry J. 211, 326, 459

Lyons, Henry J., and Associates 481

McCaffrey, Roddy 186
McCormack, Keane & Partners 454
McCormick, Liam 261, 264–5, 269–70, 273, 464, 471
   church designs 269
McCormick Tracey Mullarkey 464, 471
McCullough, Niall 50, 384–5, 448
McCullough Mulvin Architects 53, 379, 381, 384–6, 388–9, 390, 400, 480, 482, 488
McDonald, Frank 353–4, 402
McDonnell and Dixon 311
McGarry Ní Eanaigh Architects 53, 353, 398, 498
McGrath, Raymond 479
McFeely, Fr Anthony 269
McGloughlin, J. & C. 191–2
Mackay, David 52, 355–7
McKenna, Mary 41
McKillen, Paddy 331
McMahon, D. 468
McMahon, Bloomer, O'Hara 468
McNamara, Shelley 41, 419, 424, 427, 485, 496
McQuaid, Archbishop John Charles 23–4
Magahy, Laura 358
Maguire, Brian 383
maisonettes 129, 132–3, 138–9, 145, 165
'Making a Modern Street' 36, 52, 345, 357, 361, 396, 398
Marriage Bar 26–7
Martello Mews, Sandymount 463
Martin, F.X. 28
Martorell, Josep 356
Mater Private Hospital, Dublin 7 475
Matt Talbot House, Charles Street 130
Maureen Buildings, Temple Bar 381–5, 388
Maxwell, Robert 393
MBM Arquitectes 52, 356
Meagher, John 155, 165–6, 168, 171, 319, 444–8, 451, 463, 481, 496
Mee, Alan 402
Meeting House Square, Temple Bar 52, 350, 353–5, 358–65
Mendes da Rocha, Paulo 420
Merrion Hall, Sandymount 25, 70–81, 455
   neglect 71
Merrion Village, Ballsbridge 476
Meteorological Office, Glasnevin 464
Metropolitan Streets Commission 42
mews buildings 55, 163, 165–6, 443
Mies van der Rohe, Ludwig 77–8, 83–4, 89, 119–21, 124, 127, 196, 218–19
Miesian Plaza 83
Millar & Symes 368
Millennium Bridge 353, 495
Millennium Tower, Dublin 4 490
Miller, John 361
Mitchell, George 41
Mitterand, François 51
Modernism 20–1, 41–2, 66, 78, 83, 91, 119, 129, 138, 163, 196, 210, 218–20, 269, 301, 309, 321, 395, 399

Molloy, Maeve 41
Molly Malone sculpture 44
Moloney, Helen 269
Moloney O'Beirne Guy 249, 251, 259
Moloney O'Beirne Guy & Hutchinson 470
Molyneux, Thomas 62
Molyneux Asylum for Blind Females 61–2, 64
Molyneux House, Bride Street 60, 60–9, 78, 455
Monaghan, John 417
Monahan, Neill 384
Monahan, Seamus 122
Montrose House, Dublin 2 466
Morehampton Mews, Donnybrook 471
Moriarty, Paddy 114
Mountainview Court, Summerhill 130
multi-denominational schools *see* Ranelagh Multi-Denominational School
Mulvin, Valerie 41, 384–6, 388, 390, 488
Munster Technological University 317
Murphy, Jim 340
Murray Ó Laoire 53, 488

National Asset Management Agency (NAMA) 321, 444
National Bank of Ireland, Suffolk Street 87–8
National Botanic Gardens, Glasnevin, Curvilinear Range 491
National Children's Hospital 249, 256
National College of Art 26
National College of Art and Design (NCAD), School of Design for Industry 495
National Concert Hall 42
National Film Institute *see* Irish Film Centre/Institute
National Gay Federation 27
National Inventory of Architectural Heritage (NIAH) 50, 115
National Manpower Agency 215, 217
National Museum of Ireland, Decorative Arts and History collection 56
National Photographic Archive, Temple Bar 52, 359–60, 367
National Treasury Management Agency (NTMA) 329
Nativity of Our Lord Church 155
natural gas 107, 253–4
Neligan, Judy 29
Neo-Gothic 340–1
New Irish Architecture (NIA) 36, 41
New Street Housing, Dublin 8 55, 466
Newenham Mulligan 43
Newman House, Dublin 2 487
Ní Éanaigh, Siobhán 41
Northcliffe Apartment Complex, Chapelizod 469
Northumberland Square 287
Nowlan, Bill 286
Nutgrove Shopping Centre 43

O'Beirne, Jim 249, 255–6, 259, 470
Ó Beirne, Tomás 121
Ó Briain, Colm 374
Occupy Dame Street movement 202

O'Connor, Ciaran 486, 491
O'Connor, Deirdre 29, 139, 497
O'Connor, Joan 54
O'Connor, Sinéad 49
Ó Cuív, Ruairí 381–4, 386, 388–9, 390
Odhams Walk, London 141
O'Doherty, Éamonn 44
    Crann an Óir 201, 210, 213
O'Doherty, Michael 42
O'Donnell, Lily 453
O'Donnell, Sheila Sheila 41, 303, 377, 429, 485
O'Donnell, Turlough 478
O'Donnell, Turlough, & Associates 478
O'Donnell + Tuomey Architects 52, 55, 359, 367–70, 372–4, 377, 429, 433, 485, 492, 494
O'Driscoll, Br R.Q. 262
Office of Public Works (OPW) 41, 56, 151, 471, 474, 476, 480, 483, 486
    New Works V department 300
office workers 30, 121, 290
O'Grady-Doyle, Mary 29
O'Halloran, Aoife 156
O'Halloran, Brian, & Associates 458, 486
oil crises 24, 166, 252
O'Keefe, Maurice 460
O'Laoire, Sean 102, 373–4
Olley, John 302, 345, 362
O'Mahony Pike Architects 490, 493
O'Malley, Niamh 380
O'Neill, Cathal 361
O'Neill Flanagan and Partners 471
O'Reilly, John, & Partners 472
O'Reilly, Philip 294
Ormond Quay offices and housing 489
O'Rourke, Brian 476
Orwell Woods, Rathgar 473
O'Shea, Tony 49
O'Sullivan, Fr 156
O'Sullivan, Maurice 117
O'Toole, Shane 87, 89, 196, 204–5, 359, 400, 453, 478, 489
Our Lady of Dolours, Glasnevin 454
Our Lady of Mount Carmel Church, Firhouse 37, 155, 156, 165

Palmerston House, Dublin 2 457
Papadakis, Andreas 361
Papal Cross, Phoenix Park 188–99, 464
Paris 51
Parke, Edward 302
Parke, Robert 85
Parker, Alan 49
Parker Morris Report 144
Parsons Laboratory see Trinity College Dublin
Patrick Guilbaud Restaurant 467
Pavee Point/Free Church Travellers' Centre, Dublin 1 482
pavilions 175, *176*, 179, 181–2, 230, 453
Pearce, Edward Lovett 85
pedestrianisation 42, 44, 52, 96–8, 134, 353, 359
Pembroke Estate 25

Percy Lane Houses, Ballsbridge 481
Percy Place, Ballsbridge 326
Percy Thomas Partnership 412
Petersen Group 211
Phelan, Garrett, 'Our Union Only in Truth' 379
Phoenix Park 189–96
Photo Museum Ireland see Gallery of Photography
Pigeon House, Ringsend 107–8, *111*
Piggott Brothers 192
Pike, James 31, 135, 140, 196, 461
    urban context scenarios *132*
Pillar Project, Dublin 1 36, 478
Planning Act (1963) 179
PMPA headquarters, Wolfe Tone Square 118–27, 461
Poddle Bridge, proposed 53
Point Depot (3Arena) 479
Pollard, Carole 453
Poolbeg Generating Station, Ringsend 107–17
    chimneys 111–14, 460
Poolbeg Lighthouse 110
Port and Docks Board HQ, North Dock 468
Postmodernism 326, 328, 362
Power, Anne 101
Power Design 42
Power Supermarkets 264
Powerscourt Townhouse Centre, Dublin 2 42, 468
Printworks, Temple Bar 55, 392–405, 488
Property Corporation of Ireland 73
public housing 129–47
public sculpture 44

Quaker Meeting House, Temple Bar 353, 365
Quillinan, Frances *26*, 26–7

Radburn system 100
Randal McDonnell 473
Ranelagh Multi-Denominational School 55, 428–39, 494
    extension 430
Rathmines, Three Houses in 55, 497
recession 30–1, 35, 41, 49, 166, 180–1, 229, 293
Record of Protected Structures (RPS) 83–4, 115
Reddy, Anthony, Associates 498
Redmill, John 471
Regional Technical Colleges 424
Reid, Alan 420
Reilly, Brian 259
REMU Transformer Substation, Amersfoort 424
restoration 53, 56, 309–19, 443, 471, 483
Ringsend Housing Scheme 467
River House, Smithfield 457
road widening 22, 303, 442
Roberts, Ian 311, 313, 475
Robertson, Manning 19
Robinson, Mary 49
Robinson Keefe & Devane (RKD) 29, 44, 117, 175, 186, 288, 460, 464, 473

Roche, Kevin 78
Roche, Paul 483
Rolfe, Angela 41, 480
Ronan, Johnny 321, 324–6, 329
Ross Cahill O'Brien 462
Rossi, Aldo 50, 361, 385, 399
Rowe, Colin 50, 398–9
Rowlagh church 37
Royal Barracks (Collins Barracks) 56
Royal Dublin Society (RDS) 175, 179, 412
Royal Hibernian Academy, Dublin 2, gallery 479
Royal Hibernian Way, Dublin 2 477
Royal Hospital Kilmainham 56
Royal Institute of the Architects of Ireland (RIAI) 31, 121, 184, 285, 289
Royal Liver Friendly Society 227
RTÉ 196
RTÉ Campus, Montrose 29, 175, 456
Rural Electrification Scheme 113
Ryan, Archbishop Dermot 149, 151–3, 155, 189, 264
Ryan, Raymund 400–1
Ryan and Hogan 29, 454
Ryan O'Brien Handy 469
Rynhart, Jeanne 44

St Andrew's College 29, 178
St Columba's School, Ranelagh Road 436
St James's Hospital, Dublin 8
    Energy Centre 248–59, 470
    history 250
St Joseph's Industrial School 261
St Mary's Chapel of Ease/Black Church, Broadstone 485
St Mary's Church, Maghera 269, *270*
St Patrick's Cathedral 61
St Stephen's Green Shopping Centre 42–3, 479
St Thomas Community College, Bray *38*
Saint, Andrew 413
Sandymount 278–9
Schaechterle, Karl 139
Scott, Michael, & Associates 456
Scott, Michael, & Partners 83, 86, 89, 93, 456, 458
Scott, Niall 194–6, 225, 229, 231–2, 235, 468
Scott, Patrick 93, 192, 198
Scott Tallon Walker 29, 56, 120, 189, 191, 194, 215, 217, 218–20, 227, 228, 231, 460, 461, 464, 466, 467, 468, 478, 487, 494, 496, 497
Scully, Paul 478
Seagram building, New York 78, 83
Second World War (the Emergency) 108
Segar, Brian 112
Serbian Orthodox Church 261
Shaffrey, Cliodhna 379
Shaffrey, Maura 29, 41, 42
Shaffrey, Patrick 29, 42
Shaffrey Associates Architects 489
Sheahan, Patrick J. & Partners 457
Sheahan, Thomas F. 457

Sheehan, David 487
Sheehan & Barry Architects 487
Shelbourne Hotel, Horseshoe Bar 62
Shelly Banks 110
Shipman Brady Martin 105
Sisk, John, & Sons 153, 189, 205
Sister Stan *see* Kennedy, Sr Stanislaus
Sisters of Charity 335
Skidmore, Owings & Merrill 35, 351, 354
Skypixels Ireland 114
Slattery, David 483
Slessor, Catherine 355, 370
slip-form construction 112, 205
Smith, Ailbhe 41
Smith and Pearson 122
Smithfield 299, 303
    Phase 1 498
Smock Alley Court, Dublin 2 495
Smock Alley Theatre/Viking Centre, Dublin 2 492
smog 252
Snow Design 114
Soane, John 317
South City Area Research Partnership (SCARP) 339
social housing 55, 101, 144, 343
social unrest 26–7
South Wall 109, 110
Stanbridge, Clair 381
Stanhope Green, Focus Ireland housing, Dublin 7 334–47
Stanhope Street Refuge, Dublin 1 484
Stardust Ballroom fire 40
Stephen Court 31, 289
Stephenson, Sam 56, 61–9, 73, 77, 203–4, 206, 208, 210–11, 455, 459, 465, 474
Stephenson Associates 459
Stephenson Gibney and Associates (SGA) 29, 30, 39, 62, 69, 73, 75, 77, 79, 203, 455, 457, 465, 474
    offices 66
Stevenson, Samuel, & Sons 323, 325
Stirling, Robert 418
Stone Thoms Stephenson 67
Strahan, Nancy 41
Strand Street Little, Office Building 55
strikes 27–8, 181
Stuart, Imogen 269
suburbia 20, 24–5, 44, 54–5, 72, 97, 137, 149, 150–2, 155, 165–6, 169, 180, 240, 270, 275, 396
Surrender Grant 101
suspended floors 205
Swan Centre, Rathmines 472
Swan Place (Mews), Donnybrook 470
Swift, Arthur 456
Swift, Arthur, & Partners 456

Talbot Mall 283, 290–1
Talbot Memorial Bridge, Dublin 1 461
Tallaght 151
Tallaght Hospital 44, 157
Tallon, Ronnie 83, 87–93, 189, 191–6, 219–20, 454, 456, 458, 464, 467, 478,

494, 496
Taylor Galleries, Dublin 2 462
Teahon, Paddy 358
Temple Bar 44, 50–3, 350–405
   proposed Transport Hub 353–5, *355*
Temple Bar Action Plan 351
Temple Bar Centre 381
Temple Bar Framework Plan *50*, 350–1, 353, 355, 359, 362, 367, 393, 396, 482
Temple Bar Gallery + Studios (TBGS) 53, 378–391, 488
Temple Bar Properties 51, 355, 358, 382, 389, 398
Temple Bar Renewal and Development Act (1991) 51, 355, 382
Temple Bar Renewal Ltd 382
Temple Bar Square and buildings 491
Temple Bar Study Group 351
Texaco House, Ballsbridge 454
Thirteen Denzille Preview Theatre (Clarence Pictures), Dublin 2 496
Thomas Prior Hall (House), Merrion Road 408, 412
Thompson, Benjamin 482
Tierney, Paul 453
Toomey, James 42
Traditions and Directions exhibition 36, 168, 170
traffic management 25
Treasury Building, Grand Canal Street 320–33, 481
   refurbishment 329
Treasury Holdings 321, 329, 331
Trinity College Dublin
   Arts and Social Sciences Building 463
   Berkeley Library 420
   Buildings Committee 313, 317, 419
   Dental Hospital 56, 494
   Dining Hall: 42, 309, 310–15, 445, 475;
   Atrium/Loos Bar 308–19, 475
   O'Reilly Institute 494
   Parsons Building 417, 419, 421, 492
   Parsons Laboratory 56, 416–27
   Samuel Beckett Theatre 56, 312, 420, 445, 486
   Technology and Enterprise Campus 237
Troubles, the 24, 27, 40, 189, 434
Tuam Mother and Baby Home, Galway 264
Tully, James 138–9, 143
Tuomey, John 36, 300–1, 307, 371, 377, 430–1, 433, 468, 476, 479
turf-fired power 252–3
Turlough Hill, Co. Wicklow 110
Tynan, Derek 357–8, 393, 395–6, 398–9, 405, 488
Tynan, Derek, Architects 55, 393–4
Tyndalll Hogan Hurley 461, 475

U2 49, 114
Uí Mhurchadha, Máirín 261
Ulster Bank, College Green 29, 459
unemployment 25, 40, 95, 215, 217, 239
Unger, Klaus 480
University College Dublin (UCD)
   Belfield campus 29, 157
   Dublin City Quays Project 35, 303, 361, 395–6, 475
   School of Architecture 35, 303, 361
Upper Leeson Street Area Residents' Association (ULSARA) 179
urban design 52, 289, 356–7, 361, 396, 399
urban regeneration 25, 28, 49, 52–3, 56, 325, 367, 393
Urban Renewal Act (1986) 228
Urbanowicz, Anna 193
Usher's Quay Filling Station *44*, 475

van Berkel, Ben 424
Varming Mulcahy Reilly Associates (VMRA) 252, 259
Vatican II 156
Venice Biennale (2022) 380
Viking Centre/Smock Alley Theatre, Dublin 2 492

Walker, Robin 29, 31, 87–9, 93, 119–27, 194–6, 220, 460, 461, 466
Walls, P.J. 230
Walsh, Bill 77
Warren, Michael, *Noche Oscura* 225, *228*, 232, 235
Waterways Visitors Centre, Dublin 2 486
Wejchert, A. & D., Architects 29, 149, 153, 155, 157, 160, 434, 462, 483
Wejchert, Alexandra 154, 160, 175, 183–4
Wejchert, Andrzej 29, 38, 157, 160
Wejchert (Kornaus-Wejchert), Danuta 29, 38, 149, 153–4, 156–7, 160, 462
Wesley College 29
Wesley House/Litton Hall, Dublin 6 460
Weslin 190
Whelan, Deirdre 497
White Cube 379, 389
Wicklow House, Dublin 2 456
Wide Streets Commission 19, 350
Wilf Limited 275
Williams, Fr Des 152
Willow Field, Sandymount 274–81, 472
Wolfe Tone Square, Dublin 1 493
Women's Aid Refuge, Rathmines 29, 473
Wood Quay 28, *31*, 56, 226
Wooden Building, Temple Bar 445, 498
Woulfe Flanagan, Stephen 31, 121
Wright, Frank Lloyd 183, 290
Wright, Lance 23, 30, 83, 87, 91, 157, 206, 208, 211
Wright, Myles 139, 210

Yale Centre for British Art 317

Published by UCD Press (with Dublin City Council) as the third volume in a three-part series, which is based on a pioneering survey and research-based study into the architecture of the 20th-century in Dublin City.

It is an action of the Dublin City Strategic Heritage Plan 2023–2028 and supported with grant assistance from the Heritage Council's annual County Heritage Plan Grant Scheme, and the Department of Housing, Local Government and Heritage.

© Dublin City Council with the authors, Natalie de Róiste, Merlo Kelly, Aoibheann Ní Mheárain, Aoife O'Halloran, Shane O'Toole, Carole Pollard, Ellen Rowley and Paul Tierney, 2023

ISBN 978-1-910820-12-4 pb

All rights reserved. No part of this publication may be reproduced, stored in a retrieval system, or transmitted in any form or by any means, electronic, photocopying, recording or otherwise without the prior permission of the publisher.

CIP data available from the British Library

The right of the editors to be identified as the editors of this work has been asserted by them

Publisher:
UCD Press
University College Dublin Press
UCD Humanities Institute,
Room H103,
Belfield,
Dublin 4
www.ucdpress.ie

Commissioner: Charles Duggan, DCC
Design: Peter Maybury
Photography: Paul Tierney
Printing: die Keure

front cover: View from foyer, PMPA, c. 1980, by John Donat (Courtesy of Donat Collection, RIBApix)
back cover: Constructing James's Hospital Energy Centre, Steel Flues, c.1982 (Courtesy of Maloney O'Beirne collection at Irish Architectural Archive)